Standing in Their Own Light

CAMPAIGNS & COMMANDERS

GREGORY J. W. URWIN, SERIES EDITOR

CAMPAIGNS AND COMMANDERS

GENERAL EDITOR
Gregory J. W. Urwin, *Temple University, Philadelphia, Pennsylvania*

ADVISORY BOARD
Lawrence E. Babits, *Greenville, North Carolina*
James C. Bradford, *Texas A&M University, College Station*
Robert M. Epstein, *U.S. Army School of Advanced Military Studies, Fort Leavenworth, Kansas (retired)*
David M. Glantz, *Carlisle, Pennsylvania*
Jerome A. Greene, *Denver, Colorado*
Victor Davis Hanson, *Hoover Institution of Stanford University, Stanford*
Herman Hattaway, *Leawood, Kansas*
J. A. Houlding, *Rückersdorf, Germany*
Eugenia C. Kiesling, *U.S. Military Academy, West Point, New York*
Timothy K. Nenninger, *National Archives, Washington, D.C.*
Bruce Vandervort, *Virginia Military Institute, Lexington*

Standing in Their Own Light

African American Patriots in the American Revolution

Judith L. Van Buskirk

University of Oklahoma Press | Norman

Sections of the 1818 and 1832 pension material that appear in chapter 5 of this volume were originally published as "Claiming Their Due: African Americans in the Revolutionary War and Its Aftermath," in John Resch and Walter Sargent, eds., *War and Society in the American Revolution: Mobilization and Home Fronts* (DeKalb: Northern Illinois University Press, 2006). The material is used here with permission of Northern Illinois University Press.

Library of Congress Cataloging-in-Publication Data

Names: Van Buskirk, Judith L., author.
Title: Standing in their own light : African American patriots in the
    American revolution / Judith L. Van Buskirk.
Description: Norman : University of Oklahoma Press, 2017. | Series:
    Campaigns and commanders series ; volume 59 | Includes bibliographical
    references and index.
Identifiers: LCCN 2016038225 | ISBN 978-0-8061-5635-4 (cloth) |
    ISBN 978-0-8061-6187-7 (paper)
Subjects: LCSH: United States—History—Revolution, 1775–1783—Participation,
    African American. | United States—History—Revolution, 1775–1783—African
    Americans. | Slavery—United States—History—18th century. | African Americans—
    History—To 1863. | African American soldiers—History—18th century.
Classification: LCC E269.N3 V36 2017 | DDC 973.3/46—dc23
LC record available at https://lccn.loc.gov/2016038225

Standing in Their Own Light: African American Patriots in the American Revolution is Volume 59 in the Campaigns and Commanders series.

The paper in this book meets the guidelines for permanence and durability of the Committee on Production Guidelines for Book Longevity of the Council on Library Resources, Inc. ∞

Copyright © 2017 by the University of Oklahoma Press, Norman, Publishing Division of the University. Paperback published 2018. Manufactured in the U.S.A.

All rights reserved. No part of this publication may be reproduced, stored in a retrieval system, or transmitted, in any form or by any means, electronic, mechanical, photocopying, recording, or otherwise—except as permitted under Section 107 or 108 of the United States Copyright Act—without the prior written permission of the University of Oklahoma Press. To request permission to reproduce selections from this book, write to Permissions, University of Oklahoma Press, 2800 Venture Drive, Norman, OK 73069, or email rights.oupress@ou.edu.

Interior layout and composition: Alcorn Publication Design

To
Private Africa Burke
First Rhode Island Regiment
Died May 14, 1781, Pines Bridge
and
Private First Class William Raymond Hendricks
Sixth Marine Division, Fourth Regiment, Third Amphibian Battalion
Died May 20, 1945, Okinawa

Contents

List of Illustrations	ix
Acknowledgments	xi
Introduction	3
1. On Jordan's Stormy Banks: Their World before the War	24
2. A New World in Uniform	60
3. A Bold Experiment in Rhode Island	95
4. The Black Regiment: John Laurens's "Excentric Scheme" and Henry Laurens's Dilemma	142
5. On to the Next Battle: The Postwar World and the First Pension Act	173
6. Another Assault: A Frowning World and the Second Pension Act	198
Conclusion: Claiming Their Due	233
Notes	241
Bibliography	275
Index	293

Illustrations

Clothing inventory of soldiers killed in action	12
William Johnson's Revolutionary War pension application	17
View of Mulberry House and Street, by Thomas Coram	31
Tobias Gilmore's mitre	62
Daguerreotype of Agrippa Hull	86
Colonel Christopher Greene	109
Monuments to the fallen at Pines Bridge, Yorktown Presbyterian Cemetery	138–39
John Laurens, by Charles Willson Peale	155
The Death of Colonel John Laurens, by Howard Pyle	171
John Brister's discharge certificate	180
Badge of Merit for Prosper Gorton	181
Inventory of Artillo Freeman	182
Self-portrait of Hamet Achmet	221

Acknowledgments

As any historian knows, working on a project entails living in two worlds: the one that you physically occupy and the one your historical subjects inhabit. I have been inspired by people in both places and so this acknowledgment section is as much a journey with the veterans as a statement of gratitude to those who have supported me.

This project started with the African American community of Mount Vernon, New York. Right beside a revolutionary era church, I gave a Fourth of July address in 2002, after which I spoke to many gracious and generous people, including two veterans of the Pacific theater in World War II. Nobody had recorded their recollections, yet they were willing to talk. So I referred them to a project at Rutgers, which at that time was collecting soldier testimonies from the Second World War.

I don't remember their names, but on my way home I worried that these men's stories would never see the printed page. To history, they would be forgotten—like my uncle Bud, known formally as William Raymond Hendricks. He was only sixteen years old when he entered the marines and was assigned, like the African American men in Mount Vernon, to the Pacific theater. He survived several battles, including the major action at Okinawa. After the battle he was stringing communication wires across the island when a sniper shot him. He survived a few more hours, not long enough to greet his twentieth birthday. It happened to be the day when his sister (my mother) got married back home in Philadelphia. Years later my mother burned his letters because reading them was too heartbreaking. His service records burned too in a fire at a government repository in Saint Louis. All that is left of him is a box with a few belongings, including a Purple Heart. And since he had no children, there will be no kin down the ages to claim him and honor his sacrifice. The veterans of Mount Vernon and my uncle Bud blended together on that ride home and inspired me to look into the forgotten veterans of the country's founding war—the American Revolution.

At the time I started my research, the classic work on African American soldiers was still Benjamin Quarles's classic published in 1961, *The Negro in the American Revolution*. And no wonder—finding sources on poor black men in the Revolution is a daunting task. I had come upon a few African American Revolutionary War pension applications during research on my first book. I figured that if I could find one hundred of them in the eighty thousand

Revolutionary War files, a story would emerge that featured the closest approximation of their voices. I ended up with over five hundred African American pension files with the help of the best librarian around, Kathie Ludwig of the David Library of the American Revolution (DLAR). Kathie began by helping me find already-existing lists of African Americans' names compiled by researchers like David O. White, Richard Walling, Glenn Knoblock, and George Quintal. When I had a question that I thought probably had no answer, I would ask Kathie anyway, and, every time, she'd haul out some books and microfilms that constituted a solution to my problem. Not only does Kathie have an unrivaled command of the sources of the American Revolution, she also has the biggest heart in the business. Those who have worked at the David Library know exactly what I mean.

I'd also like to thank Brian Graziano and Rich Wood at the DLAR; Ken Carlson at the Rhode Island State Archives; Claire Bestwick and Paul Campbell at the City Archives of Providence; Brian Lippincott III at the Newport Historical Society; Phoebe Bean at the Rhode Island Historical Society; Richard Malley at the Connecticut Historical Society; Debra Pond at the Connecticut State Archives Law Desk; Debbie Shapiro at the Middlesex County Historical Society in Connecticut; Bette Epstein at the New Jersey Archives; Ray Russell at the Stony Point Battlefield State Historic Site; Aslaku Berhanu at the Charles Blockson Afro-American Collection; Pam Luby at the Maryland State Law Library; Ginny Dunn at the Virginia State Library; Mary Thompson at George Washington's Mount Vernon; Earl Ijames at the North Carolina Department of Cultural Resources; Harlan Greene at the College of Charleston's Archives; Carol Jones at the Charleston Library Society; and Nic Butler at the Charleston County Public Library.

During the course of my research, I had enriching conversations with Todd Braisted, Larry Babbits, Joe Becton, Ruma Chopra, Tom Corey, Marion Lane, Ann Greene, Don Higginbotham, Don Hagist, Noah Lewis, Jenea Moseley, Genny Moseley, John Rees, Wendy Wong, and my brothers Mike and Bill Van Buskirk. Thank you all!

As my research project took shape on paper, the following people gave generously of their time to read a portion of the manuscript or comment on conference papers: anonymous readers for the University of Oklahoma Press, Patricia Bonomi, Denver Brosnan, Ira Berlin, George Boudreau; Caroline Cox, John Ferling, Holly Mayer, Andrew Jackson O'Shaughnessy, Karen Pastorello, Bill Pencak, Dan Richter, Donna Rilling, Amy Schutt, Camilla Townsend, and especially Jack Resch and Greg Urwin. At the University of Oklahoma Press, Adam Kane, Mette Flynt, and Stephanie Evans were all wonderful supporters of the project. Thanks too to freelance copy editor Chris Dodge.

I would also like to thank the following organizations for their generous financial support: the American Philosophical Society, the David Library of the American Revolution, the United University Professions, the SUNY Cortland History Department's REDI grant, and the Haines Foundation.

This book has been thirteen years in the making. I owe a big hug to all those friends and family who encouraged me to persevere, provided welcome release from my books and papers, and shared my excitement in discovering new veterans.

I know it is not conventional to acknowledge one's subjects in this format, but I do feel like I traveled a road with these veterans, and I am grateful to them for keeping me going as more scholars and organizations became interested in them as well. Every time I crossed the Delaware, there were Jacob Francis and Edward Pellom, who crossed that river in 1776. When I watched Joe Becton's First Rhode Island reenactors, there in my mind's eye were Guy Watson and Prince Bent, two veterans who signed up in early 1777 and served to the end of the war. When I talked with vets' descendants, the soldiers appeared again.

And I experienced emotional reactions to my subjects, which surprised me given that they left so little written record of themselves. One man's name kept cropping up as a possible noncommissioned officer in the First Rhode Island Regiment. I looked long and hard, wanting it to be true that George Sambo had climbed up the ranks. As I came across his name in a primary source, I'd say, "There's George! And he's still a private." George Sambo had started out in Captain Ebeneezer Flagg's company in 1777, then was placed in Captain Thomas Arnold's unit at Valley Forge. Once he joined Captain Thomas Coles's company with newly minted ex-slave soldiers, he was largely absent from camp on some mission or other. In August 1779 he was off working for General Nathanael Greene. Although always listed as a private, he obviously was an accomplished soldier to be engaged in these special missions. One night I was plowing through more Rhode Island muster lists at my dining room table and turned to the October 1779 list of Captain Coles's company. I saw George Sambo's name and was about to greet him again when I was brought up short. The notation by his name read "died October 1st." It stopped me in my tracks. I stared at the letters. The only access I had to his life was via impersonal lists, yet his death registered as a shock. I was taken aback by the sadness I felt.

Along with moments of unexpected emotion, there were moments of frustration that every practitioner of history experiences. A supporter of Cuff Ashport's pension claimed that this veteran of the Massachusetts line had described to him "the face of the country around West Point" when Benedict Arnold fled to the enemy. The Continental Army was in an uproar at the time, questioning everyone's allegiance. What would we give to hear Ashport's assessment of "the face of the country" at such a critical moment. Another veteran, this time in Virginia, had regaled his neighbors with stories for decades. It was written in his obituary that Billy, still a slave at over one hundred years of age, had claimed that he "remembered all about the siege of Yorktown." And there the statement rests to this day—with no elaboration. Out in Tennessee, Jesse Grimes testified in favor of a federal pension for Mark Murry, an African American veteran of the North Carolina line. As a boy, Jesse had stationed himself by the Revolutionary War veterans at community events. He told the pension office that he had heard Murry describe campaigns and "relate incidents connected therewith which I could relate if necessary." The pension office, alas, did not take him up on his offer. Lastly, a pension attorney from Rhode Island, Benjamin Cowell, related that on some days, up to a dozen Revolutionary War veterans were in his office at once. Cowell, born in 1781, wrote a history of Rhode Island in the war, published in 1850. Unfortunately, the lure of high officials and officers led Cowell to tell the story from their viewpoint. The rank and file appear in his book only as names on pay lists, muster lists, size rolls, lists of the dead, and the like. Their "large mass of anecdote," as Cowell dismissively termed it, remains lost to the printed page.

Also lost to the historical record are the experiences of Africa Burke of the First Rhode Island. Africa lost no time in signing up when his state allowed enslaved men to serve in exchange for their freedom. His name appears on a few muster rolls and on a list of casualties from the raid at Pines Bridge. No other glimmer helps to illuminate him. I dedicate this book to him and hope that my efforts allow Private Burke and his buddies to stand in their own light, to shine for everyone to see.

Standing in Their Own Light

Introduction

One wintry night at the close of the war against the British, young Rachel Adams heard a knock on the door of her parents' log cabin in Taunton, Massachusetts. Then she heard her mother asking who was there. "A friend," a male voice answered. "Friend to whom," asked Rachel's mother. "A friend to George Washington," came the reply from outside.

As the girl made her way to the door, she heard the man "set down his musket on the doorstep" and instantly knew the identity of the mysterious voice. "Father is come," she exclaimed to her mother. "And so it proved to be," Rachel later wrote. There on the doorstep was a man in "white pantaloons [and] a Blue coat faced with red." Peter Adams, the man on the stoop with a musket and a pack, was at once a stranger and her father.

Before signing up for a stint in the Continental army, the thirty-seven-year-old Adams had built his wife and daughter a log cabin on land he owned. He could have ended his service at the end of his first hitch, but he had decided instead to see the conflict to its conclusion. As one of the "three years men" in the First Massachusetts Regiment, Adams served along the Hudson River. Over sixty years later, Rachel Adams vividly recalled the banter, the sound of the musket on the step, and the sight of her father.[1]

Scenes like the Adams's reunion occurred throughout the thirteen colonies as General Washington's soldiers walked home and reconnected with their families at the conclusion of the War for Independence. In our mind's eye, we probably see this Massachusetts veteran as a descendant of the Puritans, a white man. Nothing in his daughter's story suggests otherwise. But Adams was, in fact, one of thousands of African Americans who had shared the burden and dangers of turning the colonies into independent states.

Unlike the occasional white veteran of the Revolutionary War who left a trail of letters or a diary, African American veterans are more elusive. In most cases we tend to talk about black revolutionary war veterans as a group rather than as individuals. The history books tell us that some five thousand African Americans fought on the American side during the war. Letters written by whites might refer to "likely Negroes" building fortifications. Laws refer to "servants purchased bona fide," a euphemism for enslavement. African Americans appear in the sources, but they are usually somewhat anonymous because they left almost no letters and their stories often got lost. It is for this reason that they get such scant coverage in African American history.

Scholars of African American history have emphasized slaves and the people who worked to liberate them, abolitionists, black and white, many of whom wrote letters, petitions, and memoirs, and whose names appeared in newspapers. When mentioned at all, Revolutionary War soldiers are confined to the war years, with little more than the equivalent of "they were there too." The veterans of 1776 were largely illiterate and hence shadowy figures in the revolutionary drama. Historian Gary Nash has aptly described the African American community during the Revolution as "the forgotten fifth," referring to the percentage of the population represented by African Americans and the lack of attention subsequently paid to them.[2]

This book heralds the stories of many individuals whose petitions, protest, and service in the cause of American independence changed the world in which they lived. As you will see, Primus Tyng tells a new story about the Battle of Stony Point. Robert Laurens takes advantage of a court decision in England to leave his American master and strike out on his own. Thomas Lively loses his right eye at Monmouth, sustains a leg injury at Charleston, and survives as a prisoner of war for fourteen months but is back in the army to see Cornwallis fold at Yorktown. Judith Lines follows her husband to the Connecticut line, washing clothes for the officers until she contracts smallpox and returns home. These African American soldiers, upstarts, and storytellers moved liberation along, each in their own distinctive way. Their efforts did not convince most whites of African Americans' full and equal humanity, but they did inspire and sustain the black community whose conditions would deteriorate in the nineteenth century.[3]

The subjects of this book started their lives in a world that did not question slavery and finished their days in a world that contested the institution at every turn. Before 1765, a few African Americans in the Massachusetts courts and a few Quakers challenged the system. By 1790, the northern states had put slavery on the road to extinction. The Constitutional Convention heatedly debated the role of slavery and representation. Abolition societies and aid societies sprang up in the North and South. What had happened between 1765 and 1790? The American Revolution. Twenty years of talking about natural rights, equality, and freedom had made it such that the institution of slavery would never more be a part of the monotonous course of daily life, to loosely quote Thomas Jefferson. There are those who say that the Revolution failed African Americans because it did not free all enslaved people. They also point to the rejuvenated agricultural sector in the South, which further solidified slavery there. In the North too, free African Americans experienced increasing segregation, increased violence in the streets, and a degradation of their rights as citizens. Even many well-meaning reformers believed that deportation was the solution to the country's racial dilemma.

But I would argue that after the war not one of these developments went unchallenged by the African American community. Black people spoke out when states systematically robbed them of their civic rights. They protested and acted when slaveholders from the South tried to reclaim runaway slaves. When reformers suggested that slaves be freed and shipped off to Africa, members of black churches throughout the North roared their disapproval. They argued that colonization was a way to perpetuate slavery in this country. They claimed that this was their land and that their forefathers had spilled their blood in its defense. The abolition movement used not only the rhetoric of the American Revolution but also the example of their fathers and grandfathers who had fought to create the Republic. Black veterans had explained to their children and grandchildren how they had brought down British generals. They exhibited badges of merit and showed their war wounds to their kin. On the distaff side, black women related how difficult it had been to marry their soldier sweethearts and then keep the home front going during the eight years of war. And when the situation deteriorated for the black community in the nineteenth century, this same generation mounted county courthouse steps to claim their due as well as make sure that their role in the nation's founding was inscribed in governmental records. This book will focus on the people who pushed for decades to make the Revolution a meaningful event for not only themselves but also for their children and generations to come.[4]

Sources and Parameters

The major characters of this book, African American soldiers in Washington's forces, tend to appear primarily on lists largely representing poor, illiterate men. These lists account for men paid, men receiving bounties, men receiving new clothing, and men court-martialed. They list men present, men hospitalized, men captured by the enemy, deserters, men furloughed, and men who died while in service. There are certain lists on which the subjects of this book do not appear. African Americans in the revolution never figured on promotion lists because they were never promoted. They almost never appeared on newspaper lists of those fallen in battle as only officers typically merited that honor. To the degree that black soldiers' lives were circumscribed, the historian is similarly circumscribed.

But the lists do speak of the opportunity the war afforded black men. Whether signing enlistment papers, challenging slavery in court, or running away from a plantation, a generation stepped forward in the revolution "to stand in their own light." The phrase comes from Henry Laurens, one of the largest slaveholders in South Carolina, who would become the president of the Continental Congress. While on a trip to England in 1771, Laurens kept tabs on the doings of his numerous plantations in South Carolina and Georgia. In December that year, he advised his brother to consign Sam, a house servant, to fieldwork on another plantation. Sam had previously been "admonished," but Laurens doubted that would be enough. The slave's crime? Henry Laurens condensed Sam's infractions to his "standing too much in his own light." This was dangerous behavior, claimed Laurens, and could corrupt the rest of the slaves on the plantation. While Laurens may or may not have quelled Sam's independent spirit, the slave owner could not stop a generation of African Americans who stepped into their own light during the Revolution and made slavery forever after a point of contention in American life.[5]

The names of these people inscribed on the lists of the Revolution represent enormous risk and a powerful legacy. What follows are examples of various lists that lay out the parameters of this book. The muster list speaks to the sacrifice of black soldiers. The "List of Belongings of Fallen Soldiers" is used to explain who is included in this study. The list of "Negroes in the Engineer Department" of the British Army shows that men of color had an alternative to signing up with Washington's forces. And finally, with pension records, we see veterans themselves describing their contributions in army camps and on battlefields. The equivalent of shards of pottery and bits of bone found on an archaeological site, these pieces of paper assembled together tell a story, one of individuals with aspirations, perseverance, and humor, far beyond a list of names. My journey with these veterans led me to realize that the lists of this study add up to a movement of liberation far greater than their individual traces at first reveal.

The main focus of this book is on the black men who risked leaving the familiar to enlist in Washington's forces. Their motivations ranged from adventure to money to freedom. At the beginning of the conflict it was not easy for them to enlist. But as the war dragged on and public enthusiasm waned, white revolutionary leaders begrudgingly relented and allowed blacks to serve.

Muster rolls were used to keep track of the comings and goings of the army's companies. They were antecedents of attendance sheets and time clocks. For example, the muster roll transcribed below lists the men in Captain David Humphreys's Fourth Connecticut regiment (his name is spelled "Humphrey" in the original document) and provides a snapshot of the company in the spring of 1782. The unit is extraordinary because its privates are all black men—this in

Washington's largely integrated army. The muster hints of this. While the white officers' names are ones common in New England, featuring English and biblical sources, many of the privates have names beloved by slave masters: characters from the ancient slave-holding societies of Greece and Rome, place names, African day names, and nicknames—all unlikely to be found on New England tax lists or church records. The first and second columns of the muster roll list ranks and names, and the third column indicates that almost all the men enlisted for the war's duration. These individuals sometimes called themselves "during-the-war men" in their pension applications. A white unit typically featured an array of enlistment lengths, from duration of war to three years to nine months. As the war progressed, Washington was able to extract longer enlistments from Congress and so all-white units increasingly resembled this one.[6]

Roll and Muster of Capt. David Humphrey's Company, 4th Connecticut Regiment
Commanded by Zebulon Butler

Rank	Names	Term of Enlistment	Casualties
Capt	David Humphrey	ADC to his Excellency	
Lieut	John Ball		
Ens	John Cleaveland		
Serg	John McLean	D.War*	
Serg	Gamaliel Terry	D.War	
Serg	Daniel Bradley	D.War	
Serg	Edmund Fields	D.War	
Serg	Constant Chapman	D.War	
Corp	Abel Hitchcock	D.War	transferred to the 8th comp.
Corp	Phinehas Strong	D.War	
Corp	Jesse Vose	D.War	
Corp	Heman Rogers	D.War	
Drum	Lent Munson	D.War	
Fife	Isaac Higgens	2 years, 2 months	
No. 1	Jack Arrabas	D.War	
No. 2	Bristol Baker	D.War	
No. 3	Ceasar Bagdon	D.War	
No. 4	Sharp Camp	D.War	
No. 5	Job Ceasar	D.War	

(cont.)

Roll and Muster of Capt. David Humphrey's Company, 4th Connecticut Regiment Commanded by Zebulon Butler (*cont.*)

Rank	Names	Term of Enlistment	Casualties
No. 6	Ceasar Chapman	D.War	
No. 7	Timothy Ceasar	D.War	
No. 8	Pomp Cyrus	D.War	
No. 9	Samson Cuff	2 years, 1 month	
No. 10	James Dinah	D.War	
No. 11	Juba Dyer	1 year, 10 months	
No. 12	Ned Freedom	D.War	
No.13	Dick Freedom	D.War	
No. 14	Philemon Freeman	D.War	
No. 15	Peter Freeman	D.War	
No. 16	Thomas Freeman	D.War	
No. 17	Primus Freeman	D.War	
No. 18	Juba Freeman	D.War	
No. 19	Peter Gibbs	D.War	
No. 20	Prince George	D.War	
No. 21	Andrew Jack	D.War	lines
No. 22	Shubael Johnson	D.War	
No. 23	Prince Johnson	?	
No. 24	Alexander Judd	D.War	
No. 25	Peter Lion	D.War	
No. 26	Pomp Liberty	D.War	
No. 27	Cuff Liberty	D.War	
No. 28	Jack Little	D.War	
No. 29	Lewis Martin	D.War	
No. 30	Joseph Otis	D.War	
No. 31	John Rogers	D.War	
No. 32	Solomon Sowtis	D.War	
No. 33	William Sowards	D.War	
No. 34	Ezekiel Tophand	D.War	on the lines
No. 35	Hector Williams	D.War	
No. 36	Harry Williams	D.War	
No. 37	Cato Wilbrow	D.War	on the lines

Roll and Muster of Capt. David Humphrey's Company, 4th Connecticut Regiment Commanded by Zebulon Butler (*cont.*)

Rank	Names	Term of Enlistment	Casualties
No. 38	Congo Zado	D.War	
No. 39	Cuff Freeman	D.War	in camp? w/horses
No. 40	Peter Mix	D.War	
No. 41	Sharp Rogers	D.War	
No. 42	Cato Robertson	D.War	
No. 43	Dick Violet	D.War	deserted
No. 44	Jeff Sill	D.War	died Nov. 27, 1781, N.J.
No. 45	Prince Crosley	7 months, 10 days (enlisted May 2, 1782, for 8 months)	

I certify the above roll to be the true state of said company this 23rd Day of May 1782, John Ball, Lieut.

* Duration of war
Source: Revolutionary War Rolls, 1775–1783, RG 93, National Archives and Records Administration

This segregated unit, black soldiers under white officers, was created as the Sixth Connecticut in the Continental Army's reorganization of late 1780. As of January 1, 1781, Connecticut's nine regiments were reduced to five. The Sixth Connecticut was the only regiment not to be combined with another in the consolidation. It simply changed its name, from the Sixth to the Fourth. All black soldiers formerly of the Sixth were placed in an all-black company in the Fourth Connecticut, along with five new black recruits. Other men of color in the Connecticut line remained scattered among white regiments, as was typical in the Continental Army. The company's captain, David Humphreys, is listed on the muster as an aide-de-camp to "his Excellency," referring to George Washington. He had two jobs and so did not devote himself entirely to his unit. Indeed Humphreys's correspondence from this period has him far from his men's camp at West Point. So the everyday management of the company often devolved on the other white officers, listed on the muster in decreasing order of rank.[7]

By 1782, these black privates were seasoned soldiers. Most had enlisted in 1777, when the laws of Connecticut opened service to all males between the ages of sixteen and sixty. In 1777 the Connecticut legislature also freed slave owners from any financial liability connected with slaves they had freed. This law, combined with one that allowed men to hire substitutes for military service, assured that freeing slaves and having them serve in the stead of the master would entail no financial risk if the ex-slave could not support himself in future. And so, as the muster indicates, slaves joined the army for the war's duration with the prospect of freedom at the end. With this result in mind, many men in Humphreys's company apparently chose last names that bespoke their new status (Freeman, Freedom, Liberty), although five of these soldiers, such as Pomp Liberty, elected to retain their slave names as first names, revealing the admixture of free and slave that their lives encompassed. Whether one influential soldier started the trend or an officer made the suggestion (one Connecticut veteran said in his pension petition that his commanding officer had helped him in this regard), the idea of proclaiming one's new status caught on.[8]

Other sources fill in the story of the muster, but they can go only so far. Why was the company of black privates formed? Was it David Humphreys's idea? Did white prejudice play a role? The muster does not reveal what the men thought of suddenly being singled out in this way. Were they happy to work in a largely African American unit or were they resentful, having worked for four years with white men in Washington's army? Were they apprehensive that as former slaves they were being corralled together for future re-enslavement? Were their roles the same as those of privates in other units in the Connecticut line or were they the ones who pulled ditch-digging duty? No letters or diaries answer these questions. The muster list simply tells us who was present. But the names presented here lead the researcher to other sources that flesh out the story.[9]

Such is the case with Prince Crosley, seen on the muster roll as having enlisted in this unit in 1782. His widow applied for a pension in the 1830s, and in this application she tells the before and after of his revolutionary war service. Crosley grew up in a slave family that served the governor of Connecticut, Matthew Griswold. The governor's son later testified that Crosley was known as "Crottoo" or "Crotter" at this time. Crosley and his brother, Jim, were sold away to different masters shortly before the war. Jim lost his life in military service. Since Prince Crosley died just before the first pension act of 1818, we have no depositions from him, but numerous neighbors and veterans who supported his widow in her pension quest pieced together his movements. His daughter said he ran away from his second master and joined the army. A fellow veteran claimed that Crosley subbed for his master, who freed him at the end of three years.

Regardless of how he enlisted, we know that Crosley first signed up for a three-year stint in the First Connecticut. One veteran later recalled that he was at first known there as "Governor Griswold's Negro." He later became "Prince

Griswold" on the rolls. At the end of his three-year service, a free man, he changed his name to Prince or Prentiss Crosley. He made an impression on two of his soldier colleagues by carrying a fiddle on the top of his knapsack, an instrument "he used when at liberty." Prince also carried his fiddle to Asa Lay's light infantry company, an elite unit of the Continental Army. The best soldiers participated in light infantry assignments. Then, in the spring of 1782, he appears on our muster roll when he enlisted in Humphreys's black company.

Another veteran later testified that Crosley never recovered from a battle wound to his knee, leaving him permanently lame. Regardless, after the war Crosley married Caroline Miller, and together they had nine children. When he wanted to build a house in a certain neighborhood, a prominent white man objected until a former revolutionary war officer reminded him that Crosley had been one of the revolutionaries, saying the "old warrior . . . deserved to live among folks." Crosley must have impressed his community because when his widow needed support for her pension application in 1838, four former soldiers and seven neighbors, including the son of his former master, went to court to testify on her behalf.[10]

The muster roll certainly shows us that black men were there, but it also highlights the soldiers' length of service and the higher stakes involved in the promise of individual freedom if they survived the war. Among historians, this company is well known as an African American unit. But what of others? How does one determine whether a name indicates a man of color or not?

The scrap of paper shown in figure 1 is a visual metaphor for the lowly status of the rank and file in the army. The privates whose apparel it details were two of the three men in Captain Thomas Arnold's First Rhode Island Regiment who died on October 22, 1777, at the Battle of Red Bank in New Jersey. When the smoke cleared, a list was made of the things the soldiers left behind. Williams Kirk's clothing included a waistcoat and linen shirts, one "with ruffles," perhaps an indication that he aspired to gentleman's status. At first glance, one might miss the entry for William Sharper below the line. He apparently wore all that he owned on his back when he died. We know very little about him. He appeared in one muster list as "William Sharpo." It is possible that Private Sharpers was an African American, even an enslaved or formerly enslaved soldier since he had nothing to send home except what he wore on his feet. His name too suggests a man of color—"Sharp" or "Sharper" being common first names for male slaves. Yet no source from this period labels him as such. Thus, for the purposes of this study, he cannot be counted as an African American.[11]

There are many promising-sounding African American candidates who turn out not to have been men of color. Take Salisbury Freeman, for example.

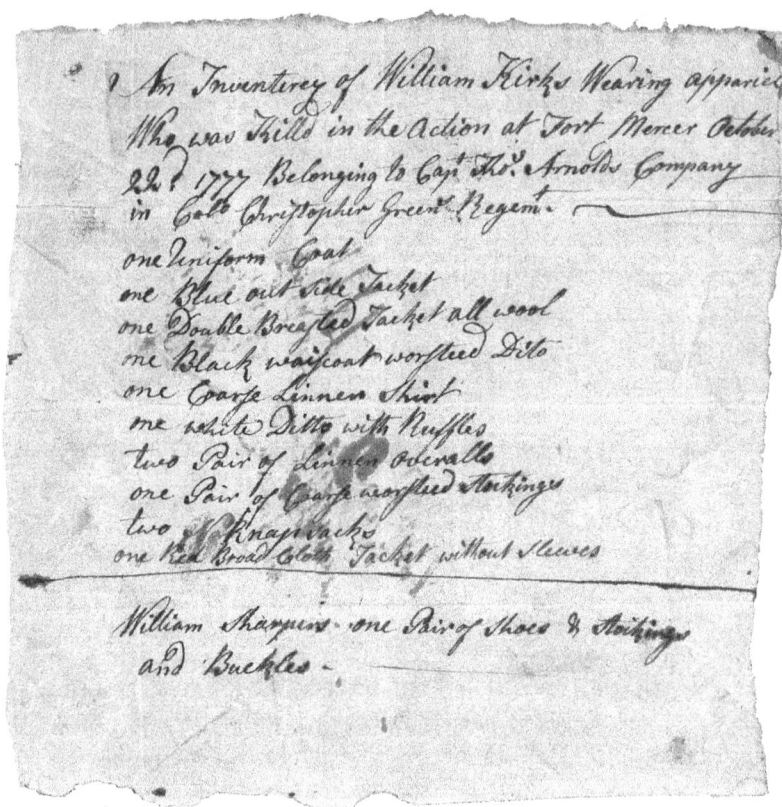

Captain Thomas Arnold company, Colonel Christopher Green regiment, clothing inventory of soldiers killed in action at Fort Mercer, October 22, 1777. Courtesy of the Rhode Island Historical Society, Providence (RHi X17 2385).

His first name is a place name, his last name is a surname chosen by many ex-slaves, and he enlisted in the First Rhode Island, which eventually became a black unit from 1778 to January 1781. Yet the First Rhode Island regimental book and the U.S. Census identify him as a white man. Similarly many masters named their slaves "Prince," but so too did parents of white babies, particularly in New England. Except for males with African names, no man passes muster in this study unless a primary source labels him a man of color.[12]

The term "man of color" encompasses American Indians, who were often labeled "Negro" or "black." Native people from New England often married people of African descent. Native American soldiers often used English names on the roll. Although difficult to properly identify, American Indians figure in this study only if they fought in American militia units or the American army or navy. Soldiers of Indian nations that fought for either side under their own banners are not to be found here.[13]

William Sharper could have been a Narragansett Indian, an African American, a white man, or a man of mixed blood. The nature and paucity of sources when dealing with poor people beget qualifying language by the authors who write about them. The reader will encounter "might" and "probably" quite a bit in this book. With respect to the scrap above, it would be helpful if other lists detailing dead men's effects existed in the archives with clearly noted racial identities attached. That way, if poor white men left clothing and poor black men tended not to, an inference could be drawn about William Sharper.

Aside from Sharper's identity, the scrap itself raises questions. Why was this list created? Were the contents auctioned off to pay the soldier's debt or to send the proceeds to the soldier's family? Did the men's effects go back into the regiment's inventory, or were they returned to their families? If the latter, what must the scene have been like when Sharper's loved ones received his shoe buckles? There it is again in this very section: "must . . . have been." "Might." "Infer." "Suspect." "Could." The terrain requires language of this sort. Historian William Dillon Piersen likened the difficulty of studying eighteenth-century African Americans to fishing. Those dealing with African Americans had to make do with whatever fish they caught, he noted, while those writing about white elites might "distain all but the trophy-sized hunkers."[14]

Although this book centers on the men of color in the Continental Army and militias, it is important to keep in mind that many more African Americans joined the British war effort. They were not necessarily musket-toting soldiers, but they provided critical support to the operations of the British army. They labored on fortifications, served British officers, delivered supplies and wood, spied, guided, and filled in whenever and wherever necessary. The British originally encouraged only those who could join His Majesty's troops. Later, they guaranteed security and freedom for incoming African Americans to pursue any occupation. The next primary source introduces men and women who bet on the British to ultimately provide them—and their families—with liberty.

The *Royal Gazette* of Charleston (then Charles Town), South Carolina, published the list, "Negroes in the Engineer Department," in March 1781, ten months after the British army captured and occupied the city. The battle for Charles Town was the worst defeat for American forces in the revolution—over five thousand men were captured. Such a resounding victory for King George no doubt encouraged many more blacks to consider a move to the British lines, particularly since His Majesty's forces had since the beginning of the war offered freedom to all slaves who deserted their rebel masters and went to work for the British. The engineering department had seen an infusion of ninety-six blacks after the British

Excerpt from "Negroes in the Engineer Department, That Joined the [Royal] Army from the Landing under Sir Henry Clinton in 1780," showing 36 of 218 employees

Owner	Negro	Owner	Negro
Peter Templat	Bristol	Thomas Rivers	Quamina
Ditto	Liberty	William King	Jethro
Ditto	July	Ditto	April
Ditto	Scipio	Joseph Ferby	Abraham
Wil. Wilkinson	John	Benjamin Smith	Cyrus
Isaac Lessesne	Gloucester	Ditto	Friday
Benjamin Cattell	George	Ditto	Scipio
Ditto	Jack	William Bailey	Jack
Benjamin Stone	John	George Smith	Abraham
Mrs. Withers	Primus	Ditto	Jack
Ditto	Bottor	John Bonneau	Quaco
Ditto	Scipio	Peter Smith	Paul
Keating Simons	Primus	Robert Johnston	Ben
John Allen	Jacob	Archer Smith	Sam
Charles Clifford	York	Christian Motte	Jacob
John McTier	Prince	Ditto	Jemmy
Charles Clifford	Moses	Tho. Middleton	Isaac
Sinkler	London	Col. John Laurens	Jemmy

Source: *Royal Gazette*, March 10–March 14, 1781. Courtesy of the Charleston Library Society, Charleston, South Carolina

conquered Georgia in late 1778. Now 208 more people, mostly men, poured into the department. Twenty had belonged to William Moultrie. A prominent rebel general, Moultrie earlier in the conflict had led an attack on a group of runaway slaves occupying an offshore island and later, in 1776, had successfully checked a British attempt to conquer Charles Town. Other African Americans on the list had worked for South Carolina's first families such as the Pinckneys, the Laurenses, and the Middletons.[15]

In the same March 1781 issue of the *Royal Gazette* are other lists of British army employees—representing the commissary, "barrackmaster," quartermaster, Royal Artillery, and general hospital departments. Mapping out the plantations of their owners, one can approximate how arduous the journey was from slavery to freedom. The number of refugees from a specific owner might indicate a severe master. A liberal sprinkling of Francis Rose's slaves staffed the British army departments. Was Rose a sadistic master, or might there have been a persuasive African American leader on his plantation who inspired others to take the risk? Although this book focuses on Washington's side of the conflict, it is important to remember that as each African American decided to work for the local regiment, join the army, or try the legal process to gain his or her freedom, there was a very real alternative with the British army, a power center that had the wherewithal to actually liberate people. Approximately twenty thousand African Americans ran away to the British from 1775 to 1782.[16]

With respect to the *Royal Gazette* list, one might wonder why the British chose to publish such a roster at this time. No such listing appears in the newspapers of occupied New York or Philadelphia. But in 1781 Charles Town there was a problem with loyalist masters' slaves who left the plantation to work for the British army. Indeed, General Henry Clinton's 1781 proclamation incited a "tidal flood" of enslaved people from rebel and loyalist households. The British offer of freedom to pursue any occupation within British lines only applied to slaves belonging to the rebels, yet this important provision seemed of no consequence to slaves who wanted to be free. Their loyalist masters subsequently complained. The British had tried to distinguish legitimate "negroes belonging to the army" by affixing to their uniforms the initial letters of the department that employed them, probably in the form of a cloth badge. This attempt failed. The British army consequently published in the *Royal Gazette* a list of 666 "legitimate black employees at work in the southern army," of whom 218 worked in the engineering department. The British took pains to name their employees' former masters, showing that they all came from rebel houses and plantations. All other blacks, ones not on the list and at work in the various departments, the army claimed, would be sent back to their masters provided the owners submitted the proper paperwork through the Commissioner of Claims office. In future the army would draw all additional black employees from estates seized from the rebels. Did these individuals survive as freemen and freewomen by the end of the war? In 1783 New York City, a list was made of British-allied blacks who had boarded ships for other parts of the British Empire. There are over four hundred South Carolinians on the list, almost all with family names, so again it *could* be that some of these people had served the British army in faraway Charles Town. But the names that appear in the *Gazette* appear only here and then disappear from the record.[17]

The anonymity of many blacks who appear on a list and then disappear has largely left the subject of blacks in the Revolution to the white Americans who commented on them, to Enlightenment thinkers who theorized about rights and freedom, or to a few black luminaries like Phillis Wheatley and Reverend Richard Allen, who left meatier sources for historians to digest. But pension records go a long way toward rectifying this problem, showing evidence provided by African American war participants or the people who knew them well. Revolutionary War pension records provide new evidence beyond the realm of lists. In courthouses throughout the country, average African American soldiers related what they had done in the Revolution. The pension documents also paint a portrait of the soldiers' lives well after the war, as it would be decades before the pensions were applied for. In 1818 and again in 1832, the U.S. government gave pensions to old veterans of 1776 provided they gave sworn depositions in their local court and produced evidence of their service—a written discharge, name on a company's muster list, or depositions, preferably of soldiers or clergymen who attested to the truth of the applicant's story. In 1836 the government provided pensions to widows, which is how Rachel Adams came to tell the story that opens this introduction.

William Johnson's pension testimony in Vermont in 1822 (figure 2) shows that he was answering questions posed by the government: When and where did he enlist? Where and when did he leave the service? The government also asked a petitioner for lists: a list of the veteran's officers, a list of his units throughout the war, the list of battles in which he had participated. Despite the fact that court clerks did not want to waste ink or risk writer's cramp by recording war stories that the veteran had been sharing with his neighbors for years, what was recorded was information provided by a black veteran. Johnson's narrative was also shaped by time. National myths and stories might have influenced the veteran as he related his own story. The events of his war years had occurred forty years earlier. The average age of the 1818 pension act applicant was between sixty-four and sixty-five. Applicants tended to remember some officers' names, but they rarely divulged the number of their regiment. Some did not recall the exact time of their enlistment, but they remembered the season of the agricultural cycle when they had joined up or recalled some big event that occurred around the time of their entry into the army.[18]

William Johnson was a sixty-six-year-old veteran when he applied for a government pension in 1822. His terse affidavit provides bare-bones answers to the handful of questions posed by the government. He enlisted in the spring of 1781 for the war's duration. He names his officers, makes no mention of any battles in which he participated, and states his discharge date (1783). By 1822 he had moved from Massachusetts to Vermont, made his living as a laborer and broom-maker, and owned a few odds and ends valued at five dollars. The State of Vermont used preprinted forms, so there was no room for war stories or other embellishments, even if the court clerk had been disposed to include them.

STATE OF VERMONT.

Caledonia COUNTY ss. } At a County Court, began and holden at Danville within and for said County on the Caledonia day of December A. D. 1822.

Present in Court, the Hon. *Isaiah Fisk* — Chief Judge.
" *Saml. Sias &* — } Assistant
" *Joseph Morrill 2nd Esqs* } Judges.

On this *12th* day of *December* 1822, personally appeared in open Court (being a Court of Record, with a jurisdiction unlimited in point of amount, and having the power of fine and imprisonment) *William Johnson* aged *Sixty six* years, resident in *Lyndon* — in said County, who being first duly sworn according to law, doth on his oath ~~declare, that he served in the Revolutionary War as follows:~~ — *make the following declaration in order to obtain the provision made by the acts of Congress of the 18th March 1818 & 1st May 1820 that he the said William Johnson enlisted into the Regement commanded by Lieut. Col. William Hull and in the Company commanded by Capt. Woodbridge of the Massachusetts Line in the Spring of 1781 for during the War and continued in the Service untill the Spring of 1783 and was honorably discharged — — and in pursuance of the act of the 1st May 1820*

William Johnson's Revolutionary War pension application, 1822. Even with a preprinted form like this one that limited the space in which a court clerk could relate the particulars of a veteran's service, one can learn details of William Johnson's war years as well as his situation at the time of his application. Courtesy of the National Archives and Records Administration, Record Group 15, Case Files of Revolutionary War Pension and Bounty Land Warrant Applications.

Luckily for us, William Johnson had difficulty providing proof of his service. He lived in northern Vermont, far away from the Boston area of his youth, and could find no witnesses for his application. He subsequently took to the road to find supporters, which led to a second document in the Johnson file—the affidavit of William Hull, the lieutenant colonel of Johnson's unit. Although Hull had not seen Johnson in forty years, the former officer recalled that this "coloured man" (underlined in the original) still retained the pockmarks on his face from the smallpox he had contracted while acting as a servant to Hull. Johnson had ridden out his illness in Hull's tent across the river from West Point. Hull mentioned that Johnson's wife, Violet, had followed her husband into the war and become "very useful in washing for the officers." When a major in the regiment transferred into a light infantry unit, he brought Johnson along to act as his waiter. After the special mission concluded, Johnson returned to the Third Massachusetts. Until the end of the war, Hull took pains to point out, Johnson had served as a soldier, even though it was in a noncombat support role. "He was much esteemed for this fidelity and good conduct," added Hull, who concluded his deposition by saying that although Johnson was deaf and in feeble health, the old vet had walked "hundreds of miles" to find an officer who knew him.

William Johnson's pension file tells us a lot about the veterans and the times they lived in. Johnson's affidavit makes no mention of race or the fact that he was pulled out of the line to act as a servant to white officers. It is Colonel Hull who underscored the words "coloured man," perhaps in an effort to explain the connection between Johnson's race and his duties in the regiment. When Johnson contracted smallpox, he was not consigned to a secluded hut but stayed in his commanding officer's tent. Johnson was not only faithful to his unit during the war but also to his wife, Violet, with whom he was still married in 1822. He describes her as sickly at that time. Violet, also a veteran of the war, could well have repeated the words of another black veteran's wife who described herself as an "old soldier's wife . . . worn out and broke to pieces."

Johnson showed perseverance and determination in moving to a frontier and then leaving his northern Vermont abode to find the required proof of his service, adding "willingness to take risks" to Johnson's list of attributes. Finally, Hull relates that Johnson was "esteemed." One does not become esteemed for kowtowing to officers. William Johnson must have carried himself and acted in a way that merited the white man's high regard. And when Johnson appeared on Hull's doorstep forty years later, the two men undoubtedly reminisced about the shiny time of their youth. At the end of that surprising visit, Lieutenant Colonel Hull had not changed his mind about Private Johnson's character.

Other pensions, particularly those that were rejected at one point or another by the government, feature veterans' responses that provide more information—even stories. Veterans who applied under the 1832 pension act tend to be wordier, as by then they had great difficulty finding veterans who could testify for them. They made up this deficiency by adding more narrative to their depositions. As you will see, the pension applications put a face on Revolutionary War veterans. The narratives based on distant recollections were shaped by what the government wanted to know and then mediated by white court clerks, but they provide African Americans a voice in the Revolutionary War story. Like no other source, they divulge that significant numbers of rank-and-file black soldiers played a crucial role in the founding of the United States.[19]

The five hundred African American pension files that are the basis of this book go a long way toward explaining why later generations of abolitionists used them to advance their arguments. The war itself provided African Americans with greater leverage in their everyday lives. With white men absorbed in the chaos of violent upheaval, people of color could negotiate better conditions on American farms and plantations. They could run away more easily. When it came to military service, they made a choice on a life-transforming level, a power they rarely had before the Revolution. They decided whether or not to join the military. Even the men who were drafted into their first stint often told the pension office that they had subsequently reenlisted on their own. It was important to them to indicate that they had made a free choice. Men who substituted might well have been coerced by their masters, but here also many masters had to offer their slaves eventual freedom for the boon of staying home and furthering their prosperity. To extract the promise of eventual freedom indicated a measure of control that men of color had likely never before had. This new decision-making power exercised by men of color was materially enhanced by the fact that they had another viable option—to join the British. For the first time in their lives, a power center in their world issued them an invitation. Escape slavery, urged a series of British leaders, by running away from rebel masters and working for wages with His Majesty's forces. It was a particularly enticing offer in light of no comparable promise from the Continental Congress. Between 1775 and 1783, men of color had options to consider as they contemplated their next move.[20]

For the pensioners on the American side, life in the military had permitted them a range of action unthinkable in civilian life. Whether complaining to an officer about some instance of inequity or besting white men on the field of battle, young soldiers of color could assert themselves in ways that civilian life rarely condoned. Mark Murry, a militiaman, demanded to receive a discharge certificate when his tour of duty was over. John Ellis of North Carolina felt the thrill of the chase in pursuing loyalists throughout the Carolina piedmont. Soldiers also effected profound changes in their own lives, creating surnames for themselves or buying relatives out of slavery. Cato Freedom, born in Africa, chose a family name that reflected the deal he had made with his master—his service for freedom, a state of being he possessed at birth but later lost when the agents of slavery snatched it from him.[21]

Operating in an integrated army, black and white privates confronted the enemy, shoulder to shoulder. Hamet Achmet, a native of Africa, and Daniel Raymond, a white native of Connecticut, both stared up the cliff they were expected to climb at Stony Point. William Taburn and Thomas Jordan saw the blood of their beloved officer pour out onto the ground at Cowen's Ford. Black and white men faced hardship and profound moments that their neighbors back home could not imagine. This shared experience often created a bond that lasted at least until the end of their service. When Mark Murry complained about his discharge, three white messmates accompanied him to their officer's tent. When black veterans needed support for their pension applications, they most often went to their white cohort, whose depositions ranged from matter-of-fact statements of the black men's presence in the line [he was there] to statements of appreciation [he was a good soldier] to occasional assessments filled with admiration and affection. When Solomon Bibbie, a veteran of the Tenth North Carolina Regiment, applied for a pension, the government office gave him a hard time about why he had taken so long to apply. Bibbie brought his neighbors into the picture when he explained that neither he nor they imagined the pension act applied to colored people. The African American veteran then got a support deposition from the son of an officer in his unit who said that his father had said about Bibbie that "no finer soler he never saw in his life."[22]

In general, this shared experience resulted in an acknowledgement of one veteran's presence in a company or regiment. It does not prove camaraderie trumping racism, but it is an opening, an appreciation between two individuals of different races. Perhaps this accounts for the Pension Office's remarkable color-blindness during the first pension act. In 1818 there were still many veterans alive who could attest to a black man's service in and out of government. By the pension act of 1832, American society had changed, and many fewer witnesses could attest to revolutionary war happenings.

In applying for their pensions, black veterans affirmed revolutionary ideals. They demanded their due like any other man. Each veteran had to stand alone in his local courthouse and resurrect another era, a time when vigilant citizens dropped their farm chores and hit the road to help their compatriots, risking their lives in the process. They spoke of gaining freedom, of spilling their own blood for it, and they condemned dastardly masters for breaking promises to their slaves turned soldiers. James Dinah of the Connecticut line, featured on the muster list in figure 1, proved his mastery of the nation's founding documents by using famous revolutionary words to explain his journey to a new home. "When in the course of human events," he said, "it is sometimes necessary to move."[23]

These funny, courageous, and persevering men had to face an ungrateful nation at war's end. Whether freeman in the North or slave in the South, a black man was perceived by the white community as "less than" because of skin color. Prince Vaughan, a five-year veteran whose toes and joints were seriously damaged at the disastrous Oswego expedition, kept an oyster stand in New York City and polished shoes to make a living. But he was also a Badge of Merit winner who treasured his discharge certificate signed by Washington and could tell his soldier stories to customers and family alike.[24] As is evident in the widows' pensions of the 1830s and 1840s, the children and grandchildren of revolutionary soldiers testified that their fathers and grandfathers had regaled them with stories of their role in the nation's founding. This later generation, in the course of agitating for abolition and equality, cited their family members' sacrifices. Newspapers, pamphlets, books, speeches—they contained the argument that people who spilled their blood on the battlefield deserved an equal share of the nation they had created. These black soldiers and their presence in the literature of liberation are a hitherto unheralded link between the American Revolution and the majestic Thirteenth Amendment.

The book opens with a chapter that places the Revolutionary War soldiers in their setting before the war. Free blacks, as well as the enslaved, lived under distinct laws aimed at shackling them to lifelong service. Each colony had its own variations. In addition to laws, work regimes and proximity to white communities also made for different cultures. I begin with South Carolina and work my way up the coast, allowing South Carolina to stand for the Deep South, Virginia to represent the Chesapeake, Pennsylvania and New York to highlight middle colony life, and finally Massachusetts to portray the New England scene. Other states will take center stage when specific issues arise necessitating this. Although each region presented its own challenges to people of color, there is little dialogue in this book about the morality of slavery in the prerevolutionary period. In all of the colonies, North and South, a master could lash out at any time with no repercussions from his community. This review of slave life ends in Massachusetts, where revolutionary activity begins. The second part of the chapter deals with the opening controversies of the American Revolution, as African Americans and racial tactics played a role. When the fighting starts, the revolutionary authorities immediately turn their attention to the role that men of color can play in the military conflict, in part because the British were a major power in North America offering freedom to the enslaved.

Chapter 2 follows the states as they grappled with the possibility of black soldiers and even of slave soldiers. Southern states sometimes opened the door to black participation in advance of their northern neighbors. Evincing many of the same motivations for joining the army as whites, black men faced unique challenges that sometimes made for different, more pressing motivation than their white compatriots. The same can be said for their daily routine in camps and on battlefields. Drawing on the Revolutionary War pension records, we see the war from the perspective of the rank and file caught in dramatic and dangerous events as well as during the long intervals in between.

Washington's army was an integrated operation. Chapters 3 and 4 deal with two states that seriously contemplated all-black regiments: Rhode Island, which implemented such a unit, and South Carolina, which failed to do so. Both states responded to the lack of enthusiasm for sustaining the war effort that characterized all thirteen states. The war was only in its second year when low enlistment reached a crisis level. Regiments typically numbered between six hundred and eight hundred men. Due to attrition, many Continental Army regiments dwindled to less than three hundred. Calls for patriotic commitment and ever-increasing bounties did not do the trick. Officers in the Rhode Island line suggested to Washington that they recruit an all-black regiment from among the state's enslaved population—this in a state that was the center of the slave trade in North America. Based on orderly books, correspondence of generals and Rhode Island officers, Continental Congress documents, Rhode Island assembly minutes, pension records, newspapers, muster records, tavern records, and even smaller scraps of extant writings of the day, this chapter addresses the racial composition of the First Rhode Island Regiment, the possibility of black noncommissioned officers, the role of the unit at the Battle for Rhode Island, the regiment's segregation from the main army, the internal dynamics of the unit, the divergent versions of the disaster at Pines Bridge, and the black soldiers' eventual segregation when the Rhode Island regiments were reunited in 1781.[25]

While Rhode Island succeeded in forming a small regiment of black soldiers, South Carolina not surprisingly failed to avail itself of this option. What is surprising is that the idea's major backer was a scion of one of South Carolina's major slaveholding families. John Laurens, son of Henry Laurens, the president of the Continental Congress, kept arguing, debating, and cajoling his father and anyone else who would listen in an effort to form a regiment from the state's enslaved population. Chapter 4 focuses not only on the famous exchange of letters between father and son but also what the Laurens's correspondence reveals about the enslaved people on the family's plantations and town house, people who fought a different kind of conflict than the soldiers in their military units.

Chapters 5 and 6 show that the black solders' fighting days were not over once the military conflict ended. The African American community wrote petitions, celebrated the anniversaries of gradual emancipation legislation in the

North, produced leaders who united and galvanized black communities, protected refugee slaves from slave owners, secured allies in the white community, and established aid societies for the growing black population of America's cities. They faced growing hostility as the battle for equality ran up against Jeffersonian democracy (for white men only) and an epidemic of fear among whites. Employment opportunities shrank for free people of color. Their right to vote was stripped from them in one state after another. But the United States did not retreat back to the Founders' formative years. The unquestioning days of slavery's existence were over.

For the black community, the war had widened the scope of discussion to include issues of equality. The Revolutionary War veterans provided a solid flank in this battle. In 1818 and in 1832 they stood in their county courthouses to relate their contribution to American independence. Hundreds of men of color demanded their due. They had fought like their white brethren, and now they braved not only county officials but also Washington bureaucracy to prove this fact. The Revolutionary War pension records paint a picture of the veterans' lives in the early Republic with respect to economic status, mobility, family composition, literacy, white allies, and their memories of the war.

The book's final section highlights individual men's struggles with the Pension Office. Pension records transform the black veterans from blurred images to focused portraits. Primus Hall of Massachusetts, Jeff Brace and Hamet Achmet of Connecticut, Sam Sutphin of New Jersey, and Mark Murry of North Carolina were not going to let anyone deny their sacrifice in the nation's founding. These men could not have dreamed of such resistance in the world in which they grew up. That world had not yet experienced the liberating potential of the American Revolution.

CHAPTER 1

ON JORDAN'S STORMY BANKS

THEIR WORLD BEFORE THE WAR

The Revolutionary War gave black soldiers a face and a voice in American history. Unlike previous wars, the Revolution's ideals spoke to the condition of the enslaved. To understand this pivotal change, one must appreciate the world in which they were formed. Work regimes, masters' and slaves' personalities, their proximity to one another, the percentage of blacks in a colony's population, the economic value of slave labor to a region, and the ability to remain in one's family—all of these mixed to produce a myriad of combinations that formed each black soldier's spirit. All, however, lived under a code of laws in each colony that set out to quash free will, stifle a sense of self, and consign people of color to the drudgery of ceaseless work. These laws went unquestioned by all but a few before the revolution. The general message of white authorities to blacks was to work and be cheerful, or at the very least to work and shut up, and this was so throughout the thirteen colonies. To speak up or go against the grain was a hazardous enterprise, reinforced by law and custom.

Thomas Jefferson, slaveholder and expert on Chesapeake slavery, distilled the essence of the institution in a metaphor convenient to all masters, calling it a state of war. Whites and blacks in America would never see true peace, explained Jefferson, because of deep-rooted white prejudice and the "ten thousand recollections by the blacks, of the injuries they had sustained." To control the enemy was therefore key. It was important that the master class not be lulled into the mistaken notion that slaves could become free and equal in this country. Such an experiment, claimed the master of Monticello, would lead to "convulsions which will probably never end but in the extermination of the one or the other race."[1]

What Jefferson had not taken into account when predicting the future were persons like fellow Virginian Tim Jones and Isham Carter from South Carolina, both men from slave societies where fabulous wealth was generated by enslaved labor. These two men took part in "convulsions" but not of the Jeffersonian variety. Both black men were on Jefferson's side in the Revolutionary War, having marked their Xs on enlistment papers of the Continental Army, where they served for several years. They saw the possibility of freedom that Jefferson did not. Tim Jones's service resulted in his freedom from slavery. Isham Carter, one of the few free blacks in South Carolina, might have hoped that his service would result in freedom for his wife and children, not to mention a more secure position for himself in the postwar world. These men not only survived the war, each was awarded a Badge of Merit. The war provided a platform for them, from which to build a legacy contributing to a world very different from Jefferson's Armageddon. All the more important it is, then, to examine the societies from which these southerners sprang. We will begin with Isham Carter's South Carolina, focusing on the legal bonds of slavery, and then move on to Tim Jones's Virginia, where the focus will be on plantation life.

South Carolina

Never was Jefferson's warfare imagery made more concrete than in the center of South Carolina's slave society, where a building called the workhouse loomed over the western fringes of Charles Town, the colony's capital. With massive towers and crenellated walls, it functioned as a "house of confinement and correction," supplementing another prison in town. For people of color, the "correction" going on within those walls made the workhouse a dreaded place to contemplate. Any blacks "playing the rogue at unseasonable hours of the night" would be deposited there. Any found on the roads without a master's pass, called a ticket, would end up in a cell there. Uncooperative slaves whose spirit could not be broken on the plantation would be handed over to professional torturers, whose techniques, it was thought, would render the resistant ones sufficiently docile to return to work. In the nineteenth century, witnesses wrote of the screams that could be heard through the thick walls of the facility.[2]

One of these, Angelina Grimke, brought up in an upper-class family in early nineteenth-century Charles Town, called the workhouse "the house of blood." Once, passing the place, she became weak in the knees, believing herself to be in "the precincts of hell." She saw the results of a stay there on individuals who had been gregarious, lively house servants before their incarceration. "But the exercise of the slaveholder's power," claimed Grimke, "had thrown the fierce air of tyranny even over these." This was the purpose of the workhouse—to drive its inmates to permanent docility and despair.[3]

When the two Griffin brothers and the three Jeffers brothers—all black Continental Army privates from central South Carolina—approached Charles Town for the first time, the outlines of the workhouse would have been apparent on the skyline, along with church steeples and perhaps the small tower over the Exchange Building, where slave auctions occurred. These soldiers fought to keep the British out of Charles Town, but to no avail. Osborne Jeffers lost his life in the attempt. Morgan Griffin and Allan Jeffers somehow survived their confinement as prisoners of war after the battle.[4]

Isham Carter joined Griffin and Jeffers in prison after the debacle at Charles Town. He was the son of an Indian woman and a black man, making him free under the laws of South Carolina. As a nineteen-year-old he had enlisted in the South Carolina artillery. He did not remember the date he signed up but reckoned it was shortly after the disastrous Battle of Brier Creek on March 3, 1779. (The patriot force in eastern Georgia was surprised and routed that day.) Subsequent battles in which Carter participated were no more encouraging: Stono Ferry, Savannah, and Charleston. He served his unit's colonel for a short time, but for the long haul he was a matross (gunner's assistant) who loaded and fixed guns until the end of the war.[5]

These African Americans, engaged in the most aggressive of pursuits, came from a society that tied their hands, where sadism, rape, and pedophilia went unchecked against people of their color. African Americans lived under special laws that applied only to them and rendered them helpless, for example, when a slaveholder laid covetous eyes on a ten-year-old. Obviously the few blacks of the South Carolina line did not fight to uphold this system into which they had been born. Each as an individual probably thought he could change his situation for the better. They were not defeatist men who shrugged their shoulders and whined "what can we do?" Along with all men of color who took active roles in the American Revolution, they lived with enormous risk in order to change their world. That world prominently featured laws that treated black people as enemies of whites, making for a virtual war, as Thomas Jefferson had asserted. Jefferson was stumped over how to resolve slavery, but he knew what he was talking about when he described volcanic masters who lost control and victimized people whose hands were legally and literally tied behind them.

Laws and Life: South Carolina

The South Carolina assembly, one of the much-vaunted examples of representative government in the colonies, passed the laws that determined who would inhabit the workhouse. Naturally those who committed a crime would be sent there. But the difference between paying a fine and languishing in prison was often determined by skin color. Certain crimes could only be committed by people of color. As the American revolutionary generation grew up in South Carolina, the code that governed the lives of "Negroes and other Slaves" was passed in 1740, one year after the Stono Rebellion, in which approximately one hundred slaves made a break for Spanish Florida, killing twenty-five whites along the way. The act clamped down on movement, assembly, and independent economic activity on the part of people of color. The preamble explained that the law kept the slave in "due subjection and obedience" as well as restrained the cruelty of the master, as if this were a matter of balance. But only six of the law's fifty-eight subsections dealt with reining in the slave owner, and those clauses were vague and very difficult to prosecute. For instance, clause 38 dictated that owners provide enough food and clothing for slaves under their charge. How was the owner brought to justice for violating this clause? A white person had to bring a complaint to the parish justice on behalf of the slave. If positive proof were missing, the owner could clear his name by taking an oath that he adequately provided for his slaves. What constituted positive proof? The law did not say. What was deemed sufficient food and clothing? The law remained mute.[6]

When it came to restricting slave behavior, however, the law was very specific. On the subject of clothing, no slave could dress above his station. Thus, a slave could wear no apparel finer or of greater value than "Negro cloth, duffels, kerseys, osnabrigs, blue linen, check linen, or course garlix or calicoes, checked cottons, or Scotch plaids." The colony's legislators bothered about this because, they claimed, slaves used "sinister and evil methods" to procure clothes above their station. But unsaid in the law was the concern that poor whites might chafe at seeing a slave better dressed than they.[7]

On violent crimes, the law was far from impartial but made a show of protecting the slave. A slave who was beaten while on business for the master got the satisfaction of seeing his attacker pay a fine that went to the local parish. If the slave were "maimed or disabled" by the beating, the attacker had to pay the owner fifteen shillings a day for "lost time" until the victim could again work. If the attacker were short on cash, he could be sent to jail until the penalty was paid. The owner here is the protected party, and the victim is lost in the penalties and fines around his monetary value to the master.[8]

But what if the master killed or cruelly used a slave? If done "willfully," a master would have to pay the very substantial fine of seven hundred pounds and would be henceforth prohibited from holding any office in the state. If a master killed a slave in the "sudden heat of passion or by undue correction," the fine went down to 350 pounds, still a substantial sum, but the master could hold office in the state. And finally, if a master willfully cut out the tongue, put out the eye, castrated, or cruelly scalded, burned or deprived any slave of any limb or member, the master would be fined one hundred pounds for every offense. The law specifically protected corrections like "whipping or beating with a horse whip, cow-skin, switch, or small stick or . . . putting irons on or confining or imprisoning such slave."

The fines noted above were substantial. A healthy, skilled slave could be purchased for two hundred pounds, so a seven-hundred-pound fine was serious money. In the wake of the Stono Rebellion, the powerful planters in the assembly indubitably thought about why the slaves had rebelled. Among the limited number of large plantation owners, they knew who among their number practiced sadism. So the assembly members were likely sending a message not only to those in their elevated fraternity but also to up-and-coming planters. The worst punishment was reserved for those without the cash to pay such a fine. If a planter could not pay a seven-hundred-pound fine, the law said that he could be—though rarely if ever was he—consigned to a frontier garrison or committed to the workhouse for seven years of hard labor.[9]

There was a way out for even these offenders because the law sanctioned violence against the enslaved in certain cases. For example, if a slave were off the plantation and defied a white person who wanted to see his ticket, he could be killed with impunity. The owner could also always claim self-defense or claim that his slave had been fomenting rebellion. And who was to bring charges against the master? A slave could not testify in a trial involving whites. Overseers and other white employees would lose their livelihoods if they turned against the owner. These laws against cruelty were at best a warning to those masters prone to losing control on their plantations. If need be, there was now a law in place to punish them in future.[10]

Elsewhere in the 1740 South Carolina act, the legislature shut down every avenue that was seen as possibly leading to rebellion. A slave could not travel anywhere without a ticket from his master. It became chancier for slaves to assemble. The law forbade more than seven slaves in a group to travel the high roads. And the farther south one traveled, the greater the risk. The colony paid good money to retrieve runaway slaves. A dead slave was seen as being better than a slave in Spanish Florida who could inspire others to flee, so the legislature paid for dead slaves too, provided one produced a scalp and two ears. The state was, of course, providing unholy temptation to kill any black man for his body parts.[11]

Slaves could not use a gun unless in the presence of a white man or with a ticket from the master saying the slave could hunt. Slaves were forbidden to carry drums or horns because they could be a means of summoning rebels to gather. (Drums were prominent in the Stono Rebellion.) No tavern or punch house could serve a slave strong liquor without express permission of the master. Slaves could no longer sell produce for their own benefit. Slaves at the market in Charles Town had to have a ticket from their masters stipulating that all proceeds would go to the master. Money meant latitude for potential rebels, seen by slaveholders as dangerous. Slaves could therefore no longer have boats or raise horses for their own benefit because both situations allowed slaves to move about. No slave could rent a room on his own because "nefarious circumstances" could follow. It was illegal to teach slaves to write (there is no mention of reading in this act), since slaves might then forge tickets. Indeed, the fine for teaching a slave to write was greater than the reward for killing a runaway slave. "Thus the legislature deemed educating slaves far more malevolent than even slaves fleeing their masters," wrote legal scholar A. Leon Higginbotham. Finally, to prevent any "barbarous murders" as had been committed at Stono the year before, any white could kill "rebellious negroes" in self-defense with no legal repercussions.[12]

Although the 1740 code included laws previously passed, the masters had further narrowed the parameters of slave life. In the wake of Stono, the assemblymen made it their business to understand the enemy. Suspects were interrogated. Masters of the slaves involved provided information about their suspect slaves to legal officials. The legislators understood that excesses in the system should be eradicated but did not move decisively to do this. The slaves' best protection was not the legal system but their economic value to their masters, and this would continue to be the case.

Three years later, when the law governing blacks was to be renewed, the assembly tacked on another precaution. To protect the population from the wickedness of African Americans, the legislators ordered all men between the ages of sixteen and sixty to attend church services with either a gun or a pair of horse pistols, along with at least enough powder and ball for six shots. One had to produce this hardware every time a church warden asked to see it. If one did not come to church loaded, there was to be a fine, half of which was to go to the church for the relief of the poor—this was inducement for the men of the cloth to cooperate. White churchgoers in Charles Town could travel lighter, as the city watch served as their first line of defense. After all, the Stono Rebellion had started on a Sunday morning. The men who benefited from the free forced labor of others had to be ever ready for action. They could never relax their guard, even in church. Houses of worship provided no asylum from the fear that planters carried with them everywhere.[13]

In the years leading up to the Revolution, assemblymen filled in any chinks in the security wall around their lives. In 1751 the assembly dictated that patrols be prompt in breaking up groups of three or more fugitive slaves who had absented themselves from the plantation for more than thirty days. No slave could carry any firearms off the master's plantations. No black could work at an apothecary shop, for fear of access to poisons. Enslaved doctors could only practice at the specific direction of a white person. There was no limit to the fear these laws manifested.[14]

To the enslaved community coming of age in the American revolutionary era, these laws presented challenges to be overcome by wits and downright guile. The laws testify to the fact that slaves continued to carve out space for themselves in their highly regulated lives. The legislature continued to concern itself about runaways (Spanish Florida was nearby, where slaves were given sanctuary), the ability of slaves to sell produce or carry guns, and their access to watercraft, indicating that the original laws were not effective. Since the fines stipulated in most laws included a cut for the informer, slaves had to be more careful in going about their business. There is some dispute as to the degree of enforcement. The laws themselves penalized owners, sheriffs, and justices of the peace for not administering punishments to slaves, an indication that there was a problem in this regard.[15]

While the enslaved learned the interstices of plantation life, they also had to respond to large events like insurrections. With respect to the Stono Rebellion, the range of the enslaved community's reaction probably ran the gamut. Were the rebels heroes or fools? Did they inspire, or did they teach what *not* to do? Up to the Revolution, white sources recorded rumors of rebellion plots. Historians of slavery dispute whether this was evidence of a broader culture of resistance or only reflected individual responses to specific conditions. What the laws show, not surprisingly, is a reinforcement of patriarchy. If anything, the laws in Stono's wake threw the enslaved back in their masters' arms as practically any law could be countermanded by an owner's note. As a corollary, however, slaves who played their cards right with the patriarch could manipulate their way to a wider scope of action. That is, if one had access to the master.[16]

Plantation owners in South Carolina typically did not live full time on their plantations. Many had townhouses in Charles Town, which was a better option than the malarial swamp of lowland rice fields. They certainly knew their house servants in town, who spoke English and tended to be lighter-skinned than the enslaved workers producing rice and indigo. Being a city servant was a badge of gentility, of rank and dignity, at least for the owner. This was driven home to a northerner, Timothy Ford, who was picnicking along the road to Charles Town with South Carolina friends when they spied a mounted man coming toward them. By the look of his dress and his horse, the northerner surmised that the man was "of some note and distinction." Not so, said his South Carolina hosts—the man was "riding without servants." Eventually two slaves hove into view, however, restoring the master's lost honor. The amazed northerner later reflected that in South Carolina "a person can no more act or move without an

Thomas Coram, *View of Mulberry House and Street*, around 1800. Oil on paper, 4⅛ × 6¾ inches. Built between 1711 and 1714 on the banks of the Cooper River in Berkeley County, South Carolina, Mulberry was a 4,400-acre rice plantation. This painting is one of seven that Coram did of Mulberry. Courtesy of the Gibbes Museum of Art / Carolina Art Association, Charleston, S.C. © Gibbes Museum of Art / Carolina Art Association.

attending servant than a planet without its satellites." Servants were the "necessary equipage" for the southern aristocracy.[17]

But it was the workers on the plantation who provided the wealth that undergirded any pretensions to gentility. And here the master depended on men with whips—white overseers and black drivers—to manage the day-to-day operations on the plantations. That management was based on quota arrangements called the task system. The owner and overseer, perhaps with some input from black drivers, set a work output quota for each slave per day—so many rows to be sown, so many barrels to be packed, so many ditches to be cleaned, so many rows to be hoed. Having completed one's quota, the slaves' labor for the master was done. They could tend their own vegetable patches, fix cabin roofs, go fishing, or engage in other activities that advanced the welfare of their families. How much time and autonomy this system gave to the slave in the mid-eighteenth century is questionable. The laws might provide a clue as to how much of the day was devoted to the master. The 1740 code set maximum daily hours of work for every slave—no more than fourteen or fifteen hours per day, depending on the time of the year. It is likely that the average field hand worked close to these hours for the master every day.[18]

With little connection to whites, historian Ira Berlin noted, the field slaves had more opportunity to maintain African customs and speak their own language, often an amalgam of African languages. There was no expectation, claims historian Gerald Mullin, for South Carolina field hands to speak English. One only has to look at the workhouse ads in the Charles Town newspapers to see the numbers of slaves who did not speak English or had facial scarring from their homelands. African ways were further enhanced by the numbers of people imported straight from Africa when slave importation resumed in earnest ten years after Stono. From 1750 onward, new waves of Gambians and Angolans passed through Charles Town, infusing African ways and languages in the slave population coming of age during the American Revolution. Perhaps this African world provided a buffer for most South Carolina slaves against active participation in the contest that tore South Carolina apart in the late 1770s. Or perhaps, as historian Peter Wood has suggested, the system so reduced them to a state of thorough submission that not many were prepared to participate in the American Revolution.[19]

Life on the Plantation

As Tim Jones's pension file revealed more than fifty years after the fact, his master, under the influence during a "drunken frolic," signed enlistment papers. Sobered up the next morning, the bleary-eyed Rolling Jones regretted his bravado and tapped his slave to go in his place. Jones's master, not Jones, got a cash bounty as well as two hundred acres of land for enlisting. Private Tim Jones served in the Third Virginia Regiment for over four years. He was taken prisoner at the Battle of Camden, exchanged, and then lost a leg at Yorktown, the last major battle of the Revolution. It does not appear that Rolling Jones returned the favor and freed his slave. As the veteran explained to the government pension office, he was given his freedom "by the country." Or as one of his supporters expressed it, Jones "was set free for the faithful manner he discharged his duty."[20]

The nature of the conversation that day after the master's enlistment is not recorded in Jones's pension application. Whether he was coerced or given a choice in the matter, whether or not his master promised him his freedom, the enslaved man completed his part of whatever bargain there was at great personal cost. Whatever deficits marred his owner's character, Tim Jones kept the surname of his master even though he had lived his first thirty years under Rolling Jones's control, under the shadow of coercion, threat, and actual force.

As in South Carolina, the numbers of enslaved people in Virginia were substantial, constituting about 40 percent of the population of half a million. Also as in South Carolina, a slave in Virginia could not raise his hand against a white, had no recourse in the judicial system, could not move off the plantation without a ticket from the master, and suffered under draconian punishments. Strictures on gun ownership, independent trading, and group meetings also characterized Virginia's legislation.[21]

As with South Carolina, it is difficult to know how scrupulously the laws were enforced. Slaves were an economic asset to the master. So long as they did not harm whites, it made no economic sense to undermine their productivity. On the other hand, rage could supersede monetary considerations, and slaves never knew when such an explosion would occur. A northerner recalled one such instance when he had been at the breakfast table of a slaveholder. The diners had just said grace when a slave woman poured out a little more molasses than usual to one of the master's children. The angry master held both of the slave's hands in one of his and beat both sides of her head with the other until his hand hurt. He then removed a shoe and continued to beat her until she screamed for mercy. The master then called in a "great overgrown Negro" to hold the woman down as the master continued to thrash her. All this, said the witness, for a slip of the hand.[22]

Another instance of unexpected cruelty concerned an eight-year-old girl whose mistress sent her to a store to pick up a package. On the girl's return, the mistress opened the small parcel, wherein lay a "raw cowhide strap," about two feet long. Seventy years later the former slave girl remembered, "She started pouring it on me, and I didn't know what she was whipping me about." In the middle of this gust of passion, the mistress managed to spit out her outrage that the girl had not called the mistress's three-year-old son "Marster Henry." The old ex-slave could not fathom it all those decades later. "'Marster' to him—a baby," she exclaimed, still in disbelief.[23]

Despite constant apprehension, enslaved people were not frozen in fear. Successive laws were generated as previous ones covering the same ground were deemed ineffectual, a sign that the subjects of the legislation had found ways to get around them. But the small atrocities of everyday life on the plantation did not rise to the level of the colonial legislature. Thomas Jefferson, himself a burgess in 1769 and a major slave owner, certainly understood this more immediate level of oppression, but his concern rested with the master class. Masters who lost their composure in disciplining slaves provided a terrible example to the next generation. What Jefferson neglected to narrate was that for every owner whose face reddened with rage, there was a defenseless victim in agony. Or as an enslaved Virginian later wrote, "the overseer's whip took no note of aching hearts."[24]

For lack of sources in the eighteenth century, abolitionists and former slaves in the nineteenth-century South provide the victim's perspective. They explain that masters did not always do the whipping. They had brothers whip brothers and mothers whip children. They made husbands and children watch as their wives and mothers were strapped down and thrashed until the blood flowed. One frustrated master had sent a recalcitrant slave to the Charles Town workhouse on multiple occasions to no avail. Ultimately the master made her wear an iron collar with three long prongs projecting out from it and then knocked out one of her front teeth so she could be more easily identified if she ran away. A genteel, churchgoing mistress had to borrow slaves from a neighbor because her own, whipped over and over, had putrefied flesh that "emitted such an intolerable smell that they were not fit to be in the presence of company." Such might have been the condition of young William Grimes, whose master took him behind an icehouse, had Grimes "horsed up" (i.e., raised upon the shoulders of another slave, who confined the victim's hands around his chest), and administered forty to fifty lashes. Grimes was only ten years old.[25]

On the rumor of a slave rebellion, patrols went through the countryside, searching for printed material, especially Bibles and hymnals. The owners of such subversive materials would be whipped. "Our slaves was told," said one former slave, "that if they ever learned to write, they'd lose the hand or arm they wrote with." Another slave related that he and some "white chaps" were playing under a tree with letter blocks when his master came by, saw the blocks, and "whipped me good." Some of the enslaved figured out that since the master so abhorred the idea of learning one's letters, it must be a good thing. So thought a young Maryland boy who would later become a great abolitionist. Frederick Douglass learned his letters from playing with white boys to whom he gave bread for instruction. These attempts to fight the system are all the more extraordinary because an impulsive white man could snuff out the life of a slave with no compunction. A visitor to Virginia knew a young man who, out hunting with his chums, saw a black man walking down the road in front of them. The white man shot him in the back. At least this white murderer had to go to trial, but once there he did not even pretend to be innocent. His lawyer argued that the defendant's mother was a widow and that he was young and had no malicious intention in killing. The young killer was acquitted.[26]

Black freemen, whether in South Carolina or Virginia, fared little better in the legal system. The view of the master class toward free people of color was clearly articulated by the royal governor of Virginia, who in 1723 had to justify to the Board of Trade in London why Virginia had limited the right to vote to free white men. The board's legal counsel had a problem with disenfranchising people based solely on race. Governor William Gooch poured himself into the task.

First of all, he said, a conspiracy had recently been discovered in which free blacks and mulattoes were suspected to have participated. The Virginians had no "legal proof" to convict anybody, but the governor assured the board that free blacks would always side with slaves in any insurrection. As to the character of freed slaves, they were, in a word, insolent. People in England could not know, said Governor Gooch, the "Pride of a manumitted slave," who looked on himself as the equal of the "best of his neighbors." This inappropriate self-esteem was magnified when the freeman had a white father or mother. Gooch felt compelled to explain that these interracial couplings involved lower-class whites only, namely imported servants and convicts. The law in question would preserve a needed distinction in society and would discourage interracial unions, or, as the governor put it, "that kind of copulation." The governor did not rule out that in the future the legislature might reconsider the law based on an individual's education and degree of African or African American descent. This was enough of an explanation to quell the qualms of the board.[27]

While slavery permitted the worst of the worst to happen on any given day, it also featured complicated relationships in which oppression mixed with care and affection. Not surprisingly, we hear most often about these relationships from those who held the upper hand. In South Carolina, Henry Laurens described a homecoming featuring his townhouse slaves engulfing him and welcoming him with tears, although one wonders about the nature of the tears, if any. On another South Carolina plantation, Eliza Pinckney's daily routine included teaching a "parcel of little Negroes" how to read. She later refined the idea to teaching two black girls who would then teach the rest of the black children on the plantation. She labeled her plan a "scheme"—shorthand for unconventional thinking.[28]

Most often the masters allowed their affection to show with respect to elderly slaves. "My honest ones are now too old," wrote Landon Carter of Virginia, "and the young ones are all rogues." Carter devoted six pages of his diary in the 1770s to very old Jack, relating how Carter had humanely moved the slave to less taxing positions as he aged. The tribute ended at Jack's deathbed, where Master Carter did what he could. Whether pressed by revolutionary rhetoric to prove himself a kind master to faithful old Jack or moved solely by affection, Carter's sentimental elegy neatly wrapped up a life of unremitting toil and placed it in the golden light of pastoral tranquility. Jack does not get to speak for himself, and consequently his version of events remains a mystery.[29]

Other slaves did speak, and they sometimes had kind words about their masters. Olaudah Equiano, the African who wrote the most famous slave narrative of the eighteenth century, "still loved" the master who, with not so much as a nod, sold young Equiano to another man. He grieved at the death of his captain, who once had needed to be pressured into saving Equiano from a Georgia slaveholder bent on Equiano's destruction. When Equiano bought his freedom, he still felt beholden to his former master and delayed his return to England in order to work on his master's ships. But Equiano was an exception. He claimed he never felt the lash. His enslavement made him a sailor who plied the Atlantic trade routes accumulating enough money to buy himself out of slavery. The former slaves who told their stories to interviewers of the Federal Writers' Project in the twentieth century lived more typical lives in slavery. They had been born and raised on plantations and farms and experienced the brutality of the ruling class. Still, some slaves in these narratives talked about caring for old masters and mistresses after their liberation. Others talked of "good masters" on the same page that they mentioned a whipping. In this twisted world where whippings were a commonplace in life, a master who rarely resorted to them was deemed a good man.[30]

Although the assemblies of the Deep South and the Chesapeake provided a legal framework for brutal exploitation, and the enormities of the system existed in both places, the work lives of the slaves in these two areas differed considerably, with implications for the culture that resulted within the enslaved community. In Virginia, at least a few of the first Africans had the opportunity to become free and attain economic stability, but the memory of that time was no doubt hazy for the revolutionary generation. Likewise hazy would have been any memories of black slaves and white indentured servants working in the same abysmal conditions. A biracial military coalition in 1676 forced Virginia's governor, William Berkeley, back to England, an event known to history as Bacon's Rebellion. But the slave laws, beginning in 1680, helped to make alliances unlikely between poor whites and blacks. By the mid-eighteenth century, free blacks comprised only 5 percent of the African American population of Virginia. By mid-century, no significant new African importation further refreshed the old country culture. And unlike in South Carolina, black Virginians lived in close proximity to their masters, who tended to live full-time on plantations. The few Africans who were imported in the mid-eighteenth century tended to go to small farms in western Virginia and so interacted with the master on a daily basis. By mid-century, many Virginia planters were converting from tobacco to wheat, which left a good part of the year when slaves did not have to work in the fields. To maximize profit, resident planters had their workers learn skills and hired them out in the slack season. By the revolutionary generation, Africans, native-born blacks, and whites in Virginia formed a creole culture that featured fluency in English, artisanal skills, and a greater absorption of English culture than existed among blacks in South Carolina. When revolutionary fervor filled the hearts of Virginia's white population, the enslaved were better situated than their Deep South kin to absorb the political ferment and act upon it.[31]

The societies in which Isham Carter and Tim Jones lived treated them as enemies. Thomas Jefferson's convenient metaphor for slavery, "a state of war," required an enemy. His organizing principle made the enslaved a veritable hostile army. These dangerous people had to be conquered in mind and spirit because they lived to varying degrees among the master class. Carter's and Jones's stories started with helplessness: their women were violated and children taken away as they watched. They had much higher hurdles to negotiate than their northern compatriots when the war came along. If soldiers were capable, selfless, praiseworthy individuals at the time that they were needed, then how could black men be soldiers? The answer came from Carter's South Carolina, where they allowed very few men of color into the lines, while Jones's Virginia tried to limit black soldiers' duties to the menial tasks of digging and acting as servants. The northern slavery system, a much looser affair, with considerably less investment in slaves and with more free blacks in the mix, generally meant an easier time in the North making the connection between brown skin and soldiering.

Laws and Life: Middle Colonies

The most striking difference between the southern colonies and the Mid-Atlantic region concerned demographics. Blacks numbered no more than 14 percent of the population of New York (the largest percentage in the North) and only 2 percent in Pennsylvania. In neither colony was black labor essential to the economy. In neither colony did whites feel as vulnerable as in colonies whose enslaved population formed a pervasive presence on the landscape. When slave rebellions occurred in 1712 and 1741 in New York City, there was never a doubt that they would be put down, and the 1741 event, although it resulted in thirty slaves being hanged or burned to death, did not precipitate a new, harsher slave code. Historian Ira Berlin characterized the difference between, for example, South Carolina and Pennsylvania as the difference between a "slave society" and a society with slaves.[32]

Like early Virginia, New York's slavery regime initially featured opportunity for slaves to better their condition under a system called "half freedom." The Dutch had settled the area before the arrival of the English. In the Dutch colony of New Netherlands, people in bondage could buy their way to free status. The free black community settled north of the walled city, in what is now Greenwich Village, forming a buffer between the city proper in lower Manhattan and the Indian population that outnumbered whites and blacks on the tiny island. When the English relieved the Dutch of their colony in 1664 and renamed it New York, all such experiments with slaves and freedom ceased. Hence the young, enslaved man growing up in prerevolutionary New York risked a whipping if he carried a gun, strayed too far from his master's home, struck a white person, engaged in independent commerce, or congregated with more than four other black persons. His master could vent his private anger on him but not to the point of killing or dismembering him. Furthermore, a master had to provide enough food for his workers. The city did not want beggars in the streets. To that end, masters were constrained from freeing old or sick slaves.[33]

By the 1750s, there were still people of color in New York who could relate stories about the 1712 slave revolt. In the early spring of that year, two dozen slaves, allegedly aggrieved by their masters, stole enough weaponry to stage their response. This mostly Africa-born band set fire to a building and then descended upon those who tried to douse the flames. Nine whites were killed. In the hunt afterward, six conspirators slashed their own throats rather than face an enraged community. Of the seventy arrested, twenty were hanged and three burned to death, one of whom was condemned to roast slowly "in torment for eight to ten hours and continue burning in the said fire until he be dead and consumed to ashes." Revolted by the extent of the punishments, Robert Hunter, the royal governor of New York, wrote to his superiors in London that New Yorkers should have emulated the West Indian colonies, which, although renowned for the severity of their laws, would only execute a few conspirators as an example. Although the governor managed to reprieve five men, the New York courts had their way and sent a gruesome message to any future rebels who contemplated force to effect their independence.[34]

The colony of New York responded by fashioning a new, more comprehensive slave code. Not surprisingly, it made burning a house a capital offense. It also made it harder for a master to free a slave. Now the owner had to lay down substantial cash (two hundred pounds sterling) to insure the colony that if a newly freed man could not support himself, the master would share the burden. To that end, the owner also had to support his manumitted slave to the tune of twenty pounds a year, and that newly freed slave could not own a house because such a property could serve as a future nest of conspirators. The alleged collusion of free blacks in the events of 1712 resulted in a weakening of the African American community, both with respect to numbers and blacks' ability in the future to support slaves deemed intransigent by the white community.[35]

When the future revolutionary war soldier walked the streets and lanes of New York City in his youth, a more recent rebellion still loomed large. In the spring of 1741 a series of mysterious fires led authorities to suspect a slave conspiracy, eventually resulting in sensational trials and the execution of thirty-four people, thirty of whom were black. Of those thirty, thirteen were burned at the stake. What is evident in the 1741 court proceedings is the teeming, disorderly nature of New York City, where blacks congregated in groups larger than four, where slaves had guns, where tavern owners served slaves liquor, where black artisans had real mobility, and where newcomers with rogue ideas circulated. The law, however, could always reach out and punish a slave who raised a white man's ire. A slave master could always apply a switch to a man's back, but the bustling economy seemed to have outrun some of the restrictive laws on the city's enslaved community. And when street protests rocked the city during the Stamp Act Congress in 1765, "Negroes" were in the surging crowds.[36]

Where noisy disorder characterized the background of the future black revolutionaries in New York, a quieter but profoundly powerful force transformed the lives of slaves in Philadelphia and its hinterland. Pennsylvania was a latecomer to the American colonies, founded in 1681 by William Penn, an English member of the Society of Friends, commonly called Quakers. The religious society's founder, George Fox, advocated that masters bring their slaves to "the knowledge of the Lord" and instructed overseers to "deal mildly and gently" with them, eventually freeing them after a certain number of years. Penn, a disciple of Fox, favored black workers on his farms because "a man has them while they live"—no hint in this comment to his friend James Harrison of manumission. Still, the Quaker belief in the light of God in every person might have assuaged the severity of the system even in the already moderate middle colonies.[37]

In 1688, settlers in Germantown, a village outside Philadelphia, penned the first written protest in the American colonies "against the traffick of men-Body." Shortly thereafter, George Keith, a Quaker reformer, also took aim at the peculiar institution. So too did the Philadelphia Monthly Meeting of Friends, which protested the slave trade in 1698. In 1711, the Pennsylvania assembly passed a statute prohibiting slave importation, only to have English authorities disallow the law. Undeterred, the assembly slapped a high import duty on each slave, which England again invalidated. The colonial assembly played an elaborate game with Britain's Privy Council through the first half of the eighteenth century concerning the slave trade.[38]

Nevertheless Pennsylvania assemblymen passed legislation in the early eighteenth century that limited black testimony in court, created a "Negro Court" for slaves and free blacks (adjudicated by a judge but no jury), prohibited slaves from engaging in trade, and fined anyone who entertained slaves without the consent of the master. A slave could receive ten lashes if found more than ten miles from his master's house without a ticket. If found drinking after 9:00 P.M., a slave could suffer up to ten lashes. For shooting off a gun at horse races, a white man was liable to pay a fine, while slaves or servants suffered fifteen lashes and six days of hard labor. All blacks, free and enslaved, who committed rape, murder, "buggery," or burglary faced a death sentence, although it was not a mandatory punishment. Whites did not face capital punishment until 1718, and then only for murder.[39]

It is not clear that the slave who received seven lashes for stealing gold buttons in Pennsylvania knew of the more draconian punishments of Virginia or South Carolina. One still had to face the pain and humiliation of a public whipping decreed by a prejudiced judicial process. Still, one might have heard stories from slaves who ran away from the southern states. One might have heard about patrols killing people there who absented themselves from the plantation or slaves suffering death for raising a hand to a white person on their third offense. There was no such thing as a ten-lash punishment in the South Carolina or Virginia slave codes.[40]

While expressing concern for the enslaved, the Quaker hierarchy moved to severely limit free blacks, whom they described in Pennsylvania's 1725 Act for the Better Regulation of Negroes, as "an idle, slothful people, often burdensome to the neighborhood." To limit the number of such characters, the assembly stipulated that masters be charged thirty pounds to cover any costs the community would have to pay if a freed slave was unable to maintain self-support. This was far less than the New York law provided, but the Pennsylvania assembly further penalized newly freed people. If a free black had sexual relations with a white, he or she would be put back into servitude for seven years. If a black married a white, he or she would be sold into slavery. Freed blacks faced the same corporal punishments as slaves. Black rapists faced possible castration. White rapists did not. All blacks could be whipped for carrying guns. And if free blacks could not pay any fines assessed by the law, a justice could put them back into servitude. The Quaker obsession for order mixed with racial prejudice made freedom a different entity for whites and blacks in Pennsylvania.[41]

Nevertheless, a black Pennsylvanian growing up before the revolution experienced an environment in which slavery was a contested subject and in which they were better equipped to protest. For one thing, Pennsylvanians did not fear literate slaves. Anglicans took the lead in educating Philadelphia's black population, starting in 1740 with a school specifically reaching out to blacks. In the same decade, the Anglicans' Christ Church was opened to blacks. Although outnumbered by other denominations at mid-century, the Quakers still exercised significant influence on the colony. Prominent men like Anthony Benezet and John Woolman wrote antislavery tracts beginning in the 1740s and 1750s respectively. While John Woolman tussled privately with individual slave owners and gently prodded them in his publications, Anthony Benezet started night classes in his home in the 1750s and eventually founded a Quaker-supported school for African Americans in 1773.

Quiet soul-searching led to an increasing number of manumissions in Philadelphia area wills. It was Benezet who urged an up-and-coming doctor, Benjamin Rush, to write an antislavery pamphlet in 1773. Rush, in turn, met Tom Paine, a recent English immigrant two years later in a bookstore. Perhaps inspired by the young doctor, Paine penned an attack against slavery in which he asked, "With what consistency or decency [could American slaveholders] complain so loudly of attempts to enslave them, while they hold so many hundred thousand in slavery?" These men—Woolman, Benezet, Rush, and Paine—were not the norm, but they kept a conversation going about slavery such that people of color knew that their lot need not be inevitable. In 1776 the Philadelphia Yearly Meeting ordered its members to release their slaves.[42]

Massachusetts

As in Pennsylvania, Massachusetts had a few early voices lifted in condemnation of slavery. John Eliot, a Puritan minister, wrote the Boston General Council in 1675 that selling "souls for money" was "worse than death." Yet despite the fact that New England did not depend on slave labor to run its economy, and its black population numbered not more than 2 or 3 percent, the institution took hold nonetheless. And like other colonies, Massachusetts forbade interracial sex and marriage, sanctioned severely whipping any black who "presumed to smite" a white person, and threw obstacles in the way of manumission. On this last point, the legislature noted in 1703 that "inconveniences had arisen with respect to the growing freed community," impelling them to assess a fifty-pound fee on masters who freed slaves. Any freewheeling ways in the freed community had to be quashed. The legislature allowed town officials to put "unruly" persons of color back into a period of servitude. (All women, white and black, who delivered children out of wedlock could also be condemned to a period of servitude).[43]

Like other colonies, Massachusetts laid a disproportionate share of the blame on people of color for disorder in the streets. In fact, "great disorders, insolvencies, and burglaries ... committed in the night" led the legislature in 1703 to impose a curfew at 9:00 P.M. Black violators would receive no more than ten stripes if the town had no house of correction. No stripes at all for whites, however. If offenders made noise at night, they either paid a fine, were imprisoned, or suffered in the stock or in the cage. By the 1750s the streets saw "tumultuous companies of men, children, and Negroes disguised by vizards [masks] and discolored faces who, armed with sticks, put on pageants and threatened people for money." The legislature ordained that if more than three people engaged in this practice, there would be consequences. Freed people either paid a fine or went to prison for no more than a month. As a courtesy to the masters, black servants could be whipped (no more than ten lashes) in lieu of imprisonment. Carrying sticks was not the issue. There was no law that prohibited people of color from carrying a weapon. But the rough and tumble in the streets had to be controlled. To that end, authorities placed restrictions on liquor sales and forbade people of color from buying lottery tickets.[44]

What distinguished Massachusetts from even Pennsylvania was the access it provided the enslaved to the courts. Slaves could legally challenge their masters. They could contest a beating. They could petition for freedom, and they seemed to enjoy the same legal protections available to whites when they were accused of a crime. In 1737 an enslaved man named James sued for his freedom based on his master's will. The courts made him wait until his mistress died but issued a writ of protection so that he could not be sold. Two years later, after the decease of his mistress, he applied again and obtained his freedom. In another case, a free black man, John Woodby, related to the court that he had been walking home from work when a watchman "bound" him and threw him into prison, necessitating a thirteen-shilling fine to obtain his liberty. The black man appealed to "Law and Justice." The Boston selectmen summoned the watchman and Woodby to a hearing. Woodby did not show and so the white man was cleared but not before being admonished to "act prudently in all such matters in future."[45]

With the taxation crisis of the 1760s, both white politicians and enslaved individuals made further forays into dismantling slavery. In 1767 a Massachusetts bill calling for an end to the "unwarrantable and unlawful practice or Custom of inslaving Mankind" and the trade enabling it went down to defeat. Four years later, the legislature passed a bill to do away with importing and purchasing slaves only to have Governor Thomas Hutchinson refuse to sign it. The enslaved community did not wait for the white power structure to budge. Jenny Slew of Ipswich sued for her freedom, charging John Whipple Jr. with enslaving her by "force and arms." Her original case did not go her way, but on appeal she prevailed. Throughout the late 1760s and the 1770s, Aaron of Newport, Caesar of Essex, James of Cambridge, Hendrick of Essex, and Cabel Dodge of Essex did not let up on the pressure they exerted on the courts. In this last case, the jury found in favor of the black man, claiming there was "no law of the province to hold a man for life."[46]

Court cases were complemented by petitions. In January 1773, the first of five appeals in two years from Boston's black community appeared. In the first, African American voices very carefully stroked the power structure to get what they wanted. They did not boldly call for freedom. Rather they phrased this idea in terms of humbly asking "for Relief"—relief from their "unhappy state" where the only future they could see for their children was a life like "the Beasts that perish." The four paragraphs that formed the body of the petition featured religious themes—God as no respecter of persons; God whose commandments they would keep, especially obedience to their masters; the Father in Heaven whose grace enabled them to live a Christian life. Their enslaved condition, however, was "unfriendly to religion" and every moral virtue except patience. The governor, council, and house had it in their power, said the petitioners, to create a condition that would make better Christians of the enslaved.

The petition also reminded the colony's politicians that they would not be alone in bringing relief to the enslaved. The petitioners alluded to the *Somerset* decision of 1772, in which a court in England had mandated that masters could not forcibly take their slaves out of the country. Judge Mansfield in the Somerset decision saw the exercise of the power by the master over his servant as legal but the exercise of that power, said Mansfield, "must always be regulated by the laws of the place where exercised." So the Somerset decision did not abolish slavery either in Britain or the colonies but simply ordained that slavery operated differently in London and Jamaica. Although on paper upholding the slavery laws of the colonies, the Somerset decision struck a blow against the institution in the colonies because it was interpreted by many to go much further than it did—that is, interpreted as eliminating slavery in Britain. The New England press reported on the case in one or two issues but then let the matter drop. The articles from London's newspapers were reprinted in the *Boston Post-Boy* as well as in other papers in Connecticut and Rhode Island. One of these articles featured the arguments from the counselors on both sides as well as the probing questions posed by the chief judge, Lord Mansfield. The Boston petitioners noted the "Men of Great Note and Influence" who argued this case.[47]

But this was about as far as these black petitioners would go in citing the developments of their time. They did not use the language of the American protest movement. They did not point out the inconsistency of clamoring for freedom while at the same time enslaving thousands. They launched no challenge in that way. They knew their audience—churchgoing politicians—and they were careful to anticipate white prejudices as well as quell white fears. They acknowledged the existence of "vicious" blacks (who, they said, should be punished under the same laws as the king's other subjects), but they pointed out that "discreet, sober, honest, and industrious" blacks, if made free (the only time "free" appears in the petition), would pay taxes and promote the common weal. The petitioners also anticipated masters' trepidations in promising that they would obey as long as bondage lasted and would seek only such relief as would not harm their masters. They say, "We have no property. We have no wives. No children. We have no city. No country." But they had a father in heaven who invested the "great and good Court" to judge what was "just and good." The petition was signed with one name—"Felix"—which stood for one-eighth of the population of Boston, most of whose lives were "embittered" by slavery.[48]

In 1774 another try at stopping the slave trade via the legislature led to the stone wall of Governor Hutchinson. Later that same year some black men in Boston offered to fight for the British if the new royal governor, General Thomas Gage, would arm them and free them. The governor gave serious consideration to their petition, but word of its content leaked out to the community, and Gage abandoned the idea. But the royal government's days were numbered, and when the new state government under total American control came into being, Massachusetts blacks petitioned again in 1777, this time using the rhetoric of the independence movement. They opened with a salvo. There were "a Great Number of Blacks detained in a state of slavery in the bowels of a free and Christian country." Instead of an emphasis on God, they spoke of the unalienable rights of natural rights philosophy. The system of slavery had "dragged" them from a "populous, pleasant, and Plentiful Country . . . to be sold like "Beasts of Burthen." Sold by whom? By a people "professing the mild religion of Jesus" but whose rational faculties could appreciate the injustice. It astonished them that there had been no connection made between the colonies seeking freedom and the slaves engaged in the same endeavor. Unlike the petitioners of 1773, they told the legislature what it should do—restore the enslaved population to the "enjoyments of that which is [their] natural right . . . in this Land of Liberty." Ever mindful of the owners, they demanded that all children should be set free when they reached twenty-one years of age. They ended the petition by reiterating the white community's "inconsistency" in clamoring for liberty from Britain while denying it to the enslaved. Only four years separated the two petitions, yet the confidence, stridency, and secularity of the second petition spoke of a black community that had absorbed the arguments of the revolutionary movement. They no longer pleaded. They launched a challenge.[49]

Crispus Attucks and the Boston Massacre

That the petitions came from the city of Boston is not surprising. Its docks and wharves were the lifeblood of the city where black sailors, maritime artisans, and dockworkers were a visible presence. As a port on the American shore of the Atlantic World, Boston had ongoing connections with Europe, the Caribbean, and Africa. Worldly black sailors lived in a society that swirled with political news and imparted that news to the land-bound communities of the English empire in America. Thus, the black community of Boston had a conduit to the latest political happenings, provided by confident black men whose travels had taken them to the source, whether that be the antislavery glimmerings in London or crowd actions on the streets of New York, Philadelphia, and Charles Town.[50]

The African American sailors themselves were descendants of black seamen whose mobility throughout the Atlantic World made them cosmopolitan characters knowledgeable about national currencies, Dutch slave forts, English maritime innovations, and Caribbean markets. These mobile, multilingual people were few in number but thrived up to the first third of the eighteenth century, when their presence on the American coast was overwhelmed by plantation slavery. By the 1770s, black sailors were often enslaved, but their life's work took place on boats and ships where all hands depended on one another, whether white or black. The collective work on a ship in the face of a mighty ocean sometimes trumped racial attitudes. Although still subject to unfair punishment and prejudice, black seamen could make better money, acquire valuable skills, and develop a more independent attitude than did their counterparts on land. When people on the streets of Boston looked for allies in their protest against the Crown, they did not have to go far to see a large, self-assertive community used to brawling and familiar with the process of acquiring more freedom from powerful forces that wanted to keep them down.[51]

Crispus Attucks, a sailor, was the first black man to die in the revolutionary cause. We know very little about this hero. The only clues to his life before March 5, 1770, the date of the Boston Massacre, indicate that he was a mulatto from Framingham, Massachusetts, who had influence in the sailor community. Indeed, in the months before the massacre, Boston's sailors had rumbled with British soldiers for jobs on the city's docks. Sailors everywhere in the Atlantic World also had to contend with impressment, whereby the British navy would pluck men out of the taverns and alleys of port cities and forcibly throw them on the decks of His Majesty's ships. Liberty had a special meaning to sailors, who shared experiences not known to landlubbers. With tensions already high between the British soldiers and the civilians of Boston, the waterfront element added energy to citywide grumbling about the arrogant, overreaching British.[52]

On the night of March 5, several boys decided to taunt a British sentry at the customhouse on King Street. They pelted the redcoat with snowballs and challenged him to respond. A crowd started to gather while British captain Thomas Preston led seven more troops out to support the sentry. Word traveled fast. The crowd joined in the drama, adding ice, oyster shells, sticks, and pieces of coal to the debris launched in the soldiers' direction. Fire bells rang out, bringing more people into the streets. As John Adams described it in a trial that would follow, "The multitude was shouting and huzzaing and threatening life, the bells all ringing, the mob whistle screaming . . . like an Indian yell, the people from all quarters throwing every species of rubbish they could pick up in the street." Two hundred people beheld the swelling scene, some witnesses said.[53]

Views would differ as to the degree of this disorder and exactly what happened, but shots were fired, and three Americans, including Attucks, died instantly. (Another wounded man died within hours, and Irish immigrant Patrick Carr would die two weeks later.) At the trials of the British soldiers held in the fall of 1770, witnesses for defense and prosecution were at odds. One eyewitness spoke of having seen "the Mulatto" with a large stick not ten minutes before the firing, at the head of twenty or thirty sailors coming from Cornhill Street, huzzaing and whistling. Another witness, of Irish descent, said that at the foot of Jenkins Lane he had run into a "tall mulatto fellow" who had two clubs and offered him one. Dropping the club in the snow, the witness had followed Attucks into King Street, where the agitated man "went on cursing and swearing at the soldiers." Another witness, a black man named Andrew, claimed that the crowd appeared to have been backing down when a number of men appeared "huzzaing and crying, 'damn them they dare not fire, we are not afraid of them.'" The mulatto, a "stout fellow," the witness said, threw himself at the British line, knocked a gun out of a soldier's hand, and then struck him over the head. This man then held the soldier's bayonet with his left hand "and twitched it and cried kill the dogs, knock them over." The crowd closed in, and then a shot rang out. Another witness said that the mulatto man was the first to fall.[54]

Still other witnesses related a different story. They denied that the mulatto was up against the soldiers. Two said he was fifteen feet away, leaning on a stick. Regardless, the mulatto was the one civilian character who stood out in the testimonies at the trials of Preston and the other soldiers. Some witnesses specified no skin color when they spoke of the man who attacked the soldiers. A defense attorney always then asked if this man was the mulatto. Some said yes, others said no. The preoccupation with skin color might have been part of a strategy to show a black man heading the mob that brought on the shots. Indeed, John

Adams, the lead counsel for the British soldiers, focused on the mulatto in his summation. Starting with a sarcastic comment about the mulatto's "heroism," Adams named Attucks as the man who had led an army on the attack. "If this was not an unlawful assembly," said Adams, "there never was one in the world." This Attucks and his "myrmidons," argued Adams, assured the crowd that the soldiers would dare not fire. "Kill them! Kill them! Knock them over!" Attucks reportedly roared. Adams went on to put a picture of Attucks in the jury's mind. This "stout mulatto fellow whose very looks was enough to terrify any person . . . tried to knock their brains out," he thundered. "This was the behavior of Attucks," Adams explained, "to whose mad behavior, in all probability, the dreadful carnage of that night, is chiefly to be ascribed." And then, resorting to the well-worn tactic that turned crowds into mobs in the eighteenth century, Adams closed by identifying Irish [Catholics] and "a rabble of Negroes" as the irresponsible participants who had provoked the tragedy.[55]

The first Boston newspapers to be published after the disaster appeared on March 8. Both the *Boston Chronicle* and the *Boston Newsletter* listed the dead and wounded. Crispus Attucks got no honorific "Mr." by his name as the others did—he was simply "a Molatto" or "a mulatto man named Johnson." By March 12, when the next batch of newspapers appeared, he had become "a mulatto man named Crispus Attucks who was born in Framingham but lately belonged to New Providence and was herein ordered to go for North Carolina." The name change could have been a simple case of confusion, or perhaps Attucks had gone by more than one name, which might have indicated that he wanted to hide something from his past.[56]

Indeed, Attucks was successful in masking his past until 1859 when a researcher found this ad in the October 2, 1750, *Boston Gazette*:

> Ran away from his Master, William Brown of Framingham, on the 30th of September last, a Molatto Fellow, about 27 years of age, names Crispus, 6 feet two inches high, short curl'd hair, his knees nearer together than common; had on a light colour'd Bearskin Coat, plain brown Fustian jacket, or brown all-wool one, New Buckskin breeches, blue yarn stockings, and a check'd woolen Shirt . . . and all Masters of Vessels and others are hereby caution'd against concealing or carrying off said Servant on Penalty of the Law.[57]

Crispus Attucks of the March 5 events in Boston shared the given name of the escaped slave. Both John Adams and the newspapers claimed that Attucks hailed from Framingham. A couple of trial witnesses said he was tall. Many runaways ended up on ships, and Crispus Attucks had allegedly led a group from the docks and was himself bound for North Carolina. The probability that the runaway slave and the crowd leader were one and the same person was further advanced by the historian who found the runaway ad. C. H. Morse took pains to locate the grandson of William Brown, Crispus Attucks's former owner, who verified that Attucks was once a slave in the family. The grandson even produced "a pewter drinking cup worn by Attucks when he fell," as well as his powder horn.[58] If these objects were legitimate, the authorities in Boston gave Attucks's last effects to the man who had enslaved him. Ultimately, the master owned what little of Attucks that was left.

Crispus Attucks, likely an enslaved man in his youth, defined liberty by freeing himself, sustaining his person in a difficult trade for twenty years, and finally leading a group of lowly men up into the faces of royal authority. John Adams pointed to Attucks as the man most responsible for what happened on the night of March 5. The event, later styled by patriots the Boston Massacre, would keep the opposition fires burning during the lull between the 1765 Stamp Act and the Boston Tea Party in December 1773. Every year on March 5 thousands of Bostonians gathered to hear a prominent orator talk of the dangers of keeping an army stationed in a community during peacetime. Bells tolled, and lantern shows reenacted the English barbarity of that bloody night.[59]

Crispus Attucks invigorated the movement that clamored for liberty. He also inspired individuals for whom the word "freedom" had a more personal and urgent significance. A young slave woman in Boston, Phillis Wheatley, wrote a poem titled "On the Affray in King Street, on the Evening of March 5th." She was the first African American to publish a book in America, but unfortunately her Boston Massacre poem was never published and cannot be found. For others, for the men who would shortly dare to fight for liberty, Crispus Attucks taught them a lesson: he did not hold back.[60]

Painted Faces and the Tea Party

Into the 1770s, the British Parliament persisted in the folly of infuriating its American subjects by passing disguised taxation called import duties. In the wake of the Boston Massacre, an article in the *Boston Gazette* surmised that the British soldiers stationed in Boston in 1770 were there to enforce the then-latest gambit by Parliament—to take money out of the colonists' pockets under the guise of import duties. The Townshend Revenue Act caused no explosion as the Stamp Act did, but protests and spotty boycotts kept the ill will going between mother country and colonies. By 1773 Parliament dropped import duties on all goods but tea. Through novel distribution methods, Parliamentary legislation made legal British tea cheaper in America than the smuggled product from abroad. The Tea Act of 1773 paired cheap tea with Parliamentary sovereignty. But alas for Parliament, Americans understood this connection all too well. American radicals seized on this latest scheme from London and created an event sure to rouse everyone's attention on both sides of the Atlantic. Not surprisingly, the most dramatic stroke occurred in Boston, where the event's major players struck the empire through a show of force on the city's docks. The nub of the problem was of concern to the city's sailing community in that it involved the movement of goods across the Atlantic and the struggle for more autonomy.

On December 16, 1773, Bostonians packed Old South Meeting House to discuss the three tea ships in the harbor. "But BEHOLD what followed!" crowed the *Boston Gazette*. Just before the meeting broke up, "a number of brave and resolute men, dressed in the Indian manner" approached near the door of the building and gave a whoop that "rang through the House and was answered by some in the galleries." Order was restored, and hundreds of people followed the disguised group headed for the docks. The painted men, some of whom colored only their faces black, methodically found and threw overboard the offensive cargo in each of the three ships. In less than four hours, 342 chests were disposed of, with no harm to the ships themselves. No raging crowds here. This was a surgical strike.[61]

The people of Boston were not unfamiliar with street theater. In the 1750s, some in the colony had tried to curtail street pageants featuring "painted or discolored faces." These revels were getting out of hand and promoted "opposition to government," one law claimed. The 1773 group chose to be Indians, a distinctly American group that had long since been neutralized in eastern Massachusetts. To the colonists, Indians were synonymous with freedom, making them an excellent symbol for a movement whose members were dedicated to getting more of it for themselves.[62] But the newspapers of the time said nothing about the deft use of the Indian symbol. That was for later commentators. Instead, the *Boston Weekly Newsletter* did precisely what John Adams had done to Crispus Attucks. It noted the disguised colonists' "grotesque ... appearance."[63]

Surrendering the chests of tea to the tides, Bostonians destroyed property at close to $1 million in today's money. Only New York City followed Boston's lead in throwing tea into the harbor, but patriots in other cities managed to intimidate ship captains from unloading the East India Company's tea, or they spirited it to another location. The Bostonians thus bore the brunt of London's rage when Parliament passed the Coercive Acts, which some Americans dubbed the Intolerable Acts. The port of Boston would be closed until the tea flavoring the city's harbor had been paid for. Even more egregious was an attack on the colony's representative government. The Crown restricted town meetings and dictated that the upper legislative house become an appointed body. The people of Massachusetts rose up—not just in port towns like Boston—but in the country, where the people closed down the empire's judicial system in

Massachusetts. No famous founder engineered this response. The farmers of western Massachusetts led the way.[64]

Americans who supported the British Empire used the same strategy as John Adams had done in 1770. The crowds were called mobs composed of n'er-do-wells, they said, like sailors, boys, and blacks. Prominent loyalist Peter Oliver, chief justice of the Superior Court of the Province of Massachusetts Bay, likened the colonials to "perfect machines wound up by any hand." They were like "a poor Negro boy" who balked at a command by his master to fetch something, said Oliver. The "poor wretch with tears in his eyes" replied, "Me 'fraid Massah Tamp Act he catch me." Oliver explained that rebel leaders put diabolical heads and cloven feet on each act of Parliament, thus paralyzing the people with fear. But when the mob moved, African Americans were at the center of incipient riots. "Boys and Negroes" made bonfires in the streets, said Oliver, "and when all was ready, the mob whistle . . . [and] sometimes the Mob Horn in unison would echo through the streets to the great terror of the peaceable inhabitants." On the night of the event called the Boston Massacre, "boys and Negroes assembled before the Custom House and abused the Centinel." Elsewhere an anonymous Loyalist pamphleteer characterized the "motly" radical crowds in New York City thusly: "People of all sizes and of all hues! redskins, yellow-skins, green-skins, grey-skins, bay-skins, black-skins, blue-skins." The pamphleteer sneeringly compared this "enchanting variety" with the pure white physiognomies of the king's supporters.[65]

The Coercive Acts impelled the colonies to unite in a congress held in Philadelphia in the fall of 1774. They listed Parliament's actions in what they saw as rising degrees of danger. They derided the "little acts of finesse" and then warned of "insidious manoeuvres," but most importantly they predicted doom in a "state of slavery." The First Continental Congress implored King George III to rectify the situation. It also established committees to enforce a boycott against imports from Britain and an imminent policy against colonial exports to Britain, and issued veiled threats that Americans would use violence to protect their rights. The Congress warned the people of Great Britain that Americans would never do what slaves did every day. "We must tell you that we will never submit to be hewers of wood or drawers of water," said the Congress, "for any ministry or nation in the world." To fellow colonists, the Congress predicted that Parliament was likely to ignore America's pleas, ultimately forcing the colonists to choose "either a more dangerous contest or a final, ruinous and infamous submission." Anticipating that their fellow countrymen would choose the former, the Congress enjoined the colonists to "be in all respects prepared for every contingency."[66]

1775: Two Roads to Liberty

And so Americans turned their sights to "the most mournful events" of an imminent dangerous contest. For Boston's people of color, there was only so far they could go in participating in any military action. A 1707 Massachusetts statute consigned free blacks to repair highways and clear streets in lieu of "trainings, watches, and other service for the common benefit of the place." Not allowed to bear arms, the law required them nonetheless to make their appearance in cases of sudden alarms when an officer would tell them what to do.[67]

New England was the site of many alarms in 1774 and 1775, the most dramatic of which took place on April 18–19, 1775. British soldiers marched from Boston to Concord in order to seize an arms cache there, and along the way they ran into sixty men on the village green of Lexington. The operation started on the night of the eighteenth. Delays meant that the British force did not make Lexington until 4:30 A.M. on April 19. The British finally arrived and exited Concord by noon. In the interim, the countryside had awakened. Men poured into the fields and lanes between Concord and Boston to take their best shots at the lobster backs. Recent scholarship has told us that the American response to the Redcoats' foiled raid was more organized than early historians described. But still, these men operated in emergency conditions, in a great deal of confusion, and in this circumstance militia leaders were likely not fussy about a man's skin color.[68]

The so-called minutemen, generally perceived as farmers in the immediate area of operation, were joined by others as the alarm spread out and men came marching to the environs of Boston from all over New England, including quite a few men of color. Silas Burdoo claimed in his pension application that he had chased the British back to Boston and promptly reenlisted in May 1775, arriving on Charles Town common while the Battle of Bunker Hill was raging. Prince Johonnot heard about Lexington in Methuen, Massachusetts, on the New Hampshire border, about twenty miles away. He marched to Cambridge to join the makeshift army surrounding Boston and was stationed in the "Center College Building" at Harvard. On hearing of Lexington, Archelaus White of New Hampshire got the permission of his master to enlist for eight months. Sampson Moore of Canterbury, New Hampshire, also volunteered when he heard of Lexington. Caesar Glover arrived outside of Boston with a mixed-race unit of sailors from Marblehead, Massachusetts, headed by Captain John Glover, later to become a prominent general. Freemen and enslaved blacks flocked to the growing army around Boston.[69]

The presence of men of color on the road between Concord and Lexington and then around Boston prompted authorities to confront the color issue. On the day after the shots at Lexington, the Massachusetts Committee of Safety, issued a resolution welcoming all freemen into the army while at the same time making it clear that slaves could not serve. And so the army surrounding the seven thousand British soldiers in Boston grew to thousands itself, many of whom had to be turned away for lack of supplies. On Friday night, June 16, 1775, the New England soldiers began to fortify two hills overlooking the town, Breed's Hill and Bunker Hill. This provocative act sent the British army into high gear.[70]

Itching to get at the American rabble, the English battery unleashed its fury, primarily on the hill that the Americans spent the most time fortifying—Breed's Hill. British ships bombarded the area then alive with Americans taking supplies to the hills' summits. British soldiers torched Charles Town, whose unlucky location at the base of the hills in contention spelled its destruction. The British commander, General Gage, ordered grenadiers, fusiliers, light infantry, and others in the foot companies to scale Breed's Hill and overwhelm the rebels. In beautiful formation, the redcoats charged right into a hail of American shot and canister. One American commander planted posts ahead of his men and ordered them not to fire until the British reached the posts. Another told his men not to fire until the enemy was within thirty yards of their position. Legend has it that he also shouted out the immortal words "don't fire until you see the whites of their eyes." The Americans ripped into the British lines, with agonizing results for the attackers. As the sun set on Saturday evening, the Americans ran out of ammunition and relinquished the hills to the British. The redcoats "took the field" but sustained a casualty rate of over 40 percent. Of "all the British officers who would fall in battle in the eight years of the Revolution," wrote historian Paul Lockhart, "nearly one-quarter died at Bunker Hill. All told, a little over one thousand professional British soldiers shed blood that day, while American casualties were half that many."[71]

Unfortunately, only one black man who lived to give a pension deposition in the nineteenth century provided any detail about the smoke, explosions, and blood of that day. Prince Johnnot joined the work party on Friday night building breastworks and then participated in the battle the next day. He said he knew the head of American forces on Breed's Hill. The rest of the black pensioners who participated in the battle simply listed it in the actions in which they had participated during the Revolution, or they figured in lists of men who famously waited to see "the whites of their eyes." In 2000 a study was done for the National Park Service by George Quintal. At that time Quintal counted 103 men of color at Bunker Hill. If in our collective mind's eye we see descendants of the Puritans engaged in deadly combat around Boston, we must add an African American or Indian man for every twenty who served that day.[72]

While historians might have overlooked the presence of men of color in the early days of the war, the revolutionary leaders did not. Washington assumed command of the armed men around Boston a little over two weeks after Bunker Hill. Prince Johnnot saw him arrive. On beholding the encampment at Cambridge for the first time, Washington saw no army although he was the commander of this disorganized collection of rowdy New Englanders.

Almost immediately Washington had to deal with race. His general orders dated July 1775 listed "boys, deserters, and negroes" as undesirable troops. In October when the Board of War was laying out the basic structure of the army, Washington asked them whether he could enlist blacks in the new army, or whether there was a distinction to be made between slaves and free blacks. The board responded that there was no distinction and so black men were to be rejected altogether. Washington's orders of October 31 and November 12, 1775, reflected this stricture, the latter of which classed men of color with boys unable to bear arms and old men whose constitutions were not up to the soldier's life. The free men of color in camp let it be known that they were "much dissatisfied" about being excluded. On December 30, 1775, Washington approved the recruitment of free blacks, but the Second Continental Congress again hemmed him in by stipulating that only black soldiers who participated in the army at Cambridge could enlist—"no others," reaffirmed the Congress. Washington cautioned John Hancock, the president of the Congress, that soldiers who felt "discarded" could "seek employ" with the enemy. Such an eventuality alarmed the Congress, which by February 1776 allowed all free blacks to enlist, excluding only "Boys, old men and slaves."[73]

The Other Alternative

The possibility of black men defecting to the "ministerial army" as the British forces were sometimes called, was compelling to Washington and the Continental Congress because the royal governor of Virginia, John Murray, Lord Dunmore, decided to entice black men to desert their rebel masters and join the British armed forces. He traded work for freedom. Although the deal only applied to certain slaves who could lend their strength to the British war effort, the fact remained that the British army freed black men while the revolutionaries did not. Just as whites yearned to fight for the cause of freedom, so also did black men see freedom personified in His Majesty's forces. This worried George Washington, who between him and his wife owned hundreds of slaves in Dunmore's Virginia.[74]

Virginia's enslaved population did not wait around for Lord Dunmore to issue his proclamation. As historian Woody Holton has explained, the actions of Virginia's blacks inspired Dunmore to act. In 1774 and 1775 Virginia was awash with foiled slave insurrections, rumors of slave revolts, and a marked rise in criminal cases involving slaves. It did not take many murders of masters to cause sleepless nights in the big house. Virginians understood that when whites were in conflict, the enslaved would plot to secure their own freedom. One week after the events in Lexington and Concord, the royal governor moved to relocate Williamsburg's gunpowder to a Royal Navy ship. Unlike in New England, no violent encounters on Williamsburg's town green ensued, but an angry crowd gathered there to voice their opposition to the idea. Lord Dunmore, not one to defuse situations, made it known to Peyton Randolph, the speaker of the House of Burgesses, that if one senior British official were harmed, Dunmore would declare "freedom to the slaves and reduce the city of Williamsburg to ashes." When independent militia companies threatened to descend on the colony's capital, a group of blacks went to the Governor's Palace to offer their services. While turning these volunteers away, the royal governor issued a proclamation promising to use any means necessary to restore order.[75]

As the situation deteriorated, Dunmore was as good as his word. On November 14, 1775, a pro-British force, composed of nearly two hundred British regulars and some thirty volunteers from Norfolk, some of whom were black men, defeated a much larger company of rebel militia (called shirtmen) at Kemp's Landing. Perhaps appreciating the wonderful synergy between regular troops and black volunteers, an elated Dunmore published his famous proclamation on the same day, calling on all Virginians to rally around His Majesty's standard. He further appealed to indentured servants, blacks, "or others" belonging to rebels by offering immediate freedom to those who would promptly bear arms in the interest of quelling the insurgents.[76]

Within a month, Dunmore had a black regiment on whose uniforms, such as they were, was inscribed "Liberty to Slaves." In short order, Scotch Tories and loyalist recruits from Long Island were tapped for officer positions in "Dunmore's Ethiopian Regiment." Black recruits were immediately put into service. A black raiding party descended on the Benjamin Wells plantation. The pro-Whig *Pennsylvania Evening Post* reported a general pillaging operation that ended when Mrs. Wells begged the raiders to spare her house, as she had sick, bedridden children therein. The armed band had orders to torch the house but acceded to Mrs. Wells's entreaty. In the newspaper article, Mrs. Wells's bravery was emphasized, not the black men's compassion. Such forbearance was not reciprocal. A week later, an overly "eager" militia unit began firing on a largely pro-British black unit without orders and "kept it up very hot for near fifteen minutes," resulting in two black men dead (one burned alive in a house) and two prisoners, also black. The Whig colonel relating the story could not control his men, who were perhaps fired up by the enemy's skin color. Word of Dunmore's Proclamation reached the black community in Philadelphia by the end of the year. The *Pennsylvania Evening Post* reported that when a "gentlewoman" reprimanded a black man after he had insulted her, the black man was anything but chastised. "Stay, you d——d white bitch, till Lord Dunmore and his black regiment come," he boasted, "and then we will see who is take the wall."[77]

There were no airy dismissals of black men's capacity to fight in late 1775. The revolutionary vanguard took Dunmore's action seriously. The publication of Dunmore's Proclamation was accompanied by a long response in the Whig press. The proclamation was "cruel," claimed a Whig writer, in that it took able-bodied men away from the aged, the infirm, and women and children, who were left behind to deal with a now-exceedingly angry master and with "an enraged and injured people," whose "fury" would be visited upon the black men's "defenseless" families. This was less a warning than a promise. The editorial went on to remind Dunmore's recruits of their fate if they fell "into the hands of the Americans." And if the English won, continued the writer, they would likely renege on any promises of freedom. After all, it was the English who prevented the colonists from stopping the slave trade. A more likely fate, concluded the article, involved transportation to a West Indian plantation.[78]

George Washington too lashed out at Dunmore, calling him "that archtraitor to the Rights of Humanity." Washington urged that the royal governor be "instantly crushed" even if it took "the whole colony to do it." Otherwise, warned the commander-in-chief, Dunmore's army would grow like a snowball hurtling down a hill. "But that which renders the measure indispensably necessary," warned Washington, "is the Negroes." In short order, Washington personally felt the effects of Dunmore's action when three of his "servants" floated down the Potomac to a British warship. His manager at Mount Vernon, a cousin named Lund Washington, reported on the dire situation there. He feared that white indentured servants would inspire the slaves to bolt. "Liberty is sweet," Lund Washington concluded.[79]

The political wing of the revolutionary movement responded to Dunmore as well. It permitted the recruitment of free blacks, not by saying so outright but by leaving them off the list of those forbidden to join the army. The February 21, 1776, general orders prohibited recruiting officers to enlist "any Boys, old Men—or Slaves," implying that free black men qualified for service. In short order, the Virginians did flush out Lord Dunmore and his adherents. Many of Dunmore's African American recruits, stricken by smallpox, were left behind as the remains of royal rule (including two hundred to three hundred members of the Ethiopian Regiment) and sailed up to New York in August 1776. The Continental Congress did not feel impelled to grant a similar program to its community's loyalist-owned slaves. But Dunmore was definitely on the mind of the thirty-two-year-old Virginia slaveholder who wrote the Congress's Declaration of Independence. Thomas Jefferson chastised King George for promoting "domestic insurrections." Jefferson saw no liberty in Dunmore's actions—only threat and ruin.[80]

Not surprisingly, the enslaved population saw Dunmore's Proclamation as opportunity, whether they availed themselves of it or not. Two black men, each involved in Dunmore's Ethiopian Regiment, fought in the war's early years but opted to go different ways at the revolution's conclusion. Harry Washington, born around 1740, had been wrenched from his Gambian village and later purchased by George Washington in 1763. He eventually worked on his master's home plantation, Mount Vernon. Harry started the first of many moves toward freedom in 1771 when he ran away, only to be returned weeks later. In the summer of 1776 he floated down the Potomac and offered his services to the British. He became a corporal in the Black Pioneers, an outfit dedicated to building fortifications and providing other support services to the British war effort. At the war's conclusion he retreated to Nova Scotia, where he owned a town lot and forty acres. But black loyalists there did not receive a compatriot's welcome from white loyalist refugees. Blacks could not vote or serve on a jury. They were promised land that was mightily slow in coming, if at all. And so Harry Washington joined half the black loyalists in Nova Scotia and New Brunswick in an experiment involving a move to Africa. There in Sierra Leone Harry prospered until he got involved with another liberation movement, this time to free the inhabitants of Sierra Leone from the corporate vise of a British company determined to reduce Harry and other immigrants to a virtual enslaved state. Harry Washington was captured, exiled, and died in obscurity.[81]

While Harry Washington gambled on a better life outside the United States, "Billy" opted to stay. Billy appeared in fewer lists so we know far less about his life. He rose to the attention of written commentary by living a long time. His obituary in 1852 tells us just about all we know about him. Born in Hanover County, Virginia, he was owned by Peter Garland and later served Sarah Ingram of Norfolk. Billy saw Norfolk burned by the British forces in 1775 and claimed he was pressed into service by Governor Dunmore. He served at the Battle of Great Bridge in December 1775 and "remembered all about the siege of Yorktown" in 1781. The obituary then jumped to a description of his body. "Strong, hale and hearty to the day of his death," Billy had been a cartman until his age, seventy-five, retired him from the job. At age sixty-eight he could roll a hogshead of sugar weighing fifteen hundred pounds on his cart without assistance. Billy was a model slave—"good humored, well disposed, and scrupulously honest"—until the day he died at age 107. The newspaper noted the fact that he lived in a household with three other elderly people, all of whom had died in the previous two years. Billy did not figure in the 1850 census with his ninety-four-year old mistress, Sarah Ingram, but rather appears in the 1850 slave schedules, where he is unnamed, with only his age listed, along with four female and two other male slaves.[82]

Billy served from Great Bridge to Yorktown. Was he coerced to serve with the British for so long? This is highly unlikely as there was ample opportunity for Billy to run away. He either was not coerced, or he ran away and joined American forces in time for Yorktown. There is no Billy Garland or William Garland in the Revolutionary War Service Records. There are two William Ingrams, one with Virginia troops and the other with the Nineteenth Continental Regiment. No race is indicated for either of these men. It is possible that Billy joined a local militia unit whose paperwork has disappeared, or perhaps he changed his name to serve in an American unit and never applied later for a government pension. It is also possible that he willingly joined Dunmore and was one of many blacks to surrender with the British army at Yorktown. It would not, however, have behooved him to resurrect this version of his life in antebellum Virginia.

Billy and Harry Washington might have known one another in Dunmore's 1775 unit, but they ended up a world apart, both geographically and in terms of station in life. Billy remained with his community and the master he knew in Virginia, and, although he fought, he served white people until he died. The only mark he makes on history is an obituary that praises him for his cheerful compliance with slave society. If the slaves in the Ingram household were family members, he was denied the satisfaction to seeing them freed. The United States denied him even a first name in the 1850 census. In the slave schedule he is reduced to a blank with an age.

Harry Washington's decision to join Dunmore led to his eventual freedom, albeit freedom to be poor and freedom to be rejected. But he also exercised freedom to own land, to make decisions for himself, to see his children as free people. He made the decision to keep his master's last name, and he fought every bit as much for liberty in far less comfortable circumstances than did General Washington. The point here is not to judge either Harry Washington or Billy. The contingencies of their lives are next to impossible to fathom, and who are we to judge? The point is that the British, in the persons of Lord Dunmore and later British generals, offered freedom to most of the enslaved people in the thirteen colonies as a matter of policy. Young, vital men were the target of this policy, but their families came in as well. That the British launched this experiment as a result of expediency rather than humanity does not take away the fact that they provided an excellent option to the slaves of rebels. The Americans never offered as comprehensive a route to freedom, providing few opportunities for people of color to fight with Harry Washington's master. As historian Benjamin Quarles explained, "The Negro's role in the Revolution can best be understood by realizing that his major loyalty was [neither] to a place nor to a people, but to a principle." Harry Washington and Billy lived in the same slave society, one on a plantation of a revolutionary leader, the other in a port city. Both places likely privileged them with communication networks that apprised them of the Battles of Lexington and Concord as well as Dunmore's Proclamation. In the conflict between Britain and its colonies, they each made a gamble and exercised a power over themselves that violated the very heart of slavery.[83]

Most eighteenth-century African Americans lived in a world that did not encourage them to think of their condition as anything but normal. The 1740 South Carolina slave code prohibited slaves from writing. Slaves could cause all manner of mischief by writing out tickets that could aid them in running away or instigating major trouble. The legislators in Charles Town at that time had less fear of reading because there were no dangerous texts for their "servants" to read. Slavery was the monotonous order of things, said Thomas Jefferson. Enslaved men had to watch as masters separated their families and abused their loved ones. All slaves had to deal with the consequences of a relatively kindly master having a bad day. Slowing the work or manipulating the master gave them some room in the vise-like grip of slavery, but these tactics were poor recompense for assaults on their loved ones as well as on their manhood.

In societies whose economic prosperity did not depend on slave labor, the situation was different. Pennsylvania's Quaker community, although outnumbered by people of other denominations, produced men who tried to foil the slave trade and educate black children. African Americans in Philadelphia heard white people take issue with the institution.

The North possessed many more port cities where a roiling maritime community was ever ready to mix it up on the streets. African Americans comprised a noticeable part of these "ne'er-do wells." Massachusetts went a step further than had other northern colonies by opening up the court system to blacks, who initiated freedom suits in the wake of the French and Indian War. Each case undoubtedly raised talk in the African American community where one of their own initiated such a legal suit. Legislative bills calling for the end of slavery, or at the least prohibitive duties on the slave trade, also induced the enslaved people of Massachusetts to think that their current lives need not be their destinies forever.[84]

This more open environment no doubt propelled African Americans into the streets as well as impelled black veterans of the army around Boston to complain to General Washington about their initial exclusion from the Continental Army. They spoke up and demanded their due as veterans of Battle Road (Lexington and Concord), Bunker Hill, and the expulsion of the redcoats from Boston. This was unheard of before the Revolutionary War gave black men the opportunity to demand and threaten, all the more so because these black troops had another alternative that many more of their brethren availed themselves of—the British, whose proclamations offered more than the Continental Congress ever did. The black veterans on the American side had a viable option throughout the war in the offers of the British.

Many others later confronted the same choice. In the privileged world of Thomas Jefferson's upbringing, few questioned the "peculiar institution" in "the monotonous course of colonial life." Black men's participation in the impending war was about to rattle the quiet, unquestioning peace of old Virginia. Slavery would never be quietly taken for granted again.

CHAPTER 2

A New World in Uniform

Whereas the early street actions and encounters with British troops afforded black men a way to exert themselves beyond the bounds ordained by civilian life, the Revolutionary War itself provided them an institution whose goal was to strengthen its recruits: enhancing confidence, developing skills, and sanctioning targeted aggression even beyond the battlefield. Military service provided opportunity to the men, who then liberated family members from slavery and proved that they were capable humans who did not abuse the privilege of being armed. They found a way to connect to white men that was not so blatantly hierarchical. They even earned the grudging respect of some white soldiers, whose new appreciation of men of color required the whites to change their way of thinking, either identifying these soldiers of color as exceptions or occasionally allowing themselves to feel a sense of camaraderie that entailed affection and being in the debt of a black man. Individual instances of affection, however, did not propel black soldiers up the ranks. But even as privates, they made decisions that meant the difference between life and death, and they made these decisions in a far larger scope of action than they ever did in private life. The first decision as prospective recruits was fraught with complexity and risk. Should they enlist?

Mark Murry, a mulatto farmer, was splitting rails, or as he called it, "mauling wood," on a farm in Halifax County, North Carolina, when his father brought news of the British capture of Charles Town, South Carolina, the south's major port. The older man ordered his thirty-year-old son to enlist, as Mark was a free man whose country needed him. The elder Murry told his son that if he wanted to return to the family farm, he would have to produce an honorable discharge. Mark heeded his father's call and signed up for a three-month stint in the North Carolina militia. At the end of his hitch, Mark handed his father the precious paper and then reenlisted two or three times more.[1]

Parental pressure aside, Mark Murry claimed that he enlisted of his own volition in the spring of 1780. By that time, whatever hesitation the states felt about free black men with guns had been partially offset by the exigencies of war. The conflict had gone on for four more years than expected, and with no end in sight it was increasingly difficult to fill the ranks. Mark's home state of

North Carolina never specifically excluded men of color from military service during the Revolution. Its April 1777 militia law specified that all men ages sixteen to fifty were draftable, leaving individuals the option of "finding an able-bodied man to take their place." In this scenario, not only free men of color could serve: a slaveholder might offer a slave to serve in the master's stead. North Carolina was surprisingly progressive in this early period by offering men of color the opportunity to join the military.[2]

Five counties southwest of Mark Murry's home lived Samuel Bell, another black man in his thirties who enlisted in the North Carolina militia "because he believed it his duty to assist his countrymen in arms in achievement of their independence." Fifty years after his decision to enlist, in 1832, Bell spoke of "their" independence, making it clear that although a member of the patriots' corps he did not benefit in the rewards of the Revolution. His word choice likely reflected recently passed laws in his home state, like the 1830 act making it an indictable offense to teach slaves to read and write, or laws passed in the wake of Nat Turner's Rebellion that forbade black men from preaching or teaching. Vigilante gangs also sprang up in the paranoia that followed the rebellion on North Carolina's border. Bell might have acquired some land with his pension money, making it possible for him to vote in North Carolina elections, but that freedom too was stripped away from the state's black freemen in 1835. And Bell had indubitably witnessed decades of clanking coffles as thousands upon thousands of enslaved people were forcibly moved to the more lucrative cotton kingdom in the Deep South and West. Back in 1782, however, Sam Bell had high hopes that when he signed up "voluntarily" in service of a cause, he would better his lot and that of his race.[3]

Most voluntary black recruits came from the North, where there were more free people of color in a population that was overwhelmingly white. North Carolina's color-blind legislation was all the more remarkable given that the state's black population comprised about one-quarter to one-third of the total. New Hampshire, on the other hand, met with an easier decision in permitting men of color to enlist as only 1 percent of the state's population was black. Although exempting black men in their 1776 militia law, New Hampshire came around with little fanfare when they permitted black men into the ranks in 1777. Sampson Moore of Canterbury, New Hampshire, heard about Lexington in 1775 and volunteered for one month, which took him down to the famous village green in Massachusetts. He waited for his state to officially welcome black men into the ranks before serving two more stints with the militia, the last of which had just ended when he "rejoiced" at hearing of Lord Cornwallis's defeat at Yorktown in 1781.[4]

Tobias Gilmore's mitre. Born in West Africa, this veteran earned his freedom by serving as a soldier in the revolution beginning in 1776. As a private in various Massachusetts units, Gilmore served at the Battles of White Plains and Monmouth and survived the encampment at Valley Forge. His interest in politics did not flag after his five-year stint in Washington's forces, as witnessed by his participation in the suppression of Shays' Rebellion and the patch sewn onto his mitre reflecting his postwar views, "FEDERALISM + LIBERTY". The Old Colony History Museum in Taunton, Massachusetts also owns a small cannon, which Toby would fire off at Fourth of July celebrations until his death in 1812. Courtesy of the Charles E. Crowley Photographic Center, Old Colony History Museum, Taunton, Massachusetts.

John Foy of Massachusetts specified in his 1832 pension application that he had neither been drafted nor engaged as a substitute. Other black men likewise sought to convey that they had fought for selfless reasons, not because coerced by a draft or the thought by pecuniary gain. Foy's state, whose population was overwhelmingly of European origin (97 percent), eased into allowing blacks to serve, doing this later than both North Carolina and New Hampshire. Despite the fact that some men of color had served the colony in the French and Indian War, Massachusetts in its 1776 militia act specifically forbade Indians, Negroes, and mulattoes to serve. By the end of the war, in an attempt to ascertain the number of males who had reached their sixteenth birthday (ostensibly to see how many military-aged men existed in Massachusetts), the state instructed its bureaucrats to count "Indians, Negroes, and mulatoes." By March 1778, the recruitment laws "did not fully answer the good purposes intended," and so on March 13, Massachusetts completely revamped its militia law and allowed men of color to serve, not by specifically addressing them in the law but by listing no exemptions to the statute. In the following month, the legislature resolved to fill up the continental battalions with drafted men from the training band and the alarm list. If a drafted man did not pass muster, it was his responsibility to find an able-bodied man in his stead. Again, no racial exemptions kept men of color from serving as substitutes.[5]

With legislatures opening the way, African Americans entered the military for a variety of reasons. An able-bodied man of any color could make some badly needed cash by serving as a substitute for someone else. Elisha Parker pocketed some money each of the three times he subbed in the North Carolina militia. Jacob Francis of New Jersey remembered getting seventy-five dollars in continental money for allowing another man to sit out his military obligation. This money could have helped when Francis eventually bought his wife out of slavery. Some men replaced neighbors, others filled in for family members, and still others for masters. Joseph Brown subbed for his master in the Rhode Island militia and then completed a second stint for the master's son, who went off privateering. Amos Read, a freeman from Virginia, served several enlistments for neighbors, including his former master.[6]

Virginia, whose black population topped all other states in rebellion, was the first colony to use a portion of its black manpower, achieving this by passing a militia law in July 1775 requiring all free males from sixteen to fifty years of age to participate. A later militia law stipulated that free mulattoes could only serve as drummers, fifers, or pioneers. As such, they were not likely the part of the militia who checked on the black quarters for unlawful assemblies or watched out for slaves "trolling about from one plantation to another" without a pass. On the heels of the militia law, the General Assembly addressed the problem of filling Virginia's quota in the Continental Army. Any two militiamen who produced an able-bodied man for three years or for the duration would never be subject to any future drafts. The state legislators took the trouble to list exemptions, but skin color and free status of blacks were not among them. So the masters of Virginia willingly volunteered their slaves to save them the inconvenience of serving their state.[7]

Virginia had a monumental problem in filling its military obligations during the Revolution. The ruling class felt that soldiering was the job of the lower classes. The lower classes, in turn, exercised their liberty by driving a hard bargain to enlist or refusing outright to serve. In October 1777, the burgesses offered prospective recruits twenty dollars over the continental bounty. In the May 1778 session, the legislature offered a thirty-dollar bounty, a complete suit of regimentals, an extra gill of alcohol daily, exemption from drafts for a year after the soldier returned to civilian life, and exemption from taxes for a year. These benefits reaped only 716 men of the 8,000 requested of Virginia by the Continental Congress. Such a poor turnout did not inspire the legislators to ease up on requirements for black recruits. Instead the General Assembly moved against slaves who presented themselves as free men to local recruiters. Henceforth, said the legislature, all black men needed to produce a certificate signed by a justice of the peace attesting to their free status. Restricting recruits in this manner did not help boost Virginia's numbers in the field. Thus the state offered more inducements for those who signed up for the duration—a $150 bounty, a new suit of regimentals every year, exemption from taxes for life, and full pay for life if disabled. It wasn't enough. In the October session, the bounty for duration soldiers rose to $400 in addition to the continental land bounty, the annual suit of clothes, a life disability pension, and a new inducement giving widows of dead soldiers a lifelong pension.[8]

The government of Virginia tried drafting certain groups, "expendable" poor men whenever possible, and once they tried single men over the age of eighteen with no children. But they never succeeded in finding the right combination of targeted recruits and tempting inducements. In a society where "equality" was a byword, the middling farmer bridled at slaveholders who could easily afford to pay for a substitute and whose land was tended by slaves in the master's absence. If wealthy Virginians shirked their duties, then local militia units had to find recruits, and the short straw could fall to any local farmer. Resentment led to resistance. Few white Virginians who were drafted went into the army. They rioted. They moved. When the British invaded Virginia in 1781, some militiamen organized a barbecue to rally resistance to the draft rather than confront the redcoats. In October 1780, after the disastrous defeat at Camden, South Carolina, the government tried more incentives, including a new one. Soldiers who signed up for the duration got a $12,000 bounty (runaway inflation accounts for this high number), a three-hundred-acre land bounty (up from two hundred) and "a healthy, sound negro between the ages of 10 and 30," or sixty pounds of gold or silver at the option of the recruit—both were assets that, unlike paper currency, did not lose their value. Did any black Virginians avail themselves of the slave bounty? In the cases of those veterans who lived long enough to detail their service in the nineteenth-century pension records, most enlisted before 1780. For the handful who enlisted in the fall of

1780 or afterward, most served eighteen-month stints, which qualified them for bounty money but no slave. It is possible that in practice Virginia authorities drew the line on this incentive based on the race of the recruit.[9]

Like Virginia, the state of Maryland, also rattled by the fall of Charles Town and the defeat at Camden, took action in its October 1780 legislative session, but unlike any other southern state it specifically noted that enslaved men could serve. In "An Act to Procure Recruits," the law dictated that Marylanders could recruit able-bodied men between the ages of sixteen and forty-five to serve for three years. Each recruit could "be either a freeman or a slave," provided that the master agreed to the enlistment in the presence of the recruiting lieutenant. While other states danced around the charged word "slave," Maryland invited slaves outright to fight for national freedom without any guarantee that they would earn their individual liberation through filling the state's military quotas.[10]

As North Carolina and the Chesapeake states responded to the disasters in South Carolina in 1780, the Mid-Atlantic states felt no compunction in letting down the barriers to military service for men of color. South Carolina was far away from Philadelphia and Albany, but the British base of operations, New York City, was right in their vicinity throughout the war. Thousands of enemy troops occupied the islands of New York Bay from 1776 to the end of the conflict and provided a haven for the slaves of rebel masters. Yet a sense of calm pervades the Pennsylvania statutes, unlike the apparent urgency of Virginia's acts and resolves, for example. The Quaker State limited militia service to whites throughout the war. When filling Continental Army battalions, on the other hand, there was no exemption for men of color. Only white men were expected to take the oath of allegiance. Still, a look at Pennsylvania's muster lists and the famous White Plains "List of Negroes" in 1778 yields very few men of color. Of the five hundred pensioners of color I identified in my study, only four were from Pennsylvania.[11]

Elsewhere in the Middle Colonies, New York also restricted black enlistment, but its war with the Iroquois Confederacy impelled it to relent. In the summer of 1779, General Washington sent General John Sullivan to wage total warfare against the powerful Iroquois. The army was to destroy everything in its path. In March 1780, New York opened the way for free blacks, and "all the male inhabitants (slaves excepted) of the age of 16 years and upwards" had to participate. But as a New Hampshire commentator observed about the Indian population after Sullivan's operation, "The nests are destroyed but the birds are still on the wing." Despite the devastation of their homeland, the Iroquois warriors regrouped after Sullivan and continued to defy the forces of Washington. The need for able-bodied soldiers did not diminish. So in March 1781 New York provided an avenue for slaves to join the war effort. As was already the case, all male non-slaves sixteen and older had to participate. But now slaveholders could deliver slaves to serve for a three-year enlistment in exchange for a generous land grant. The enslaved recruit would become free after his discharge. In contrast to the Empire State, New Jersey allowed "bought servants" to enlist as early as mid-1777, provided the master approved. The slaveholder then received monetary compensation for the departing worker. A "bought servant or an apprentice" could be submitted as a substitute as well. No racial modifiers accompany "bought servant," and so slaves entered the New Jersey line.[12]

The stalwart draft dodgers of Virginia aside, enough money provided sufficient inducement for many recruits, regardless of race. Poor white immigrants joined the Pennsylvania line in significant numbers. One soldier in five joined the New York line as a substitute for more affluent neighbors. But for black men, money could mean even more than keeping oneself and one's family afloat. London Atis, formerly known as London Lyon (his former master's last name) served on privateers off the coast of New England and used his prize money to buy his freedom. Richard Leet, a native African sold off in America at the age of five, also used sea service to liberate himself but offered none of his wages to his master back in Connecticut. He must have calculated that twenty-seven years of service was compensation enough. Perhaps for this reason, Leet settled in Rhode Island after the war. Pomp Sherbourne, in the New Hampshire line, used his bounty money to buy his wife out of slavery. Jeremiah Virginia appreciated the bounty money as well, but he was impelled to serve a second time because a white man claimed that he had purchased Virginia from his former master. The veteran explained in his pension application that "rather than be subjected to slavery," he had enlisted in the army again. Unlike previous generations, these men had absorbed the rhetoric of freedom and finally had the means to realize their liberation or that of their family members through service to the cause.[13]

Both white and black men served for selfless ideals and had self-interested motives. They also shared a sense of adventure with friends and family members. Prime Coffin and Prince Light were friends who signed up on the same day. Abednego Jackson of Maryland volunteered with fifty buddies when they heard General Washington was in need. In Massachusetts, Samuel Dunbar was one of six brothers who fought on the American side. Also from Massachusetts were several Indian men from the Mashpee Plantation who joined units throughout the army. They were variously described as men of color, black, mulatto, "negro," aborigine, and Indian, probably reflecting various degrees of intermarriage between the Indian and African American communities. From Granville County, North Carolina, the Tabourn family supplied three soldiers who would all apply for government pensions. From Connecticut, one of the Simon family's stories that survived into the nineteenth century concerned the Battle of Trenton, in which one of Lycus Simon's brothers aimed at a Hessian and missed his mark, prompting the other brother to fire his musket, bringing his sibling's target down.[14]

Wives sometimes followed their husbands into the army camps. Judith Lines related that the summer after her marriage to John Lines, he "sent for her." She spent three to four months in the Hudson Highlands, there contracting smallpox at camp. Nevertheless, she worked alongside her husband, who was a waiter to Colonel Isaac Sherman. Most likely she laundered for her husband's unit. This was the most common job that women camp followers performed for the army. George Washington looked askance at the number of women in his army family. They consumed resources, anywhere from a quarter ration to a full one depending on the work they performed. Officially units got sixteen rations for every fifteen men—the extra ration allotted to a woman camp follower. Women could also disrupt operations and distract the soldiers. The genteel southern lady of Washington's acquaintance was a far cry from the tough washerwomen of the regiments. By 1780, unmarried women had to leave the army. But Washington could not afford to bear down on married women. His men might decamp with their better halves. However skeptical he was about women camp followers in general, George Washington liked Mr. and Mrs. Lines. According to a friend of Lines, the general wanted them to move to Virginia after the war. Mr. Lines was willing, but Mrs. Lines was not, so they remained in New England. Fifty-six years later, in her widow's pension application, Judith Lines parted with a precious letter written by her husband in 1781, which she included as proof of her marriage. It is one of the rare extant letters written by an African American soldier in the war of the revolution.[15]

Most young men of color did not enjoy the luxury of following their fathers into the army to act as servants, as many white boys did. Although the evidence is often only suggestive, some black men appear to have served their civilian masters in the military. Prince Hull of the Connecticut line served a Captain Hull. Aaron Brister's pension application was supported by Captain Benjamin Brister. Richard Fortune started out life as Richard Putnam, a slave to Israel Putnam, later a general in the Continental Army. In other instances, the veteran would spell out his relationship to a master-officer. Joseph Johnson of New York at first stated that he enlisted in Captain James Rosekrans's company, fought in Sullivan's campaign, and was discharged at the end of the war. The government rejected his pension application because muster rolls indicated that he deserted in 1780. The soldier appealed this rejection and explained to the government that his captain was his master's son. When Captain Rosekrans lost his sanity and was discharged in 1780, Joseph Johnson left the company to take his master's son home. Perhaps he was ordered to do so and never returned, or perhaps he made a decision to decamp with the man who shared his childhood.[16]

Whether moved by money, revolutionary rhetoric, or future hopes, some black men might have been coerced into enlisting or substituting. African Americans in the loyalist pension claims often talk about being "compelled" or "obliged" to take up arms for the Americans. Of course, it behooved a loyalist applying for aid from the British government to characterize military service with the Americans as being forced. It likewise made sense for a Continental Army veteran to emphasize free choice in applying for a U.S. government pension.[17]

African Americans shared many of the same motivations for enlistment as their white counterparts. In the early going, all experienced the raw excitement of the times, providing a visceral impetus to join the cause. The black men at Bunker Hill, the soldiers who protested Continental Congress's refusal to admit them into Washington's army, the black man and his neighbors who charged down the road to Lexington—all of them felt the inexorable pull of the times.

Camaraderie, commitment to a cause, adventure, and financial considerations all figured into a white or black man's decision to join or stay in military service. But for black men, each of these reasons takes on a different slant by dint of their position in society. Camaraderie takes on a new meaning when a black recruit gets to work as a free man in a largely African American environment, be it in First Rhode Island Regiment or in an all-black company within an integrated regiment. Massachusetts considered following Rhode Island's lead of establishing an all-black regiment but tabled the idea in 1778. Still, there appear to have been at least two all-black companies in the Massachusetts line. Cicero Sweatt (Sweet) claimed in his pension application that he was part of a black company commanded by Captain Matthew Chambers in Colonel Calvin Smith's Sixth Massachusetts Regiment. Another pensioner, Edward Sands, enlisted in Captain Jeremiah Miller's "company of blacks" in Colonel Joseph Voses's Massachusetts regiment. There also appears to have been an all-Indian company in what is now Maine. Nicholas Hawwawas, a Passamaquoddy man reputed to be the son of a chief, said in his pension that he was a lieutenant of an Indian company. Hawwawas claimed to have owned a sword given to him by George Washington. He also kept a French musket as a souvenir after the war. Connecticut too shied away from legislating a distinct black regiment, but it too had an all-black company, headed by Captain David Humphreys in the Fourth Connecticut. One Connecticut veteran, Caesar Shelton, claimed in his pension application that he had served in an all-black company in the Leather Cap Regiment (Sixth Connecticut—later to become the Fourth Connecticut in the army reorganization of late 1780) headed by Colonel Return Meigs. Peter Jennings, another New Englander, from Rhode Island, claimed that he had enlisted in 1776 in the "Fifth Regiment of Artillery of Blacks" in the continental line. In all his militia stints, James Kersey saw action only once, and that was with "a body of Negroes above Charlestown." These units were exceptions to the rule. Most men of color worked in an integrated unit and so had an enhanced opportunity for a positive relationship with men whose skin color would have precluded such interaction before the war.[18]

Adventure too, in the sense of an undertaking involving risk, looked a shade different to an African American recruit. Who could tell if the state governments and masters would live up to their word? Would black soldiers serve as cannon fodder? Adventure, in its second meaning, the rush of seeing faraway places, would have been all the more exciting to men whose mobility had been the most limited before the war.

With respect to financial considerations, both black and white men grabbed at the chance to better their lot, but for African Americans money could mean redeeming themselves or their families from slavery's yoke. And finally, commitment to the cause of liberty was fundamentally different for black and white men. White men, who envisioned themselves enslaved by England, had "masters" who were three thousand miles away. Even the royal governor's touch was light indeed on their everyday lives. A black man's master, on the other hand, was in the neighborhood, and his minions could beat and rape, and they could pull apart families.

Adventure, fellowship, passion for the revolution's ideals, hope for a better future, hope for escape from poverty—all these motivated black and white men alike. But, with the exception of a poor apprentice who wanted to part from his master, white veterans could not begin to appreciate the higher stakes experienced by men who had been enslaved for life. Laws opened the way for black participation in the war, but the men themselves had to make the decision. They had to calculate the odds that state laws would be honored after the war, that masters would live up to their word, that they would survive to reap the benefits. None of these scenarios was a foregone conclusion when African American men made their marks on enlistment papers.

The War

As men of color faced recruitment officers, white people commented on their presence in the army, navy, and militia, mostly limiting their expressions to surprise at the number of dark-skinned men in the lines. Others registered a range of emotions from outrage to enthusiasm. Alexander Graydon, an officer from Pennsylvania, despaired at the state of the American army in 1776, including "the miserably constituted bands from New England." A notable exception in this group was Glover's Regiment from Marblehead, Massachusetts. But, added Graydon, "Even in this regiment, there were a number of negroes, which, to persons unaccustomed to such associations, had a disagreeable, degrading effect." Graydon does not say whether he felt degraded or not. In inserting the phrase "to persons unaccustomed to such associations," Graydon might have betrayed his own hesitation in denigrating these above average soldiers. But Captain Persifor Frazer, also of the Pennsylvania line, made no such qualifying statements. He conveyed his disgust at the miserable appearance, and worse, the miserable behavior of the New England troops. Sickened by their deportment, and convinced that the Yankees were not fit to endure hardships, Frazer fretted, "There is the strangest mixture of Negroes, Indians and whites, with old men and mere children, which together with a nasty, lousy appearance made a most shocking spectacle." Both Graydon and Frazer fought in Pennsylvania units where there were noticeably fewer men of color in the ranks.[19]

Alexander Hamilton, on the other hand, felt no such disgust when he contemplated black men in the mix. He had been on Washington's staff for two years when he wrote to John Jay to support the idea of South Carolina raising black regiments. "I have not the least doubt that negroes will make very excellent soldiers with proper management," wrote Hamilton. He acknowledged the uphill battle that recruiting black soldiers would be. Public perception was not on his side. Hamilton attacked this perception in two ways. With respect to the notion that blacks were "too stupid to make soldiers," Hamilton rejected any inherent inferiority, asserting that proper training and good officers would make these men fine soldiers—better, in fact, than white men because blacks had lived lives of subordination. They were used to taking orders. Secondly, Hamilton pointed to society's role in fostering this inaccurate perception. "The contempt we have been taught to entertain for the blacks makes us fancy many things that are founded neither in reason or experience." Greed too, claimed Hamilton, conveniently colored perceptions.[20]

James Madison, one of Virginia's representatives in the Continental Congress, agreed with Hamilton. The war was in its fifth year when Madison suggested that Virginia liberate some of its slaves to serve as soldiers. Rather than use slaves as bounties for white recruits, Madison favored liberating them and making them soldiers. The war was, after all, he argued, a "contest for liberty." Anticipating the objections of his fellow Virginians, Madison saw no "imaginable danger" as white officers and a majority of white soldiers would control the situation. And Madison's experience had shown, he wrote, that a freed slave immediately loses "all attachment and sympathy with his former fellow slaves." Although sorely pressed, said a friend of Madison's who was a state legislator in Richmond, Virginia refused to consider creating black regiments, deeming it "unjust" to sacrifice the property of only a part of the community. If Virginia instituted such a "negro scheme," the English would respond in kind, resulting in the ruination of the southern states.[21]

Despite resistance from the legislatures, thoughtful leaders of the revolutionary elite, like Hamilton and Madison, had seen enough of black soldiers to recommend their further participation in the military struggle. Men of color were in every military theater. Their recollections in the nineteenth-century pension records tell the story of the American Revolution from the ground level. These stories enhance our knowledge of what it was like to fight on an eighteenth-century battlefield and at times challenge the standard historical narrative based only on views of the high and mighty. Four veterans—Jacob Francis, John Roe, Pompey Woodward, and James Depuy—provide windows onto the everyday and the extraordinary, from their days as fresh-faced privates to their experiences as battle-hardened veterans.

Jacob Francis and the Dimensions of Soldiering

Jacob Francis had as illustrious a military career as any veteran of the early Revolutionary War. Born in Amwell Township, New Jersey, he was bound out—sent to work as a servant—by his mother until his twenty-first birthday. Traded off to a series of masters, and acquiring the name of one of them (Jacob Hulick), Francis ended up in Salem, Massachusetts in 1775. In the fall of 1775, he enlisted for one year. Francis fought for General Washington at Long Island and was one of the few faithful who remained in Washington's force on the banks of the Delaware River in December 1776. He could have abandoned the army like so many other soldiers had done after the debacles in New York and New Jersey. Francis's enlistment was up, and he could have walked away having fulfilled his contract. But he decided to stay on for the daring raid at Trenton. Shortly thereafter, Francis left the army and returned home to find his mother ill. She told him his real surname. Francis thereafter stuck close to home and served in militia units under his family's name. He served at Monmouth, New Jersey, in June 1778, but did not serve, he later admitted, in the heat of battle. After the war Francis settled in New Jersey and married a woman whom he had to buy out of slavery, and he applied for a pension at age seventy-eight. Originally rejected by the pension office, Francis went to court again and swore out a thirteen-page deposition, which was enough to convince the bureaucrats in Washington to enter his name on the pension rolls.[22]

In the detailed accounting of his youth in the military, Jacob Francis reminds us of important aspects of eighteenth-century warfare—its limited dimensions and the proximity of fighting men on both sides of the conflict. While still near New York City in the fall of 1776, Francis related that his unit was encamped so close to the enemy Hessian force that he could hear them only about a quarter mile away. Another African American veteran, Benjamin Lattimore, in the same area around New York, recalled that after a skirmish, a truce was declared "for the purpose of burying the dead."[23]

Both men's testimonies point to intimate warfare, where one could see the enemy's face, hear his banter, and negotiate accommodations that made the conflict a bit more humane. The Revolutionary War's modest dimensions facilitated these aspects, as was highlighted by the African American veterans as well as their white cohorts. At the Battle of White Plains, where Private Francis ate his grub within earshot of the enemy, there were four thousand soldiers on both sides who actually fought in the battle. At Freeman's Farm, one of the battles of the Saratoga campaign, American forces numbered eighty-five hundred while the British had seventy-five hundred effectives. At Yorktown, the final battle of the Revolution, a joint American-French force of eighteen thousand cornered an enemy force of eighty-three hundred. Such numbers would not even fill a modern sports stadium. Within a century of these great revolutionary battles, Americans would see 165,000 of its sons in the armies that clashed at Gettysburg, with 51,000 casualties over the battle's three days. In Jacob Francis' day, a soldier's imagination could better encompass the extent of the battlefield in which he was engaged than a later generation would be able to do in the Civil War.[24]

Francis not only found himself in close proximity to the enemy in October 1776 at the Battle of White Plains, he was also in extremely close quarters with soldiers on his side of the battlefield. Eighteenth-century infantry guides dictated that men form a line in battle, often shoulder to shoulder. A firing line was typically two or three deep, with the men in the front row on one knee, the men in the second row each slightly to the side of the man in front of him, and each man in the third row just to the side of the man in front him in the center row. If a two-line formation, the first row would fire and then fall back to reload while the second row moved up. Six feet behind these soldiers were the "file closers," who served as replacements for the fallen. Surrounded by the men of one's company, a soldier faced enemy fire. Luckily for soldiers in tight formation, the enemy's fire was wildly inaccurate. In addition, even in good weather the flintlock musket fired only half the time. In rain or damp weather it did not fire at all. The British "Brown Bess" musket's official range was two hundred yards, but a more realistic assessment would place it at eighty yards—far less effective than a bow and arrow. Only 5 percent of all musket balls found their mark in another soldier. As historian Daniel Headrick put it, "Soldiers commonly shot away their weight in lead for every man they killed." Soldiers pointed their sixteen-pound muskets in the general direction, fired, and hoped their shots would hit the enemy. With no repeating weaponry, each soldier had to reload after every shot—an operation that could take an expert fifteen to twenty agonizing seconds to perform. A more accurate rifle, the Pennsylvania long rifle, was not unknown to the revolutionary battlefield, but its effectiveness was hampered by the smoky fields of battle and the length of time it took to reload—three times as long as the average musket. A battle opened with the two opposing sides three hundred to six hundred yards apart. Artillery would begin to soften up the enemy, followed by the lines moving forward. When only fifty to one hundred yards away from the enemy, the line would stop to issue its first volley, answered by the other side. To find one's mark, a soldier had to look into the eyes of his opponent far more often than a soldier would in later wars. When an American officer ordered his men at Bunker Hill to fire only when they saw the whites of their opponents' eyes, he understood a thing or two about the wild trajectory of a musket ball and the odds of hitting one's target.[25]

When two opposing infantry lines closed in and clashed, another weapon became of prime importance. The offset-blade socket bayonet began to be affixed to guns at the turn of the eighteenth century, allowing a soldier to protect himself after firing. By the revolution, commanders appreciated the terror-inducing properties of a bayonet charge. British generals attributed their earliest victories in the New York campaign to the bayonet and became convinced that American soldiers, particularly the militia, would lose heart and run in the face of these charging blades. The Americans, for their part, learned of this latter-day pike's value. After the Paoli raid of September 20, 1777, when British bayonets did grisly work on Brigadier General Anthony Wayne's forces, the American general responded with a surprise attack of his own on the seemingly impregnable British position at Stony Point. Disabling the firing mechanism on their muskets, the Americans prevailed with the element of surprise and their bayonets. Jacob Francis had seen the efficacy of British bayonets on Long Island in the fall of 1776. And in his integrated regiment, he stood shoulder to shoulder with white comrades, who many years later testified that Private Francis was a "good soldier and always did his duty well."[26]

John Roe and the Battle of Stony Point

On receiving the glorious news of the taking of the seemingly impregnable fort at Stony Point on the Hudson River, an amazed George Washington remarked that General Wayne's troops had primarily used bayonets to secure the victory, "scarcely firing a gun," he said. Two months before, in May 1779, the British had moved up the Hudson and captured the fort at Stony Point and one across the river at Verplanck's Point, just fifteen miles south of West Point. Wayne's successful surprise attack on the west bank fort shocked the British out of occupying the Hudson Highlands. It was at once a drama and a significant battle, although there is no evidence of either element in the pension depositions of the rank-and-file soldiers involved in the action.[27]

One such soldier, John Roe, a "free man of color" in Virginia, stepped into the Botecourt County courtroom on January 12, 1819, to swear that as a private in the Second Virginia Regiment, he had participated in the Battles of Monmouth, Stony Point, and Yorktown. The record is silent on what he saw, what he did, and how he felt there. We know that Roe was in the thick of things at Monmouth because he tells us that he was wounded there. Among his black comrades at Stony Point was a Massachusetts soldier named Primus Tyng. Tyng did more than mention his participation at Stony Point. He recalled that he saw the first man go into the British works, and it was not the field officer cited in the history books but a lowly private named David Drury.[28]

The veterans' matter-of-fact listing of the battles in their nineteenth-century pension applications often left out the drama of events. Back in the summer of 1779, Roe and Tyng were both battle-hardened veterans, solid enough to be chosen for a top-secret operation led by General Wayne in the neighborhood of West Point. They were likely members of light infantry units, the elite of the Continental Army. As they assembled around West Point, the ranks were probably abuzz as to where they were headed. Roe and Tyng were not the only African Americans in light infantry units. Thirteen other black pensioners listed Stony Point on their roster of battles as well. Their officers told them nothing about their final destination. Roe and his comrades received further evidence that something special was in the works because shortly before they were scheduled to pull out, each man received a cap, a blanket, two shirts, a pair of overalls, and a pair of shoes. This was unheard-of largesse on the part of the commissary. On the morning of July 15, Roe and the other members of the light corps turned south on country roads so rutted and narrow that the men had to march single-file for most of the distance. They marched silently over mountains and through ravines. At 8:00 P.M., the corps arrived within two miles of Stony Point. Roe had probably guessed by this time what was in store for him. There was still plenty enough light to see the British stronghold rising 150 feet above the Hudson and jutting about half a mile into the river. Surrounded on three sides by water and on the fourth by swampy terrain, the fort was secured by a fence of sharpened tree branches and three redoubts. Roe and his fellow soldiers were told that they were to dismantle the perilous fences, storm up the hill, and capture the fort.[29]

This was a tall order. The British described Stony Point as a second Gibraltar. To encourage the American soldiers, General Wayne offered monetary rewards that would be given to the first five men to enter the British works. As a last precaution, the men were given pieces of white paper to be put in the "most conspicuous part of his hat" so as to distinguish friend from foe—not exactly a reassuring detail for those who looked up the hill. At about midnight, the action began. John Roe was more than likely in the right flank attack group led by Wayne that sloshed through waist-deep water, reached the fences under a withering fire of grapeshot, buckshot, and stray bits of metal called legrange, and started up the hill. Luckily for Roe and his fellow soldiers, much of the British fire went over their heads. British cannons were set to fire on likely targets on the river, not down the face of a sheer drop at the base of the hill. As members of a Virginia company, Roe played a key role as Virginians comprised the advance party of the right flank and largely made up the twenty-man elite team called the Forlorn Hope that preceded the others and was responsible for dismantling the abatis on the hill with long, hooked poles. It took only half an hour to overcome the British, with bayonets only. Once in control, the Americans let out three long and loud cheers that, as one soldier explained, "reverberated in the stillness of night amidst rocks and mountains [that] sent back an echo to cheer the hearts of the victors." With the exception of some diversionary fire, not a shot issued from the American light corps that night. Sixty English soldiers died of their wounds while seventy survived their bayonet wounds. On the American side, fifteen soldiers lost their lives, while eighty-five were wounded. We do not know if John Roe or Primus Tyng were sickened by the sight of so many mangled bodies or whether they were sufficiently battle-hardened after Monmouth to allow themselves only the feeling of relief at having survived the assault. Wayne, who was himself wounded, sent George Washington a message that might have resonated with black soldiers. The general wrote, "Our officers and men behaved like men who are determined to be free." Wayne became famous that night. He received plaudits from Congress, and a gold medal was struck in his honor. Risky exploits like this one would eventually affix the adjective "mad" to his name for all posterity. The American survivors of Stony Point received a monetary reward from Congress distributed according to their ranks. The rewards for the first men into the fort went to five officers, headed by a French lieutenant colonel, Francois Fleury.[30]

Forty years later, court clerks and pension bureaucrats would not have known that Primus Tyng was rewriting history by acknowledging a lowly private as the first man into the British works. Tyng's voice joined the chorus of people who had disputed who did what on that summer night in 1779. The unsung hero, Private David Drury, disappeared from the records. A white man named David Drury does appear in the 1790 census in Andover, Vermont, but whether this is the elusive veteran from Tyng's account will never be known. In the confusion, smoke, and motion, there were likely many "first men in the works" at Stony Point, depending on one's vantage point. But that there was not one private in that golden circle of five seems somewhat unlikely. In all, at least thirteen black pensioners were part of this elite group under Wayne that night. There were indubitably other black participants who did not live long enough to swear out a pension application. But of the pensioners who claimed Stony Point as part of their service record, over half were from southern states, proving that state laws like those of Virginia that sought to confine black men to roles that did not require a gun were not enforced on the ground.[31]

Pompey Woodward and Bennington, Vermont

Tyng was not alone in challenging the official version of the war's events. The rank and file often relate aspects of battles not found in a war's official history. Pompey Woodward provided one such detail. In July 1777, when British general John Burgoyne descended from Canada and took Fort Ticonderoga, Woodward was part of the force that evacuated the fort and fought a rearguard action at Hubbardton. Slowed by American forces and the terrain, Burgoyne was not far from his destination, the town of Albany, when he decided to send a Hessian detachment east to secure his left flank and to wrestle up "large supplies of cattle, horses, and carriages."

Woodward, in a Massachusetts unit, was one of the soldiers to meet the largely Hessian detachment near of Bennington, Vermont. His later recollections were not of the battle but of its aftermath. The patriots having won the day, Woodward saw the Hessians put into a meetinghouse where "there was a disturbance among the prisoners in the night." He remembered "that they were fired upon by the sentries while in the meeting house and that some of them were killed." This gunning down of prisoners of war did not figure in the generals' reports. Brigadier General John Stark, who commanded American troops at Bennington, likened his men to military luminaries of the past. "Had they been Alexanders or Charles[es] of Sweden," Stark crowed, "They could not have behaved better." Major General Benjamin Lincoln, also on the scene that day, described the troops as having behaved "in a very brave and heroic manner." Woodward and his fellow soldiers, most of whom were militiamen, certainly laid their lives on the line, obtaining revenge for Hubbardton and, using Major General Horatio Gates's word, slowing the "impetuosity" of Burgoyne's approach. A few of the men, however, overreacted at the meetinghouse. Given the gushing of American generals, it is small wonder that the meetinghouse episode did not appear in the history books until 1997, when Richard Ketchum found a source written by a woman who tended those particular Hessian wounded. Yet in 1832 this memory had lodged in Private Woodward's mind for over fifty years. His story was lost in the thousands of pension files for another 175 years.[32]

James Depuy and the Frontier

While Pompey Woodward fought in a well-known battle that turned the tide of the war, James Depuy engaged in ongoing warfare on the New York frontier. Born into slavery in Mamakating, New York, James Depuy served one master through the Revolution, after which he was sold to a series of masters named Depuy. Aside from keeping guard on the Neversink River, "he assisted in building Fort Depuy about a mile below DeWitt Fort." This picket fort surrounded Benjamin Depuy's house and barn and protected approximately nine families. Woodward served as a sentry on the hills surrounding the fort and was frequently in scouting parties in the woods. On one occasion, the Iroquois leader Joseph Brandt, with a party of Indians and Tories, attacked the little fort. When alerted of Brandt's imminent arrival, the occupants of Fort Depuy fled to the better fortified and larger Fort DeWitt. James Depuy preceded the refugees, pulling down fences so that the rest could pass through with their wagons. Once behind fort walls again, Depuy saw Joseph Brandt step in front of his men to set fire to a barn outside the fort walls. Before retiring, the Brandt party "burned Fort Depuy, killed a number of cattle and hogs, and destroyed considerable property." Depuy's conduct during the crisis so impressed a local captain that the officer gave Depuy a musket and a cartridge box. This was to be the only reward Depuy would receive for his service in defense of the frontier. When he applied for a pension in 1832, the government turned him down, claiming that New York state law had not allowed slaves in the militia at that time. The pension office stood firm on this point despite the efforts of James Depuy's neighbors to educate the government bureaucrats. Two white soldiers attested to Depuy's service. One of these men explained that on the frontier the people had to depend on themselves. Occasionally a few soldiers came down from the "North River" (the Hudson), he explained, but most times the community had to shift for itself. They built three forts, and the contingent that guarded them were "old and young boys, white and black." Another neighbor added that "wives and children" helped build the forts. And finally, claimed the sister of one of Depuy's white supporters, they called up *anyone* who could bear arms.

James Depuy's story tells us of the improvisational quality of frontier warfare. The isolation of the Neversink River settlements meant constant vigilance on the part of the settlers. They could not afford to make distinctions with respect to age, gender, or race because they needed everyone's muscle to pull through. Survival superseded state law. Indian and Tory contingents killed livestock and burned buildings. In communities far from populated areas, this destruction of food and shelter inflicted a particularly heavy blow. When George Washington's attention turned to Indian raids on the frontier, he advised Major General John Sullivan to aim at "the total destruction and devastation of their settlements and the capture of as many prisoners of every age and sex as possible." This total warfare did not exist elsewhere in New York. Sullivan's expedition in 1779 laid waste to much of Indian country in the state. But the destruction of "14 towns and most flourishing crops of corn" did not knock the Indians out of commission. Hence, James Depuy states that although he occasionally worked on his master's farm, he spent most of his time "keeping guard and scouring the woods" to prevent the Indians and Tories from scoring another victory against the little forts on the banks of the Neversink.[33]

Rank-and-File Memories

For the most part, black and white pensioners tell remarkably similar stories about their war experiences. Some of this can be explained by the fact that black veterans were moving through a pension process dominated by whites. The likelihood of getting government money would not be enhanced by revealing inferior treatment based on race. Pension agents likely prepped the veterans before their day in court. A story told to a neighbor might be stripped to bare essentials by a court clerk, anxious to move on to the next case. But the above factors would more likely account for what is not in the pension deposition rather than what *is* there. The similarities in the pension accounts reflect a military life lived in close proximity to others during the formative years of young manhood. In between the heart-stopping moments on the battlefield where fellows of one's company were indispensable, the soldiers of Washington's integrated army shared the tasks of keeping warm, fed, and entertained during the long days of camp life. Some may well have developed an appreciation for their fellows that in the crisis trumped skin color. They certainly shared the dangers of their occupation but also absorbed a similar culture that led them to express their war experiences in a certain way. Such was the case with labeling battles. Practically all veterans tended to label the great patriot victories with the names of the defeated British general. Before the history books assigned place names to identify these battles, the veterans had personalized them by calling them "the taking of Burgoyne" [Saratoga] or "the capture of Cornwallis [Yorktown].

These humble soldiers were, of course, claiming an integral role in the fall of these great men. The only American disaster to be labeled with a general's name was the Battle of Camden, South Carolina. That debacle appears in a couple of pension applications as "Gates's Defeat"—the blame here was with the head of American forces, not with the rank-and-file soldiers. Washington's name was not attached to any of his victories or more numerous defeats. Indeed, one notable exception to the similarities of white and black pension depositions is the number of Washington sightings. White pensioners mentioned him quite a bit, while African Americans rarely referenced him.[34]

Black and white men shared the physical danger of engaging with an enemy. Southern states tried to detach black men from guns. Virginia tried to limit free blacks to service as drummers, fifers, or pioneers. South Carolina eventually instituted a similar law. Although North Carolina's 1777 militia act demanded that all men had to serve, the state had passed laws early in the war disarming persons of color. Despite these restrictive laws, the pension applications indicate that black men found their way into battle. Whether as line soldiers or as fifers and drummers providing crucial communication links during battle, black men served in the line of fire. Seventy-five percent of the black southerners in my sample noted specific battles in their pension applications. While being present at a battle does not necessarily equate to a combat role, evidence of a wound would indicate that the veteran was likely in the thick of the action. More southerners in this study noted being wounded than soldiers from north of the Maryland-Pennsylvania border. Morgan Griffin's daughter claimed that her father was wounded seven times during his service in the South Carolina line. Other soldiers lost limbs. Elisha Hunt of North Carolina lost his right arm at Charlestown. Tim Jones lost his leg at Yorktown. Thomas Lively of the Eighth Virginia survived the Valley Forge encampment only to lose his right eye at the Battle of Monmouth in 1778. Most men would have retired from military service after such a blow but not Private Lively. In the spring of 1780 he was wounded in the leg during the siege of Charles Town and then had to recuperate in prison as he was confined as a prisoner of war for fourteen months. In October 1781, this indomitable veteran hobbled into Yorktown, where he participated in the siege and saw the fall of mighty Cornwallis. If purple hearts and service medals could be given posthumously, Thomas Lively of Petersburg, Virginia, certainly deserved all the accolades his country could bestow. After the war he was penniless when he applied for a pension.[35]

That these men survived their injuries and lived to an old age is a miracle given the dangerous, unchallenged microbes of everyday life and the state of battlefield medicine in the eighteenth century. The likes of Thomas Lively and Morgan Griffin beat the odds by living well after the average life expectancy then of fifty-five years (they had survived infancy too, as many did not), particularly noteworthy given their early residence in military hospitals. There dysentery, typhus, smallpox, and various fevers accounted for 90 percent of the soldier deaths in the war. If wounded, the odds to beat increased dramatically. Most medical practitioners in the revolution were not licensed or professionally trained. On December 12, 1777, George Washington "desired" that all regimental surgeons attend "a course of lectures on Anatomy and operations of surgery," it was said. They did not understand the connection between lice and typhus, or between contaminated fluids and typhoid fever. Trained specialists of the time like Benjamin Rush believed that there was more blood in the body than there actually was, and so when doctors bled their patients they sometimes took out too much. The medical consensus was that bleeding a person relaxed the tension of a "feverish illness or infection." One of the instruments used in extracting blood from the body was called a lancet, leading one wit to claim that more Americans died of the lancet than the lance. Asepsis (sterile conditions) and antisepsis (combating infections) were decades in the future. Anesthesia was likewise seventy years away. Amputation was the general rule if a limb were even partially shattered. If he was lucky, Tim Jones (the vet who lost his leg at Yorktown) had a surgeon with a sharp saw, two strong men to hold him down, some rum or opium mixture to serve as anesthesia, and surgical instruments that did not have too many pathogens from the half dozen men who had preceded him on the table, door, or plank that served as an operating table. If not passed out during the amputation, Tim might have bitten on a bullet as his stump was cauterized with a hot iron. Today one may bite the bullet metaphorically—to overcome a difficult situation—but the excruciating pain of the phrase's origin has been lost.[36]

Morgan Griffin's daughter said that her father had lead in his body when he died. Surgeons extracted musket balls that they could access, perhaps in some fleshy part of his body. They left others in the soldier with the hope that they would not poison the patient to death. Caesar Shelton was both cut with a sword and shot. Punctures made by swords or bayonets were "clean" wounds compared to the jagged wounds produced by musket balls. "Unlike the hardened bullets of the late 19th century," explains historian Richard Blanco, "the low velocity lead balls flattened on impact . . . tore flesh savagely, traumatized tissue, splintered bones, and implanted bits of clothing in the injury.[37]

Seriously injured soldiers like Elisha Hunt or Tim Jones most likely got to a military hospital by springless wagons, exposed to the elements and feeling every bump and rut. There were no beds in most hospitals. Overcrowding was endemic. Lack of hygiene prevailed. Patients had no choice to be in these houses of carnage, as Anthony Wayne called them. The people who worked in these "cesspools of human life," as Benjamin Rush described them, *chose* to work there, exhibiting bravery that rarely merited a medal. A far higher percentage of medical personnel died during the war than officers of the line. One in four soldiers died in the hospitals, one estimate claimed, while the odds of surviving on the battlefield were 98 percent. Although doctors were not then familiar with the role of bacteria, they understood that cleanliness was a condition to strive for, that diet affected health, and that crowding might bring on infection. On the orders of the Board of War, Doctor Rush republished his pamphlet on preserving the health of soldiers. In it he extolled the benefit of vegetables and clean clothing, as well as changing the straw on which a soldier lay and exposing blankets to the sun. But the need for Rush's pamphlet speaks to the appalling conditions in the average hospital. After visiting some military hospitals in New Jersey, Governor William Livingston urgently recommended reforms before Washington became "a General without an army." Black members of that army might have had further odds stacked against them because of skin color. Color-blind triage might have prevailed on the battlefield and in the hospitals of the Revolution, but just as likely is the possibility that men of color came last, just as they did in other aspects of life. None of the pensioners mentioned this kind of treatment, but they might have realized that such an assertion would be interpreted by white decision makers in the Washington pension office as "sullen" and "ungrateful."[38]

While listing their own wounds, many veterans, both black and white, related instances in which they saw their officers fall on the field. The government wanted to know the names of each applicant's officers. Perhaps some privates thought to enhance their applications by adding important details about their officers. Or perhaps they wanted to convey to the Pension Office that they shared the dangers of war with higher ranked individuals or masters. Some stories are very matter-of-fact. Allan Jeffers, a South Carolina veteran, saw Brigadier General Casimir Pulaski wounded at Savannah and related that "his thigh [was] cut off and he died." Peter Jennings of Rhode Island saw Lafayette wounded at Brandywine and was at Germantown when General Francis Nash was killed. Andrew Pebbles saw Lieutenant Colonel John Laurens die at a skirmish almost a year after Pebbles himself had sustained three wounds at the Battle of Eutaw Springs: in his shoulder, in his left hand (he lost a thumb), in his belly, where he was bayoneted. Perhaps these men were very attached to their officers. The court scribes recording their testimony may have edited out the emotion as they wrote down the facts. But elsewhere the black veterans managed to convey their attachment. At the Battle of Camden, Edward Sorrell and three other men tried to carry a wounded Colonel Charles Porterfield off the battlefield. Under hot fire, they had to leave him there to be taken prisoner.

After collecting wagons and teams for the army in western Virginia, Sorrell was chosen with some others to go retrieve Colonel Porterfield who had been accorded a parole by the British. They found the officer "confined a prisoner," facing rougher conditions than typical for an officer POW. The colonel died five days after they arrived, Sorrell had the honor of taking the colonel's baggage back home.[39]

William Taburn, a "free man of color" from Granville, North Carolina, paid a full-throated tribute to a general felled in battle. Taburn joined the army on the Catawba River just opposite the enemy. The Americans took the offensive and attempted to cross the river. Taburn "was stationed very near Brigadier General William Lee Davidson who rode upon a black horse when he received the ball that put a period to the life of the ablest, kindest, and best officer that ever commanded an army." When hit, the general called out, "Help me down, Boys. I am a Dedd man—give the news to the men at the Island and above." These were Davidson's last words, recollected and recorded for history by a black private. The enemy took advantage of the death of "our beloved general," continued Taburn in his pension application, and made his unit "scamper for life." Stopped by their field officers to form a line, they met the enemy commanded by Banastre Tarleton in the pouring rain. "Like a torrent," it was, Taburn remembered. Tarleton's mounted infantry charged the militia, whose guns were so wet that they could not discharge them. Taburn and his fellow soldiers "were all put to flight." Taburn "fell in with an old Horse without Saddle or a Bridle" and rode all that day and into the night only to find out the next day that he was only twelve miles from the same farm where Tarleton had routed them. Decades later, as an octogenarian, Taburn recalled the emotions of that fateful day: the frenzy of running for his life, the panic of clicking the trigger to no effect as armed horsemen closed in, and the loss of a great leader whose death had unleashed this train of events.[40]

When it came to enemy officers, all veterans seemed to know Burgoyne and Cornwallis, the big losers on the British side. The next name on that list did not command an army but made a considerable impact on rank-and-file Americans. Major John Andre lost his life at the end of a noose on a charge of spying. He was Benedict Arnold's British contact when Arnold planned to sell West Point to the enemy. Arnold's treachery in 1780 shook the foundations of the revolutionary movement. Arnold was a military hero whose leg had been shattered in the Saratoga campaign, where he turned the tide of battle in favor of the Americans. Washington did not succeed in capturing Arnold, but American militiamen did manage to intercept the dashing, handsome Andre with the plans for West Point hidden in his boot. Andre's hanging was an event that many veterans mentioned forty years later in their pension applications, black veterans included. Prince Light of the Third New Hampshire simply stated that he was there. Cuff Ashport of the Connecticut line said he saw Andre's execution but mistakenly located it at West Point. (It was at the Tappan encampment.) A supporter of Oxford Tash's pension application did not remember the date of his acquaintance with Tash, but it was around the time of Andre's execution, he said. The soldier also felt compelled to tell posterity where he had been (a mile or two away) when the execution occurred. John Foy in the Massachusetts line not only saw the execution but also guarded the British officer in the days before his demise. Finally, Primus Coburn of Captain Miller's company of the First Massachusetts said that his regiment was drawn up and surrounded Andre at his execution. Coburn was part of a unit that another veteran of color described as a black company. It could be that Andre's last glimpse of this world included a group of black soldiers watching his ultimate defeat from a prominent position around the gibbet.[41]

Riveting events like the Benedict Arnold conspiracy with John Andre or great battles where thousands of soldiers clashed were rare occurrences. Soldiers (all white) who left diaries of everyday life in camp wrote of the quest for food, the battle with rain, snow, and heat, and the fight with boredom. Here again, black and white veterans shared these experiences. The rare glimpses of fun that black veterans allow us in the pension applications bring them to life as people and provide a colorful backdrop to the great historical events.

Jeffrey Brace, a native of Africa who served in a New England regiment, related that he and his buddies stole a pig from a loyalist who, with "frothing anger," followed them back to camp and complained to their commanding officer. As slaves often outsmarted their masters, Brace and his comrades outwitted both white men, with the result that the angry loyalist got no satisfaction for his loss. When Brace applied for a pension, he had trouble convincing the government bureaucrats of his service because he had changed his name since his army days. So he went to Ansel Patterson, a fellow veteran of the Connecticut line. Patterson did not know Brace but remembered a "Jeffery" in the all-black company. The two men conversed. Patterson claimed that Jeffrey Brace related "transactions" in the service that only a veteran could do, like where and when a mutiny had occurred, including the ringleader's name and where he was hanged. Brace also related stories about "Negro Boxing" and the "many tricks performed by a Negro boy nicknamed "The Cat." It was these details of camp life that convinced the white veteran to state that Brace had indeed been a soldier.[42]

Between battles, good-natured fun certainly lifted the spirits of cold, dirty, hungry men. A white soldier in Jacob Francis's unit related that after a reconnaissance mission, the black man rode into camp at the front of his unit sporting a cow's tail on the back of his head in imitation of the fashion of gentlemen officers who wore a queue. Inspired by the black man's caper, his fellow soldiers promptly "elected Francis their leader." Camp life events also secured a pension for another black soldier, Pomp McCuff. McCuff's soldier witness, also a man of color, remembered him at Valley Forge because they used to play ball together on the grand parade. This field was famously the place where Inspector General Friedrich von Steuben drilled the ragtag American army and reputedly made them into a professional fighting force. But there is another more human side to the field's story—Valley Forge was filled with thousands of young men who shifted for something to do amid their duties. These cold, hungry men in the middle of nowhere may have briefly forgotten their sad situation by playing ball to pass the time.[43]

Also at Valley Forge was a mixed-race black and Indian man who amused himself by singing French songs from his earlier life among the Jesuits. One morning a young French officer was greatly surprised to hear a fashionable French opera song sung by "a supernatural voice." The officer, Peter Stephen Du Ponceau, went in search of the voice and found Louis Cook, "a tall Indian figure in American regimentals." The two struck up a conversation wherein the mixed-race soldier explained that his people thought of the French as "fathers," while the English were merely "brothers." Cook respected the French far more than he did the English. Although fighting for the Americans, Cook yearned for the return of the French to his region and asked Du Ponceau why the French had abandoned the Indians. The two men ended up breakfasting in Baron von Steuben's tent. With a little more training, thought Du Ponceau, Cook "would have made a valuable acquisition to the French Opera."[44]

Mark Murry also entertained white citizens as part of a troupe of sorts. Murry's North Carolina unit was on the way to join General Gates in the summer of 1780 when they came upon the Great Pee Dee River. Intending to cross there, they were intercepted by "some gentlemen in the neighborhood" who convinced the general to linger so as to provide an entertainment for the people of the county. Murry's pension application notes that the general complied with their "urgent request," and on the next day, a Sunday, a "large crowd came in composed of Ladies and Gentlemen." They were treated to a "sham battle," the likes of which was "regularly fought," much to the approval of the assemblage. This reenactment of sorts kept the men of Murry's unit from General Gates's defeat at Camden. Playing war while in the midst of one was somewhat unusual, but sham battles were not unknown in the eighteenth-century world. Much to the delight of Londoners, British army units conducted sham battles in London's Hyde Park, where the soldiers could perfect their maneuvers at the same time they acted out the drama of a battle.[45]

Another bit of levity, in which a black private took on the persona of an officer, featured Private Agrippa Hull, an enslaved man whose wit, intelligence, and "readiness in repartee" made him a favorite among the officers. He ended up a groom serving Thaddeus Kosciuszko. This Polish officer had brought with him to America a costly uniform, "brilliant with adornments," along with a cap replete with "a showy cluster of ostrich plumes." The temptation was too much for Agrippa, commonly called "Grippy." On a night, when the Polish officer was away, Grippy threw a party for all the black servants in camp. He donned his officer's extravagant uniform and "blackened his legs in order to make them shine like boots." The well-wined assembly was toasting Grippy as General Kosciuszko when the real Kosciuszko suddenly appeared in their midst, "causing as much commotion as if Satan himself crossed the threshold." The partygoers stampeded out, leaving a mortified and fearful Grippy to confront the Polish officer. The black man begged for a whipping. But instead, Kosciuszko continued the drama by addressing the black man as an African prince, making him don the ostrich cap, and parading him across the camp to General John Paterson's quarters (Hull had served Paterson before Kosciuszko). There a mock throne was erected, and a white throng saluted Grippy as royalty, affording the revelers "a world of sport." Paterson's biographer, his great-grandson, claimed that the black man suffered as if at a crucifixion that night, although in old age Grippy had swallowed his mortification and delighted in regaling one and all with his caper.[46]

Black men's relationships with officers ranged from good-natured ribbing to hardnosed bargaining. William Taburn's story featured the latter. Unlike Agrippa Hull, Taburn was a free man who had completed several enlistments in the state militia. On one occasion he bargained with his officer to allow him to forego one of these commitments in exchange for the use of his wagon and team. The company was desperate for wagons to move the unit's baggage. The one problem with the deal was that Taburn could not procure a driver, and so he made a second deal with a wagoner who would take charge of Taburn's wagon in exchange for which Taburn would tend the wagoner's crop. (A white comrade later verified this story.) On another stint, a captain left the army, and Taburn ended up with his rifle. It was Taburn's fellow veterans who related in their support depositions that Taburn took a young white soldier under his wing and used to carry the smaller man across deep streams. A half century later this white veteran returned the favor by testifying in support of Taburn's pension application.[47]

The men got a break from camp life when they went home on furlough. As was the case with many young civilian men, their precious time off often revolved around the women in their lives, either wives or sweethearts. The sight

Daguerreotype of Agrippa Hull. This picture, taken in 1844 by Anson Clark, is the basis of an oil painting of Hull that now hangs in the Stockbridge (Massachusetts) Library. Clark did not have the benefit of chemicals to seal the image to the plate. This probably accounts for the drawn-in tie. Luckily for us, someone took a photograph of the daguerreotype before it further faded. Courtesy of the Historical Collection of the Stockbridge Library, Museum, and Archives, Stockbridge, Massachusetts.

of a man in uniform was said to impress young girls mightily. Flora Taggert admired her beloved Pomp Sherbourne's "uniform coat and cocked hat." Another girl noted the red facings on her man's uniform as well as the letters USA on his buttons. Young African Americans who wanted to marry often faced the obstacles that slavery presented. Most young soldiers from New

England were in the process of freeing themselves through military service, but their prospective partners were often still enslaved. Phillis Hinkley's old mistress forbade her to marry Cuff Wells. When she finally relented in April 1783, Phillis immediately got one of her master's old clerks to write a letter to camp, urging Cuff to return home. The soldier lost no time. He was back, resplendent in his uniform, within a month, and so the two enjoyed a May wedding. The soldier then returned to serve out the rest of the war. Another master forbade a suitor from even seeing his slave Molly. Undeterred, Mingo Pollock went courting with the help of a ladder. Having negotiated that obstacle, they went on to marry.[48]

In the North, such a marriage ceremony usually took place in the house of a white person. Some family members could not attend because their masters needed them where they were. When Aaron Carter of the Connecticut line and Rachel Bolles married in the home of a justice of the peace, they were subjected to a condescending lecture by the functionary about the number of unfaithful couples of color who violated the "mutual obligation" expected of married persons. The official's son later remembered that his father had "admonished them for some time on that subject, strongly recommending them not to conduct [themselves] in so dishonorable a manner as others had previously done, some of which cases he mentioned to them." The lecturer, John Watrous, a descendant of the Puritans, certainly knew how to put a damper on joy. He needn't have worried, however. The Carters remained husband and wife for over twenty years, their status only broken by Mr. Carter's death.[49]

After the ceremony, a couple would visit neighbors or sponsor a dance (or both). One veteran exchanged his superior musket for a white man's lesser model and realized some profit, which he used for his wedding. Another couple had a post-wedding dance that townspeople still recalled fifty years later. This became a problem for Molly Pollock, who had to prove her marriage when she applied for her widow's pension in 1837. Her seven supporters all remembered only the party afterward. A fifteen-year-old boy at the time of the wedding did not attend the ceremony, but he did not miss the dance. The man at whose house the dance occurred was probably too busy preparing for it to attend the ceremony, likewise his son. The son explained in his deposition that dances were the custom in that part of Connecticut. An eight-year-old girl at the time, whose grandfather brought up the bride, glossed over the marriage to relate her delight at being permitted to hold the Pollocks' first child in her arms when it arrived after the wedding. Another deponent, who would later become a state senator, related that he had been the fiddler at the dance. Yet another supporter said that his grandfather had owned a "public house" at which the wedding party had made a call for "refreshments and anecdotes on and about the wedding." Unfortunately, as was typically the case with the marriage of many enslaved people, the Pollock's marriage was not recorded in the town or church records. But Molly prevailed. The sheer number of partygoers, including a musically gifted future state senator, must have sufficiently impressed the Pension Office, which put her on the rolls.[50]

Many soldiers used their furloughs to connect with their already established families. Rachel Carter had four children when her husband enlisted in the Connecticut line in 1777. As she had never learned to read or write, Rachel could not write letters to her husband as Abigail Adams had done to her husband, John. But it is a certainty that Rachel fought the Battle of Colchester as surely as Abigail had engaged in the Battle of Braintree. One could fight the war at home, as these women had done, or support one's husband in camp. Sarah Green's betrothed had been a soldier for several years when they got married in January 1782. Immediately afterward, they "both went on and joined the army" at her husband's unit in the Second Massachusetts, serving until the end of the war. Soldiers, whether black or white, pursued their private lives as best they could while keeping the Revolution alive with their military service.[51]

While sharing food and clothing, coping with insufficient shelter, and partaking of both the dangerous and lighter moments of their profession, black and white soldiers did not see exactly the same war. Some aspects of the conflict only applied to men of color. Once enlisted, African American men served longer stints in the Continental Army than most of their white comrades. Black pensioners had spent on average almost five years in the military, compared to three years for whites. The army was a better option than civilian life for the poorest and most vulnerable men. Some of the state programs offering enslaved men freedom for their service demanded a commitment for the duration of the war. Another difference from their white counterparts was that a greater percentage of military men of color were born in the colonies. Only 4 percent of the black pensioners claimed to be of African birth, and all but one of those had served in New England regiments. Most African-born veterans matter-of-factly mentioned their birthplace. In marked contrast, Prince Bailey spelled out the injustice of his kidnapping by explaining that he had been "stolen from Africa," his native country, at the age of eight. Other African veterans could barely be understood even in old age. Peter Maguira's supporters said that only those who knew him well could make out what the old vet was saying. Although struggling with the English language himself, Maguira, along with his wife, saw their children attain literacy, at least to the extent that both their son and daughter could sign their names to court documents. In another case, a court clerk in Middleton, Connecticut, claimed he had made a mistake in recording Africa-born Hamet Achmet's pension deposition because the clerk could barely understand the sixty-two-year-old Achmet. These extraordinary men actively participated in two profound events in world history—the Middle Passage and the American Revolution. They were among the few African-born men to survive enslavement and then to free themselves by fighting in the Revolutionary War.[52]

The pensioners played down any racist treatment that they experienced in the military. Caesar Shelton from Connecticut went about as far as a black veteran could go in describing the racist behavior on the part of his white cohort. Although he adopted the family name of his master, Shelton explained that in the army he was called "Caesar Negro or Caesar Nig." In mentioning this in his pension, it is not clear that Shelton was offended by such usage. He may have been. But he also could have been warning the Pension Office to look for "Caesar Negro" when examining the muster rolls for proof of service. Elsewhere a buddy of Thomas Gardner told the Pension Office that the musician-soldier had been known at West Point as "Black Tom" or "Black Drummer." While signaling this to the office, Gardner's white supporters could not say enough about their comrade's great qualities. Shelton and Gardner could not escape their skin color, as whites, even those positively disposed toward them, continued to mark them as different.[53]

Even if not subjected to racial labels, black men saw that their lot was not the same as other soldiers. They were far more likely to fill certain jobs. Plato Turner of Massachusetts was a waiter to a major. Isham Scott of North Carolina was "taken for a servant" to another major. Agrippa Hull of Massachusetts served two of his six years in the army as a servant to General John Paterson, the remainder as a servant to Thaddeus Kosciuszko. Virginian John Harris was pulled from the ranks to serve Major James Monroe, with whom he served at the Battle of Monmouth. (It was during James Monroe's presidency that Harris applied for a pension.) Waiter, servant, orderly—all these jobs entailed tending to another person's needs. Many of these veterans did not note that their skin color had anything to do with this kind of service. In none of these cases did the veterans serve their fathers or older brothers as many young white boys did in the military. Some black veterans did, however, point to their skin color as a reason they were treated differently from whites. William Walton from Rhode Island explained that "as a coloured man," he could had not been able to enroll in the militia but he had been able to serve as a substitute. Other veterans felt the need to explain why they did not immediately assume combat positions in their companies. James Hawkins of Virginia explained that "being a coloured man" he was "taken as a waiter to Major Crughan." Of Joel Taburn it was noted that "being very young and a person of colour, he was first taken and employed as a servant to the officers," but a short time later he was put in the ranks, the record states. Reuben Bird of North Carolina never got the satisfaction of bringing down British generals as he was "a colored man and kept as a bowman," hence he actively participated in no battles during the war. Pomp Magus of Massachusetts related that "being a man of colour myself, . . . some others [and I] were left on fatigue." In other words, Magus was left to do menial jobs.[54]

Even if distinguishing himself as a fighting soldier in the line, a black man was not promoted into the officer class. Neither the Continental Army nor the state militias made it possible for black men to command white soldiers. Claims have been made by historians about certain individuals, but none of these are backed up with evidence. A glimmer of possibility comes to us from a pensioner in Charles City County, Virginia. James Harris claimed in 1818 that he had been an officer but for the purposes of obtaining a pension he claimed a rank of private. Had Harris persisted, he would have had trouble proving officer status because the extant muster rolls label him exclusively a private. It is more likely that a man of color could obtain noncommissioned officer rank in a unit of blacks or Indians. Nicholas Hawwawas, a Passamaquoddy man from Maine, led "a body of Indians," according to his pension record. Although probably not an official unit in the Continental Army, Hawwawas's men received rations from the Americans. As we will see in the next chapter, it is possible that black men achieved the rank of corporal in the all-black Rhode Island Regiment. But with these few exceptions, the military of the eighteenth century did not defy convention and make men of color authority figures.[55]

Few men of color went into specific details about their duties, but among those who did, many noted a servant's role. Others provided a range of jobs that highlight how the Continental Army operated on a daily basis. In the North Carolina militia Drury Walden made gun carriages, cannons, and canteens. He also built barracks and guarded the Halifax jail, said in is pension deposition to have been "full of Tories." George Buley of Maryland guarded prisoners after Yorktown. Buley could have eaten beef provided by Silas Burdoo, a Massachusetts soldier who collected cattle in Connecticut bound for General Washington in Virginia. John Pinn, "a descendant of the Aborigines," could have partaken of Connecticut cattle provided by Burdoo and operated a cannon made by Drury Walden. As a very young man, Pinn joined the Virginia artillery with his father, a "mustee," along with two brothers. He served as a powder boy on "Gun #3" at Yorktown. Andrew Pebbles, also of Virginia, was assigned with twelve other men to a gun, likely a cannon. Samuel Dunbar of New England claimed that he had gone on a secret expedition to Rhode Island but unfortunately gave no details about it. Moses Knight, a South Carolina soldier, claimed he had been a "press master," a position that gave him the power to make men do jobs for the military. He said that while taking a boatload of arms down a river he had "pressed hands." The army could requisition a civilian's property and also make civilians work, usually the poorest and most vulnerable. Although it is unlikely that a black man in South Carolina could make whites do anything, it is possible that, having been raised by General Alexander MacIntosh, the black man had been entrusted by the general to round up black men for service. Knight's claim to a role as press master was bolstered by another veteran, who testified in court that he had seen Knight in a press master's uniform.[56]

Far more common were the men who drove the wagons—a noncombat role that was essential in provisioning an army and guaranteeing its mobility on campaign. The army hired civilians to drive and also placed soldiers in that capacity. The distinction became important when these men applied for pensions after the war. Daniel Williams, of Accomack County, Virginia, claimed he had been a wagoner for five years, but the Pension Office rejected his application, saying that Williams "did not serve in a military capacity." Indeed, Williams proffered no officer names, making it likely that he was the equivalent of an independent contractor. Amos Robinson, on the other hand, was a wagoner in the Rhode Island Line who "every month joined the company to answer to his name." He got a pension. Regardless of how they were paid, Robinson and Williams were part of a legion of wagoners whose function was highly prized by George Washington. The perennial shortage of wagons could be addressed in two ways: either requisition more vehicles and pay civilian drivers, or limit the amount of items to be carried. Washington tried the latter when he ordered officers to limit the niceties they packed. He threatened severe reprimand if he found one more officer's heavy bedstead on a continental vehicle. He also warned drummers that their instruments were not to clog up any army wagon.[57]

The best-paid position a man of color could hold in the continental line was that of fifer or drummer. Primus Slocum, as an old man in the pension process, could still recall the exact day he became a fifer—June 12, 1782. The discharge certificate he treasured through almost four decades of moving around noted his distinction from a common soldier—"Primus Slocum, Fifer," it read. Fifer Slocum's position meant no command over other men. It did mean his pay went up (once they got their instruments, the army's musicians were responsible for maintaining them), and it also meant that he played a crucial role, along with drummers, in battle. The musicians of a company sent crucial signals to their fellow soldiers. A certain beat meant that the men were to advance, another meant that they were to move to the left. To distinguish them on the battlefield, they wore the reversed colors of their regiment. If the privates wore a blue uniform with white facings, the musicians typically wore a white uniform with blue facings. They stuck out for the enemy too. At the Battle of Rhode

Island, Caesar Babcock saw a drummer named Card "filled [felled] by a shot in the breast." At one of the southern battles, Jim Capers of South Carolina said, a ball had passed through him and killed the drummer behind him. The musicians had no muskets, each just a sword or a knife, giving them a chance of survival if the lines collapsed. Still, their odds were poor when confronted with an enemy soldier whose fifteen-inch bayonet on a five- or six-foot musket barrel came closing in. If they survived the occasional battle, the musicians continued to sound reveille, call for meals and work, and signaled when to retire. They alerted men on the approach of the enemy and provided a beat for marching soldiers. These important signals were sometimes scuttled by the drummers themselves as they played their drums when the spirit moved them or just wanted to practice. Orders on October 27, 1776, declared that the "constant beating of drums on all occasions is very improper." The general soldiery might not distinguish between play and the real deal, so specific times were set up for practice—5:00–6:00 A.M. and 4:00–5:00 P.M. The morning session was later moved to a more civilized nine o'clock. Musicians at times were also called to administer punishments dictated by courts-martial. The importance of fifers and drummers was highlighted in the spring of 1782 when it was noted that "the duty can scarcely be done for the want of them." Although not comprising as high a percentage of soldiers as wagoners or servants among black soldiers, musicians could develop a reputation for their skills. This can be seen in the pension records of the nineteenth century. A white veteran said that after Eutaw Springs, he heard that the "great drummer, Jim Capers under [General] Marion was wounded" at that battle. Another white veteran claimed that Thomas Gardner was considered one of the best drummers in the two regiments of artillery at West Point. Capers and Gardner were not the only two black soldiers to develop a skill and be lauded for it years later. Cuff Wells of the Connecticut line served as an apothecary in his unit. Years after the war, he was still known in his neighborhood as "Doc" or "Doctor Cuff." Sampson Cuff, after exposing the peculation of a steward aboard a ship, himself replaced the dishonest seaman.[58]

The military provided an outlet to prove one's competence and to assert oneself in ways unheard of for black men in peacetime. Record Prime, a poor freeman from North Carolina, described how he was part of a group that "whipped" powerful white men at the Battle of Guilford Courthouse in March 1781. Even though the field was claimed by the British that day, Prime was correct in bragging that "we whipped the British and Tories" because the British were forced to retire to the coast for supplies. Another veteran, Oliver Cromwell, named for a famous British revolutionary and general, informed the pension office in 1818 that "we knocked the British about lively" at Trenton and Princeton. The uniform permitted men of color to use force, requisition supplies, and move around. George Sambo of the First Rhode Island was often absent from camp. The muster rolls marked him "on command," meaning that he was out and about on his company's business. Virginians marched into Pennsylvania. Rhode Islanders got to see the plantation system in Virginia. Most Americans at the time, white or black, never ventured more than a few miles from their birthplace. The army provided protection for black men on the move.[59]

But the army also furnished its share of trials. Coping with daily encounters with mud, infection, and hunger helped these soldiers bond. In the winter of 1779–80, George Washington wrote Congress that he could neither contain nor condemn soldiers who plundered. He had already taken Indian corn meant for horses and had it ground to compensate for a lack of flour. In January 1780, the general marveled at the men's patience. Many had not consumed any meat for five days and eaten only a little bread. They were reduced to "maraud and rob the inhabitants," a practice that Washington had not the power to repress. A white soldier at that encampment filled in the details. "We were absolutely, literally starved," he wrote. With not a morsel of food for four days, he was reduced to gnaw on black birch bark. He saw some of his fellows roasting their old shoes and eating them. Another veteran lost his unit but found it again by following bloody tracks in the snow. If one could run the gauntlet of military service, one proved something to oneself. Most men of color who did not originally sign up for the duration ended up committing to another enlistment. The army offered sparse rations, drafty quarters, and considerable danger, but the uniform also meant mobility, adventure, the opportunity of teaming up with a white countryman in pursuit of a lofty goal, and recognition for skills and talents that might not otherwise have come to light in the tobacco fields and servant quarters of civilian life. This led many vets immediately after the war to say that they would serve again. Cato Boose, a five-year veteran in the Rhode Island line, told his neighbors that "he would fight again if there was another war." A similar sentiment was expressed by Edward Harman, a six-year veteran from Delaware. One of his pension supporters said that he remembered Ed's return to town after the war with a group of Delaware troops, all uniformed and with their equipment. Townspeople had taunted Harman, called him a fool to have spent so much time in the army with no pay. Although having survived the disastrous Battle of Camden, Harman replied matter-of-factly that he was willing to go again and hoped that he would "git paid at some time."[60]

Edward Harman got more than pay from his service in the Continental Army. He, along with the other black veterans, must have developed a new muscularity that trumped simple payment for services. He might have thought about the depreciation of the continental currency when his neighbors taunted him. But more likely he knew he had whipped the enemy and proved his manhood. He came home to a community familiar to him yet different, because his old friends and relatives, who had not traveled more than twenty miles from where they lived, could not understand the scope of his experience. Others did, however, and not just black veterans. White and black soldiers shared a bond to the extent that they were connected by experiences. They had shared the same mud, the same cold, the same hunger, the same lead shot flying by them. They had depended on one another on the battlefield. Who else could understand the storming of Stony Point but another soldier who were there that July night? Certainly there were few people that white veteran Daniel Raymond could talk with about scaling that cliff under fire. But "the little black drummer," Hamet Achmet, was one of them. When Achmet needed a support deposition for a pension, Raymond stepped up.

Similarly, Edward Harman (mulatto) and Mitchell Kershaw (white) understood what it was like to be overrun by the enemy at the Battle of Camden. Whatever his racial views were generally, Kershaw, later a lieutenant colonel in the Delaware militia, swore out a support deposition for Harman, a soldier who had not been able to climb the ranks like Kershaw, because of his skin color. Soldiers could, to a certain extent, break through societal conventions in the army, but the institution remained stiff-backed with respect to general societal restrictions concerning African Americans and advancement. The crisis of the war, however, did shuffle society's priorities so that race dropped down the list in importance, at least for some in the military for the duration of the war. James Depuy told us this about the New York frontier. Many African Americans conveyed the same message by their presence in elite light infantry units.

The legacy of this promising bridge building had everything to do with where the veterans ended up at war's end. The widely disparate economic systems of North and South created two different worlds. In the North, black veterans could make new alliances with whites concerning their status in society, despite deteriorating conditions there. White southerners, on the other hand, vigorously reinforced slave labor and created a poisonous ideology to justify slavery in the land of the free. These distinctly different outcomes can be detected during the war in the way that Rhode Island and South Carolina encountered the possibility of fielding a black regiment. The following two chapters will continue the story of black military involvement on the American side by examining the power structures that determined the contours of their service. These led to the colossally different destinies for people of color in the North and South.[61]

CHAPTER 3

A Bold Experiment in Rhode Island

Samuel Tenny was not a man to mince words. A doctor in the Rhode Island Regiment, he managed to keep his sense of humor in the midst of his taxing job, and his letters show that he was not awed by the British army that had just outwitted and out-soldiered the Americans. From his "den at Valley Forge," Tenny wrote home in January 1778 to his friend Elihu Greene that his regiment was throwing up redoubts "to prevent impertinent visits from Billy Howe." Sir William Howe had just administered a royal drubbing of Washington's army in the Philadelphia campaign, but that did not prevent Tenny from reducing the British commander-in-chief to the level of incorrigible child. However much he joked about Howe, though, Tenny worried about the next campaign.

In the winter of 1777–78, the Continental Army lived in a frozen-over encampment while the British enjoyed the hearths of Philadelphia's solid brick houses. Valley Forge's campfires did not attract recruits to fill the army's half-staffed regiments. Tenny contemplated the numbers of men needed to implement the upcoming spring's campaign. "But Lord only knows where they are to come from," he wrote. Tenny lamented the lack of will among his countrymen that made the army's situation so forlorn. "We depend on the small remains of American virtue," he explained to Greene, "to recruit an army diminished by the Sword, Sickness, and Desertion."[1]

Tenny was not the only soldier to feel abandoned in the wilds of Pennsylvania. Nathanael Greene of Rhode Island, the quartermaster general of the distressed army, must have wondered where the republican virtue had gone that was supposed to clothe the soldier and provide his ration. It was Greene's job to distribute the everyday requirements to keep the soldiers alive. He wished that civilians back home could hear the screams of the wounded. "The troops are worn out," he explained in an early-January letter, and although "the Rhode Island troops have done themselves great honor," there were not enough of them to carry on the fight. Greene's belief in politicians' ability to solve the army's shortages of men and materiel was at a very low ebb. He wrote that he thoroughly appreciated a colonel's "drole description" of a legislature whose "ignorance and confidence" comprised "the true characteristic of the spirit and genius of Administration." The politicians' sunny forecasts, in other words, were poor substitutes for substantial support on the ground. "It is an ancient Proverb," wrote Greene, "that when the political pot boils, the scum rises."[2]

It is also a truism that emergencies often produce inspired ideas. Such was the case at Valley Forge when Rhode Island's troop strength was half of what it was supposed to be. A group of that state's officers, headed by Brigadier General James Varnum, went to George Washington with the proposal of filling Rhode Island's quota with slaves whose masters would be reimbursed and whose training would be conducted by Christopher Greene, the hero of a recent battle with Hessians outside Philadelphia. Washington might have been more amenable than usual to risky tactical moves because he was in the unenviable position of begging for more supplies and troops from a Congress that had to tough out a winter in the rural burgs of western Pennsylvania thanks to the commander-in-chief's failure in the Philadelphia campaign. Washington gave tepid approval to the Rhode Islanders by requesting that the state's governor give "all the assistance" to the officers "in this business."[3]

As the Rhode Island contingent headed home to sell the idea and then implement it, their compatriots back at Valley Forge—at least those who knew about the plan—noted it in their letters. Sam Tenny hoped that "the scheme for raising a Regiment of blacks" would meet with suitable encouragement. "It is very much applauded in camp by all that have heard it," remarked Tenny. The doctor further opined that the all-black regiment might serve as a precedent for other states to liberate the victims of "our unbridled avarice." Nathanael Greene explained to his correspondent that the two half-strength Rhode Island regiments would be combined into one, with the all-black regiment completing the line. His third cousin, Christopher Greene (known in the family as Kit), would oversee the whole project. Nathanael Greene was on the fence as to the idea's success, but he was willing to support it in light of the crisis in Washington's army that winter.[4]

Innovators such as James Varnum and Christopher Greene, along with the risk-takers who populated the new black regiment, came from a tiny state that had produced antislavery voices before the war. Rhode Island and Providence Plantations started as a religious haven, welcoming sects that could not find acceptance in the surrounding New England colonies. Among those who settled there were the Society of Friends, who as early as 1717 felt "a weighty concern on the importing and keeping of slaves." As conversation continued in this minority group, many of its members acceded to high positions in government, including the governor's chair. Not unlike Pennsylvania, the Quakers' influence exceeded their numbers. In 1760, the Yearly Meeting at Newport adopted one of the first anti–slave trade resolutions in American history. In 1773 the same meeting ordered all Friends to free their slaves or face expulsion from the society. In 1774 the Rhode Island assembly passed a bill that prohibited the direct importation of slaves. Replete with loopholes, it nonetheless chipped away at the institution in Rhode Island, a major player in the slave trade. The following year a bill for the gradual abolition of slavery was defeated. Despite the fact that the powerful slave trade lobby prevailed, Rhode Islanders, white and black, were privy to a public conversation about the morality of slavery. They had even seen Moses Brown of the prominent slave trading family defect from the lucrative business, free his slaves, and join the Quakers in their abolitionist endeavors. In 1778, when Samuel Tenny wrote about the victims of "our unbridled avarice," he was not speaking from a vacuum. Nathanael Greene too did not have to be convinced of the humanitarian side of Varnum's plan, as Greene had grown up a Quaker and no doubt heard the arguments of his minister father.[5]

Although exposed to antislavery sentiment, the decision makers at Valley Forge were soldiers, and they had to be sufficiently confident that a black regiment would be effective in battle. Otherwise the idea would never have left the encampment. Into their calculations came the black men of the Rhode Island line who had faithfully and effectively served over the previous two years. Forty-two percent of the black Rhode Island veterans who lived long enough to claim pensions said they had entered the military before the Slave Enlistment Act. Their combined experiences not only provided proof to Varnum and Greene, they also provide a narrative of the war's earliest and at times darkest hours. Andrew Frank, living in Massachusetts at the time, turned out for service outside Boston in Rhode Island's Army of Observation and participated in the Battle of Bunker Hill in June 1775. As described in chapter 1, there Frank and over two thousand other Americans surprised the British by fortifying a hill overlooking the occupied city of Boston. To dislodge the Americans, wave after wave of redcoats tried to climb the hill and scale the American works at the top. Three attempts only meant an increasing number of British soldiers on the ground. After three hours of battle, the Americans ran out of ammunition and withdrew. Did Frank see the red line advance? Did he shoot an enemy soldier? Was he part of the effort to get supplies to the top? Was he in the thick of the action where musket balls whizzed by his ear and landing cannon balls blew dirt and debris into his eyes? Was he disappointed that after all that effort the Americans withdrew? How long was it before he knew the full extent of the British sacrifice in taking the hill? The British suffered over one thousand casualties, with less than half that experienced on the American side. None of these questions are answered in the one piece of paper left behind by the African American veteran—Frank's pension deposition. He simply mentioned his unit at the famous battle—Captain Slocum's company. From the high drama of Bunker Hill, Frank returned to Rhode Island and did the plodding duty of standing guard along Narragansett Bay for two hours every night during the British occupation of Newport.[6]

Philip Rodman, a free black, also fought in the critical battles of the war's first year. He enlisted in October 1776 and in that same month participated in the Battle of White Plains. Once the Americans dislodged the British from Boston, His Majesty's troops focused on New York. In the fall of 1776, British general Howe and his forces swept the inexperienced American army off Long Island, chased them up Manhattan Island, and then crossed the river to the little town of White Plains in Westchester County. Maneuvering under heavy rain, each army had about thirteen thousand effectives although, a fraction of those actually participated in the action. Like most Americans that day, Rodman did not fire a shot. Only about sixteen hundred men from Delaware and Maryland poured fire into the British ranks. The weather then provided a reprieve, during which time Washington left a portion of his army east of the Hudson and led the rest down the length of New Jersey to the Delaware River. Rodman was one of that number and probably shared the despair of seeing the army's strength plummet from thirteen thousand to twenty-five hundred. Perched on the Delaware's southern bank in Pennsylvania, Rodman was among the first to hear Tom Paine's immortal summons to stay the course after Washington ordered it to be read aloud to his troops. "These are the times that try men's souls. The summer soldier and the sunshine patriot will, in this crisis, shrink from the service of his country; but he that stands it NOW, deserves the love and thanks of man and woman." Fortified by these words and little else, the soldiers under Washington recrossed the Delaware in ferociously bad weather on Christmas night and captured the Hessian outpost at Trenton by the next morning. Rodman and his comrades survived the icy crossing and the driving hail to at last furnish the Americans with a clear-cut victory. Nine hundred Hessians were captured that day. In the midst of elation, Washington was desperate to keep his army together as most enlistments were up at the end of the year. Rodman claimed that Washington asked him to stay another month. Washington did indeed assemble his men and asked them for another six weeks of service in exchange for ten dollars in hard money each. Among the soldiers that this Virginia slaveholder begged to stay were battle-hardened black men. Most clichés go right to the heart of the matter. In this case, war most certainly made for strange bedfellows.[7]

Another black veteran, Peter Jennings, provided some detail about the Trenton and Princeton campaign in his pension application. He had enlisted in 1776 in what he called the "Fifth Regiment of Artillery of Blacks in the

Continental line." His unit was split, and Peter ended up marching south to Washington's army and entering a unit commanded by a Major Talbot in a company led by Captain James Starling. Jennings remembered that the night of December 25, 1776, he crossed the Delaware about nine miles north of Trenton. He recalled that troops under Generals "Ewald" [Ewing] and Cadwallader were also supposed to cross the river but could not because of ice floes. Regardless, "we obtained a complete victory over them," exalted Jennings, "killing many of them and taking several hundred prisoners, who were principally Hessians." He also recalled a Hessian colonel shot dead and an American captain named Washington being wounded. He remembered the captain's name because it was the same as the general's. After the battle, Jennings was part of the massive operation of getting the prisoners and captured stores back across the river. He returned to Trenton to find a newly arrived British force closing in and firing on Washington's forces. Jennings and his cohort were ordered to light campfires along the front of their lines and then were ordered to march off—all for the purpose of "deceiving the enemy." Next morning Jennings arrived in Princeton, where another skirmish took place. Here, said Jennings's pension, he had "a perfect recollection for an occurrence which took place during this engagement which will never be effaced from his memory." As the Americans fell back as a result of British fire, General Washington seized a flag and rushed to the front of the troops, exclaiming, "Come on, boys." He rallied the troops and exposed himself to one round of fire from each side but remained untouched. Soon thereafter, Jennings was shelling a public building in Princeton, which resulted in the surrender of the British troops who fled from there. Finally he remembered a General Mercer (Hugh Mercer) from Virginia who was wounded and might have died afterward. Mercer did die of his wounds. In this and in his other recollections of the Trenton and Princeton campaign, Jennings was remarkably accurate.[8]

In the next battle season of 1777, the British closed in on the seat of the Continental Congress, Philadelphia. Only a few miles outside the city, Washington tried to check the British advance at Brandywine Creek. Here Jennings saw Major General Lafayette wounded in the right leg and heard that another American general was wounded (Jennings had forgotten his name by the time of his pension application). Brandywine was a scene of "great loss." Two or three weeks later Washington received reinforcements from Virginia and tried to break the British lines again, this time at Germantown. Jennings related the confusion experienced by the redcoats in the early-morning attack. As in so many Revolutionary War engagements, weather was crucial. Jennings said that the "cloudy foggy morning" caused confusion on the American side. Germantown resulted in a "retreat with great loss" and also the death of another American general, whom Jennings identified as Nash (Francis Nash of the North Carolina line). After this debacle, the Americans retreated to Whitemarsh, expecting an attack that never came. Jennings and his fellow soldiers proceeded to Valley Forge to take up winter quarters.[9]

Jennings related the highlights of his soldier life fifty-five years later in a courthouse in western Tennessee. The eighty-year-old veteran may not have recalled what he had done the previous week, but he vividly remembered the highlights of the great wartime dramas in which he participated. He got some of the details wrong. He confused Hessian Captain Ewald for Brigadier General James Ewing at the crossing of the Delaware. He mentioned the two abortive crossings that night as being upriver from the encampment, when they were both downriver. But he accurately remembered the fog at Germantown and the deaths of major officers. Veterans of later wars have claimed that they could remember minute details of a long-ago battle and not remember what they had for dinner a couple of days before.[10]

While Jennings and the remainder of his largely black artillery unit dug in at Valley Forge, another contingent of Washington's army did its best to foil the British to the east of Philadelphia. These soldiers occupied two forts that guarded obstructions in the Delaware River, preventing the British navy from supplying the troops occupying Philadelphia. One fort (Mifflin) occupied an island in the middle of the river, while another installation, Fort Mercer (named after the general Peter Jennings saw fall at Princeton), perched on an embankment on the New Jersey side. Colonel Christopher Greene, the future leader of the First Rhode Island, and four hundred Rhode Islanders were responsible for holding this second fort. Among the black soldiers in this group was Richard Potter, who as a sixteen-year-old enlisted in May 1776 for three years. Known as Dick in the regiment, he helped make major renovations to the fort recommended by a French engineer, including a ditch ringed with pointed wooden spears and an interior wall that was not visible to an attacking force. The British sent Hessian regiments numbering twenty-four hundred with ten artillery pieces to clean out Greene and his men. A black guide whom General Howe sent along, showed the Hessians "a hidden route" to the fort. On October 22, their leader, Carl von Donop, sent a note to Greene demanding surrender, or no quarter would be given. Greene refused. One of the Hessian officers called Greene's response "a spiteful refusal." In one of the press accounts after the assault, Colonel Greene played a "very good deception" on the enemy soldier delivering the ultimatum. Greene concealed all but fifty men and told the messenger that "with these brave fellows, this fort shall be my tomb."[11]

Buoyed with the news of a paltry few defenders, the Hessians went to work. They had no axes to deal with the abatis. They sustained losses as they filled the ditch as best they could with bundles of branches called fascines. They thought that they had breached the American line and started a healthy round of huzzahs when they stumbled upon the newly built interior wall with many more than fifty Americans amassed at the top. Now the unfortunate Hessians found themselves in a confined space looking up at American muskets. The killing commenced, and in the space of forty minutes, the Hessians lost four hundred men, including a mortally wounded commander. The assault on Fort Mercer, also known as the Battle of Red Bank, provided an enormous boost to American morale. In the official letter sent by Greene's major, Samuel Ward, a special mention was made of "the greatest bravery" by officers and privates alike. Colonel Greene was voted an honorary sword from Congress as acknowledgement of his and his soldiers' bravery. The British eventually leveled Fort Mifflin, necessitating the Americans' withdrawal from Red Bank. The significance of the battle, however, lay in putting to rest the myth that Hessians were invincible super-soldiers. At Trenton the weather had helped Washington trounce the unprepared Hessians, but at Red Bank the Germans were awake and armed and were ultimately defeated.[12]

In the same month that Greene and his men rained death on the Hessians, other Rhode Islanders still at home tried to dislodge the British from Newport, the state's capital. Esek Roberts, described in his pension as "a man of colour," enlisted in West Greenwich in June 1777. He was part of a unit of state troops numbering nine thousand men under General Joseph Spencer who marched forward on October 26, 1777, only to have bad weather and the late arrival of a brigade scuttle the operation. Spencer had to answer to a court-martial, while Roberts finished his nine-month enlistment and signed up for another year in 1778. He was thus fated to meet and see the black regiment in operation.[13]

Jennings, Frank, Rodman, Potter, and Roberts joined various Rhode Island units before the passage of the Act to Enlist Slaves. They were joined by many other men of color, so when the Rhode Island continentals were reorganized into a unit called the First Rhode Island in January 1777, men of color served in all its companies. According to Louis Wilson's research, their numbers in these pre-February, 1778 companies ranged from 10 percent of Captain Elijah Lewis's unit to almost one-quarter of Captain Thomas Coles's company to half of Captain Silas Tolbut's privates. African Americans and Indians comprised less of the Second Rhode Island's manpower. Still, the presence of men of color was not a rare occurrence in the Rhode Island line. When Varnum and Greene broached the idea of enlistment of slaves to General Washington, they might have had more confidence than most that blacks and Indians would make solid soldiers.[14]

Armed with an endorsement from General Washington, Varnum and Greene, now the hero of Red Bank, left Valley Forge in early January 1778 to convince Rhode Island legislators to take the leap. A month later the Rhode Island assembly passed the Act to Enlist Slaves. Nathanael Greene's estimation of politicians must have gone up a notch. The law that had passed was a real innovation. As such, the legislators took special pains to justify their decision in the act's preamble. First and foremost, the "rights and liberties" of the United States required that every effort be made to preserve them. Secondly, Generals Washington and Varnum requested this proposal. History too nodded in approval, the act suggested, as the "wisest, the freest, and the bravest nations" had used their slaves as soldiers with the ultimate reward of freedom. And finally, the enemy was not simply at the door but in the house, as the British occupied Rhode Island's capital and chief port, Newport.[15]

Having established the need and its precedent, the lawmakers went on to spell out the program. They invited "every able-bodied negro, mulatto, or Indian man slave" to enlist for the duration of the war. These recruits would receive the same "bounties, wages, and encouragements" as any other soldier. Once approved by Colonel Christopher Greene, the slave was to be immediately discharged from the service of his master or mistress. To underscore what this meant, the assembly declared these recruits to be "absolutely FREE," as though they had never been enslaved. What is remarkable about the act's major provisions is that nowhere does it say that slaves had to have their masters' permission to enlist. Placating the masters, then, comes next on the act's agenda. The legislature acknowledged the owners' property rights, and so compensation up to 120 pounds per slave would be paid to the master provided he handed over all the slave's clothing. Here again, this clothing stipulation implies that some masters would not be happy with their slave's choice— most slaves did not have a wardrobe worth anything. A committee would examine each recruit and fix the value to be paid to the owner. Upon enlistment, the masters would receive a certificate discharging the recruit from any service to them and another certificate indicating the slave's value. The money for this program would be paid by the state with funds provided from the Continental Congress.[16]

The act provided for no appeals on the part of the owners, and some owners in the legislature, unsurprisingly, protested vigorously against the law. They said that there were not enough blacks who would want to enlist and that the expense of raising such a regiment would exceed the expense of raising a regiment of white men. "Great difficulties and uneasiness" would arise with masters, many of whom would not be prepared to part with their slave at any price. But the longest of the legislators' objections had to do with what people would think. Constituting a black regiment would highlight to the world the inconsistency of having slaves fight for the state's rights and liberties. Neighboring states would greet the news with contempt, as black troops could not equal white ones, it was said, and thus Rhode Island would not be credited with raising the troops required by Congress. The enemy too might glean that this idea sprang from desperation, as not enough of "our own people" would take the field. It also provided a delicious opportunity for the British to use the same language employed by Americans against Dunmore's regiment. And lastly, Rhode Island's action might "suggest" to the British the idea of raising a black regiment of their own. In short, this "abortive" and "fruitless" idea would rain down all sorts of mischief on the already embattled state.[17]

The protest, signed by six members of the legislature, was an interesting exercise in selective thinking. The reason that Rhode Island's governor and legislature even entertained the idea of a black regiment was that they could not induce enough white men to enlist. The dissenting legislators acknowledged the irony of having slaves fight for another's liberty without seeing the inconsistency of slavery embedded in the "land of liberty." To quiet the fear that other states would refuse to credit Rhode Island for its black regiment, the dissenters only had to look at their own government in Philadelphia. States chose men to serve in the Continental Congress, and it was this body that was to pay for the experiment in the first place. On the subject of Rhode Island's example encouraging the British to launch black regiments of their own, the British needed no precedent from the Americans because they had already constituted military units in Virginia (though not incorporated into the British army or, with one exception, into the provincial corps) and had been encouraging black men to work in the British army since the beginning of the conflict. Finally, if a black man was not the white's equal, perhaps it would be advantageous for the British to form all-black regiments as well.

On two points, the unhappy legislators were spot-on. The British could expose the Americans as hypocrites given the ridicule the Americans "so liberally bestowed . . . on account of Dunmore's regiment of blacks." While no reserve of biting sarcasm flowed from the Tory newspapers, they did at least report on the act. The Whig-controlled *Providence Gazette* remained absolutely mute on this story. The Tory-controlled *Newport Gazette*, on the other hand, jumped on the news in its February 5 edition, editorializing that "we hear they (blacks) have in general refused their freedom upon such dishonorable terms."[18]

Another accurate prediction was the resistance the idea would engender. There may have been a grain of truth to the *Gazette*'s story because, as the dissenting legislators predicted, Rhode Island's enslaved men did not volunteer in sufficient numbers to fill a regiment-sized unit. Only 130 new privates and musicians entered the First Rhode Island, at least eighty-seven of whom were slaves. The remainder could have been from the militia or state lines, or they were perhaps freemen who had decided to give military life a chance. There were many possible reasons why Colonel Greene was not inundated with recruits. Enslaved men could have elected to stay with the devil they knew. Perhaps they feared being used as cannon fodder or never seeing their families again. Word of the army's depleted condition at Valley Forge might have found its way home. Could they trust the white man's word? The British in Newport had already extended an invitation to Rhode Island's slaves, and the British looked to have the upper hand there in 1778. In the process of making such a weighty decision, the enslaved man, not realizing how narrow the window of opportunity was to be, could have taken too much time to make up his mind. But none of these scenarios was as decisive as the possibility that Rhode Island's slaveholding class could refuse to part with its slaves. There is no indication in the law that the masters had any say in their slaves' departure. Indeed, the law's detractors mentioned the "great difficulties and uneasiness" that would arise from the price the state was willing to pay for its recruits. If the masters could have simply said no, there would have been little malaise. Yet it is undeniable that masters exerted tremendous power over their slaves' lives. So while the law remained mute on the masters' right to cooperate, they could indeed have controlled the situation on the ground.[19]

On the other end of the social scale, Rhode Island's legislators also faced a complicated set of considerations in passing this novel law. There were forty-six delegates in the Rhode Island assembly, 55 percent of whom had house slaves, according to the 1774 Rhode Island census. (The census does not indicate the number of slaves on any farms that the legislators might have owned.) The largest slaveholders, Benjamin Underwood and Christopher Lippitt, each had six people of color working for them in their homes. These legislators ran the risk of losing some slaves, although not all house slaves were able-bodied men. Underwood and Lippitt, along with the majority of the legislature, voted for the slave enlistment act. Of the six legislators who protested the Act to Enlist Slaves, five were slaveholders, and according to the 1774 census they owned more slaves than the average legislator. Perhaps to soften the blow for the dissenting members, one of their number, Samuel Babcock, was appointed to the committee charged with setting a value on each black recruit. He might have swallowed hard, because one of his slaves, Primus, was one of the last to sign up legally before the law was repealed.[20]

Among the black soldiers in the Rhode Island line were individuals with the same surname as the protesting slaveholders—Babcock, Northup, Gardner, Gorton—although it is not always possible to ascertain in which specific household these men of color resided before the act's passage. Most of the Rhode Island legislators who owned slaves voted for the act. The crisis that faced the state could well have propelled them to act in the way they did. William Greene of Warwick emphasized the lack of enthusiasm for the legislation when he wrote to Nathanael Greene in March 1778, "As to the state bill, I dare say you have as great a liking for it as many have this way, but as it was earnestly recommended by Congress to make a trial, the Convention thought proper to adopt the measure."[21]

So in February 1778 the great experiment began. Officers of the First Rhode Island fanned out across the state to convince black men to take the leap. One of the recruiters, Elijah Lewis, found himself in South Kingston, the major town in an area with a considerable number of black farmworkers. On his arrival there, Lewis saw "large numbers" of black men "apparently desirous of enlisting." Lewis's hopes were dashed, however, by one enraged white man, Hazard Potter, who showed up at the enlistment rallies, hurled "injurious expressions" against the officers of the army, and "censured highly" the legislature that had passed the Slave Enlistment Act. More damaging for Lewis's mission was the picture that Potter painted of the black recruits' future in the military. Potter found three ways to express "cannon fodder": blacks would perform the most dangerous service; blacks would be in the vanguard of every battle; blacks would be the equivalent of breastworks protecting the white soldiers. Then Potter predicted that, if taken prisoner, blacks would be sold into slavery in the West Indies. Captain Lewis was so upset that he replicated Potter's rant in a letter to the Speaker of the Rhode Island assembly. If unchecked, he wrote, such conduct would damage the public service. And indeed, Lewis's estimate was spot-on.[22]

Of the Rhode Island veterans for whom we have enlistment dates, only five men from South Kingston enlisted in the days after the tumultuous meeting, a far cry from the "large numbers" who were interested enough to attend. Newport Champlin, a five-foot-three sixteen-year-old, fearlessly disregarded Potter's warnings and signed up at the meeting. Two days later, five-foot-nine Peter Hazard made his mark on the enlistment papers. He towered above most recruits, who averaged five foot five. Generally speaking, the men who freed themselves under the act were mainly from Providence, East Greenwich, South Kingston, and Warwick. The average age at enlistment was twenty-five, ranging from Champlin and sixteen-year-old Mingo Rodman who signed up as a drummer, to fifty-three-year-old Pharaoh Hazard, a grey-haired mulatto shipwright. They made a calculation in favor of the Continental Army.[23]

As the newly liberated black men joined up, the assembly had to iron out the details. What if a recruit had been apprenticed to another master? The assembly decreed that the owner would get the principle of the sum the slave was appraised at, while the current master would get the interest on the appraised sum until the expiration of the apprenticeship. What if the recruit enlisted and then deserted before he was mustered and valued? The assembly would still pay the master the appraised value. What if slaves from another state enlisted, as a recruit from over the Massachusetts border did in the spring of 1778? The assembly would discharge said recruits and send them back to their masters. On the subject of remuneration, the solicitous assembly tried to blunt the blow for slaveholders who were inconvenienced by this sudden shift in their lives.[24]

Meanwhile, the masters had to make do with absence of workers. They could have used their refund money to purchase other slaves, but the war disrupted trade, and there was no surplus to be had in New England. Beriah Brown of North Kingston, in March 1778, wanted his "Negro Boy," Scipio, to be returned from the army. Browne claimed that the new recruit had been only fourteen years and three months old when he enlisted. With another of his slaves in Greene's regiment, he had "no other Boy to Do anything." Lest anyone accused Browne of depriving the patriots' cause of needed hands, he pleaded his advanced age and claimed that he was as ready as anybody to defend his country. Browne wrote his petition one day after Scipio had left—one day too late, as the army had Scipio now and was not prepared to give him back. Although only five two, the newly freed man claimed he was eighteen years old when he committed himself for the war's duration. He appears on muster lists in Captain Ebeneezer Flagg's company as a drummer. He continued in the military until the end of the war.[25]

While Scipio's master had to get used to doing work himself, another slaveholder tried to game the system by claiming that because he did not have the proper certificates he had not been reimbursed under the terms of the act. He wanted either the money or the return of his mulatto slave, Frank Gould. The master, Dr. Thomas Eyres, would settle for the money, however, as "the said Frank [was] esteemed by his officers an excellent soldier." But Eyres's slave had not enlisted under the February 1778 act. He was one of many black men who enlisted before the act's passage—in Frank's case, in June 1777. Eyres was entitled to no certificates or money. His six-one slave had managed to enlist, describing himself as a twenty-three-year-old mariner when he entered the Rhode Island line. The army would not budge when it came to returning its recruits.[26]

Despite a slow start in South Kingston, enlistments could all but empty a farm or household of its laborers. The 1777 military census of the town counted 218 black males sixteen years of age and older, eighty-five of whom were able to bear arms. Some of the households there with multiple slaves, like those owned by Matthew Robinson and John Smith, managed to retain all their able-bodied men. Others were not so lucky. John Rose saw three out of four black laborers leave for the army. All three of Stephen Champlain's able-bodied men of color joined the service. William Case, a master in his sixties, had to muddle as best he could when all three of his black laborers left the farm. We do not know the conditions under which master and slave parted company in each case, but to see all one's laborers leave had to have been hard.[27]

For this reason, and most likely the Continental Congress's distressed financial condition, (Continental Loan Office certificates were definitely not hard money), the state's masters applied enough pressure to get the state assembly to repeal the Act to Enlist Slaves. Just three months after the law's passage, the legislature characterized their groundbreaking action of February as having been temporary, making the enlistment of any "Negro, mulatto, or Indian slave" impossible after June 10, 1778. The window was open for only four months. The army served the legislature, and so now the First Rhode Island's officers had to fall in line and return the slaveholders' property after June 10. The last enslaved man to benefit from the act was London Hall, who enlisted in Captain John S. Dexter's company on the June 10. Men of color continued to join the Black Regiment, particularly some who enlisted for a three-year hitch in the first half of 1781, but their status as freemen or slaves is not noted on the muster lists. The few slaves who enlisted after June 1778 were likely to have been substitutes for white men.[28]

The white man who took on the responsibility of leading a black regiment, Christopher Greene, left Valley Forge and headed back home to advance the idea among legislators and prospective recruits. Greene was forty-one years old when he started this adventure. He came from a prominent family and was a great-grandson of Puritan theologian Roger Williams. His father was a judge who educated his son and turned over the family's milling business for him to manage. Christopher Greene's neighbors in Warwick elected him to the Rhode Island assembly, where he followed the growing breach with England and became convinced of America's grievances and right to defend itself from tyranny. When the community decided that military action might be called for, Greene enthusiastically joined the newly formed Kentish Guards and became a lieutenant. When the stakes were raised by events at Lexington and Concord, Rhode Island formed an "Army of Observation," headed by Greene's third cousin, Nathanael Greene, whose immediate mission was to support their aggrieved neighbors in Boston. Christopher Greene headed an infantry unit on the outskirts of Boston and then was tapped by George Washington to lead a battalion to Canada as part of an effort to bring that English colony into the resistance movement against the mother country. Greene's commanding officer, Benedict Arnold, led his part of the operation through the wilds of the Maine woods, no mean feat with seven hundred men, a supply train, and several cannons. The army arrived exhausted at the stronghold of Quebec, where they met with the other half of the American expedition, led by Richard Montgomery. The Americans threw everything they had at the Canadian fortress to no avail. In one of those actions, Christopher Greene was taken prisoner on December 31, 1775. After the Americans retreated, he was left behind, a man of action in business, politics, and soldiering, suddenly sidelined and coping with a prisoner's monotony. As an officer he was more than likely not incarcerated in a prison cell or interred in a miserable camp. Still, he had to wait until finally swapped in a 1777 prisoner exchange. We'll never know the effect of this forced inactivity on Greene. He was not a prolific diarist or letter writer. But once exchanged, he was fit enough in body and spirit to jump back into a colonel's role, leading the Americans to victory at the Battle of Red Bank. At Valley Forge, he endorsed Varnum's proposal to arm enslaved men in exchange for freedom. It is likely that Greene was thinking of the perilous condition of his native state, whose major city, Newport, was occupied by the British. Greene's wife, Anna, and his eight living children—ages twenty, nineteen, sixteen, fourteen, twelve, nine, four, and one—were only nineteen miles from the British outposts. The British conducted sorties out into the countryside at various times.[29]

The spirit required to repulse a determined enemy on the field of battle was one kind of courage. The bravery it took to lead what was to be a very controversial enterprise was another. Before February 1778, Rhode Island allowed individual blacks to enlist and scattered them throughout the militia and the companies of the state's two continental regiments. Here these men of color were controlled by the considerable majority of whites in these units. Other New England states did the same. Freemen enlisted, as did slaves whose masters agreed to the arrangement. In the Act to Enlist Slaves, on the other hand, the state itself liberated slaves and then made a distinguishable black regiment of them. This was a high-profile act that many powerful men in the state considered dangerous. The Rhode Island assembly was further weakening slavery. The sight of newly returned free soldiers would hardly reconcile the still-enslaved to their plight. What was next? Might the assembly that had already constrained the slave trade go ahead and do away with it altogether? Rhode Island's prosperity hinged to a great degree on the slave trade. Christopher Greene was staking his reputation on overcoming certain resistance to a black regiment and on his ability to instill into former slaves the boldness and enterprise needed for soldiering—qualities not encouraged by their masters.[30]

The first man to sign up for this grand experiment was Cato W. Greene, who on February 15, 1778, made his mark on the enlistment papers that sealed his fate until the end of the war. In marked contrast to the white officers of the regiment, we know next to nothing about him—no date or place of birth, no education record, no land or business papers—not even a mention in his master's correspondence. Cato W. Greene was owned by William Greene, the man

Colonel Christopher Greene of the Rhode Island Brigade, by J. C. Buttre, 1864. Print of ink on paper. Courtesy of the Rhode Island Historical Society, Providence (RHi X17 272).

who would soon become the governor of Rhode Island. It is possible that the prominent politician was sending a message to other slaveholders in the state about the sacrifice required to win the war, leading by example. The only insight we have into the slave-turned-soldier is the fact that he signed up. Two weeks after that, Cato marched to East Greenwich and received some training there. He, along with the other slaves-turned-soldiers, made their first appearance on a May or June 1778 muster roll. In Captain Flagg's company he joined thirty-two other black privates and musicians, all of whom had signed up between February and June. No seasoned hands stayed on from Flagg's previous unit to help guide the fresh recruits. George Sambo and Windsor Fry, both black men in Flagg's April muster joined all the other black men already serving in the Rhode Island line in Captain Thomas Arnold's large company of fifty-two black and Indian privates. Even the noncommissioned officers and musicians were new names by the time black privates entered Flagg's company.[31]

Cato W. Greene was joined by three other men named Cato. Masters often named their bondsmen for classical figures, a reminder that the Greek and Roman civilization had slavery as well. The Roman Cato was an orator and statesman who challenged the tyranny of Caesar. It took a cruel brand of humor—or a degree of ignorance—to name the lowliest in society after grand historical figures like Cato, Titus, and Caesar. In the same vein, four men in Cato's company were named Prince. Other masters commonly chose place names for their slaves. Cato attended the morning roll call with men named Newport, Britain, Africa, Bristol, and Boston. Biblical names like Sampson, Saul, Job, and Jacob could remind the master of the Bible's support of slavery. Some men retained their African names. There were two Cuffs and one Cudgo among Cato's cohort, both names from Whydah (Ouidah) and the Bight of Benin in Africa. Other men in Cato's unit had nicknames like Jack, Tony, and Frank. Only three men in Cato's company answered to names typical of white men of the time—William, Nathaniel, and John. The black men's last names were likely those of their masters. Slaves were typically denied the dignity of surnames, but in the military one had to distinguish the many soldiers sharing a first name. Africa Burke's master was James Burke. Jack Coddington's master was John Coddington. Titus Pierce's master was William Pierce. As the war went on, some former slaves changed their names, thus shedding their identity as bondsmen, but most retained their masters' names when they applied for pensions as old men. In marked contrast to other units, the all-black company in the Connecticut line featured soldiers who changed their names to reflect their new status in life: Freeman, Liberty, et cetera. Influential officers or black recruits in Connecticut may have started the trend toward proclaiming freedom in a basic signifier of their identity.[32]

The recruits of the First Rhode Island stepped into a perilous situation, fraught with ambiguity and adventure. They left their homes and the strictly structured regime of slave life to move around like never before. This movement could have been at once liberating and a real trial. The army did not guarantee wheeled vehicles and sturdy shoes. In fact, when it came to the terms of everyday comfort, the army was not necessarily a step up. As a servant to Rhode Island's governor, Cato W. Greene had probably gotten enough to eat and would have found himself by a warm fire when northeasters slammed into New England. The army was not known for creature comforts. As early as August 1777, a colonel of the Second Rhode Island wrote the state's governor that his nearly barefoot unit, "scandalous in its appearance," elicited disagreeable taunts throughout New England and New York that could be condensed, said Colonel Israel Angell, into the phrase "the Ragged Lousey Naked Regiment."[33]

To put up with month after grueling month, the men of color had the state's assurance that they were free men. Whether the state would honor its commitment once the war was over was probably a subject of conversation among the black recruits. When they let their daydreams wander to the future, they may have wondered what the status of their children would be or what they would do to earn a living after the war or when (or if) they could accumulate enough money to buy family members out of slavery. The promise of the Revolution, freedom, resonated more profoundly with the former slaves of the First Rhode Island than for average recruits elsewhere. But for the moment, the black soldiers were paid the same as white soldiers and shared the discomforts of camp life as any lowly private did in Washington's army.

The logistics involved in creating a new regiment within the Rhode Island line provided a special challenge to its all-white officers. The month before Cato Greene appeared on the muster list, Captain Flagg had commanded close to thirty privates with the help of two sergeants and two corporals. His men were seasoned soldiers. Many, like Winsor Fry, a mustee from East Greenwich, had marched to Boston in 1775. Others in the Rhode Island line had participated in the rout around New York and subsequently crossed the Delaware River with Washington at his lowest moment of the war and then recrossed to defeat the Hessians at Trenton and the English at Princeton. Most of them saw action at the victory of Red Bank and had braved the winter at Valley Forge. Five of them had not survived the diseased environment there and died in April. Flagg's seasoned unit was primarily white, with six men of color. All the NCOs and musicians were white as well and had served throughout the eventful year of 1777.[34]

With the turn of a calendar page, Flagg's world had changed. As of February 1778, all of his white privates had gone to the Second Rhode Island Regiment. His black and Indian privates did not accompany them. They were placed in

Captain Arnold's First Rhode Island along with all the other men of color in the First Rhode Island and those few from the Second Rhode Island. His four NCOs were gone, to be replaced by three new ones. Even his drummers and fifers were new. Flagg likely left Valley Forge to go meet his new unit in Rhode Island and participated in their recruitment and training. There he met Cato Greene for the first time along with thirty other fresh recruits. Although he did pick up two lieutenants and one ensign, he still had to start from scratch again, with only two sergeants and one corporal. Flagg's fellow captains, John S. Dexter, Thomas Cole, and Elijah Lewis, faced the same challenges—a change in personnel with new "colored" recruits and fewer NCOs.[35]

The captains of the Second Rhode Island had a lighter load to bear. They saw their companies double in size as the white men from the First Rhode Island streamed in. These men at least were experienced soldiers. They maintained their esprit de corps because all of the white First Rhode Islanders in any one company were transferred together into one company of the Second. Thus, all of Dexter's First Rhode Island white men went to Captain William Humphrey's company in the Second. These new, larger companies did not include their black soldiers. Those men of the Second Rhode Island were transferred to the Captain Arnold's company in the First Rhode Island. Arnold's May 1778 muster list was the only one dating from Valley Forge. It appears that all the men of color within the Rhode Island line at Valley Forge were deposited in Arnold's company. These men of color were in the minority in their pre–May 1778 units. Now, in Arnold's company, they worked in a largely African American environment, despite the fact that their officers were whites. Rather than place all the seasoned black soldiers in one unit, it might have made more sense to leave them in their former companies to act as trainers for the new recruits. This was not to be, perhaps because these experienced men would serve as a model company for the new recruits, a common practice in eighteenth-century armies. Another possibility was that they were there at Valley Forge and convenience dictated that they stay put.[36]

A striking feature of the muster lists is the total absence of corporals as of July 1778. A common saying in the army even today is that the NCOs (sergeants and corporals) run the army. To have new recruits and no corporals to train and control them would constitute a nightmare for a commanding officer. Corporals are the men who oversee the guard. It is inconceivable that a regiment with new recruits should lack corporals, let alone a unit about to fight a major battle. It is conceivable, however, that this lowest rung of noncommissioned officers in the First Rhode Island was manned by black soldiers. To have acknowledged them officially by noting their names on the muster list would have offended white sensibilities of the time. When the inspector general, Steuben, filed his report in September 1779, he noted that the noncommissioned officers in Greene's regiment were "very bad" because "being white men [they] cannot be reduced or their places supplied from the ranks." But three months before, Colonel Christopher Greene's order at the East Greenwich encampment on June 9, 1779, mentioned having the "white corporals" accomplish a task. He would have no reason to specify skin color unless there were black corporals as well. So it is a distinct possibility that in the First Rhode Island muster rolls, the blank space under "corporal" hid the fact that there were corporals who were men of color.[37]

In the summer of 1778, the men of the First Rhode Island trained at the East Greenwich camp. It did not take much imagination to figure out where they might see their first fighting. Just a few miles south of their camp lay Rhode Island's principal port city, Newport. Occupied by the British army since December 1776, Newport was the British army's one and only outpost in New England. Like New York City, it lay on the water, enabling the Royal Navy to provide crucial cover to the occupying force.

Unbeknown to the men of the First Rhode Island, a French fleet had arrived in American waters in the summer of 1778. As a result of the American victory at Saratoga the previous fall, King Louis XVI of France had agreed to an alliance with the fledgling American nation. The signatures at Versailles would eventually impact the First Rhode Island, as the French fleet would lead Washington to believe that finally the Americans could liberate Newport. The American commander in Rhode Island, Major General John Sullivan, a thirty-eight-year-old former attorney and mill owner from New Hampshire, put out the call for five thousand militiamen to augment his thousand-man force. Washington sent two veteran brigades to assist, along with two accomplished senior officers, the Marquis de Lafayette and General Nathanael Greene, a Rhode Island native. The First Rhode Island found itself surrounded by frantic activity as thousands of men converged on the area around Aquidneck Island, on which stood the garrisoned city of Newport with its 6,700 British and Hessian soldiers. The arrival of the French fleet was a surprise to the British command. A civilian woman in the city described their hasty efforts to shore up the lower part of the island. "Heavens! With what spirit the army undertook to repair the old batteries," she wrote to her husband in the American army. "With what amazing quickness they threw up new ones! The Night did not retard them, so earnest were they to give the Count [French admiral D'Estaing] a proper reception," she wrote with great admiration.[38]

The American general and the French admiral agreed to start a joint operation on August 10. The men of the First Rhode Island felt for the first time the excitement of moving as a force of thousands of men. A black militiaman said in his pension application years later that the soldiers of the Black Regiment were the first onto the island. The arrival of a British fleet sent French land forces back into their ships. As the two navies sized one another up, a massive storm hit and scattered both squadrons along the coast. This "perfect hurricane," said the woman observer in town, brought rain that rivaled the great biblical flood. She described the British soldiers as "drowned rats" and said their tents had "blown to pieces." She could just as well have been describing the American forces that saw much of their gunpowder destroyed in the rain. One Rhode Island soldier called the tempest "the French storm." The British, as if acknowledging that all bad things came from the rebels, called it "the continental storm." Much to the chagrin of General Sullivan, the French admiral decided to take his battered ships to Boston to be repaired. Poised to start their final assault, the American commanders, along with Lafayette, pleaded with D'Estaing to stay another couple of days. The Frenchman canvassed his officers who responded with a definite *non*. When Sullivan received intelligence that another British fleet had left New York bound for Rhode Island's Narragansett Bay, he withdrew his soldiers to the north of Aquidneck Island, whereupon the British came out of their works to pursue the Americans.[39]

Surrounded by storms and fleets and booming artillery, the black men of the First Rhode Island accomplished their maneuvers in the mud without the leadership of their colonel, Christopher Greene. Sullivan had pulled Greene out to head a brigade that would occupy the center of the American lines. His black and Indian recruits were placed on the far right flank, led by Major Samuel Ward, an officer who was involved with the Black Regiment idea from the beginning. The First Rhode Islanders were not the only inexperienced soldiers in this battle. Sullivan reported to the Congress that not more than fifteen hundred troops had even seen action before. In their pursuit of the Americans at dawn on August 29, the British first encountered light infantry, one unit of which was led by John Laurens, a young lieutenant colonel from South Carolina. The First Rhode Islanders could no doubt hear the battle advancing toward them. Elements of the light infantry under Laurens fell back toward the First Rhode Island position, and in the words of one of their number, the light infantry group was relieved "by the Black Regiment." By 9:00 A.M., the "perfect storm" had descended onto the First Rhode Island. Hessian troops had seized territory that provided a clear field of fire into the American right flank, consisting of four brigades anchored by the First Rhode Island. British ships sailed up the Narragansett Bay to lob cannon fire into the same right flank. Sullivan said that the enemy "bent their whole force" on his right. Perhaps espying the black unit up ahead, crack Hessian troops decided to concentrate on that point in order to break through the American lines. Sullivan later remarked that their choice sent "considerable bodies of infantry" to assist men already there. Despite being caught in artillery crossfire and a murderous attack of Germans storming their way, the men of the right flank, including the black novices, held. The Germans sent two "furious onsets" of battle-hardened veterans into the American line, and these engaged the African Americans in hand-to-hand combat. The men of color held again. Finally the Hessians decided to go around the First Rhode Island, leaving the black men surrounded by deafening sound and teeth-rattling explosions. The First Rhode Islanders then saw the frantic Hessians retreat back to the British lines. Of one officer at the battle it was later written, "It was the first time in his life he found that men could endure more hardships than horses."[40]

When General Sullivan called it a day in late afternoon, the black unit, along with the rest of the army, must have been relieved, having had no food or rest for thirty-six hours. The next day Sullivan heard that the British fleet would soon be upon them. In a textbook retreat maneuver, with enemy sentries only two hundred yards away, Sullivan spirited all his troops, supplies, and guns off the island. On August 31, he reported 30 killed, 137 wounded, and 44 missing. By that date the First Rhode Island had reported two killed, thus constituting 7 percent of the men killed in the battle. The next day nine more men died in the First Rhode Island, bringing the count to eleven. Among the First Rhode Island companies, Captain Lewis lost two men: Query Sweeting and Caesar Eldrage. Captain Flagg lost two men, Jacob Hazard and Cuff Tilinghast. Captain Jonathan Wallens lost five men: Ganset Perry, Abram Pierce, Derrick Vanzober, John Nocake, and Moses Weeks. Captain Cole lost one man, Warren Mason. Captain Dexter lost two men, William Babcock and Prime Gardner. It is possible that some died from non-battle causes, as many were reported sick in the August 22 muster. Nine First Rhode Island soldiers died on September 1. It could be that the hurricane and resultant saturated conditions weakened already ailing soldiers. Whether killed in action or dying of disease, the First Rhode Island made its sacrifice to the cause. They were not the only troops on Sullivan's right flank, but in "entering pell mell" with the Hessians, the first of the Black Regiment's men died in battle.[41]

In the flurry of congratulations that ensued after the battle, the best that could be said at that time about the First Rhode Island was that they did not disgrace themselves. In his message to the troops, George Washington related that "some persons" had criticized the First Rhode Island, whose conduct had not been "equal to what might have been expected," and that "their commander in the battle," Major Samuel Ward, was "much dissatisfied." Washington wanted to assure the men that no censure had been laid against the unit. "Doubtless in the heat of the action," explained Washington, "Major Ward might have said something to hurry the troops on to action which being misinterpreted gave rise to the Report." Washington went on to commend the First Rhode Island, which in his estimation was "well intitled to a proper share of honor of the Day." Even the naysayers had to admit that the newly minted soldiers of the First Rhode Island, many of them in their teens, had held their position. This is the first and only time that a whole unit within the Continental Army was publicly vilified. Individual commanders, like Lee at Monmouth, as well as undisciplined militia came in for their share of calumny, but the men of color are the only group of continental soldiers to be so accused, however inaccurately.[42]

In the first three years of their service in the First Rhode Island, there was nothing quite like the soldiers' first six months. Former slaves left their masters, entered training, and became full-fledged soldiers in the spring, only to be thrown three months later into a crucial part of the American line at a battle where they confronted seasoned enemy soldiers. The stress must have been enormous. But for the next three years the First Rhode Island settled into the daily grind of patrolling, mustering, and maintaining decent living conditions as best they could in Rhode Island. Muster rolls reveal typical notations concerning furloughs, leaves, guard duty, and special missions outside the camp. They repaired boats. They made fascines. They patrolled the coast.

The army was supposed to provide life's basics but carried out that responsibility with chilling ineptitude. The First Rhode Island did have the advantage of staying close to home, so the governor and assembly were in the neighborhood and could see firsthand the condition of the regiment. Their families were close by too and gave what support they could. A "Return of Purchases" for the First Rhode Island indicates that they ate beef, onions, salt, flour, and rice. They consumed gallons of port wine, Indian rum, New England rum, and French rum. It is doubtful that the rank and file got the good stuff, but all this rum averaged out to one gill a day per soldier, a gill being one-half a cup. To contain drinking, Colonel Greene forbade sutlers (outside peddlers who followed the army) from selling any kind of spirits to the regiment. The daily ration ordained by the Continental Congress included one pound of beef or three-quarters of a pound of pork or one pound of salt fish, along with one pound of bread or flour and one pint of milk. Other items like vegetables (three pints per week) and spruce beer (one quart per day) and later whiskey (one-half cup per day) were often absent from the army's larders. As any officer's correspondence will attest, the ration was an ideal that fell far short of being realized.

At times the men took their wages and frequented Preserved Pearce's establishment in East Greenwich for a dram or a dinner. Occasionally there is evidence that captains treated the rank and file, as when Captain William Potter paid for Prince Watson's breakfast and dinner. Captain Lewis bought yarn for thirteen men, only two of whom were in his company. Perhaps in their spare hours the men knitted hats, socks, and scarves for themselves. Individual soldiers had accounts in Pearce's establishment for supper and drams to wash it down. Along with the rank and file, noncommissioned officers and field officers also frequented the inn, the latter often paying charges for their horses. To supplement rations and food eaten at the occasional trip to local taverns, some men, like soldiers everywhere in this period, stole from local farmers. A September 1778 orderly book entry in Greene's regiment noted complaints about soldiers stealing corn and potatoes. There was always tension, during the Revolution, between civilians and soldiers regarding food. Foraging parties took supplies, issuing worthless pieces of paper to the owners in return. General Washington wrote reams to the Continental Congress about food and supplies that never arrived in camp. The soldiers saw well-fed civilians and might have figured that a few less potatoes in their larder would do them no harm. Still, this was deemed "unsoldierlike behavior," and Greene ordered his soldiers to restrict themselves to not more than one mile from their quarters.[43]

On the clothing front as well the army struggled to supply its men. In the Account of Clothing for 1780, Windsor Fry, a First Rhode Island private, received for the year one coat, one vest, one pair of woolen overalls (no linen), one stock (tie), two pair of socks, two shirts (no hunting shirts), one hat, one pair of shoes, and one blanket. Although there were "breeches" and "stockings" on the list, the rank and file did not get them. These were officer items like the port wine. Shoes were always an issue. In June 1779, the quartermaster asked officers to submit requests for shoes for the privates and noncoms, but only if the men were "so badly shod as not to be able to march without receiving a pair of shoes each." In February 1780, Captain Stephen Olney wrote to a Mr. Hazzard, asking Hazzard to front him twenty pair of large shoes in order to supply a detachment about to go out on a mission. Hazzard would be repaid once the state parcel of shoes arrived. Although Olney expected some shoes from headquarters in a day or two, he (Olney) doubted their quality, so Hazzard was wise to wait. The Rhode Island assembly got involved in shoe requisition when in September 1780 it ordered 116 pairs for noncoms and privates, but each officer had to get his pair first. Even at war's end, the army had still far from perfected their delivery of decent clothes to the soldiers. After the battle of Yorktown, the regiment (now combined with the Second Rhode Island) suffered an outbreak of fever, during which their clothing, termed "dirty rags," was consigned "to the flames."[44]

There is no evidence that the men lacked for the tools of war. Each soldier had a musket and bayonet, a scabbard, a gun sling, a bayonet belt, a cartridge box with cartridges and flints, and a knapsack. Gun-cleaning materials like gun worms, screwdrivers, brushes, and "prickers" were issued as well as drums and fifes. At times the tents meant to cover all this equipment were in short supply.

In the first summer of their service, the First Rhode Island recruits were told to build huts or "brush houses" because tents were not to be had. Three summers later the men were assured that tents were on the way, but in the meantime the men were to use the best of the old tents. With the essentials often a question mark, the men's health suffered. In September 1778, almost three weeks after the Battle of Rhode Island, the "Return of the Sick" listed seven men with dysentery, two with fever, two lame soldiers, one with bad cough, and six recovering from illness. About 10 percent of the men were out of commission. In the dead of winter two years later, men were also struck with pleurisy, pneumonia, rheumatism, and "bilious fever." Venereal disease also occasionally appeared.[45]

While challenged on the front of everyday necessities, the First Rhode Island performed their duties as any other strapped unit in Washington's army. Muster rolls have the men on guard, on special assignment with specific officers, or "on command," which indicated a mission outside the camp. Enlisted in 1777, George Sambo was constantly "on command" once incorporated in an all-black unit. He operated out of camp until his death in October 1779. With one exception, when he is "on command" with General Greene, the musters remain mute as to the nature of his assignments. Yet his officers entrusted him to operate outside the limits of strictly regulated camp life, testifying to his dependability, resourcefulness, and intelligence. Strength was another advantage that led to special projects. As orderly books indicated, skilled oarsmen often found themselves on special assignment. In October 1779, Colonel Greene summoned a sergeant and eight good oarsmen at 4:00 A.M. to go to Aquidneck island (the island also known as Rhode Island, on which sat Newport) on a flatboat with a platform laid for carrying horses. Although the British had evacuated the island five days before, Greene might have feared that British ships still lurked in the vicinity, necessitating this mission in the dark of night. Earlier in the war, black militiaman Sampson George was one of three oarsmen to row Colonel William Barton to the environs of Newport, where he and his forty-man force kidnapped the commanding British general, Richard Prescott. Prescott was later exchanged for continental general Charles Lee. Other special missions included searching for deserters and requisitioning supplies. In addition to being restricted to within one mile of their quarters, the soldiers also had a curfew. In Colonel Angell's regiment, tattoo beat at eight, all lights were out by nine, and after ten no person could pass without the proper countersign. At times the men played with the passwords of the day. Typically the sign and countersign were place names or famous men's names or inspiring words like "independence" and "liberty." But after the Battle of Rhode Island, the men had fun. When greeted with the word "soldier," one's answer was "to your quarters." A guard might ask, "Are you charged?" The proper response: "not yet."

On a subsequent night, the parole was "Who is there?" and the countersign was "come and see." Shortly after the battle for Newport, the parole was "Cornell," the name of a battalion commander next to the First Rhode Island on the field, and the countersign was "here we are."[46]

Joking around with the parole and countersign injected a little levity into essential but boring guard duty. With no diaries or memoirs from the enlisted men of the First Rhode Island, we do not know what they did for entertainment. The lists on which their names appear provide no entries for the lighter side of life. Other soldiers' diaries mention ball games, singing, and card games. Noah Robinson, a New England sergeant, and his mates made an apple pie on a particularly dreary, rainy day. On another he played quoits with officers. On March 3, 1778, the town of Warwick celebrated Pancake Day, and presumably the order of the day was to eat more pancakes than usual.[47]

The only hint we often get about what the soldiers did in their spare time was when they violated rules or orders. Bad behavior in a military unit ran the gamut from sleeping while on duty to disorderly conduct (often in connection with alcoholic beverages) to desertion and mutiny. The First Rhode Island soldiers were no different from other military men in qualifying in all of these departments. The articles of war laid out the rules under which the army operated. They did not specify punishments for each infraction, but they did stipulate the maximum penalties. For sentences short of capital punishment, the articles of 1775 mandated no more than thirty-nine lashes, a number harkening back to Mosaic law. During the French and Indian war, American soldiers looked on with horror as the British thrashed their own soldiers well beyond the biblical limit. Colonials had no stomach for five hundred lashes, well laid on. In fashioning their own punishments in 1775, the Americans, who emulated the British in most respects, chose to depart from British practice and adhere to biblical law. In short order, George Washington realized that thirty-nine stripes was no deterrent whatsoever. He explained to General William Heath that most soldiers would willingly submit to the maximum penalty for a bottle of rum. "I might almost as well attempt to remove Mount Atlas," wrote Washington about the thirty-nine-lash limit's ability to discourage plundering. The revised articles increased the maximum number of lashes to one hundred. In early 1778, Washington was informed that "100 lashes are considered . . . a trivial punishment," and so still more daunting numbers were put in place. Drummers and sometimes fifers were the persons administering the lashes, with a drum major in attendance to see that the punishment was done—and done properly. Of course, some crimes, like desertion and mutiny, could land one on the gibbet, but courts-martial or the commanding officer could be generous. Regardless, death sentences had to be approved by Washington.[48]

Before the introduction of the formerly enslaved black men into the Rhode Island line, there was a fracas in 1777 sufficient in severity to be termed a mutiny. Six NCOs and seven privates, all white men in the First Rhode Island, faced a court-martial for mutiny and behaving in a disorderly manner. All were absolved of the mutiny charges but suspended or reprimanded (or both) for disorderly behavior. Two years later another mutiny, this time in the Second Rhode Island, occurred on July 29, 1779, at their encampment on Barber's Heights. The first sign of trouble in the diary of the unit's commander (who was away from his unit at the time) concerned a sartorial protest. Colonel Israel Angell wrote on July 24, 1779, that two-thirds of his sergeants "had conspired together and ript [off] the bindings of their hats contrary to orders." Angell ordered his men to reaffix the bindings by next guard mounting or they would be reduced in rank and tried for willful disobedience of orders. A week later, Angell received the "disagreeable news" of his men mutinying. Angell traveled through the night to reach his unit, arriving to find "all in peace." He thanked the Kentish Guards and militia for putting down the mutiny. The regiment was ordered to parade and then received a general pardon. Only one mutineer, a private, was put in irons and sent to Providence to be court-martialed.[49]

The First Rhode Island, while primarily a black regiment, committed no mutinies and saw very few instances of disorderly conduct. Actions that did reap physical punishment in the Black Regiment were most often being absent during roll call (typically punished with twenty to eight lashes) and being asleep at one's post or sitting at one's post. July Champlain, Prince Gardner, and John Pomp each got twenty stripes for succumbing to their fatigue. Leaving camp for a night or two usually meant more pain. Newport Champlain got one hundred lashes for his absence. He claimed that he'd had permission to leave camp but that he overstayed his furlough and then was afraid to return. His officers remained unmoved. Prince Bucklin absented himself all night and missed the next day's roll call. He received fifty stripes. Occasionally a private engaged in prohibited activities and was not punished. When sergeants called a private to play cards while the private was on duty, it was the sergeants who were court-martialed. Presumably the private was only following orders when called to play cards. Sergeant William Kipp was reduced to a private, while Sergeant Remington was demoted and transferred to another regiment, never to be a sergeant again. Usually these kinds of demotions were temporary. Commissioned officers never received lashes. For more serious offenses, they were drummed out of the army. Noncommissioned officers might be demoted and then lashed.[50]

Moving up the scale of offenses, theft was a common problem throughout the army. Anthony Griffin pled guilty to stealing rum and beef out of the continental stores. He received "fifty lashes on his naked back" and had to return the provisions. London Thompson was found not guilty of stealing a blanket but was whipped thirty times for trading his own blanket for a shirt. Other men brought up for theft received greater punishment, probably because they had committed previous offenses. Sharper Gardner got one hundred lashes for theft in June 1779. Two months before, he had deserted the regiment, for which he had suffered sixty lashes. Less than a month after the theft charge, he was lashed one hundred times again, this time for a charge called "skating." In the space of three months, Gardner endured 260 lashes to his back. One may well question how a man could survive this degree of punishment, but Gardner did, serving until the end of the war. He died in New York City around 1793.[51]

Another repeat offender, Winsor Fry, graduated to the ultimate penalty. He started in early 1780 with breaking into the commissary, stealing beef, candles, rum, and cornmeal. He then deserted on February 5. Retaken, he submitted to a court-martial that on April 12, but George Washington deemed this "irregular" and ordered a retrial. Another court-martial, on May 9, found him guilty and sentenced him to death. On May 19, Fry bolted and remained at large until sometime in September. He had missed his execution date of June 1, 1780. In mid-October, with Fry again in custody, Colonel Greene wrote to General Washington that times had changed and that there was no reason to exact the death penalty. An example had been needed back in June, argued Greene, but not now. A week later Washington concurred, as his policy was to approve death sentences only as a deterrent. Greene must have had a soft spot for this soldier who had served since the war's commencement. Fry lived to be an old man thanks to Colonel Greene, who used a special power delegated by General Washington to grant Fry a "full and free pardon." In 1818, Fry went to the East Greenwich courthouse to claim a pension for his services in the revolution. He claimed that he had first enlisted in the spring of 1775 and then joined Greene's regiment in 1777, serving to the end of the war. "During all that time," Fry said in his pension application, he was "absent but once." In fact, according to the regimental book of 1781, Fry left without leave for eight months in 1780, along with one brief hiatus in 1779. Overall, however, he served his country for nearly eight years. When it came time to apply for a pension, both a district judge and one of his former captains successfully supported his claim.[52]

This kind of intercession on the part of a commanding officer happened intermittently throughout the service. But it seems to occur less frequently in the Black Regiment. Colonel Angell in the Second Rhode Island interceded for his men more often than Greene. On one occasion he suspended a corporal's lashes provided he behaved himself in future. In another instance, a private's sentence of forty stripes was suspended "in light of previous good behavior."

A Second Rhode Island court-martial found three of its soldiers guilty of an attempted rape on an eighty-year-old woman. The first perpetrator got one hundred lashes, the second thirty-seven lashes, and the third was forgiven. It is hard to believe that any black man in that scenario would be let off so lightly. It took a dramatic sentence in the First Rhode Island to call out the commanding officer to intervene. Colonel Greene had saved Windsor Fry's life in 1780. After Greene's death in 1781, the new colonel of the black regiment, Jeremiah Olney, interceded for Fortune Stoddard, who was convicted in civil courts of manslaughter. Olney argued to the Continental Congress that Private Stoddard had killed a man in the line of duty. General Washington concurred, and he explained to the secretary of war that it would be "extremely unjust and cruel that the soldier should any longer be confined or should be sold to pay the charge of prosecution." Stoddard survived his confinement and returned to Newport after the war.[53]

While George Washington said what could not be said of a white offender, namely that he be "sold to pay the charge of prosecution," the average sentence did not vary much from black to white soldier. A couple of extreme punishments, however, occurred in the black companies. On one day in late 1779, a court-martial in Greene's regiment tried six men for two instances of theft. Ezekiel Dimond and Caesar Harris, both of Captain Dexter's company, were charged with stealing rice from a Mr. Burk's store. Dimond pleaded guilty, but Harris claimed he had nothing to do with the theft although he consumed some of the haul, knowing it was stolen. The court sentenced Dimond to two hundred lashes, while Harris got one hundred.[54]

The next case that day concerned Peter Hazard and Frank Gould, a former mariner who had enlisted before the Slave Enlistment Act. They were found guilty of breaking into the commissary and two windmills to lift pork and grain. Perhaps inspired by the previous case, Gould pleaded to an accessory charge with respect to the commissary. Gould claimed that Peter Hazard, then a sentry, performed the crime while Gould looked on. Still, he admitted to the windmill heists and to eating the pork that Hazard had stolen. His tactic did not work. Gould suffered 200 lashes.[55]

The court-martial went on to determine the guilt of John Remington and Ned Rose. Remington, as a sentry, allegedly had allowed Rose and Peter Hazard into the commissary, while Rose was accused of stealing candles, soap, and rum. Remington and Rose garnered two hundred lashes each, while Hazard, for whatever reason, was not tried or punished. At the end of the court-martial, the scribe who recorded the proceedings took the trouble of adding up the lashes prescribed that day. One thousand lashes at one court-martial might have struck him as an anomaly.[56]

Judging by the types of offenses committed by the African American soldiers in Greene's unit, it appears that they used the same strategies against their officers that they had used against their former masters. They slowed down the work, they took extra supplies, they ran away. One of the charges all but absent from the First Rhode Island records is disorderly conduct, along the lines of mouthing off or challenging officers. Ex-slaves knew this was a risky practice—far better to strike back in less overtly confrontational ways.

Again, a comparison with the Second Rhode Island is helpful. Often the unit's colonel could talk the men down before they engaged in an actionable offense. Before the mutiny of July 1779 in the Second Rhode Island, Colonel Angell's men joined a mutiny sparked by Connecticut troops who marched to the barracks at night to recruit more men. Angell had to talk to his men "some time" before they dispersed and troubled the peace of the night no longer. Six months later, Angell experienced the "mortification" of the July 1779 mutiny. Six weeks after that, the beleaguered colonel heard that some soldiers asserted that their enlistments were for three years, not for the war's duration, and threatened to leave on their third service anniversary. The colonel assured the men that he had checked their enlistments and that their commitments were for the war's duration. If they bolted, they'd be tried for mutiny.[57]

There were individual acts of insubordination in the Second Rhode Island as well. A private defied a sergeant of the guard and received forty-two lashes as punishment. A captain absented himself for four days and also behaved "unbecoming the character of an officer and a Gentleman" in frequently associating with the wagon master. He was discharged, but like so many officers he was reinstated with no demotion. Even the women in the regiment gave Colonel Angell a hard time. Mrs. Thomas, a soldier's wife, stole a gown. The colonel ordered all drums and fifes to parade her out of the regiment with a paper pinned to her back that read, "A Thief." Thus, said the colonel, "she went off with Musick." Another woman's mouth, this time that of a Mrs. Grant, earned her a mention in the orderly book. She exhibited "insolence and disrespect" directly to the colonel, thus engendering "the most dangerous Consequence to the good order and obedience of the Guard." She was ordered away but reappeared like a bad penny. The colonel was not amused. He ordered her on the road by eleven the following morning or else her second leave-taking would not be nearly so pleasant as the first.[58]

This kind of mouthing off was rare in the First Rhode Island records. The one time a black soldier, Caesar Updike, mixed it up with his corporal, his punishment was mitigated from fifty to twenty lashes because "there were circumstances of particular indecency in Corporal Stafford's behavior to Caesar Updike's wife." Only extraordinary circumstances pushed the black man to directly challenge an officer and spark a court-martial.[59]

The women of the First Rhode Island were not always as careful. A Mrs. Updike was one of several women who generally washed clothes and provided nursing services to the regiment. These women who drew rations were as subject to the military justice system as the soldiers. When Sarah Oatly and Hannah Wanton hid a deserter, they were tried at a regimental court-martial headed by Ebenezer Flagg, now a major, and sentenced to fifteen lashes on their naked backs and then drummed out of camp as far as a certain bridge, a healthy distance away from the soldiers. Flagg remitted the stripes, "flattering himself [that] the disgrace of drumming [them] out of town" would be sufficient punishment. He then ordered that their departure be carried out at 2:00 A.M., with all the guard present except sentries on duty.[60]

On the whole, the punishments accorded people of color did not noticeably vary from the punishments of whites. For absenting oneself from camp or sleeping at one's post, the typical soldier suffered twenty to fifty lashes. Theft typically carried a penalty from thirty-nine lashes to one hundred lashes. Exceptional two-hundred-lash sentences appear in a couple of First Rhode Island cases, but otherwise punishments for theft fell into the typical range. Desertion sentences also carried a penalty of between thirty-nine and one hundred strokes. If, however, a soldier deserted and then offered his services to the enemy, he was likely to suffer death. In June 1782 General Washington approved a death sentence for a black soldier in the Rhode Island regiment who had gone over to the British. Four months later, a white soldier from Rhode Island suffered the same penalty for the same crime. With the exception of directly confronting officers, a phenomenon more common in the Second Rhode Island, black and white soldiers got into the same trouble and suffered the same punishments.[61]

The Battle of Rhode Island in the summer of 1778 was the last attempt at dislodging the British from Newport. The enemy obliged the Americans by decamping on its own. On October 11, 1779, a fleet of fifty-seven ships arrived from New York, all of which appeared to be empty. Nine days later, an informant who lived in Newport reported that the British had loaded heavy baggage and their cannons onto the ships. Two days later, on the anniversary of the Battle of Red Bank, the officers of the Second Rhode Island provided a dinner where the soldiers were joined by hundreds of country people who climbed a nearby hill hoping to see the British fleet's departure. They had to wait three more days. Finally, just after sunset on October 25, the British lifted anchor and sailed into the night.[62]

Both Rhode Island regiments marched into Newport to find it in shambles, although the British left some admirable examples of fortification, or as Colonel Angell termed it, "some of the Beautifullest works that I ever saw in my life." The First Rhode Island took up their quarters on Goat Island in the Newport harbor. They would be isolated there and in the vanguard if the British decided to return. Two days later, all the continental troops were ordered to march west to the major encampment of the Continental Army in the Hudson Highlands. With the British gone, Washington saw no need to retain them in Rhode Island. But the state's nervous assembly asked that a regiment stay behind.[63]

The First Rhode Island, therefore, hunkered down in its native state and led a somewhat placid existence until a new general arrived in Rhode Island to disturb the daily round of muster, drill, and work. The *Providence Gazette* heralded the arrival of Major General William Heath and his suite on June 16, 1780. Heath was a peppery New Englander who had seen action in the Revolution's earliest days at Battle Road and Bunker Hill. A major general by August 1776, he led an unsuccessful siege against a fort guarding the Hudson River, for which Heath was censured by General Washington. However limited Heath's talents as a saddle general, he did impress Washington with his organizational skills. He never commanded troops in action again, but he did oversee the major encampment in the Hudson Highlands, and when Washington needed a man to arrange for the arrival of the French fleet at Newport with its six thousand soldiers, Heath was the man for the job.[64]

Upon arrival at Providence, Rhode Island, Heath was appalled at what he considered to be the poor state of military preparedness. Ammunition was stored in a wooden house surrounded by other wooden houses. An explosion would fire the town, warned Heath. Unguarded cannons were scattered here and there, an inviting target for any loyalists in the neighborhood to disable. There was not so much as a sergeant's guard or a sentinel posted in Providence during the day, groused the general. Admitting that it was outside the scope of his assignment, Heath nonetheless felt compelled to report this sorry state of affairs to the commander in chief. Heath likely dressed down Christopher Green, the man responsible for the situation. But he got nowhere, reporting to Washington that Greene's "very small . . . Regiment of Blacks" was at North Kingston making fascines. Heath's letter drips with disapproval at this curious choice of priorities. Although he wisely foregoes spelling out his censure in his letter to Washington, he surely expressed himself more overtly to the Rhode Island officers. They informed him that General Washington himself had ordered the First Rhode Island to do precisely what they were doing. Indeed, a month before, Washington had even specified the dimensions of the timber used to make fascines—twelve to eighteen feet in length and ten inches thick. A frustrated Heath was thus immobilized between Washington's orders and Colonel Greene's intransigence. Furthermore, Heath and Greene argued about an officer matter concerning pay and rations. The fact that Heath was a pencil pusher of sorts, while Colonel Greene was a bona fide war hero, could not have helped matters.[65]

Heath spilled these contentious issues into his first communication to Washington. The next day he found a pretext for using Greene's officers who were, after all, not making fascines. The Rhode Island assembly had enacted that six hundred men were to be recruited for a six-month stint in the continental lines starting July 1. Heath proposed taking two or three officers from Greene's regiment, along with some NCOs, to train the new men. He pointed out that not one regimental officer could be found in Providence—another swipe at Greene. Two days later, in another missive to Washington, Heath warned of trouble ahead in meeting troop quotas, saying "many are adverse to being incorporated with the Blacks." To alleviate this concern, Heath proposed to have officers from the Second Rhode Island (the white regiment) come up from the major Continental Army encampment to march the rank and file of the First Rhode Island back to General Washington, leaving the First Rhode Island officers and musicians behind to train the new men. Heath then ordered Greene's regiment to make itself ready to march on the shortest notice, all the while continuing with the fascine project. Heath wanted the black soldiers out of Rhode Island. He wanted to clear the way for the skittish white men to sign up. So too did the Rhode Island Council of War and the state assembly. On July 25, the former wrote to Heath that the state had requested to retain the presence of the First Regiment but now wanted the rank and file to march to the Grand Army. That is, with the exception of "the greater part of the Musick." The state legislature went one step further, ordering that the new recruits be put into a "corps separate and entire" from the existing regiments. In so doing, the state legislature guaranteed new recruits that they would not serve with black men. The imminent arrival of the French fleet and army would also obviate the need for the First Rhode Island's 120-man unit.[66]

Now caught between the state legislature and Washington's orders, Heath begged for a reply from Washington, preferably before July 1, the deadline for new recruits. In the meantime, he went about putting into action exactly what the Rhode Island Council of War suggested. On June 26, Heath ordered Captain John Holden of the First Rhode Island to arm, equip, and drill the new recruits. On July 27, he ordered Major Flagg of the First Rhode Island to lead the black soldiers to Washington's camp, taking ammunition, clothing, tents, and accoutrements. He enjoined Flagg to keep the men from "loitering or straggling or inflicting any injury or abuse" on the good people of the towns through which they marched. Heath further cautioned Flagg to maintain a heightened sense of alert as the unit approached New York State given the prevalence of the enemy there. Always keep an advanced flank and rear guard, ordered the man who well knew the perilous situation along the Hudson. With everyone lined up, Heath finally officially informed Colonel Greene that Greene's men were to march "with all possible dispatch" to the main army. Heath literally isolated Greene from his men by ordering the colonel to remain in Newport, while ordering all his officers to Providence to receive further orders. Heath did not care to share with Greene what these orders would be, nor did he solicit Greene's opinion about anything concerning his own regiment. Hearing nothing from Washington by July 1, Heath ordered Flagg and the regiment to shove off, allaying new recruits' concerns about joining a black unit. His orders included an interesting addendum, however. He told Flagg that this order could be remanded, so the unit was to march slowly in the first two or three days because it might be called back. If after the fourth day Flagg had heard nothing, he was to pick up the pace "with all possible dispatch."[67]

Heath's caution was well advised. Sometime in early July he finally received a reply from Washington, dated June 29. The commander in chief nixed the Rhode Island assembly's idea of creating a third continental unit. Yet he understood the recruiting problem connected with white men serving in a black unit. The solution would be to march the First Rhode Island *and* the new recruits together to the main army and, once there, distribute them between the two existing regiments. "The objection to joining Greene's Regiment may be removed," explained Washington, "by dividing the Blacks in such a manner . . . as to abolish the name and appearance of a Black corps." Washington reiterated that the black corps should not be moved until the new levies were trained. In the interim, they were to continue with the fascine construction. In a letter to Rhode Island's governor, written on the same day, Washington explained that the First Rhode Island was "too small to afford any material reinforcement and could be more usefully employed where it was [Rhode Island]." Unsaid in the general's letter was the concern that the arrival of 120 more men at his Hudson River camp would mean more mouths to feed, and the fact that these men were black could also rile up an army that had not seen this unit for a couple of years.

Now Heath was caught between Washington's order and a First Rhode Island Regiment on the march westward through Connecticut. The beleaguered general hastily scrawled the order to bring them back. Whether evincing a real concern for their health or a desire to delay their return, Heath recommended to Flagg a pace commensurate with the excessively hot weather at the time. When Flagg returned, he was one of two officers to oversee the recruitment of the new six-hundred-man levy. His orders, issued by Lieutenant Colonel Jeremiah Olney, stipulated that "Negroes will not be received, nor any but able-bodied effective men." This blatantly racist pronouncement, along with those of Washington and Heath, speak to the racial prejudice that permeated white society at that time. So also does the fact that the only all-black regiment in Washington's army served as a labor battalion for over a year.[68]

In addition to the power politics among colonels, governors, and generals, Heath had to pay attention to the men in the ranks. No letters or diaries exist about the feelings of the black privates throughout this upheaval in their lives, but the muster rolls tell a story. The men were deserting in significant numbers. From March through July, twenty-eight men walked away from the military service, almost one-quarter of the unit. From early March to the first week of June, the men left in ones and twos. But in the two-week period of Heath's plan to send the First Rhode Island to the main army, fifteen men deserted. That was around 13 percent of the unit. They might have wondered what kind of conditions would exist in the main army when basic supplies were wanting at home. Seven men had died in camp through early July. The soldiers might too have despaired at the length of the war. For the previous two years they had been isolated from the rest of the army, with little martial activity and the esprit de corps that can go with it. Outside factors too might have played a role in their departure, like familial emergencies or the lure of a privateer. But the fact remains that fifteen of them left in the period when they were preparing for and marching to their new post in New York. They acted like many militiamen who loathed the idea of leaving their home territory.[69]

The relationships of the men who deserted are not clear. Two of the men who walked out on June 20 were from Captain Lewis's company, and both had served in Captain Slocum's unit before that. Of the four soldiers who left on July 3, one was an Indian who had just enlisted in March. The other three men were veterans who had joined the continental line before the Slave Enlistment Act of February 1778 and so had probably been freemen when they enlisted. The four who walked on July 4 were all enslaved men who had taken advantage of the Slave Enlistment Act. The same applied to the two men who deserted on July 7.[70]

Such was the number of desertions from the First that the legislature asked Washington and Heath to pardon the men if they returned within a reasonable time. Heath complied, setting September 1 as the deadline, and Washington extended the pardon to *all* soldiers in the Rhode Island line. Until the publication of these pardons, the newspapers gave no clue that anything was amiss in their local continental regiment.[71]

The desertion problem and the pardon announcements appeared in all of the Rhode Island papers, but the big news in mid-July was the arrival of the French fleet of forty-four sail and "6,000 very fine troops." Newport was a ruin after the British occupation, but the little town perked up and sponsored fireworks to welcome its long-awaited ally. Glittering dinners were had. Heath in his memoirs recalled ordering in "considerable supplies for my table," including "good" sugar and the "best" salt and fish for the occasion. Delegations of

Oneida and other Indians had dinner with General Rochambeau and Admiral de Ternay, performed war dances, and in turn saw French soldiers drill. The word went out that farmers would receive good money in exchange for vegetables and hay. Perhaps the men of the First Rhode Island could have earned some extra money in this friendly invasion of their world. But the French might also have caused disaster within the black regiment. In the last week of July, six black soldiers died, including Cato W. Greene, the first enslaved man to have signed up under the 1778 act. In the much-reduced unit, that was a 5 percent mortality rate in one week. It is possible that the men suffered some camp distemper, but it is also likely that they picked up microbes from the newly landed French. One-third of the French force was sick on its arrival. Heath had set up a hospital for the French near Providence. It is possible that these sick men passed through the black encampment or that black soldiers helped them to get to Providence. Regardless, the French arrival coincided with a near end to the string of desertions—there were only two more for the rest of 1780.[72]

Although charmed by the French officers, General Heath longed to return to the main army. His assignment in Rhode Island was essentially to make the French officers happy. So now the hapless general found himself under the thumb of Rochambeau while General Washington persisted in firing off orders. The French needed a decent road between Providence and Newport. The French needed the First Rhode Island in the area. Rumors abounded that the British planned to move on the French army, so any future displacement of the First would be Rochambeau's decision. Dismiss the militia and contain expenses, ordered Washington, provided that Rochambeau had no need of the militia. Washington also leaned on Heath to make sure that Colonel Greene and his regiment were doing their job, as if Heath needed to be told that. "Is Green fixing the boats?" queried Washington. Has Greene found the planks of wood left there last year? Is Greene giving his "constant attention" to disciplining his men? Is Greene ready to march "the moment he is ordered to do so?" Either Washington believed that Greene had to be ridden to do anything, or he was placating a ruffled Heath with respect to any possible dispute between the two officers. At any rate, Washington ended Heath's exile from the main army when on October 1 he called the New Englander back to run West Point in the wake of the Benedict Arnold treachery. Heath later recalled in his memoirs that he took "affectionate leave" of the French officers, not mentioning a word about the American officers he left behind.[73]

With Heath out of the way, Colonel Greene resumed his direct correspondence with Washington. He wrote in mid-October that the lack of supplies and provisions had hindered the completion of projects in Rhode Island. The Massachusetts militia, for example, was behind in building fortifications on

Butt's Hill, just north of Newport. As the Massachusetts men's terms of enlistment were about to expire, Greene pointed out that if Washington did "not call my Regiment to join the Army, they would undoubtedly be very usefully employed" in completing the job. Greene also reminded Washington that the enlistments of the six-month recruits would end by January 1 so it made no sense to send them to the main army. Although Greene ended the letter by saying that he personally would like to return to the main army, the overriding message was that he and his men should stay.[74]

Greene could well have timed this letter in light of the October 1 reorganization of the army that dictated that Rhode Island have just one regiment, not two. The writing was on the wall as to the First Rhode Island's return to the main army. The existence of a distinct black unit would disappear with the merger. Washington asked Rochambeau to release the regiment. "If they should be of no use to you," wrote Washington on November 27, "give your order to Colonel Greene to march to West Point." On the same day, the commander in chief wrote to Greene about the probability that Rochambeau would be ordering the colonel and his regiment to West Point. The sojourn in Rhode Island was over. The First Rhode Island marched west to the Grand Army and, conformable to the reorganization plan, was amalgamated into the Second Rhode Island, forming a new unit called "the Rhode Island Regiment." As of January 1, 1781, the new regiment had nine companies, eight regular and one light infantry, two of which were composed of men of color only, except for commissioned officers. One of these companies was headed by Zephaniah Brown, a familiar face to the First Rhode Island, and the other company was headed by Dulee Jerauld, formerly of the Second Rhode Island. Former First Rhode Island captains Cole and Holden each headed a white company. Corporals reappeared in force on the muster rolls of the Rhode Island regiment, and these men were all white. Although headed by Christopher Greene, it is obvious that the decision makers in the army wanted to shake things up.[75]

The newly reformed Rhode Island line encamped outside of Peekskill, New York, near the Croton River. They named their base of operations Rhode Island Village. Another of the changes the First had to negotiate was the presence of the enemy. But despite being only fifteen miles from the British lines outside of New York City, the Rhode Islanders saw few British troops. Rather, the continentals had to contend with an audacious loyalist unit under James De Lancey, former sheriff of Westchester County. Called De Lancey's Corps or sometimes "the Refugees" (because they had lost their homes), these Americans faithful to the British Empire continually raided towns in Westchester County, burning houses and taking prisoners. They also were called cowboys because they corralled sheep and cattle to take back to the British lines. Washington would send soldiers to ferret out the loyalists, occasionally coming back with a couple of prisoners. Such setbacks did nothing to dampen the ardor or activity of De Lancey's men. So at the time of the First Rhode Island's arrival in New York State, there was a full-fledged *petit guerre* occurring between the lines of the two armies.[76]

Just beyond the American lines was a small outpost on the Croton called Pines Bridge. An advanced unit was stationed there. Its usual duties included checking the flags of truce that accompanied movement back and forth between the lines, often comprised of families that wanted to go to British-occupied New York City. These often consisted of women and children who sought to be reunited with husbands and fathers. Men of the eighteenth century held a sometimes-fatal assumption that women were not interested in or capable of conveying information to the enemy. A woman was to be treated in a courteous manner by gentlemen. Women were consequently permitted a latitude of movement unavailable to most men. It is possible that an observant woman carried back valuable information about troop dispositions at this outpost. The unit responsible for guarding the lines in May 1781 was the Rhode Island Regiment, along with units from the New Hampshire line.[77]

Early on the morning of May 14, 1781, a band of approximately 250 loyalist soldiers led by James De Lancey thoroughly surprised the sleeping outpost, killing eight, wounding four, and carrying twenty-four prisoners back to New York City. Major Flagg was shot in the head while still in his bed. Colonel Greene tried to put up a fight and was bayoneted to a stupor and then carried out to the woods where he expired. Most of the others killed were black men, who either died that day or of their wounds shortly thereafter. Most of the prisoners taken were white men.[78]

As the officer in command of these men, Greene must carry the responsibility for this debacle. It appears that De Lancey knew that Greene's sentinels retired at dawn and timed his attack accordingly. Greene knew that the Refugees were a power to be reckoned with. Back in the summer, General Heath had criticized the First Rhode Island for the very same practice of retiring sentinels during the day in Providence. Heath had also cautioned Major Flagg to be ever vigilant about the Tory rangers once the regiment reached New York State. Heath, the faultfinder, the persnickety know-it-all paper pusher, turned out to be right.

Contemporary accounts of the events leading up to the massacre as well as recollections afterward fill in the story's bare outline. One month before the event, Greene wrote a breezy letter to Samuel Ward, a military colleague and friend from Rhode Island. In it Greene touched on three items that would prove crucial to what was to come. He had just recently been on the lines at Pines

Bridge and noted that he had only two hundred men, including officers, to guard twenty miles but expected that once many of his men came out of the smallpox inoculation process, he'd have three or four hundred. "I have been much indulged and consequently lazy since I arrived here," he wrote. Dining out was the most regular duty he had been called upon to perform. But Greene was not unaware. In the next paragraph, he wrote about the "Cowboy" raids and how the laws of the state were not sufficiently punitive. "I have heard of many being taken," he wrote, "and none hanged."[79]

Three weeks later, Greene wrote Heath about calling back troops on command so that they could join the "little force" on the lines. He also mentioned that the troops had not eaten any meat in the previous five days, acknowledging the difficulty of procuring such provision when the teams pulling the wagons had no grass or hay to eat. Indeed, the provision issue had Washington "distressed beyond imagination." The commander in chief decided to send General Heath to New England to implore the states there to contribute to the continental larder. Consequently Heath wrote to Greene that he would send his black servant back to the lines and would delegate Greene's provisioning issues to a major in Heath's absence.[80]

The element of surprise was evident in all the contemporary accounts of the raid. General Heath received word of the action a week after it happened. Greene, a "brave and intrepid officer," in Heath's estimation, had nevertheless been "surprised" because it was his habit to call off the guard at dawn, thus making a passable ford in the river like an open door. The enemy was upon the camp before the soldiers knew what had hit them, wrote Heath. The brother of one of the dead officers related that the river was thought *not* to be fordable. De Lancey divided his command, sending troops to two places that morning. They fell upon soundly sleeping sentinels. Jeremiah Greenman, a lieutenant who headed a guard unit that night, related in his diary that the appearance of De Lancey's corps of Refugees was so sudden that there was no prospect of escape. He surrendered himself and his men.[81]

Two individuals who well knew Colonel Greene and his men both related their recollections well into the nineteenth century. The Marquis de Lafayette on his American tour in the 1820s centered his story around Greene's black servant, Prince. Lafayette incorrectly labeled the attacking force as British soldiers sent to capture Colonel Greene and Major Flagg. According to the Frenchman, the two continental officers, along with Prince, had been hunting on May 13 and chose a deserted hut to spend the night. At daylight, Prince heard footsteps but too late to rouse his companions before an enemy officer was in the room demanding their surrender. The continentals refused. Instead of taking them prisoner, Lafayette related that Greene and Flagg were bayoneted "before they could rise from the ground." Prince threw himself on Greene as the bayonets tore him apart. The only soldier named Prince who was wounded that morning was a veteran soldier, Prince Childs, who had just passed his fourth anniversary in the Continental Army on the day before the attack. He died a week later of his wounds.[82]

The most poignant of the recollections of that sad day was provided by Major John S. Dexter, an officer who served with all the men who fell. Dexter was one of the five captains who had trained the new black recruits back in 1778. He was in the vicinity when disaster struck. Two black men who had previously served under him died that day. Two friends with whom he had served since 1777 also fell. In the nineteenth century, when members of the First Rhode Island applied for pensions, it was Major Dexter who verified the veterans' service from the "Regimental Book of Occurrences." His matter-of-fact reports appear everywhere in the Rhode Island pension files. When a widow of one of the soldiers captured on May 14 applied for a widow's pension, Dexter provided more than the typical enlistment date and duration of service. He described how the soldier, posted as a picket, had been captured by De Lancey's men near Pines Bridge and then taken to New York City, never to return. Totally out of character, Dexter filled a whole page of narrative and then dutifully signed the document. But he was not finished. On the next page, as if still in the coils of an event that would not let him be, he continued:

> As I have in the preceding certificate mentioned the manner of Wilkenson's capture, I beg permission to narrate some melancholy circumstances which attended or made a great Part of that unfortunate Event. The attack on the Picquet [picket] was at early dawn: Colonel Greene and Major Flagg, who the preceding night lodged near the Picquet for the benefit of procuring Forage in the neighborhood, and nine privates were killed and lieutenant and an Ensign, one sergeant and twenty-one Privates were taken Prisoners and carried into New York; of the latter one died in Prison and three were claimed by the Enemy.

In a matter-of-fact way, the old major managed to convey his emotions fifty-five years later as the names in his regimental book brought back a flood of memories.[83]

Another of the elements that characterized the Pines Bridge disaster was the carnage associated with a military action that was not a fair fight. Lafayette's version has Flagg and Greene still on the ground when the bayonets and sabers did their work. In Henry Flagg's narrative, his brother, Ebenezer, was shot in the head through an open window by his bed. When the enemy broke into the room, they thought Flagg was still alive and being "sullen." So they tried to rouse him with "several sword cuts on the back." When they finished with Greene, he was an "inhumanly mangled corpse," according to Flagg. Stephen Olney's version has Greene still alive when the attackers put him behind one of the enemy's horsemen who rode out into the woods only to have Greene's body fall to the ground. That is where his men found him later in the day.[84]

The only documentation we have of the wounds sustained by any private was recorded decades later when a supporter of a pension application described Prince Robinson's blind eye and lame leg received when "the Black Regiment was cut to pieces." Scars from a saber wound to the head extended from his temple, over the eye, and through one side of the opening of the nose. Left for dead, a white soldier noticed sign of life in Prince Robinson and took Prince "in his arms from among the dead and wounded in the field and carried him into camp." Prince survived and lived to be an old man before he died in 1830.[85]

Almost all of the accounts of Pines Bridge (sometimes referred to as "Crompond" in the soldier pensions) provided by contemporaries of the event emphasized the plight of the officers who fell. The emphasis on officers had a special resonance for the eighteenth-century public. Men above the noncom rank, as men of honor, were considered to be gentlemen who had to be treated with courtesy. Both sides routinely kidnapped enemy officers mostly to effect prisoner exchanges. De Lancey was an experienced practitioner of this gamesmanship. His men typically did not kill continentals. That would defeat the purpose of a mission. On the battlefield and off, officers were a separate class. When captured, an officer was not typically thrown into a prison cell as were the rank and file. When Lieutenant Greenman was taken to New York City on May 14, he was treated "very politely" and then separated from his men, who were put into the city's dreaded Sugarhouse prisons. Greenman signed a parole and was quartered with a family on Long Island. He read novels, sewed new clothes, sampled the area's churches, and socialized with the neighbors. This "sedentary" existence, as he referred to it, continued until he was exchanged.[86]

What happened on May 14 to Flagg and Greene violated the code of military civility, at least from the continentals' perspective. There was no fair fight. "Unmanly rage" was said to have run through the attackers. Their leader, James De Lancey was said to have "stooped so far from the Dignity of a Gentleman as to command a Regiment of freebooters." This critique characterized the Whig newspaper accounts of the event. The *Newport Mercury* and the *Providence Gazette* carried identical coverage. De Lancey's band of 260 men came "down on their [the Rhode Islanders] backs," it was written, implying cowardice on the part of soldiers who did not face their enemy. They began the attack "by firing into the Houses, and cutting down all before them, in the most inhuman manner before our People could be formed." Colonel Greene was "cut to pieces,"

Major Flagg "was inhumanely murdered in his Bed." As for the other victims, they were "cut and mangled' in such a way that the wounded could not possibly recover. And, finally, the marauders were chased off by "a small party," implying that this rabble could not face even a few well-armed and fully awake men. The *American Journal and General Advertiser* departed from the journalistic convention of the time by listing *all* of the casualties of May 14 in its Fourth of July edition. Exemplifying what Tom Paine called the high price of freedom and what Lincoln would later call "the last full measure of devotion," the simple listing of the casualties on the front page reminded the paper's readers of the sacrifice needed from all the country's citizens to win the war.[87]

The pro-British press in occupied New York City told another story. No mention was made of the time of day this attack occurred. One-third of the report in the *New-York Gazette* detailed the difficulty of getting across the Croton River. Its "unusually deep" condition required cavalry members to hoist up their feet. Some men had to swim across. Having successfully conquered the natural barrier, De Lancey divided his men into two groups, the first of which, under a Captain Kipp, descended on "the rebel Colonel Greene [and] a number of Continental troops." No mention was made of the sleeping men, just the results. They killed Colonel Greene, Major Flagg, and twelve privates, taking one doctor and twelve or thirteen other men prisoners. Meanwhile Captain Knapp of the cavalry attacked the widow Griffin's house about one-half mile away, where he killed eight and took twenty-one men prisoners. On their return, three more were killed and five militiamen taken to New York City. The newspaper account boasted that not a man of the attacking party was killed. One lieutenant suffered a toe wound and one private was slightly wounded in his side. The result in numbers on the American side, it said: twenty-two killed, two wounded, and thirty-five prisoners, including one ensign, two lieutenants, and a surgeon. "The above service," boasted the article, "was completely effected in 24 hours." In every way, reported the newspaper, a satisfactory day's work. Or was it?[88]

That some officers were killed in a military action was not surprising, but the one-sidedness of it all might induce people to wonder if killing the officers was absolutely necessary. This certainly occurred to the people at the loyalist newspaper. More justification had to be supplied, and so the article ended with a sentence pointing out that Colonel Greene had headed the force at Red Bank, where a Hessian colonel had been killed. But again, any reader who was familiar with the action at Red Bank knew that the raid at Croton River was not the same thing. At Red Bank, two prepared forces clashed. At Pines Bridge, the element of surprise was so complete that not one of the attacking party even suffered a serious wound. In an attempt to vindicate De Lancey's men that day, the paper inserted a postscript in italics:

> N.B. *After the rebels had on a summons consented to surrender, they fired out of the windows of a house into which they had retreated, thereby provoking the conquerors to storm it.*[89]

The various versions of the event highlight different aspects, disagree about others, and convey distinct messages. What is clear is that this was not the typical De Lancey raid. First of all, De Lancey led this attack, although the unit was typically led by other officers. Secondly, his men usually descended on a place in the no-man's-land between the armies, rousted animals, burned some buildings, kidnapped people, and perhaps in the process killed one or two individuals. The attack on Greene's men manifested a fervor that resulted in the "mangled bodies" mentioned in the Whig sources and the "storming" of the rebel cowards in the loyalist account. Although Flagg was allegedly shot before he was stabbed repeatedly, the others were torn apart, indicating that the weapons of choice were the bayonet and the saber, silent killers tailor-made for a surprise attack in the vicinity of the main army. The exaggerated number of killed soldiers and the underestimated number of wounded given in the loyalist paper could be a case of simple exaggeration or an honest mistake made by men who so badly mauled the enemy that they thought the Rhode Islanders on the ground were all dead. The Whig newspaper doubted that the wounded would survive. Private Robinson was believed dead on the ground. The list in the pro-independence newspaper on July 4 noted that only ten died, two of whom expired of their wounds sometime later. Regardless of the exact numbers, this bloody thrust on the continentals might have been payback for everything the loyalists had lost—homes, livelihoods, reputation—or perhaps revenge for a previous continental attack on Morrisania, De Lancey's base of operations in what is now the South Bronx.

That the subject of race might have accounted for the ferocity of the attack is a possibility. Most of the rank and file killed were black men. Of those taken prisoner, only three of the twenty-four soldiers were men of color. On the other hand, the men around Greene were reported to have attempted resistance, while Lieutenant Greenman immediately surrendered his men. Whatever their motivations, the victors in this engagement had some explaining to do. And their activities were curtailed after Pines Bridge. De Lancey does not appear in General Heath's memoirs again until August. Once more, there are multiple ways of explaining this. It could be that Westchester County became too hot for De Lancey's Refugee force. Perhaps Washington sent more patrols out to the no-man's-land. Another possibility is that the English put the brakes on De Lancey. The mangled corpse of Colonel Greene might have been a public relations problem for the British side. It would not have been the first time that the British regular army and the loyalist units clashed on how to conduct the war.[90]

Another of the notable elements of the May 14 raid was the excellent intelligence gathering on the part of De Lancey's men. Henry Flagg's narrative mentions that De Lancey had good information. The loyalist newspaper had the raiders attacking Greene "directly after crossing the river." The other loyalist unit knew that more men could be found at the widow Griffin's, a half-mile away from Greene. When Greenman was overtaken by the loyalists, he related, they informed him that they had killed Greene and Flagg. They knew exactly who these men were. Who provided this intelligence? It has been suggested that observant civilian eyes under flags of truce could have imparted useful information, but such persons could not have had the opportunity to procure Colonel Greene's sentinel schedule. Greene had complained about being understaffed, and so the forward lines could have been porous enough for unauthorized movement back and forth. But whoever it was, the person had to be close enough for long enough to know when the sentries returned to their beds and also where Greene might be on the lines when he visited his forward-stationed men. It is likely that there was either a mole in Greene's operation or that a recently deserted soldier took this detailed intelligence straight to Colonel De Lancey. At least one sergeant and three privates had deserted the Rhode Island Regiment after the unit's arrival in New York and certainly had been privy to all the information that made De Lancey's raid such a smooth operation.[91]

Years later, when they applied for pensions, some of the black men involved in the massacre mentioned that they were at "Crompond." Other black veterans who were not there strained to connect themselves to the event. Ben Lattimore from New York State related in his pension application that on a march to Peekskill he had passed through Crompond. Jack Rowland, a black veteran from Connecticut, recalled that he had enlisted in Crompond. For New England veterans, it was a significant moment, alongside Red Bank and Yorktown. The Rhode Islanders remembered the disaster as "Crompond" probably because Colonel Greene and Major Flagg were buried in the Crompond Presbyterian Churchyard. A large stone monument erected in 1900 marks their sacrifice but remains mute on the contribution of African American soldiers who fell that morning in 1781. At the time of the revolution, the church would have been the largest landmark in the countryside surrounding it—its ground made all the more sacred by the soldiers whose bodies were buried there. Hence, the raid's surviving participants from the First Rhode Island most often remembered April 14 as "Crompond." But not all the veterans in the area did so. Others remembered it as "the death of Colonel Greene." White veterans typically labeled the action "Pines Bridge." The white and black communities

Monuments to the fallen at Pines Bridge, Yorktown Presbyterian Cemetery. The monument erected in 1900 (*above*), mentions only the commissioned officers slain at Pines Bridge and then buried in the cemetery. In 1982 Westchester's African American community told the rest of the story of Pines Bridge by erecting a monument (*opposite*) honoring the black soldiers

also saw the raid differently. Their identification with their own race continued to the twentieth century and can be seen in the Crompond cemetery. Alongside the large granite marker commemorating white officers is now a stone honoring the fallen black soldiers of the Rhode Island Regiment.[92]

Although described as literally and figuratively "cut to pieces" that day, the Rhode Island Regiment fought on until the end of the war. The men of

who died at that engagement, often termed by black participants "the Battle at Crompond." The monuments differ as to when the raid took place. Most contemporary sources indicate May 14, 1781. Photographs by Lisa Flanagan, First Presbyterian Church of Yorktown, Yorktown Heights, New York.

color worked in two segregated companies, a minority of the consolidated regiment, comprising at most 20 percent of the privates in the Rhode Island line. Five months after Crompond, they marched south with the French army they had known back in their home state to finish off Lord Cornwallis's troops in Virginia. An aide de camp of General Rochambeau noted that the Rhode Island regiment was "the most neatly dressed, the best under arms, and the most precise in its maneuvers." The Marquis de Chastellux met up with a detachment of the Rhode Island Regiment in January 1781 and referred to it as "the same corps we had with us all last summer." They looked like new men to Chastellux, though, because they were now properly clothed. "The majority of enlisted men are Negroes or mulattoes," said Chastellux, "but they are strong, robust men, and those I saw made a very good impression." No longer a regiment but still constituting a recognizable force, the black men of the Rhode Island line helped to provide the stroke that would eventually convince the British to lay down their arms and go home.[93]

The First Rhode Island Regiment was in a position to answer the critiques about black men's abilities as soldiers because they were a discernible "colored" unit within Washington's army. Except for a few companies, other black men, scattered about the army, were a minority in their units, making it difficult to single them out for assessment. But there was no denying that the First Rhode Island, whose rank and file were men of color, comprised a key component of General Sullivan's unbreakable right flank at the Battle of Rhode Island. Indeed, their color attracted the notice of "some persons" in the army after the battle who complained about the black men's alleged ineptitude. This assessment rose to the level of the commander in chief, who dismissed the rumor and praised the regiment's performance. Inadvertently George Washington's support might have caused more problems, because his defense of the First Rhode Island went out in orders to the entire army so all the soldiers would now know of the allegations. At no other time during the war did the rank and file of a continental regiment come in for criticism about their performance in battle. Racial prejudice could well have accounted for this chapter of the First Rhode Island's history. Later letters from Rhode Island commanders and General Washington amply demonstrate that race negatively figured in their decisions about recruitment. And perhaps this prejudice in the army played a role when Rhode Island requested that some continentals stay in the state once the British had decamped. Washington decided to leave the First Rhode Island behind. Isolated from the main army, the black soldiers whiled away their time making fascines for the rest of the army. General Washington acted like a true Virginian when he ordered the Black Regiment into a purely supportive role. His native state had dictated just such jobs in the legislation allowing black men to serve in Virginia's military.

A little over two years later, in the army reorganization, the two Rhode Island regiments were merged into one at the main encampment on the Hudson River. In the new arrangement, black men comprised two segregated companies, while some other men of color belonged to the new regiment's elite light infantry unit. It was at this time that foreign soldiers praised the black men's appearance and competency. When the Americans stormed one of the two British redoubts at Yorktown, the Rhode Island Regiment's light infantry company under Captain Stephen Olney led the charge. In the thick of this action, black soldiers of Olney's company followed Alexander Hamilton up into the British fortification, making the British position at Yorktown untenable.

From the black men's perspective, a history encompassing such achievement and such persistence in the face of white prejudice must have engendered a sense of solidarity among the rank and file. They represented their race like no other unit in George Washington's army. Known at the time as the First Rhode Island or "Greene's regiment," the rank and file, along with their white officers, became known as the Black Regiment in the nineteenth century. Working for two years in a largely black unit, with perhaps black corporals, the men might well have experienced liberation beyond their departure from slavery. They did not have to defer as much to other white soldiers. They could relax in not having to pay as much attention to white sensibilities. They could understand one another's jokes and accents, which meant less chance of unpleasant misunderstandings to occur. And they moved forward, accomplishing each task and mission as a body of black men.

The number of states that considered an all-black regiment and then decided against it makes the Rhode Island experiment all the more extraordinary. Whether soldiers before the Slave Enlistment Act, former slaves turned soldiers, or subsequent recruits, the black men of the First Rhode Island played a significant role in the Revolution, such that their colonel, Jeremiah Olney, addressed them at the end of the war, praising them and promising his help for the rest of his life. The black recruits' gutsy decision to make a large down payment on their freedom in the capital of the American slave trade would also merit special recognition from nineteenth-century black abolitionists. These abolitionists carried on the fight, armed with a history that they demanded include the sacrifices of their forefathers.

CHAPTER 4

The Black Regiment

John Laurens's "Excentric Scheme" and Henry Laurens's Dilemma

Unlike Rhode Islanders, South Carolinians would not see their way clear to fielding a black regiment, even though one of the state's most powerful politicians, a slaveholder himself, eventually recommended it. Goaded by his idealistic and vainglorious son John, Henry Laurens dealt with the issue of blacks as soldiers in the context of his relationships with slaves in his service. During and after the Revolutionary War, the North and South made turns in opposite directions with respect to African Americans' freedom. An examination of Laurens's dilemma shows how powerful a hold slavery had in the mind of an relatively enlightened slaveholder. An examination of his slaves shows that they dealt with the issues of slavery and freedom as assuredly as did black soldiers. Laurens's slaves would not get the opportunity to join the continental line. Their struggle took place on different terrain. As we will see, Scaramouche, Sam, and Mary claimed their freedom by doing battle with the everyday constraints of their situation. Another of Laurens's slaves, Robert Scipio Laurens, would also encounter constraints on his freedom in the cosmopolitan world of his master's abode in England. John Laurens's scheme to enlist the military services of slaves would connect his father and these slaves in a new way by encouraging the elder Laurens to envision capable and brave black soldiers, a far cry from the docile and obedient drudges of Henry's worldview. As it turned out, this was a dangerous idea to white South Carolinians, as incendiary as any British bomb.

    The man who had actually written out the letter from George Washington to the governor of Rhode Island concerning the formation of a black regiment was a young aide on the general's staff, John Laurens. This twenty-four-year-old soldier hailed from one of the most prominent slave-owning families in North America. No other state joined Rhode Island to form a black regiment, but the most unexpected attempt at fielding one came from South Carolina. Only a month after writing out Washington's letter, this young maverick defied his

Charles Town neighbors and began to persistently pressure his father to transform slaves into soldiers, and then into free men.[1]

Hundreds of miles of bad roads separated Rhode Island from South Carolina, yet the ties that bound these two colonies were profound. Rhode Island's business community had a hand in procuring the Africans who would work in South Carolina's rice and indigo fields. In addition to economic connections, there were social ones as well. Newport was a popular summer refuge from Charles Town's heat and disease. Known as the Carolina Hospital, Newport saw an influx of southerners every May and June who stayed until October or November. Unlike any other affluent refugees from the American colonies, the South Carolinians merited frequent mention in the *Newport Mercury* after their ten-to-fifteen-day voyage on the Atlantic. Well-known families, like the Rutledges, the Legares, the LeMottes, and the Gibbeses debarked on Newport's Long Wharf to start their summer vacations. Their ships also brought back prominent New Englanders from their jaunts to Charles Town. Men's names headed the published lists of luminaries. Only women traveling on their own with children were mentioned by name. These elites were certainly accompanied by slaves, who made a rare appearance in the newspaper as "servants." These southern visitors arrived in a city where blacks totaled 13.5 percent of the population, the closest a northern city would come to Charles Town's 50 percent. They saw black men performing a range of duties, from hefting crates and lugging baggage on the city's docks to serving dinners at their friends' homes. The southerners socialized with the Newport elite like the Browns and the DeWolfs, whose firms delivered Africans to the American colonies. The elegant townhouses and exquisite Chinese porcelain that graced the burgeoning port city of Charles Town were the result of a vast trading system that put similar niceties in the lives of New Englanders. There is no mention of Laurens family members cooling off in Newport, but there is enough of a connection, perhaps of the business kind, to find Henry Laurens donating money for the founding of Rhode Island's college, later to become Brown University. By the time that Rhode Island started its black regiment, Henry Laurens was president of the Continental Congress and his son John worked on General Washington's staff.[2]

John Laurens grew up in a slave society whose population was 60 percent black, with a concentration of these slaves along the coast. He understood that his father's workers represented more than brute labor. Africans from the rice-growing regions of their homelands brought innovations that made that staple the most lucrative crop in South Carolina. When his father had traded slaves, he had advertised sales of Africans, often featuring people from the "Rice Coast" or "Windward Coast"—present-day Liberia and surrounding countries.

His family's slaves continued to make improvements on the family's plantations. Despite this background, young Laurens saw no innate inferiority in slaves but rather a system that robbed its victims of the "manners and Principles" of free men. A regiment he proposed to lead would shoot down the enemy a well as the "absurd arguments" that supported the institution. As Laurens put it, he would advance those "unjustly deprived of the Rights of Mankind" and provide a period of time for the men to adjust from slavery to liberty.[3]

The young Laurens was not whistling in the wind. He had every reason to expect his father's support. Henry Laurens was a critic of the institution of slavery although he owned hundreds of slaves on eight plantations in South Carolina and Georgia. The elder Laurens started his career as a part of a slave trading company. After amassing a fortune, he pulled out of the business in the early 1760s, privately expressing his opposition to slavery while publicly claiming in 1769 that the "Goodness of my Heart" had nothing to do with it. The aggravation was not worth the money, he said. His opposition to the idea remained firmly in the realm of the theoretical and had no impact on the reality of his rice and indigo plantations. Believing that slaves were the heart of the South Carolina economy, Henry Laurens would "proceed with caution" on the subject of freeing his own slaves, believing that some day the time would be right. Laurens was not at all sure if that day had arrived when his son's letter reached him in 1778.[4]

The elder Laurens's hesitation is understandable given the world that he inhabited. Here slavery was embedded in the colony's economy, landscape, and in its homes. Founded in 1670, South Carolina saw an influx of settlers from the Caribbean islands, where sugar had created fabulous fortunes for a few on the backs of African laborers. To the north, the Chesapeake region thrived on tobacco, a crop planted, harvested and cured by enslaved people. The enterprising founders of South Carolina looked for their moneymaker and found it in two crops—rice and indigo. Both required significant labor. This was a far cry from Rhode Island, where dairying, fishing, lumber production, and simple staple farming could be handily done by families. Furthermore, Rhode Island's slave-trading empire did not require the presence of black people in its society, so arming slaves was not nearly as terrifying an idea as it was in the Deep South.[5]

Henry Laurens could also look back in his own life and find reasons to temper his young son's enthusiasm. His maternal grandfather had met his end in the 1712 slave rebellion in New York City. Twenty-seven years later, Henry himself, at the tender age of fifteen, lived through South Carolina's most serious slave rebellion. On Sunday morning, September 9, 1739, an indeterminate number of slaves met at the Stono River and broke open a store to obtain its stock of guns. They proceeded to head south (probably toward Spanish Florida), killing whites in their path and picking up more recruits until their force numbered between sixty and one hundred men. Their fatal mistake was to pause in a field to celebrate, and there militiamen caught up and defeated them. Bands of these rebels escaped the field, however, and caused great fear among whites in the lowlands for weeks afterward. One leader was not caught until 1742. Sixty people lost their lives, twenty-five of whom were white. The rebellion was not nipped in the bud like others had been. It happened. Blood was spilled. There was no reason to think that an enlarged version of Stono could not happen at any time. South Carolina elites passed a new slave code in 1740, tightening up the conditions under which the enslaved would live. They also slapped a prohibitive duty on new slaves arriving from Africa or the West Indies. For the next ten years, as Henry Laurens was growing into manhood, very few slaves from abroad descended gangplanks into Charles Town.[6]

The impending catastrophe of slave insurrection looming over sunny Carolina dampened any public criticism of slavery or its harsh enforcement. Early Anglican missionaries might express qualms about slavery in their reports back home, but their public stance sustained the system by preaching obedience and humility. Henry Laurens's church, St. Philips, was built with the proceeds of rum, brandy, and slaves. The minister there received a compensation package that included a male and a female slave. The institutions of Laurens's world—governmental, religious, and cultural—remained virtually mute on the morality of the institution. But for the private scruples of men like Henry Laurens and the letters of missionaries, there was no questioning of the system—that is, until the British decided to tax the American colonists.[7]

Depriving the colonies of their property and hence their liberty led to reams written of a British plot to enslave Americans. When this dispute ripened into military conflict, the presence of able-bodied men of color could not be ignored. When the Laurenses considered the idea of a black regiment, their frame of reference was the enslaved population who shared their lives. The core of the proposed regiment would consist of these people. It is worthwhile, then, to attempt to plumb the Laurens's complicated relationship with their slaves. Clarifying this relationship can also shed light on the complexity of arming slaves and then freeing them in a slave society. Examining the slaves at Mepkin Plantation also reveals the ways in which enslaved people living in a slave society fought against the status quo during the war.

On one end of the relationship are individuals who are difficult to know. Most of the enslaved people on Henry Laurens's plantations most frequently appear in the family's correspondence as anonymous characters. Groups appear more often than individuals. In 1771 at Mepkin, the main Laurens plantation,

Henry promised well-behaved slaves the best material for clothing. In 1773 Mr. Casper, an overseer, was dispatched to look for three runaways. Occasionally a name makes an entrance for one or two scenes and then disappears from the records. Satira's right arm was seriously burned by a lightning strike. Leverpoole had to see to the wild indigo seed. Old Cufffy was abused by an overseer who in Laurens's mind did not measure a "tythe in virtue of that Black Man." When Laurens was in Europe, he would sometimes ask his correspondents in South Carolina to convey his regards to certain named slaves—always in some form of "howdy."[8]

But the slaves who most often appeared in the family's letters were those who were too assertive, too daring, too uncooperative—sticky cogs in the wheel of a smoothly functioning plantation. Ironically, these same individuals demonstrated initiative and courage—qualities found in good soldiers. Scaramouche was one of a small group of slaves whom Laurens hired out. In 1772 Scaramouche disappeared after he was supposed to take a boat from Charles Town to Mepkin. This "desperate fellow" was caught and left at the workhouse in Charles Town, a place where masters sent their most recalcitrant slaves. Described as a man whom "nothing but chains could hold," Scaramouche was brutalized at the workhouse into changing his behavior. After forty-one days that must have been excruciating, he returned to Mepkin Plantation. Aside from being noted as threatening to run away in June 1777, he never appeared in his master's letters as a troublemaker again. By the end of the war, he is termed faithful, and faithfulness is a far cry from the qualities most offensive to the master—artfulness, sauciness, and impudence. But Scaramouche was replaced on the roster of the uncooperative by Sam and Mary. Sam drank too much, but his owner indicted him for independent behavior. "He stands in his own light," claimed Henry Laurens, "and his example must be exceedingly pernicious to my interest." Laurens was convinced that Sam could be brought into line by just the threat of the workhouse. Mary was a far more serious case. She "corrupted and ruined" valuable men on the plantation, Laurens said. Her son, Doctor Cuffee, ran away with another valuable man, named March, in the fall of 1777. Cuffee's value might have been enhanced by the possibility that he knew something about herbs and the healing arts, as suggested by his name. As Laurens explained it, Cuffee had been following in the footsteps of his mother, "who had long been the bane of my Negro families."[9]

Also placed on Mary's doorstep was the behavior of one of the plantation's most valuable slaves. March was a driver, and as such he was responsible for making sure his workers brought in the requisite amount of crop. Four months before he ran away, March was confronted by the overseer, a Mr. Casper, for stealing rice out of the machine house. The "very saucy" March fended off the overseer's attempt at laying hold of him and threw the white man to the ground. The overseer ordered the other slaves present to seize March, which they refused to do. Later on, the overseer heard "a noise in the Negro yard." Upon investigation, he found that the "desperate fellow" had cut off his left hand "above the thumb," which did not hinder him from advancing on Casper with his bloody knife. Sent to Savannah to be cured, March was then to be thrown in the Charles Town workhouse and faced possible later punishment from Casper in "the presence of all the Negroes." March certainly had inducement to run, either before or after Casper's revenge.[10]

Four months later, Henry Laurens held Mary, Doctor Cuffee's mother, responsible for March's "temerity." Before "his connexion with her," said Laurens, March had been an "honest, orderly fellow." Mary could start a "contagion" and so had to be sold far away from any of Laurens's plantations. Her son shared a similar fate when he was found nine months later. His friend, March, was moved from the Georgia plantation to be strictly watched on the Mepkin property. Mary, as one of the "great transgressors," as well as Scaramouche and Sam, threatened to spread to other workers what Henry Laurens would call willfulness, but what the enslaved might have characterized as their determination to act as free people. Slave rebellions began with individual leaders. Henry Laurens, the professional slave master, understood this.[11]

It is doubtful that Scaramouche, Sam, or Mary had much contact with the Laurens family, being workers on the outer plantations. But Robert Scipio Laurens worked at the family's townhouse in Charles Town. He exhibited assertive behavior that gave his master pause. He became a freeman in England with disastrous results. The example of his life may well have influenced and complicated how both Henry Laurens and his son John approached the notion of freeing slaves through military service.

Scipio was a young, trusted slave who ran errands and messages for his master. From the beginning, he comes across in the sources as his own man. In February 1770, he was instructed to travel far from Charles Town for a letter from a planter, rest for forty-eight hours, and then return to the city with the letter. Instead Scipio rested for seven days and then saddled up without obtaining the letter. This "precipitant conduct," as Laurens called it, did not get in the way of Scipio's entreaties to accompany Laurens and his three sons to Europe in 1771. Scipio must have been a person of great charm or at least a young man who knew how to work Mr. Laurens. Scipio convinced his master to take him along as the family's servant. On arrival at the British port of Falmouth, the slave announced that he would no longer answer to Scipio and that he was now Robert Laurens. His master obliged him in this regard, referring to him ever afterward as Robert, perhaps because Henry Laurens felt that "no Stranger could serve me so acceptably as he" could. Most of Robert's duties revolved around the Laurens boys. He rambled in the fields with Harry and Jemmy. He accompanied the youngest Laurens boy to another town for the Whitsun holidays. He was inoculated with Laurens's sons, and in a line at the end of Laurens's letters, he was often mentioned with them.[12]

Whether caring for the boys, delivering a message, or working for others when the elder Laurens was out of town, Robert Laurens exhibited an independent streak that manifested itself in behavioral problems for Mr. Laurens. In the early days of their European stay, Henry had Jemmy and Robert inoculated against smallpox. Afterward the former had only one eruption around the injection area, while Robert's face and body erupted with pocks. Laurens postulated that it was Robert's lifestyle—irregular eating plus smoking, chewing tobacco, and "hovering around the kitchen fire too much"—that produced "a larger crop" of pocks. Although never sick enough to be bedridden, Robert was not shy about complaining about his condition, or as Laurens put it, his servant "grunted according to his Way, abundantly." Nor was Robert shy about informing his master that the two new shirts just purchased for him were not enough, necessitating Master Laurens to have two more "strong Dowlass shirts" made for him.[13]

In the latter half of 1772, Robert and his master butted heads enough for Laurens to label Robert as "troublesome." By December 1772, Laurens informed a correspondent that he did not want Robert to have access to his trunks. He warned a man who would be putting Robert to work in his master's absence that the black man might pose a problem. Henry's complaints escalated in the spring of 1773. Robert was a spendthrift and a slacker. Laurens gave some hint about the timing of these problems, however, in that the troubles began after the 1772 *Somerset* case (*Somerset v. Stewart*) at the King's Bench in England.[14]

The case revolved around Charles Stewart, a merchant from Massachusetts, who had brought a slave he had purchased in Virginia to England to serve him. Two years later, the slave, James Somerset, ran away and was recovered, only to be put on a ship bound for Jamaica, where it was his master's intention of selling him. Friends of Somerset obtained a writ of habeas corpus, and he appeared before a court, claiming that he was had been unjustly detained. Laurens first noted this case in a letter to his plantation manager back home. He referred to "a long and comical Story of a trial between a Mr. Stuart and his Black Man James Somerset." If not for the fact that supper had just been announced, he wrote, Laurens would have gone on at some length about the case. By the date of this letter, there had been four days of arguments before the chief justice, Lord Mansfield. The one and only time that Laurens put words into his bondsman's mouth concerned the *Somerset* trial. Resurrecting

Robert's slave name, his master wrote, "My Man Robert Scipio Laurens says the Negroes that want to be free here [in Britain] are Fools." It is possible that Robert was of that opinion. He could have compared his lot with the desperately poor on London's streets or he could have been telling his master what the master wanted to hear. As if to confirm Robert's statement above, Henry Laurens wrote that Robert had "behaved a little amiss one day," which led the elder Laurens to tell his slave that "he would not be plagued" by Robert and that "if he did not choose to stay with me, [then he ought to] go about his Business." But Robert would "serve nobody else," reported the master, "and has behaved excellently well ever since."[15]

Laurens's next mention of *Somerset* in his letters occurred a couple of months after the court decision. It was no longer "a comedy." Lord Mansfield had ruled that no master could take a slave from England and sell him or her abroad. The decision was interpreted by many to mean that slavery was abolished in England. Although that is not what Mansfield said, the judge did term slavery as being "odious." Laurens did not hold forth on this case, but he did criticize the slave master's attorney. By this time, his own servant, Robert, began to make his master seriously fret, and the news from back home in South Carolina brought no comfort. An overseer on one of Laurens's plantations was reported to be abusing the slaves. Perhaps affected or threatened by the abolitionist air of London, Laurens wrote to his brother James to "submit to make less rice . . . keeping the Negroes at Home in some degree of happiness, in preference to Large Crops acquired by Rigour and Barbarity to those poor Creatures." He also issued a stern rebuke to the overseer involved, admonishing him for his "violent passion and badness of temper."[16]

Robert, in the meantime, worked for an associate of Laurens, while Laurens traveled to Geneva to see his eldest son, John, in school. In Geneva John had imbibed Enlightenment thinkers and become an accomplished theoretical abolitionist. By late July 1773 Henry Laurens had returned to London, but not one word appeared in his correspondence about Robert for the next seven months until Laurens received word of a "Comical narrative of Bigamy and Burglary which . . . will close the Scene of my foolish Rascally Robert in deep Tragedy." Robert had been arrested for housebreaking and robbery. Laurens figured that Robert's punishment would be "transportation" to America, and, if this were so, Laurens wanted to pull strings and have Robert shipped to Charles Town. "If he is transported to America," wrote Laurens, "it will be impossible for him to escape from slavery," the implication being that Robert was not in slavery in England. It could be that as a result of the *Somerset* decision, the only way that Robert could be forced to return to South Carolina was by a court-imposed punishment for crime. Robert Scipio

Laurens disappears from Henry's letters as of March 10, 1774. He had not at that point been sentenced in the robbery case. To the last, Henry Laurens saw himself as "too indulgent" and the bondsman as an ungrateful scoundrel. Henry's son John knew Robert but for the most part was studying in Switzerland and so was dependent on his father's version of the story.[17]

Throughout his years in Europe, Henry Laurens corresponded with his plantation managers, casting himself as an indulgent patriarch. He had the obstreperous chastised. In 1773, while in England, Henry got word of an overseer who put the slaves in "Violent Labor," as he referred to it. He asked that his manager on the site find some way of getting rid of the cruel overseer and even took the time to write to the overseer to "conduct himself with humanity." Laurens understood the implications of power on the plantation. He was a professional in the business of slavery in a way that a shortsighted sadistic overseer was not. Laurens's measured approach perpetuated the system he privately abhorred. In many ways, a plantation owner resembled a general in his appreciation of power. He understood that beatings were a temporary fix that should be judiciously administered. He appreciated the two-way flow of power, however uneven, between those who commanded and those who were expected to obey. He comprehended that to allow overseers free rein to exercise their zest for inflicting punishment could bring the whole system down. The overseer's whip versus the slaves' numbers—it was a relationship to take seriously. Laurens saw himself and his slaves caught in the throes of a rotten system. His role was to mitigate the suffering, particularly of slaves who worked hard and kept quiet. While concerned with his slaves' happiness, he did not flinch when plantation managers sent men to the workhouse, when family members were wrenched from one another, when stripes were administered to a slave woman's back. But only so much of this could be encouraged. The overseer, in this case seeing the handwriting on the wall, found employment elsewhere.[18]

Although Laurens ceased his involvement in the business of the transatlantic slave trade, he remained very active in advising others on how to make a profit out of it. He arranged deals between the British slave trader Richard Oswald and the man managing the Laurens's plantations in America, John Lewis Gervais. On one occasion he advised a prospect on how to go about signing up on a "Guinea man" (referring to a slave ship). On another he told a potential buyer that a ship of his would serve well for this purpose. Laurens continued to buy slaves, one time from Gambia or the Gold Coast, another time from Ghana. As a private individual he also sold them for other companies. In one shipment, a woman hanged herself with a "piece of small vine," Laurens wrote, prompting his cool calculation that "her carcasse was not very weighty." In a typical example of Laurens's split self concerning slavery, he demonstrated a sliver of humanity by calling the woman a "poor pining creature" while reducing her body to that of a dead animal.[19]

On other occasions Laurens used enslaved people as counterpoints to the perfidy of the English. Whenever aggravated by prominent whites or those he called "riding on four wheels," Laurens compared them negatively to superior slaves on his plantation. He wished, for example, that the British ministry were as honest as his slave Quaco. Part of the problem, as Laurens saw it, was that parliamentary seats could be bought and sold, resulting in legislators who had no business running an empire. If this pernicious practice continued, Laurens could see a day when blacks, "through the mediation of Money and an active Broker," could accede to a seat in Parliament.[20]

Years of self-justification continued up to the outbreak of the Revolution, and neither public nor private abolition came to pass. Meanwhile, Henry Laurens disciplined his slaves by having overseers whip the recalcitrant, by sending slaves to the workhouse in Charles Town, and by threatening to send the "saucy" to the outer plantations. In the spring of 1775, Laurens, as president of the Council of Safety, joined other southern slave holders in fretting over possible slave insurrections. This "amazing bustle" among fearful whites culminated in the uncovering of an alleged plot in mid-June headed by a freeman-pilot named Thomas Jeremiah, commonly known as Jerry, and abetted by two or three whites. "Strong Negro evidence" brought these nefarious individuals to light. In the following week, Laurens reported to his son John that there was very little foundation to the story. Nonetheless, authorities had decided that a few slaves should be "severely flogged and banished." Laurens wrote that if they were guilty of insurrection, the law prescribed execution, but flogging the innocent was "strange doctrine indeed." Yet an alarmed citizenry needed punishments, and the two major players, Jerry and a white preacher named John Burnet, would have to further answer to authorities.[21]

In Burnet's case, the white man had to defend himself before the St. Bartholomew's Parish Council of Safety. A slave named Jemmy had accused Burnet of inciting fifteen black preachers (including two women) to spread insurrection. Another black witness at the trial had heard one of the insurrectionists speak of a book given by God to the King of England that was to "alter the world and set the Negroes free." In clandestine meetings in the woods, Burnet had allegedly told his enslaved followers that "they were equally entitled to the Good Things of this life in common with Whites."[22]

On his day before the committee, Burnet claimed that he knew nothing of the book and indeed had only the salvation of "those poor ignorant Creatures" in mind when he preached obedience to their masters and urged them to reconcile themselves to their lot in life. Despite the fact that he was warned to stop private meetings with slaves back in 1773, the committee urged him to behave himself and vacate the neighborhood. He complied in part because Henry Laurens appears to have given the errant minister a job on one of his plantations in Georgia.[23]

While "Negro evidence" was not good enough to convict a white man, it was more than satisfactory with respect to the black defendant, Jerry. This freeman was different from the average black man because he had money and white supporters. At the trial, those who supported Jerry argued that the act under which Jerry was accused (Negro Act of 1740) did not apply to freemen. In reporting the case to his brother in Europe, Henry Laurens mentioned that one of Jerry's advocates even "threw the Magna Charta in the Faces of the People." Laurens reported that "uncommon pains" were taken on Jerry's behalf, including visits to his cell by clergymen. Despite his advocates' arguments and Jemmy's recantation of his evidence against Jerry, the black defendant was hanged and then burned on August 18, 1775.[24]

Laurens was satisfied because the other witnesses did not recant and because Jerry had lied when he claimed at first that he did not know Jemmy, an alleged co-conspirator who was Jerry's brother-in-law. But equally damning in Laurens's mind was the defendant's personality. Jerry was "a forward fellow, puffed up by prosperity, ruined by Luxury and debauchery and grown to an amazing pitch of vanity and ambition . . . a very silly Coxcomb." Like Laurens's slave Sam, Jerry stood too much "in his own light."[25]

The freeman's death did not close the books on this case, as there was an epistolary scuffle between Laurens, as president of the provincial congress, and the governor's office over the fate of Jerry. The controversial case made its way to London, where the British press reported that during the parliamentary debates on the Prohibitory Act (that expelled the rebellious colonies from the empire), Lord Sandwich, the First Lord of the Admiralty, opined that the colonial governments were so "tyrannical" as to tar and feather three women and "murder a free negro of Property in Carolina supposed to be a Friend of Government." The use of the word "murder" put Henry Laurens's son John, then resident in London, on the defensive. John walked his father's version of Jerry's case to a prominent London newspaper in the hopes of vindicating his countrymen and his father. Henry Laurens had convinced his son that Jerry had urged his compatriots to wait for the British soldiers to arrive and then strike for their freedom.[26]

Seven months after Jerry's execution, Henry Laurens advised his agent in Georgia to recommend that authorities there move against a group of "fugitive and rebellious slaves" on Tybee Island off the coast of Savannah. To use Henry's words, however awful the business, however horrible the prospect, sanguinary measures had to be employed, whatever the threat from Tybee Island. This was not a straightforward case of defending a community from aggressive foes using deadly force. The rules of war allowed a community to defend itself. These slaves were not armed. What Laurens was suggesting struck him as "awful . . . horrible . . . inglorious" so much so that he agreed with his correspondent that Indians would be "the most proper hands" to do the dirty work, with some "discreet" white men to lead the way. Having prescribed harsh measures, Laurens then had to provide some heavy rationalization for the men who were to authorize this operation. If the matter concerned only one colony, he explained, such "sanguinary measures" would not be needed. But whatever was happening on Tybee Island could bring down Georgia and then South Carolina and then the "defeat of the American cause in which the happiness of ages unborn is included." With the stakes this high, the prudent and humane thing to do, according to Laurens, was to kill them all. And of course, the owners of the dead slaves had to be indemnified. This horrifying situation might have prodded Henry Laurens to speed the day when slaves would be free and so not be induced to support the state's enemies. But this connection never made it into Laurens's writing. He had convinced himself that he could do nothing. His hands were tied by outside forces.[27]

Outside forces, most notably the role of the English in slavery, figured large in Henry Laurens's musings almost a year later to the day of Jerry's execution. The slaves on Laurens's plantation, he asserted, were "indebted to Englishmen" for their enslavement. The English Parliament employed a phalanx of "Men of War, Castles, Governors, Companies, and Committees" to extend the trade, almost totally prohibiting Americans of any profits therein. This does not explain how the Rhode Islanders did so well, but perhaps Laurens was not realizing enough profit to stay in the business. He evidently found that using Africans as laborers was more profitable than transporting them across the Atlantic. Of one thing Henry was sure. The English were the ones who currently made a profit through Dunmore's Proclamation as they stole the slaves and then sold them to "ten fold worse Slavery" in the Caribbean. "O England, how changed! How fallen!" lamented the elder Laurens.[28]

Focusing on forces larger than himself, Henry Laurens could sidestep his own complicity in the peculiar institution. He had no influence on Parliament and the big British trading companies. But ultimately the slaves worked in his rice paddies and made food for his family. Turning his gaze to his own plantations, Laurens still managed to exonerate himself. He was born into a slave society, he explained, where Christianity and slavery existed simultaneously. He used the word "abhor" to characterize his feelings toward the institution. Almost as if anticipating the charge of hypocrisy, Laurens explained to his son that he could sell all his slaves tomorrow and realize a tidy profit, but he elected instead to find a way to manumit them. Although his neighbors might see him as a promoter of "dangerous doctrines," and his children might bristle at being deprived of their inheritance, Laurens vowed to "do as much as I can in my time and leave the rest to a better hand." Knowing that there was a day in the hazy future when he would manumit his slaves, Laurens could comfortably sit in the here and now, riding the status quo to continuing prosperity, all the while assuring himself that he was a different creature than his avaricious countrymen.[29]

Such was the older man's passion about the subject (at least on paper) that the son had to slow his father down. In an October 1776 letter, young John heartily concurred with his father's idea but cautioned the older man that freeing slaves should be a process, not done in a moment. Perhaps Robert Laurens's experience in England influenced John, but he resorts in his letter to an earlier example. History tells us, opined the junior Laurens, that Rome suffered from "swarms of bad Citizens" who were freemen. A little more than a year before John Laurens divulged to his father his plan to enlist slaves as soldiers, he was putting the brakes on the senior Laurens's wish to free his slaves. When John subsequently wrote about his plan to create a black regiment, which would provide an interim period of military service between slavery and freedom for the Laurens's slaves, he had every reason to expect parental support, given the elder Laurens's critiques about the institution and his plans to free his slaves sometime in the future.[30]

But John Laurens's 1778 letter dashed his father's hazy musings about abolition at some distant future date. This was a demand to do something here and now. Tired of what he perceived as being the creeping conduct of the war, John wanted his share of the family slaves with which to augment the army's forces. His father's first tactic in responding to his son was to call for "mature deliberation." Implying that John was acting in a foolishly hasty manner, Henry warned him that he risked ridicule if this plan came to light. John was not deterred, which required a more pointed response from his father. Henry responded with three arguments. First, John would need at least twenty supporters who shared his enthusiasm for this quixotic project. Had John consulted Washington? Secondly, John's share of the Laurens's slaves numbered three hundred individuals, out of whom perhaps forty would be soldier material—not enough for a "bold stroke." And lastly, the enslaved individuals involved would deem this scheme to be of "the highest cruelty," exchanging a tolerable and comfortable life on the Laurens's plantation for a life away from wives and children with the possible loss of life or limb. Still, said the exasperated parent, "you shall have my honest sentiments and then do as you please."[31]

John Laurens, by Charles Willson Peale, 1780. Watercolor on ivory, 1½ × 1⅛ in. This portrait dates to when Laurens was a prisoner of war in Philadelphia. Exchanged later in 1780, he left for Europe to represent his country in a diplomatic capacity before returning to resume his soldier duties. Courtesy of the National Portrait Gallery, Smithsonian Institution/ Art Resource, New York.

John responded with the energy of a young man impassioned with an idea. The force of his convictions blew up his father's concerns one by one. He would risk the "monster popular prejudice." He would transform "irrational men" into "well disciplined soldiers." He felt confident that these men who toiled for the luxuries of merciless tyrants would enthusiastically support the plan given this opportunity to liberate themselves from "a state of perpetual humiliation." So far John had articulated an agenda that would have made any Enlightenment figure proud. But then he moved to solve the manpower dilemma by proposing a less enlightened idea, namely exchanging women and children in his lot for able-bodied men. With chillingly cavalier indifference, John was prepared to break up families in the interest of gaining soldiers for the cause. He assured his father that his ambitious plans met with General Washington's seal of approval. The commander in chief expressed to Henry Laurens that "the numerous tribes of blacks are a resource not to be neglected." Finally, John reminded his father of the elder Laurens's desire to end slavery. What better time to do this than the present, he wrote, when enfranchisement could serve the immediate crisis. Satisfied that he had answered his father's queries, John went on to contemplate his regiment's uniforms (white faced with red, providing "a good contrast with the complexion of the soldiers") and to consider possible candidates for officer positions in this black regiment.[32]

Such pleasant reveries were broken by his father's next letter. Perhaps Henry had not meant his previous letter's points to be debatable. Perhaps he bridled at his son's characterization of the enslaved as "toiling for the Luxuries of Merciless Tyrants." In response to John's doggedness, Henry did not mince words in this next letter. He laid out his frustration in the first sentence, accusing his willful son of writing a six-page missive on his "Negro scheme" without any visible plan. Furthermore, there was not a man in America, claimed Henry, who shared John's views. In opposing the "opinions of whole Nations," John would look the fool to his children's children. Henry went on to ask what right John had to "exchange or barter" women and children given that John claimed he had no moral right to them as property. Henry suggested that his son free his prospective black soldiers first and then see if he could recruit them. The elder Laurens would be surprised if four in forty would enlist. Although not "an advocate for slavery," Henry confessed that the more he thought on the scheme, the less he approved of it. Effectively closing the door to parental approval, Henry pretended to leave it ajar by saying that his son could take as many of Henry's slaves as he wanted, all the while hinting at John's selfishness by reminding him to leave a just number for his father and siblings. Believing that this harebrained scheme sprang from his boy's desire for glory and command of a regiment, Henry urged John to return to South Carolina to raise a regiment of white men. He ended his letter by praying to God to add discretion to his son's knowledge and learning.[33]

John got the message. In his next letter, he admitted that any pursuit of the "excentric Scheme" would be unpardonable given his father's rejection of it. The young officer bridled at his father's insinuation that only ambition drove John to pursue "the Negro Scheme." Not so, replied his father. He only wanted to spare his son from the charge of "singularity, whimsicality, and caprice" in putting energy into a fruitless pursuit. "You would not have heard the last jeer till the end of your life," assured the father.[34]

And there the matter rested until the British turned their attention southward in an effort to find the right combination of terrain and loyalism to bring the Americans down. In December 1778, a British force invaded Georgia and took Savannah with the help of an African American who guided the British to the rear of the American lines. John wrote to his father in February that only two possibilities would liberate Georgia: either Spain would enter the war and attack from Florida, or southerners, impressed with the "impending calamity," would adopt his (John Laurens's) "Black Project." For his part, John was ready to transform the "timid slave" into a "firm defender of Liberty." John asked his father, who sat in Congress at the time, to push for a congressional recommendation on the subject of black troops. He also asked for his father's advice on how to deal with the South Carolina legislature.[35]

The elder Laurens consulted with General Washington, who saw no sense in arming blacks until the enemy did. If the Americans initiated the idea, said

Washington, then the British would follow, and they had the muskets to give—the Americans did not. Furthermore, freeing some people would render slavery "more irksome" to those who remained in its grip. In much the same way that Henry Laurens dealt with his son, George Washington chose not to definitively close the door on the idea by saying that arming blacks had "never much employed my thoughts." Surprisingly, no reference was made to the First Rhode Island throughout this correspondence or the fact that blacks in irregular units on the British side had fired guns. Even the South Carolina legislature had already opened the door for black troops in April 1776 when it stipulated that arming slaves or Negroes could be done "for the better defense of this Colony against all enemies whatsoever who shall invade or attack the same, or endanger the safety thereof."[36]

While Washington's response made its way to Philadelphia, the congressional committee in charge of the defense of the southern states warned Congress that the South's people of color could rise up in rebellion. This dire news may have come from Isaac Huger, an emissary sent from Governor John Rutledge of South Carolina. The militia, he explained, could not be counted upon because they had to remain home "to prevent insurrections among the Negroes" and to prevent their desertion to the British, who, claimed Huger, try to "excite them either to revolt or to desert." The South Carolina delegates in Congress, along with Huger, suggested a novel solution—draft Negroes, who would make a formidable force and who were accustomed to discipline. How did arming black men square with the danger of insurrection? The South Carolinians explained that the "most vigorous and enterprising" blacks would be enlisted, thus depriving any possible revolts or desertions from the best leadership. The Congress promptly resolved that three thousand blacks should be raised, to be commanded by white commissioned and noncommissioned officers. Congress would reimburse the owners up to one thousand dollars for every able-bodied man no older than thirty-five years of age. These draftees would get no pay or bounty but would be fed and clothed. They would gain their freedom and $50 each if they survived to the war's end. Since this plan could involve "inconveniences," Congress decided to let the state governments of South Carolina and Georgia choose to adopt it or not. To sweeten the deal, the Continental Congress would pay all the expenses. An ebullient John Laurens was commissioned a lieutenant colonel, and George Washington gave him leave to spearhead the project. John was no longer a lone wolf. Everyone was falling into line. Once an "excentric Scheme," the project now had the backing of Congress. Even his father told him to "do everything respecting" the family's slaves that John and the plantation manager saw fit. And Laurens's plantation manager, Gervais, had already expressed his support of the idea, claiming that the cause could save money on less pay and clothing for black troops. John had every expectation that faced with British invasion, South Carolina might finally authorize his black regiment.[37]

Despite South Carolina's predicament, the state's Privy Council rejected Congress's recommendation. A prominent assemblyman, Christopher Gadsden, called the arming of slaves to a "very dangerous and impolitic step." As Henry Laurens, an old hand at South Carolina politics told his son, "you have been defeated in your first battle in the Field of Politics." With the British poised on their southern frontier, South Carolinians not only refused to use black troops but also refused to do much of anything to help themselves. They initially had refused to supply North Carolina militiamen bound for battle in Georgia until General Benjamin Lincoln, the Continental Army's southern commander, diplomatically twisted their arms. They refused to draft men to fill up the South Carolina regiments, preferring instead to entice its citizens to join with a bounty of one hundred acres of land and a slave. They even proposed to a British force at the gates of Charles Town in the spring of 1779 that the state remain neutral until the war's end with its status to be negotiated at that time. Perhaps not believing his ears, the British general passed on this incredible offer. South Carolina at first refused to move its militia outside the state when General Lincoln sought to dislodge the British from Savannah. The militia refused to put itself under the command of continental officers even though it was paid and supplied by Congress. In February 1779, the legislature had a change of heart and passed a new militia law pledging one-third of its militia for three-month enlistments to help any sister state in need. Refusal to turn out would land the slackers in a Continental Army regiment for up to twelve months. The people of Georgia might well have scratched their heads at the timing of such a bill because their state had just been overrun by the British. The Franco-American attempt to retake Savannah with South Carolina continentals and short-term militia, along with one thousand North Carolina militiamen, ended in miserable failure. The allies lost one-fifth of their force, including General Casimir Pulaski, a Polish volunteer, now brigadier general, who led cavalry units to no avail in the action. A black soldier in the Third South Carolina regiment, Allan Jeffers, saw Pulaski wounded—"his thigh cut off and he died," said the black veteran in his pension application. Jeffers went on to defend Charles Town, was taken prisoner, and then paroled. The foreign officer and the black man whose profile was the stuff of South Carolina slaveholders' nightmares braved the British bombs and volleys in the stead of white South Carolinians who refused to fill up the state's regiments.[38]

While the state of South Carolina made no extra exertions for Savannah just across the river, it did move to protect its capital city, Charles Town, but that effort primarily called for sacrifice from the state's African American population. South Carolina renewed its call for black laborers to work on the city's defenses. It had passed legislation to put African Americans on public works projects at the beginning of the war. But the local committees who were charged with administrating the program slacked off from their duty, necessitating another ordinance four months later that placed the state's governor in a position to force slave owners to cooperate. Now, with the British at their door, the legislature doubled the wage allotted to slaveholders and compensated them further for any injuries sustained by their slaves on the job. Public service ads to this effect continued on regularly throughout the year. By March, the city needed a manager to "overlook the overseers and Negroes" on public works. Even the most shortsighted politician realized that bodies had to accompany breastworks if the English were to be kept out of Charles Town. The South Carolina legislature turned its attention to the state's own less-than-stellar minutemen. Any militiaman who neglected to turn out for inspection properly armed would pay a fine and, on refusing to do so, would end up paying that worst of all penalties—a stint in a continental regiment. To help fill these unenviable units, the legislature allowed for substitutes. If a draftee called up for militia duty could find an able-bodied substitute willing to serve for sixteen months in a continental regiment, that draftee would be exempted from all militia duty for sixteen months. No race exceptions were mentioned with respect to substitutes.[39]

Having swept the state for vagrants to enter the army, the assembly also tried to lure men into the continental regiments with bounty inducements. In March 1778 land bounties were offered. In January 1779 the state offered cash bounties on a sliding scale, depending on how soon after the law's passage the men enlisted. By September 1779 a recruit got a five-hundred-dollar signing bonus and a bounty of two thousand dollars and one hundred acres of land at the end of a twenty-one-month hitch. Still, some men were not enticed and thought it would be a better option to get a British parole that would prohibit them on their honor from any further service in the American forces. The legislature moved to end this shameful abandonment of the cause. To further buttress the failing South Carolina regiments, the assembly thought to form independent companies or perhaps a battalion composed of the foreign residents of the state. Newspaper articles entreated the militia to "rouse" themselves. To further provide inspiration, the Whiggish propagandists reported on victories up north, like Stony Point and Paulus Hook.[40]

The average citizen of South Carolina remained uninspired. In October 1779, as the British were poised to attack South Carolina, a petition appeared in a Charles Town newspaper from militiamen who announced that they had "cheerfully done a tour of duty" and wanted to go home. In their heart of hearts,

South Carolinians perhaps realized that all this activity did not begin to meet the emergency, so they resorted to asking for God's help. Governor Rutledge issued a proclamation designating a day of fasting and prayer. Given South Carolina's paltry efforts, the state needed divine intervention.[41]

While the power structure dithered in half measures, the state's slave population was on the move. Conflict among whites always provided more leeway for the enslaved. Early in the war, Henry Laurens told his brother James, away in England, that some slaves did not turn over their wages from being hired out. "Your Negroes in some measure govern Themselves," the exasperated Henry wrote. Henry also had to contend with two slaves of fellow planter Lachlan McIntosh, who ran away and were retrieved by Henry in Charles Town. Refusing to return to McIntosh's plantation, they were "rather an incumbrance" at Henry's Mepkin Plantation. He tried to sell them to no avail. Seven months later, Henry had them at his Charles Town house, making nuisances of themselves in Henry's kitchen. (They must have been doing something useful for Laurens to keep them.) Hearing nothing from McIntosh, who was in the army, Laurens thought to send them off to public works service, although he knew there was a risk of losing them in that . When Charles Town was besieged by the British in 1780, slaves had to be pressed into service because their masters did not want them working on the fortifications. Henry Laurens was no different. In March 1780, one of his managers promised Laurens that he would keep Laurens's slaves out of public service.[42]

It was during the war years that enslaved March threw the overseer to the ground, that Mary proved to be a bad influence on the young men around her, and that several of Laurens's slaves took to the roads. They did not all flee to the British or to Spanish Florida. Many ran to other plantations to be with their families. Charles Town's runaway ads back to the *Gazette*'s inception in the 1730s frequently mention a family connection, and the revolutionary period was no different. In 1777 Gervais, Laurens's senior manager, mentioned the problem of slaves from Mepkin coming uninvited to the house in Charles Town. He decided to make an example of Collonel, a slave sent to the workhouse for "a gentle whipping." While there, Collonel saw another man executed for attempts to spirit himself, three women, and two children onto a British ship. Collonel mistakenly thought he was next and was "well satisfied," said Gervais, of his "gentle correction." The following year Henry Laurens received the news that several slaves at his Santee Plantation had run away to his Wrights Savannah property. The overseer at Wrights Savannah seemed very pleased to get the extra help, while his counterpart at Santee seethed that the runaways were not sent back. Gervais told the aggrieved overseer to act like a regimental commander and retrieve his deserters.[43]

When reported by whites, slave disappearances from the plantation were almost always conveyed in the passive voice. Slaves were "carried away" by loyalists or were "carried off" by British cruisers, as if they had no choice. Certainly, some of the enslaved were kidnapped and sold, but there were few white masters who admitted to a slave's free choice in leaving. African Americans, on the other hand, did not massage the verbs. Samuel Massey, a literate mulatto slave, wrote to Henry Laurens that some slaves "went off with the king's troops" after a couple of raids on Mepkin. He later related that "two soldiers and three Negroes" had raided Laurens's major plantation as well, and finally he said that "robbers and the Negroes" had left those remaining at Mepkin "in the dreading way." In the black man's recitations, the people of color are active about their business. There is no sign that they were forced to do anything.[44]

The Revolution had emboldened men of color to take off with Henry Laurens's mahogany furniture, papers, and horses, emulating the British and Hessian soldiers in this regard. The Revolution's ideals inspired some of these runaways. An ad in the Charles Town newspaper told of a slave, a former drummer, who had made off with a drummer's uniform from the local militia company. Another ran away with a cocked hat featuring a cockade. Yet another had "lately been much with the army." The ad for a slave named Andrew simply warned that the runaway claimed he was free. One master, whose fury shouts out from the newspaper page, advertised for Limus, of "yellow complexion," who had "absented himself" from Mr. Joshua Eden. Of "saucy and impudent Tongue," this black man had three of his fingertips cut off his left hand, probably as punishment for past mouthing off. Eden gave permission to whomever captured Limus to flog him short of his life. It was the black man's tongue that really irked the master because Limus had faced Eden and boldly rejected the master's power over him. The slave had "the audacity to tell me, he will be free," claimed Eden, "that he will serve no man, and that he will be conquered or governed by no man." The ad ran for two weeks, after which Limus disappeared from the record—whether returned to Eden, employed by masters of vessels, harbored at another plantation, or beaten to death—most of Limus's options were not to be envied.[45]

We don't know what precipitated Limus's actions, but many slaves joined him in flight due to the war's dislocations. The war uprooted many masters and threatened many more with the prospect of financial disaster. Such misfortune, however, fell most heavily on the enslaved, most tellingly at the time of an estate sale. At any time, the death of a master must have occasioned high anxiety in the enslaved community on the plantation. However horrible one's life, the enslaved individual dealt with the devil one knew, had learned what set off a master and his wife, and had the support of the enslaved community on the plantation. But a master's death threatened to take all that away. A few slaves might specifically be given to family members. But there were also instances of large groups being sold off to strangers to cover funeral expenses and any outstanding debts. Here the enslaved individual lived with the stress associated with being torn from one's family and community. Would he or she be among the group to go? When Samuel Elliott died, he gave certain slaves to various family members. He also stipulated that all debts and funeral charges had to be paid before any legacies were distributed. It was his wish that no slaves be sold for that purpose unless "absolutely necessary." His executors would sell thirty-five slaves. Wrenched from their worlds, these unlucky individuals faced the terrifying day on the block. Some estate sales occurred on the plantation, others at various venues in the city, like Jacob Valk's Long Room and the Exchange Building, still standing at the base of South Street. Elliott's concern for his slaves is rare in the wills of other Charlestonians. More typical is William Raven, who instructed his executors to sell any part of his estate to satisfy creditors. One hundred and twenty "prime Negroes" were promptly sold.[46]

As the Revolution closed in on South Carolina, ads for more of these estate sales appeared in the newspapers. In the November 3, 1779, *South Carolina Gazette* we learn that the estate of John Gibbes sold off 260 people, including an "entire gang of Negroes" along with drivers, coopers, carpenters, sawyers, boatmen, and house slaves. Thomas Shubrick's estate offered (for cash only) two hundred blacks, among whom were included two entire "gangs" along with a coach and one hundred head of cattle. Other owners did not wait for death to divest themselves of their human property. As one owner explained it, he sold his slaves because of "the precarious situation of the State." Another owner wanted to "put his money at interest." A group of refugee owners from Georgia pooled their "disposable" slaves at one sale. These slave masters needed liquidity as they faced the vagaries of war. The people on the block faced the unknown as well, but with no control over their fates. They could, however, run away once established in their new situations. Many ads for escaped slaves indicate the likely plantation to which the newly purchased runaway fled. Two months after the 260 slaves of John Gibbes were sold, a slave named Sarah ran away, "recently purchased from the estate of John Gibbes," explained an ad. A month later, seventeen-year-old Harry ran away, having been recently purchased in an estate sale.[47]

Individual acts of rebellion were bad enough, but the prospect of a full-fledged uprising was never far from the white population's minds. As Henry Laurens put it, "Tories and Negro slaves [could] rise in our bowels." Local South Carolina politicians warned their representative in the Continental Congress about the possibility of domestic insurrections. Such a calamity was made all the more possible by Sir Henry Clinton's proclamation of 1779, a reiteration of Dunmore's Proclamation of 1775, offering the freedom to pursue any occupation of one's choosing to "every Negro who shall desert the rebel standard." The invitation was a timely reminder to African Americans in the South that their liberation could come from the king's forces. Enough people of color in Georgia and the Carolinas heard the call to materially help the redcoats in their quest to finally control a substantial swath of territory. The British advance on Savannah in December 1778 included a slave and his overseer who made their way into town, assessed the number and disposition of troops there, and reported back to the British on the location of American fortifications and artillery. Armed with this information, the redcoats advanced on the rebels with the help of a slave owned by the exiled loyalist governor, who informed Lieutenant Colonel Archibald Campbell of an unguarded road that enabled the regulars to turn the American right flank, resulting in a resounding victory. When the rebels and their French allies tried to retrieve the city in the fall of 1779, 620 black men were part of the force that threw them back, serving in the artillery, navy, pioneer units, and two new armed companies of soldiers, as well as in the traditional roles of servants to officers. The British were doing with some success exactly what John Laurens wanted to do.[48]

In early 1780, with his home state awaiting the British arrival, John Laurens's hopes for a black regiment were raised when his father, Henry Laurens, moved from the Continental Congress to the South Carolina House of Representatives. John asked his father to use his influence to raise "a few black battalions," as the Continental Congress had again requested. This time the idea of using the state's black population got some encouragement in the form of ten thousand British soldiers closing in on Charles Town. If ever a desperate hour rang out in South Carolina's struggle for independence, this was it. So it is not at all surprising that the civil and military authorities bestirred themselves—if only to a point. In January 1780 Governor Rutledge stated that it was "impracticable" to procure enough blacks to work on the fortifications of the town. As to filling the continental regiments, "no recruits" had been procured. He urged his legislature to focus on the crisis, particularly with respect to economic controls. The head of the southern army, General Benjamin Lincoln, would have the legislature focus on troop strength. He again requested "arming some Blacks agreeable to the repeated recommendations of Congress." He realized that South Carolina had rejected the Continental Congress's proposal to do the same just nine months before, but Lincoln justified his return to this idea by pointing out that "circumstances were different then. It was a providential measure, now it is an absolutely necessary one." Henry Laurens's committee responded to the general's plea by approving the acquisition of one thousand blacks, with "ample reparation." Three days later, on February 4, 1780, the South Carolina legislature narrowed the scope of action for these one thousand men by stipulating that they were to "act as fatiguemen and pioneers or as oarsmen and mariners on state vessels but not to serve in the artillery." The enslaved would wield a pickaxe, not shoulder a gun, and freedom from service figured nowhere in the deal. A frustrated member of the Continental Congress from Massachusetts, James Lovell, summed up the picture from his perch in Philadelphia. "The State of Sth Cara. have *thought* we neglected them, we *know* they neglected themselves. They will not *draught* to fill up their battalions, they will not raise *black Regiments*, they will not put their militia when in camp under Continental Rules." Yet, complained the baffled northern congressman, "we must exert ourselves for them in every Way." The Laurenses, both father and son, shared Lovell's irritation.[49]

By March, John was writing to his father from the besieged town, lamenting that the Privy Council of South Carolina had rejected his proposed "Janissaries," the term a nod to the brown-skinned artillery soldiers in the Ottoman army. Meanwhile, the city's defenders dug furiously and lobbed shells into the encircling enemy. General Lincoln pitched in to help build fortifications. British forces enjoyed the help of over five hundred black men who busied themselves building earthworks. The British were closing in, with the help of a slave named Lycus who served as a guide. With undermanned South Carolina regiments totaling fourteen hundred, Lincoln depended on the aid of troops from other states. North Carolina provided one thousand militiamen and a contingent of six hundred regimentals. Just before the battle commenced in earnest, 750 Virginia continentals arrived under General William Woodford. Assorted others brought General Lincoln's force up to five thousand men. But it was not enough. On May 12, 1780, General Benjamin Lincoln surrendered the city, along with around five thousand troops. It was the worst military disaster of the war on the American side.[50]

Among the soldiers who participated in this action were African Americans, largely from outside South Carolina. A couple of North Carolinians, Charles Hood and James Kersey, were lucky in that their unit had only made it to ten miles outside the city when the Americans surrendered. They avoided capture. Other fortunate characters, like William Clark, shared their officers' fate. Since Clark was an officer's servant, he left the British lines with his officer after the white man was paroled. John Womble of the Tenth North Carolina learned about this practice and attached himself as a servant to a doctor in order to avoid the prison ships. Others were not so fortunate. Ambrose Lewis of the Second Virginia found himself imprisoned in a barracks and then on a prison ship. Elisha Hunt of the Second North Carolina lost his right arm during the siege. Thomas Lively of the Eighth Virginia nursed a wounded leg for fourteen months while languishing in prison. Some prisoners, like Isaac Perkins and William Lomack, escaped and served on—Perkins in the militia until the end of the war and Lomack staying in South Carolina to fight at Eutaw Springs. Other African American prisoners of war pretended to have accepted a British offer to work for them and become free, only to desert at the first opportunity. Drury Scott of the Tenth Virginia would write in his pension application that, as a prisoner of war, "he then deserted from the British" and ended up at Yorktown. Ephraim Hearn suffered in Charles Town prisons for nine months before he was taken to New York City. There he escaped and made it back to Virginia. Finally, there was a small cluster of black men from Richland County, South Carolina, around present-day Columbia, who served in a company of the South Carolina line that was almost 20 percent black. Morgan and Gideon Griffin were brothers who left the quiet of an upcountry farming community to experience the incredible din of artillery fire during the siege. Allan and Berry Jeffers, from the same county and unit, lost their brother Osborne Jeffers at Charles Town. So although the South Carolina legislature refused to establish an all-black fighting unit, the state saw some black soldiers fighting for its interest when few South Carolina militiamen were willing to do so.[51]

Two days after the city's surrender, Henry Laurens brought up the black regiment to the South Carolina delegates in Congress. Without meaning "a reproach or even reproof to anybody," Laurens posited that had South Carolina "made a wise disposition of a few of those miserable Creatures to whom we owe some gratitude," Clinton, the British commander in the South, would not have prevailed. The thousands of unused muskets in Charles Town could have been "shouldered in our defense," he said.[52]

Once the British forces moved into Charles Town, they used the help of refugee African Americans. Of the 304 people who worked for the British in the Engineering Department, twenty were former slaves of Continental Army general William Moultrie. Of the twenty blacks in the Quartermaster General Department, three had the Laurens surname. Ninety-four worked in the Royal Artillery Department as artificers, drivers, and laborers. The Barrackmaster Department employed 79 blacks. Eleven men worked as laborers in the General Hospital, while twenty women served there as nurses. It is not clear that all these people were free. While the British liberated the slaves who ran away from rebel masters, they kept enslaved those slaves taken on raids of rebel plantations. There were also loyalists' slaves who remained enslaved. Loyalist masters at times provided the services of their slaves to the British, perhaps picking up some extra cash. Such might have been the case for a twenty-one-year old carpenter named Prince, previously employed by the Quartermaster General

Department, who ran away while in town. Runaway ads appear throughout the *Royal Gazette* during the British occupation. Slaves from loyalist plantations escaped to the city and to other plantations where family members lived. A group of six workers in the Quartermaster Department harbored fifteen runaways, both groups owned by the same loyalist master. Other slaves from loyalist plantations escaped to the city and to other plantations where family members lived. The British army proved a magnet for loyalist slaves who wanted to disappear into the army support departments where slaves of rebel masters legally worked. This problem reached such a magnitude that the army published a list of black workers who "legitimately" served the British, declaring that all others would "be returned to the respective owners."[53]

While dispirited masters from both sides lamented the flight of their property, American generals had to figure out how to get the city back. With a discredited Lincoln out of the picture, the Continental Congress appointed Horatio Gates, the commanding general at America's most important success in the field, Saratoga. Gates promptly went down to defeat at the Battle of Camden in August 1780. His army was routed, and a story spread that the general, on a fleet horse, won the race to get away. Two of the blacks in attendance later called the battle "Gates' Defeat" in their pension applications. George Washington did not hesitate to name Gates's successor.[54]

Nathanael Greene hailed from Rhode Island. His cousin, Christopher Greene, had headed the predominately African American First Rhode Island Regiment, whose reputation for service and fidelity had largely remained unquestioned over the previous three years. Yet General Greene at first made no request to give guns to South Carolina's enslaved men. He arrived in British-occupied South Carolina in December 1780, gathered what forces were left, coordinated action with the state's militia, and devised a strategy that rid the South Carolina countryside of Cornwallis and his redcoats. By July 1781 Greene had largely flushed the British back into Charles Town and Savannah while inducing Lord Cornwallis's force to head north into Virginia. Three months later, a combined French and American force reversed the defeat at Charles Town by capturing seven thousand British and loyalist troops at Yorktown. Fresh from his return from a diplomatic mission to Europe, John Laurens was in the middle of the fighting at Yorktown and was the American point man in negotiating the British surrender.[55]

Men of color also played significant roles in the crucial Virginia campaign. When news arrived that Cornwallis was penned in at Yorktown, Rhode Islander private Peter Jennings followed General Washington south to find Lafayette's men already involved in "some severe fighting with the enemy." He later recalled the "constant cannonading" and the French fleet that had barred His

Majesty's ships from a last-minute rescue of the British force. Jennings related that two days before the enemy's surrender, fourteen British soldiers deserted and provided information on the situation within the English fortifications. Jennings was also witness to the official surrender ceremony but from his vantage point did not fully understand the scene. He related that when Cornwallis surrendered his sword to George Washington, the American general stepped back and allowed General Lincoln to accept in his stead. An enlisted man like Jennings would not have recognized Cornwallis. The man who actually offered Washington his sword was not the commander in chief of the British army but his deputy brigadier general, Charles O'Hara. O'Hara first approached the French general, Rochambeau, who pointed toward Washington. Recognizing the insult, Washington declined the sword and indicated that his second in command, General Lincoln, take it. Whether Jennings was close enough to see this exchange or whether he heard about it is unknowable. Jennings's service concluded when he escorted British prisoners of war to Winchester in western Virginia. On his return to Yorktown, he was honorably discharged.[56]

Peter Jennings's role at Yorktown was not as the occasional African American player among a cast of whites. Just weeks before the battle, officers in the French Army noted with surprise the number of black troops at the White Plains encampment. One of these officers mistakenly noted that three-quarters of the Rhode Island Regiment were black men. After the Rhode Island regiments were consolidated into one unit called the Rhode Island Regiment in January 1781, not more than 20 percent of the privates were African American. It could be that the European saw a group of Rhode Island and Connecticut men (the Rhode Islanders camped next to the Fourth Connecticut with their all-black company) and assumed they were one unit. French officers noted the "naked" condition of the continental forces in general and could have confused who was who at White Plains. Regardless of the numbers, the French army officer saw a group of black men that day whom he described as "the most neatly dressed, the best under arms, and the most precise in its manouevres."[57]

Once at Yorktown, the army dug in under French supervision, creating trenches in parallel rows that advanced the Americans ever closer to the enemy. When two heavily fortified British redoubts had to be taken, the French professionals in siege warfare drew the more difficult of the two ("Redoubt 9") while American light infantry attacked the other ("Redoubt 10"). At the vanguard of the American column was the light infantry company of the Rhode Island Regiment under Captain Stephen Olney. Among the numbers of this elite unit were three African American soldiers who faced every piece of metal that British guns could hurl at them. Their commanding officer believed his men were "no doubt thinking that less than a quarter of a mile would finish [their] journey of life." Once the British line was breached, hand-to-hand combat ensued on the parapet—another bayonet battle that ended in success for the Americans. Washington later bragged to Congress that the American group "advanced under the fire of the enemy without returning a shot and effected the business with the Bayonet only."[58]

Yorktown, or as the soldiers called it, "the capture of Cornwallis," convinced the British Parliament that the cost of waging war in America was too high. But the price paid by African Americans was also evident to the soldiers of both sides who wandered around the area of the siege. Hessian captain Johann Ewald painfully recorded the "cruel" decision by the British to expel "our black friends" out of the British lines. The British, low on provisions, cast their former allies out "to face the reward of their cruel masters." Ewald, later on a "sneak patrol" at night, came across a great number of these desperate people wandering in the no-man's-land between the armies. "We should have thought more about their deliverance," Ewald concluded. American soldier Joseph Plumb Martin saw "herds of Negroes," famished and sick in the woods, set adrift by the British. As Martin surveyed the area, he saw "dead and dying" blacks "with pieces of ears of burnt corn in the hands and mouths, even of those that were dead." Another American, St. George Tucker, summed up the misery with a short and to-the-point sentence. "Immense numbers of Negroes have died in the most miserable manner at York."[59] Ultimately the expulsion of the people of color did the redcoats no good. They surrendered a couple of days after their enemies took the crucial redoubts, with John Laurens, a veteran of Redoubt 10, playing a major role at the surrender ceremony.

The victory was a joint French-American operation. Just as foreigners made note of the significance of the African Americans at the battle, so also did African Americans note the French contribution to the American war effort. Jennings noted Lafayette's land force as well as the French navy hemming in the British. Another African American veteran from a Virginia regiment later noted that the battle had opened on a Sunday morning when the French stormed the Poplar redoubt. The next day, the African American soldier found himself in that redoubt, transforming it into a gun battery. Private Ailstock may not have known that General Rochambeau and his siege engineers had run the operation, but he acknowledged their importance in starting the battle.[60]

The soldiers' acknowledgement of the French contribution at Yorktown was well merited. French assistance to the American cause began much earlier than the Yorktown campaign. Even before the official treaty bringing the French into the war, France funneled close to a million dollars to American commissioners, with which they went on a shopping spree in French arsenals: two hundred cannons, thirty mortars, twenty-five thousand muskets, twenty-five thousand tents and uniforms, and finally two hundred thousand pounds of gunpowder. By the end of 1777, 90 percent of the gunpowder used by the Americans came from France. King Louis extended millions of dollars in credit, acted as a guarantor on loans from Holland and Spain, and finally furnished the Americans with outright grants. When the three French expeditionary forces came to America, they spent millions of dollars of French gold to buy supplies for the troops. Could Americans have won at Yorktown on their own? The British army of sixty-five hundred men was trapped between fifteen thousand French sailors and marines, in a French fleet of thirty-eight ships of the line that defeated the British relief squadron, and a land force of seventy-eight hundred Frenchmen and nine thousand Americans. The expertise at Yorktown was also French. General Rochambeau and his siege engineers ran the operation.[61]

Although Yorktown was the last major military engagement of the American Revolution, the participants did not know that. The British were not finished. General Greene was convinced of that. The British still had four times as many soldiers as the Continental Army. In November King George tried to rile up Parliament with a fiery speech urging that England not flinch in frustrating "the designs of our enemies." The Charles Town *Royal Gazette* featured the speech in its March 2, 1782 issue, prompting General Greene to write to Washington that "the enemy are determined to prosecute the war."[62]

General Greene's forces were badly mauled by the campaign in the Carolinas, and the British still controlled the Deep South's two major cities: Charles Town and Savannah. Even before reading the king's speech, Greene went to where many had tried before him—to Governor Rutledge of South Carolina—concerning the arming of black men. Perhaps with the advice of John Laurens, who was in Greene's camp at the time, Greene went right to the pocketbooks of the South Carolinians. He reminded Rutledge that without more American troops the British could easily recapture "the most fertile parts of his country." Why not, said Greene, utilize "the natural strength" of the state that in numbers consisted much more of black men than white? In another nod to the big planters Greene lectured, "The cultivation of the country is so important an object, and so much dependent upon trade and commerce, and both so connected with the possession of Charlestown, that the whole body of the people are deeply interested in the measure." And, he added, the advantages of such a plan far outweighed the expense. Greene said nothing about the bravery of the First Rhode Island whom he had commanded at Newport. Rather, he spoke to the South Carolina fear of armed blacks turning their weapons on the white population. This he found to be highly unlikely because raising black troops would "secure the fidelity" of the black community rather than fomenting discontent or mutiny. In order to dislodge the British from Charles Town, Greene asked for four regiments whose men would be freed and who would be "clothed and treated in all respects as other soldiers."[63]

South Carolina responded with a resounding no. Instead the legislature went about raising troops by offering a slave for each year of service to those who enlisted for the war's duration or for a three-year term. Undeterred, John Laurens urged Greene to press on for the "black levy plan." Two months later, Greene took this plan to Governor John Martin of Georgia, fully realizing that "private interest and imaginary evils will frighten the legislature." Despite Governor Martin's support, the Georgia legislature lived up to Greene's expectations.[64]

So, despite the fireworks crackling throughout the states over the victory at Yorktown, Greene still had the British entrenched in Charles Town, with South Carolina men still loathe to sign on as continentals. General Greene found an impassioned ally in the legislature, as John Laurens took a seat in the South Carolina House of Representatives in February 1782. There he proposed a plan "to take slaves confiscated as Loyalist property and form them into regiments." Instead the legislature set these slaves aside for bounties promised to recruits and reserving them for the army's supply of wagon drivers and servants. Young Laurens was foiled again. John poured out his anger and frustration in a letter to George Washington. The "Voice of Reason," he wrote, "was drowned by the howlings of a triple-headed monster in which Prejudice, Avarice, and Pusillanimity were united." His only consolation was that the vote was closer this time. One of Laurens's greedy cowards, Governor Rutledge, hoped the idea would "rest forever and a day." By 1782 most South Carolina elites were more concerned with getting their slaves back. Slave owners who were allowed in Charles Town shortly before the British departure wrote to their friends in disgust that they were consigned to entreat slaves in the city to stay when the British left. For the previous three months, wrote Christopher Gadsden, he had Billy, Sam, Nancy and others in his house, using every argument to convince them to return to their masters. John Laurens did not know that his time had passed.[65]

George Washington, on the other hand, understood the planter grandees. Writing back to young John, he explained the ways of the world, conveying that he totally sympathized with John's plan (although he had never publicly endorsed it). "I am not at all astonished by the failure of your plan.... The Spirit of Freedom which at the commencement of this Contest would have gladly sacrificed everything to the attainment of its object has long since subsided and every selfish Passion has taken its place." Washington bade republican virtue farewell by saying that "it is not the Public interest which influences the Generality of Mankind nor can the Americans any longer boast an exception."

The Death of Colonel John Laurens, by Howard Pyle, 1899. Oil on canvas, 5⅜ × 12⅛ inches. Illustration for James Barnes, "The Man for the Hour," *McClure's Magazine*, December 1899. Courtesy of the Brandywine River Museum of Art, Chadds Ford, Pennsylvania, and a Private Collection, 2008.

Washington may not have been disingenuous in sympathizing with Laurens. They might have been talking past one another, with Washington thinking about the lack of support he was getting for his own priorities.[66]

In late spring 1782 the unstoppable Laurens turned his attention to Georgia, writing to George Washington that he planned to submit a proposal to the Georgia assembly "with all the tenacity of a man making a last effort on so interesting an occasion." Indeed, this was John Laurens's "last effort," as he lost his life on August 27, 1782, in a raid at Chehaw Neck that most of his contemporaries characterized as foolhardy on his part. With him died (until the nineteenth century) any prominent public voice in South Carolina on the righteousness of freeing the enslaved population.[67]

Like any fallen soldier, John Laurens left behind personal belongings, but in his case these included two of his father's slaves, one of whom was likely Shrewsberry, who had served Laurens in the army from the beginning of his service in 1777. The two black men could well have lifted Laurens's body off the field, cleaned it, and wrapped it. They must have wondered what would happen to them. If any promises had been made, they were as dead as the body in front of them. Any consideration they might have expected due to their connection to Laurens was promptly put into question by a Frenchman who claimed all of Laurens's "linen and Clothing" by dint of a European custom likely unfamiliar to Americans. The French claimant relied on Thaddeus Kosciuszko, a Polish volunteer officer, to explain to General Greene how it worked in Europe. Kosciuszko complied but added his own addendum. Whether prompted by the black men in camp or coming from his own sense of right, Kosciuszko advised Greene that once Laurens's baggage arrived in camp, that Greene divide the linen and clothing between the Frenchman and Laurens's two slaves. The black men, wrote Kosciuszko, were so deficient in "shirts, jackets, and Breeches" that they could be termed naked. The Polish officer did not divulge any further thoughts on the pitiable condition in which Laurens left his servants, but he did add that "their skin can bear as well as ours good things."[68]

John Laurens's black regiment plan may or may not have been known by Andrew Pebbles, a black private from Virginia who noted Laurens's death in his 1818 pension application. On the day before his discharge, Pebbles, who had been wounded in the shoulder, hand, and stomach at Eutaw Springs, participated in the action that spelled the young Laurens's demise. Pebbles noted that Laurens had replaced another officer, Lieutenant Colonel Henry Lee, who had gone home to get married. The black man did not know that Laurens disobeyed orders when he led his men against a British foraging unit. He did not mention that in a last futile attempt at glory, young Laurens had put his men's lives on the line. Indeed, three men died, two on the field and one later on from his wounds. Thirty-six years later, when Pebbles recounted his revolutionary service for the court, this African American veteran's wife and child were still enslaved. The entangled stories of blacks and whites are evident in the case of the Laurenses and Andrew Pebbles. As a free black soldier, Pebbles personified John Laurens's aspirations. The old veteran's family situation, on the other hand, reflected Henry Laurens's failure to make his private convictions a reality in his lifetime.[69]

CHAPTER 5

ON TO THE NEXT BATTLE

THE POSTWAR WORLD AND THE FIRST PENSION ACT

In February 1797, Caesar Tarrant of Hampton, Virginia, being "sick and weak but of sound mind and memory," made a will. He left everything to his wife, including his houses and the lot on which they stood. After she died, however, he wanted all his belongings sold, one-half of the proceeds going to his daughter Nancy, and the other half to be applied toward liberating his daughter Liddy from slavery. In the event that that money was not enough, Nancy would inherit the whole estate, but upon her death, all of Caesar's property would be sold once again and all the proceeds directed "towards liberating my daughter Liddy." Any money remaining would be split between Liddy and her son, Sampson. Fourteen years after the close of the Revolutionary War, this war veteran was still trying to buy his family out of slavery. Perhaps he had purchased Nancy and Sampson first. He neared the end of his life still fretting about the last precious child. In 1797 he found himself in the unenviable position of trying to keep his wife and free daughter afloat in the hope that any excess funds could bring Liddy back to the family.[1]

As Caesar Tarrant's will attests, the American Revolution did not live up to its rhetoric for people of color. Some scholars today consequently label the Revolution as a failure for African Americans. Dismissing the Revolution, however, leaves one with a wide gap between 1775 and the Thirteenth amendment. The black abolition movement did not dismiss the Revolution. It added the glorious language of liberation created in the revolutionary age to already existing biblical liberation language. Along with inspiring words, the African American community added the heroic examples of black men who bought freedom for the country, as Caesar Tarrant was trying to do for his daughter Liddy.

Despite the Revolution's fine words, the Republic meant an increasingly dire time for people of color. The Euro-American culture spun ugly stories about dark-skinned people being inferior. The economy leaned more than ever on slave-produced cotton. No leadership from Washington, D.C., struggled to remind the people of the Revolution's promises to all. The country would just as soon have forgotten the fact that African Americans had participated in what was then the highest form of citizenship, namely the sacrifices of soldiery. Into the generally declining situation for people of color in the new republic stepped the old veterans whose figurative battles with the federal government animated their children and grandchildren, and provided them ammunition with which to throw off a load even heavier than the British redcoats—the institution of slavery.

In the fluid period of war and its immediate aftermath, black people worked in different ways to unite their own communities and to awaken white consciences to the evil they had created. It would not do for them to stand on a soapbox and declaim what to modern readers seems obvious. Most people were dealing with their particular situations. An enslaved man might free himself through military service. A black freeman-soldier might expect more respect and opportunity once he returned to civilian life. As free and gainfully employed, these men could make a better life for their children. Their tactic had been to aid the whites and hope for the best. Did not Tom Paine say that "it is dearness only that gives everything its value"? Men of color had bled and sacrificed themselves. Surely the hardest-hearted white man would recognize a debt to be paid. But despite participating in the most aggressive of employments, these young black soldiers did not push the white community about the larger issues of slavery and equality. For the most part, they were poor and illiterate and had their hands full with simple survival, whether that be in camp or at battles as grand as Bunker Hill and Yorktown or as small as the dangerous engagements at Pumpkin Hill, Bettis's Bridge, and Piss-Pot Swamp. While the soldiers exercised force in the field, there were other engagements during the Revolutionary War at which people armed with nothing but determination struck right at the belly of slavery. We could call these struggles the "Battle of Worcester" and the "Battle of Great Barrington," but their fields of action were not hills and swamps, they were courtrooms.

Worcester, Massachusetts: Quock Walker (1781 and 1783)

The Worcester, Massachusetts, "battle" began with an enslaved man, Quock Walker, who left his owner's farm to work for a neighbor as a free man. A previous master had promised the adolescent Walker his freedom once he reached the age of twenty-five. By that age his master had died, and his mistress had married another man, Nathaniel Jennison. She too passed on, and when Walker claimed his freedom certificate from Jennison, the white man refused. Walker did not flee. He declared his independence and walked over to the Caldwell farm and started to work there. Jennison found him, beat him, and had to lock him up in order to contain him. Once released, Walker found an attorney, asserted his freedom, and sued Jennison for assault and battery. Jennison, in turn, sued the Caldwells for abetting his property in walking off. The cases came to the Worcester Court of Common Pleas in June 1781. The jury declared that Jennison had no right to strike Walker because the young man of color was a freeman. The same court, however, found the Caldwells at fault and awarded damages to Quock Walker's master. These decisions were inconsistent. If Walker were free, the Caldwells should not have had to pay a fine. [2]

This legal conundrum was resolved by the appeals that both sides lodged in the state supreme court's September session. The court threw out Jennison's appeal for lack of the required paperwork. The Caldwells' case, however, began to address questions that spoke to a much wider audience than that of a neighborhood dispute. The jurors who had freed Quock Walker left no explanation as to why they found for the plaintiff. It could be that they believed that Walker had a deal with his former master, in which case one black man was free. Or they could have referenced the new 1780 state constitution that proclaimed that "all men are born free and equal and have certain natural, essential, and unalienable rights." If so, they were freeing all slaves in the Bay State. This important distinction remains shrouded for lack of records. The defense attorney in the Caldwells' appeal made sure that the jury thought about the larger issue. He maintained that slavery was contrary to natural law and God's law. The jury found for the Caldwells, saying that since Walker was a freeman, the Caldwells had every right to employ him. But here again there is no evidence that the jury based its decision on a specific deal made between slave and master or on the loftier plain of basic human rights.[3]

Despite a definitive loss for Jennison in his annus horribilus of 1781, the judicial system had not finished with him. There remained criminal assault charges for his attack on Walker. The case was not heard until the spring of 1783. One of the five judges in *Commonwealth v. Jennison*, Chief Justice William Cushing, stated in his instructions to the jury that he believed that the 1780 Massachusetts Constitution declared all men to be free and equal, thus clearly faulting Jennison and clearly abolishing slavery. The jury came back with a guilty verdict, but there is no indication that Judge Cushing's charge had resonated with the jurors. In one of his legal notebooks, the judge, himself a former slave owner, wrote that "slavery in Massachusetts was forever abolished" with this case. But it is not clear that others saw it that way. The clerk of the state supreme court wrote in 1798 that "as there was nothing of that [the constitutional issue] committed to writing, nothing could be recorded to distinguish this case from any other common assault and battery." Indeed, four months later, Judge Cushing ordered South Carolina slaves to be released from a Boston jail, claiming he was not ruling on whether their permanent status should be free or not. No Massachusetts newspapers in either 1781 or 1783 highlighted either of these cases as ending slavery in the state.[4]

Great Barrington, Massachusetts: Mumbet

"Any time, any time while I was a slave, if one minute's freedom had been offered me, and I had been told I must die at the end of that minute, I would have taken it—just to stand one minute on god's [earth] a free woman, I would." So said an elderly former slave from western Massachusetts who helped Quock Walker push the state's authorities to truly acknowledge their own constitution. Her battle started when Elizabeth, known affectionately as Mumbet, was a much younger woman. At age thirty-six, the widow of a Continental Army soldier, she was a slave, the legal property of John Ashley, a judge and major landowner in Berkshire County. In 1781 she asserted her freedom in a Massachusetts court. Interviewed decades after the trial, Mumbet claimed that the words of the revolutionary movement had induced her to sue for her freedom. Although she did not mention the Sheffield Resolves—the anti-British manifesto of rights, drawn up in Sheffield, Massachusetts, on January 12, 1773—she did work in a house where conversations about its concerns raged. Words such as "equal," "free," and "independent" bounced off the walls of her master's home. "God and nature have made us free," the Resolves declared. More inspiring still were the words of the 1776 Declaration of Independence, although the most pertinent document to Mumbet's case proved to be the same Massachusetts Constitution referenced in Quock Walker's case. As her biographer Catharine Sedgwick (who was brought up my Mumbet) said, "Such a resolve as hers is like God's messengers—wind, snow, hail—irresistible."[5]

Like Walker, Mumbet needed white allies. A prominent lawyer and militia officer, Theodore Sedgwick, took on her case. Just one month before Quock Walker's original motion, Mumbet and Sedgwick, along with legal scholar Tapping Reeve, started the process that resulted in *Brom and Bett v. Ashley*. (Referring to another of Ashley's slaves, Brom's name might have been added to prevent the court from throwing out an individual woman's suit).[6]

The court's decision came in August, two months after the first Walker cases (of which there were three). Although the jury found for Brom and Bett, no trial transcript revealed the legal rationale for its decision. What distinguishes Mumbet's case from Walker's is the fact that no distracting issues like a previous deal with a master clouded the picture. Mumbet simply claimed that she was free. The only way the jury could find for Mumbet was to turn to the state's constitution. But no formal court document said this. Mumbet's master promised to appeal. Two months later, Ashley dropped the idea, probably because news of the *Jennison v. Caldwell* case had convinced him that a favorable conclusion to his own suit would be highly unlikely. Although not publicized in the press, Ashley saw the writing on the wall. After the trial, Mumbet acquired a surname, Freeman. She went to work for her former attorney, Sedgwick, and, along with raising a child of her own, brought up Catherine Maria Sedgwick, who would become a noted novelist and would later record Elizabeth Freeman's version of the case.[7]

Both Quock Walker and Elizabeth (Mumbet) Freeman availed themselves of blacks' access to the court system in Massachusetts and undoubtedly drew inspiration from the African Americans before them who had petitioned the government and taken their masters to court with positive results. Although there were no banner headlines about the demise of slavery in Massachusetts, both the Mumbet and Walker cases were part of a trend in that direction. Word of these positive developments could well have circulated among the soldiers. Agrippa Hull and Frank Duncan, both from Stockbridge, Massachusetts, enlisted into the continental line. Humphrey Hubbard, a black private, served in the militia regiment headed by Colonel John Ashley, Mumbet's owner. A man from a nearby town, James Storm, was recruited into the army by Theodore Sedgwick, Mumbet's attorney. Although it is unlikely that these black recruits had received news of the court case from these elevated personages, they could well have heard about the Mumbet and Quock Walker cases from other Berkshire County soldiers who brought word of local doings to the army. At the main army headquarters in the Hudson Highlands, companies from other states worked right beside the Massachusetts soldiers. It is likely too that black men formed a special line of communication based on skin color. In 1780 soldiers in the Pennsylvania line had their own great news to spread concerning an event that clearly spelled the end of slavery in their state.[8]

On March 1, 1780, the Pennsylvania assembly passed An Act for the Gradual Abolition of Slavery. The law's opening section expressed empathy with the enslaved population by dint of the enslavement that Philadelphia had suffered during the British occupation of the city. This dubious analogy was overshadowed by Section 1's paternalistic appeal to better the condition of a people whom God cherished equally with all his creation:

> It is not for us to inquire why, in the creation of mankind, the inhabitants of the several parts of the earth were distinguished by a difference of feature or

complexion. It is sufficient to know that all are the work of an Almighty Hand . . . he placed them in their various situations, hath extended equally his care and protection to all, and . . . it becometh not us to counteract his mercies.

Such sentiments might lead one to believe that the act freed all the slaves in Pennsylvania. But the legislators in Philadelphia concurred with the "Almighty Hand" only to a point. Politics on the ground dictated that the slaveholders had to be pacified. Thus, all slaves born before March 1, 1780, remained enslaved for the rest of their lives. For those born after this date, they remained in a kind of indentured servitude until the age of twenty-eight. The gradual nature of the new law was not a novelty to the state's African American population. They saw various forms of limited servitude in their society. Pennsylvanians who freed their slaves frequently put them into long-term indentures. Around half of the English, Scottish, and German emigrants in the early 1770s were servants under a contract. Young children bound out by their poor white families did not see the end of their indentures until around twenty-one years of age.[9]

While not outright emancipation, the Pennsylvania law created better conditions for blacks in the scope of a lifetime. Even those born before March 1, 1780, could envision the end of the arbitrary breakup of their families and the elimination of a whole host of restrictions on their children's lives. A young soldier contemplating marriage to an enslaved woman would know that their children would lead a better life than their own. And who knows, perhaps the powerful could be nudged a bit more to reduce the age of emancipation or add more protections for those enslaved.

The Revolution that these soldiers had a major role in sustaining had created possibilities unheard of before the first tax act protested by American colonists in 1764. Even southern black soldiers could be optimistic at the close of the war. Virginia loosened its manumission rules in 1782. A year later the state assembly chastised masters who had promised freedom to slaves who substituted for them in the army or militia and then reneged on their promise. All slave substitutes were declared free as "they contributed towards the establishment of American liberty and independence," proclaimed the Virginia legislature, and so should "enjoy the blessings of freedom as a reward for their toils and labors." There were other hopeful signs for black southerners. The soldiers' discharges were signed by a Virginian. Some may have known that a Virginian wrote the Declaration of Independence. Echoing a line from a famous play, yet another had declared, "Give me liberty, or give me death!"—an idea that resonated particularly with soldiers who had withstood a bayonet charge or survived an artillery barrage. But the southern veterans would soon realize that these positive glimmerings could not withstand the profit motive and its powerful impact on African American lives. For the man who wrote the Declaration would soon write a devastating assessment of black people, while the man who proclaimed "liberty or death!" would never free his slaves, simply because of "the general inconveniency of living without them."[10] The revolution was not done for veterans of color.

The Setting for the 1818 Pension Act

In the summer and fall of 1783, the soldiers of the Revolution simply walked home. It is difficult to know how these men felt about the event before the event acquired a capital R. For some, military service meant three meals a day, however meager, a sense of brotherhood, and a promise of land after the war. The soldiers of color might have worried what would happen to them after they were not needed so much. As Rhode Island veterans walked from the Hudson River cantonment to Providence, Rhode Island, they passed through towns whose white inhabitants might have stared at them with belligerence and distain—the same old treatment. But still, the war had given them the chance to be forceful men—compelling the enemy to retire, toppling the greatest empire on American shores, and humbling the lordliest lords of the British army. Civilian life had few if any comparable outlets for youthful swagger and manly exploits.

The soldiers of the Continental Army left their military lives with a printed form attesting to their service to the country. These discharges identified black men with their first and last names, followed by the words, "a soldier"—not "a black soldier" or "a man of color" or "a Negro private." Oliver Cromwell's discharge identified this former slave from New Jersey as a soldier like all the rest. George Washington personally signed most of the Continental Army discharges. At the bottom of these forms was a space to honor soldiers of particular merit. Signed by an officer of their unit, extraordinary service earned the soldier a badge of merit, acknowledgement of great soldiery by one's leaders—a distinction that a black man could earn, one many white men did not. The military acknowledged that a man of color could outperform a white in a job of great daring and courage. No other institution in American life was saying as much in 1783.[11]

The soldier no doubt placed his military discharge certificate in a pocket of his uniform, another physical manifestation of his service in the war. During the conflict, the uniform gave the black soldier temporary immunity from much of the demeaning treatment of civilian life. When the soldiers returned home, their proud families and friends noted the regimentals they wore,

> **By His Excellency GEORGE WASHINGTON, Esq;**
> General and Commander in Chief of the Forces of the United States of America.
>
> THESE are to CERTIFY that the Bearer hereof _John Brister, Soldier_ in the _Second Connecticut_ Regiment, having faithfully served the United States _from May 1777_ to _15 June 1783_, and being inlisted for the War only, is hereby DISCHARGED from the American Army.
>
> GIVEN at HEAD-QUARTERS the _8th June 83_
>
> _G Washington_

Discharge certificate dated 1783, contained in John Brister's pension application. At the end of the war Brister received this certificate signed by George Washington. Most veterans, black and white, no longer had their certificates at the time of the pension acts. Some certificates were handwritten scraps signed by officers other than Washington, like General Henry Knox or Colonel Jeremiah Olney. Courtesy National Archives and Records Administration, Record Group 15, Case Files of Revolutionary War Pension and Bounty Land Warrant Applications.

however tattered. In 1846, the sister of Humphrey Hubbard, the soldier from Mumbet's town, "well recollected of his coming home at the close of said war ... with his war regimentals on." A white neighbor recalled that as an eleven-year-old boy he had seen Humphrey come home in his regimentals. When a group of Mashpee Indians "paraded" into town at the close of the war, they had on their "soldiers' uniform dress," reported a witness. For family members, the uniform undoubtedly represented the achievement of their loved ones, being physical proof that their neighbor or loved one had made this extraordinary contribution to the nation. New England veteran Agrippa Hull summed up the importance of the uniform when he submitted proof of his indigence under the 1818 pension act. While putting a dollar value on the few pieces of crockery

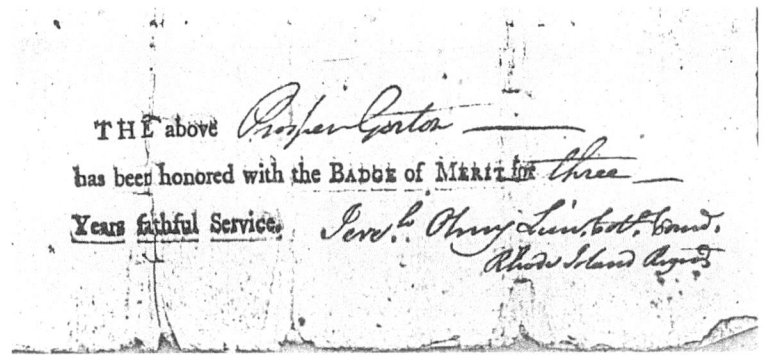

Badge of Merit for Prosper Gorton, a private in the First Rhode Island Regiment. This badge of merit appears at the bottom of Gorton's discharge certificate. Courtesy National Archives and Records Administration, Record Group 15, Case Files of Revolutionary War Pension and Bounty Land Warrant Applications.

and clothing he possessed, he also included a line for "revolutionary uniform," which he estimated as "invaluable."[12]

Revolutionary veterans brought their war experiences home to vastly different situations. The starkest contrast unsurprisingly came from the societies divided by the Mason-Dixon line. Whites in the southern states continued to make fortunes with an economy based on slave labor. Within ten years of the end of the war, southern slave families were torn apart by Virginia's new inheritance laws that permitted owners to divide their estates and all the "property" on them. Virginia's master class also found a pot of gold in selling "excess" slaves to cotton planters in the Deep South as well as to western planters in their own state. More Virginians subsequently had a stake in slavery and simultaneously saw free blacks, whose numbers grew by more than one-third from 1790 to 1800, as a threat. Virginia had long since forbidden free blacks the right to vote, but the state legislature lost no time in moving against free blacks by passing laws that could re-enslave them, limit their numbers in Virginia, and penalize anyone with a hefty fine if they assisted a slave in bringing a suit to court that proved unsuccessful. The state even went after free black orphans by forbidding the overseers to teach them how to read and write.[13]

The postwar struggle of African Americans in the North took on a different cast, but the veterans still experienced a mixed message from the power structure of the new nation. Northern states continued to adopt gradual emancipation laws, thus putting slavery on a course of extinction north of the Mason-Dixon line. But most were not prepared to give African Americans the same political rights as whites. Of the original thirteen states that allowed

Inventory of Artillo Freeman, private in the Massachusetts line, contained in his pension application. Freeman, along with all other applicants of the first general pension act, had to provide an inventory of their belongings because the pension was meant to apply only to men in poverty. Many veteran applicants stretched this definition. Consequently applicants had to supply a list of their belongings certified by local officials. Courtesy National Archives and Records Administration, Record Group 15, Case Files of Revolutionary War Pension and Bounty Land Warrant Applications.

black freemen to vote during the war, Connecticut, Delaware, Maryland, and New Jersey had taken away their right to vote by 1820. In 1821, New York imposed high property requirements for voting only on its African American freemen. North Carolina and Pennsylvania followed suit in the 1830s.[14]

New Jersey was the first northern state to take back a basic right from its citizens. New Jersey's first state constitution, hastily drafted and adopted in the tumultuous summer of 1776, based voting privileges on age, property, and residence—these requirements applying to all citizens with no race or gender exceptions. In the ensuing years, attempts were made to invalidate elections because women and blacks had voted, but these objections were thrown out. New Jersey's enlarged citizenry duly cast their ballots with no concern for the few black men who voted, until the African American community attracted the special attention of the Democratic-Republican Party—the party of Jefferson—because African Americans consistently backed the Federalist Party. The Democratic-Republicans went to work. They pointed out (probably correctly) that the framers had never intended that "all inhabitants" meant just that. If women and Negroes continued to vote, warned the alarmed Jeffersonians, they could become public officials! In case this appalling prospect did not move New Jerseyans to act, the Democratic-Republicans claimed that already there were inappropriate people casting ballots under the current law. They pointed to a Hunterdon County election in 1802 that had hinged on "the vote of a Negro slave." No specifics or proof were proffered. Ultimately the Democratic-Republicans, along with some Federalist support, thought they had set right "the true sense and meaning of the Constitution" as well as insured "the safety, quiet, good order, and dignity of the state" by denying the vote to "aliens, females, and persons of color or Negroes." Jacob Francis, a fifty-three-year-old black resident of Hunterdon County, who had marched to Boston in 1775 and crossed the Delaware in 1776, watched as "No Taxation without Representation," an idea for which he had fought, became an empty shell for anyone who looked like him.[15]

While New Jersey seemed content to let a few women and blacks vote for at least twenty-five years, the slave state of Maryland moved more promptly to cut off the privilege for its free black citizens. Like in New Jersey, Maryland political leaders wrote a constitution in 1776 that did not specify voting for whites only. "All freemen" who met age, residency, and property requirements could vote. In 1783, while freeing any slaves newly brought into the state contrary to law, Maryland's white leaders made sure that those newly freed men had no political rights. These black freemen, no matter when freed, and their children were denied the right to vote. In its 1792 constitution, Maryland tried to cover every eventuality. "No negro or mulatto whether born free or manumitted, or made free under any past, present or future law of this state" could vote in any election. The children of such people were also disenfranchised. To make up for its sloppiness in 1776, the state covered even unlikely scenarios when it prohibited people of color from ever being elected to the legislature or elected or appointed to any office whatsoever.[16]

With blacks safely banned from the ballot box, the Democratic-Republicans now in control of the state added to their core constituency by eliminating the property requirement to vote and instituting the secret ballot so people could vote in private. Previously voters announced their choices at the polling place, viva voce. To this day, the party of Jefferson gets much deserved credit for widening the suffrage to poor people and instituting the secret ballot. But history books rarely chastise them for closing the door to African Americans. While liberating the election process for poor whites, an 1802 constitutional amendment specified that "every free white male citizen of this state, and no other" could vote. An amendment ratified in 1810 reiterated this exclusion, with no need to mention "others." It simply limited the vote to "free white male citizens."[17]

From his farm in Caroline County, Maryland, Thomas Carney, a "during the war man" who had survived Valley Forge and fought at White Plains, Brandywine, Germantown, Monmouth, Camden, Guilford Courthouse, Ninety Six, and Eutaw Springs, watched the grandees of his state declare him unworthy to exercise the basic right of citizenship. Thomas Jefferson's election as president is typically touted as the Revolution of 1800, a revivification of 1776. Andrew Jackson's presidency (1829–37), we are taught, brought an additional infusion of democracy to American life. But the more sordid side of the movements these men inspired is often forgotten. As Gary Nash once expressed it, we have been "lost in the fog of our historical amnesia" when it comes to African Americans.[18]

Perhaps most surprising in the list of states that disenfranchised its citizens of color was the only New England state to do so, Connecticut. In May 1814, the state legislature decreed that only free white males could be admitted a freeman in any town. It could be that accumulated prejudice had reached a tipping point resulting in reactionary legislation. Or perhaps such prejudice might have received added urgency from the slaves who in the second decade of the nineteenth century entered the free population thanks to what amounted to a gradual emancipation proclamation. By the time that Connecticut had written it first state constitution in 1818, the state had seen its share of intense partisan gamesmanship, with Federalists and Democratic-Republicans each trying to lessen the other side's constituency by changing voting requirements. By 1818 the Federalist governor and Federalist domination of the assembly were at an end. Despite the 1814 law, voting rights were one of the "important disputable questions" at the 1818 state constitutional convention. Most of this debate on voting issues centered on property requirements, but race was a concern to the very end. One prominent legislator, unhappy with the voting requirements under discussion, wondered, "How white or black must a voter be? How much tax must he pay? How much military duty must he perform?" But ultimately his primary concern was about poor white men voting, men who in his opinion were even less qualified than "our accomplished females." Other legislators focused on race. Even after the first draft was submitted in full, Judge Nahum Mitchell proposed an amendment erasing "white male" from the eligibility section. Judge Mitchell was soon to be an important supporter in securing revolutionary war pensions for African Americans. But at the constitutional convention he failed to rally the support needed to topple white supremacy. The final tally on the sixth article, with the inclusion of the word "white," was 103 supporting the article as written versus 72 nays. When the constitution went out to the voters of Connecticut for ratification, it narrowly passed by only fifteen hundred votes (13,918 to 12,364). This vote was all that was needed to seal off polling places to people of color.[19]

One of the people expelled from full citizenship was sixty-five-year-old Robin Starr, a resident of Litchfield County, whose six-year stint with the Second Connecticut included the battles of Lake Champlain (even before his enlistment as a militiaman), Danbury, Germantown, Monmouth, Norwalk, and Yorktown. Wounded in the first and last battles of his service, he was also a part of the elite light infantry that scaled the cliff at the Battle of Stony Point. He received a discharge, signed by Washington, with a Badge of Merit. He had signed up for the war's duration and served a total of six years, entitling him to two Badges of Distinction (one for each three-year period), which he wore on the left shoulder of his uniform coat. Another veteran in Connecticut, Pero Moody, cowrote a petition in 1823 reminding the legislature of his sacrifices. "And shall he be told," wrote Moody in the third person, "that the cheering sentiments which he then heard promulgated and which animated him in the contest were but idle declamation?" Subsequent petitions by others throughout the 1840s noted the sacrifice of the petitioner-veterans, the blood of fathers and grandfathers that had sealed a "sacred compact," and the part played by "the colored sons of 'Old Connecticut' in "that noble army of men." Other witnesses of the pullback on black voting in Connecticut included those survivors of the muster roll featured in this book's introduction—men who back in the heady days of 1782 had changed their names to Liberty, Freeman, and Freedom. One of these survivors, Peter Freeman, was quoted in an 1851 newspaper article as saying that he "keenly felt the dishonor and injustice put upon him when, after fighting side by side with his white brother . . . he was denied the privilege of going up with him to the ballot box."[20]

African American Communities Respond

With gradual emancipation statutes in place, northern legislatures had to decide what to do with the free blacks in their states. The African American communities, for their part, rallied their forces and gently pushed state assemblies to see people of color as citizens when each new challenge to their basic rights came up. The Revolution had provided both inspiration and leadership toward that effort.

When Pennsylvania passed its gradual emancipation bill, it stipulated that masters had to register their slaves by November 1, 1780, or those slaves would be free. "Great numbers" obtained their freedom this way, claimed a group of African American petitioners. But by March 1781 the assembly considered amending that part of the act, giving masters until January 1, 1782, to register their slaves, thus re-enslaving people who had been declared free. A group of unnamed blacks petitioned the assembly to defeat the measure. A letter appeared in a city newspaper signed by "a poor negro" named Cato who quoted the high-minded preamble of the Gradual Emancipation Act. He also called on the "worthy good gentlemen" to remember their own contention that the king of England kept slavery alive. To throw blacks back to angry masters would belie the words and sentiments of the very law that had been passed the year before. Although massaging the "honorable assembly" with respectful argument, Cato all but called them hypocrites if they went back on their word of honor.[21]

Like their colleagues in Pennsylvania, Massachusetts legislators attempted to push men of color back, this time by disenfranchising them. In 1778 voters defeated a new state constitution drafted with this proviso therein. Back at the drawing board, legislators heard from a group of free blacks led by Paul Cuffe, a prosperous ship owner and former prisoner of the British in occupied New York City. Their petition made the argument that as taxpayers they had to vote for the politicians who would tax them, thus reminding the lawmakers of the famous revolutionary phrase "No Taxation without Representation." Whether acknowledging this inconsistency or not, legislators took out the racial disqualifiers in the new 1780 constitution.[22]

The famous phrase about taxation without representation was not the only revolutionary talk adopted by black activists. A group of largely urban slaves in Virginia turned Patrick Henry's immortal words around, vowing "Death or Liberty" in their attempt to free themselves by force of arms. In the spring of 1800, Gabriel Prosser, a literate, skilled slave who worked in Richmond, came to the conclusion that words and arguments were not enough to free his people. Inspired by the successful slave revolt in Santo Domingo—the Haitian Revolution—and taking advantage of the fact that particularly contentious political disputes consumed the attention of white elites, Prosser went about enlisting recruits for an armed insurrection. The more he recruited, however, the more likely that someone would squeal. That could not be helped, though, because armed insurrection required numbers. In the end, Prosser recruited between five hundred and six hundred men from as far away as Norfolk. The wonder is that in the four-month recruitment period nobody betrayed the operation to white authorities. However, on the day when the revolt was to start, a terrible lingering thunderstorm forced everyone to stand down. In the confusion that followed, a couple of men alerted their masters to what was afoot.

There would be no second chance for Prosser and his fellow freedom fighters. At their trials, many of the accused were said to have "displayed a proud 'sense of their [natural] rights [and] a contempt of danger.'" One of the accused highlighted the hypocrisy of his accusers and the court: "I have nothing more to offer than what General Washington would have had to offer, had he been taken by the British and put on trial. I have adventured my life in endeavoring to obtain the liberty of my countrymen, and am a willing sacrifice in their cause."[23]

The vulnerability of the free blacks in southern states prevented them from organizing and petitioning. But a few individuals who played an active role in the Revolutionary War petitioned state assemblies for their freedom. In 1786, James, a slave of William Armistead, related to the Virginia assembly that with his master's permission he had entered the service of the Marquis de Lafayette in 1781. "At the peril of his life," he had circulated in the British camp, bringing valuable intelligence back to the Americans. James petitioned the legislature to set him free. Reimbursing the master, the lawmakers did right by James, who changed his name from Armistead to Lafayette.[24]

Another Virginian, Saul Mathews of Norfolk, had served as a spy and petitioned for his freedom in 1792. The state spoke of his "many essential services." The Marquis de Lafayette, Nathanael Greene, and Baron von Steuben had praised him. The legislature freed him. Finally, Caesar Tarrant, the man who appeared at the beginning of this chapter as a father desperate to get his daughter out of slavery in 1797, was himself released from the yoke in 1792 by the Virginia assembly, which described his "meritorious service." Tarrant, it was said, "very early into the service of his country . . . [had] continued to pilot the armed vessels of his state." The state fittingly reimbursed this sailor's master out of its Lighthouse Fund.[25]

Other southern states freed black individuals who served in the war. North Carolina did so but then passed a law permitting the re-enslavement of blacks freed for any reason other than "meritorious service" in the late conflict. It was as if the state had to couple humane action with a correspondingly inhumane act toward its black citizens. The net effect could not be positive. When a group of sixteen North Carolina blacks fled their native state in 1797 and made it to Philadelphia, the city's black's leadership took up their cause. James Forten, a black man who saw action against the British navy and was imprisoned on the notorious *Jersey* prison ship in New York City's waters, joined two churchmen, Richard Allen and Absalom Jones, in submitting the first petition from Philadelphia's black community to the national government on the subject of ending slavery, or at the least canceling the Fugitive Slave Law.[26]

Connecticut too coupled a positive step with a correspondingly negative one by emancipating slaves and then denying them the franchise. Although only boys during the Revolution, two black residents of New Haven, Tobias Stanley and William Lanson, knew all about taxation without representation. They realized that the prejudices against people of their color were so strong in Connecticut that they did not expect the lawmakers to reinstate the vote for blacks. Instead they sought what "the legislatures of all the old thirteen states repeatedly and solemnly declared . . . an act of justice," namely to cease taxing anyone with no representation in the government. Inspired by a phrase from Crispus Attucks's time used against the British Empire, and citing in their petition Paul Cuffe's argument on the same theme launched against the Massachusetts government, Stanley and Lanson continued the tradition of challenging white authorities with their own revolutionary words.[27]

Stanley and Lanson were not alone in arguing for equal rights. Through the 1840s, black citizens in New London, Norwich, New Haven, Middletown, Hartford, and Framington fired off petitions to the Connecticut General Assembly concerning the right to vote. At times African American veterans headed the list of signatures. On behalf of militiaman Pero Moody it was asked, "Shall he be told in the period of his short life that the cheering sentiments which he then heard promulgated and which animated him in the contest were but idle declamation?" A petition from Middletown, headed by black veterans, pointed out that "some of us in common with soldiers of a lighter hue bore arms, fought and bled in a glorious struggle." Into the 1840s descendants of these veterans from around the state provided unwelcome history lessons to the men in power about "coloured sons of 'Old Connecticut' . . . who carried their lives in their hands till victory was declared on the side of justice." Still others spoke of "our ancestors [who] . . . fought, bled, and died sealing with their blood, in common with other heroes, that sacred compact." A recurring theme is that black veterans were no less invested in "the emancipation of the country" than were white soldiers. Using words common in the abolition movement, like "emancipation" and "justice," the petitioners reminded the assembly that the work of the Revolution was not done.[28]

Churchmen, veterans, and businessmen in the African American community found white allies in the major cities to form aid groups and abolition societies. Early groups such as ones in Pennsylvania and Rhode Island started abolition work by retrieving African Americans who had been kidnapped for the purpose of being sold back into slavery. In 1791 Colonel Jeremiah Olney wrote to Rhode Island's abolition society, informing them that two of his former soldiers, Jack Burrows and Jack Champlin, were then held in slavery when they should have been free. Olney, the leader of the First Rhode Island after Christopher Greene's death, had made another payment on his promise to his men at the end of the war that he would help them in whatever way he could for the rest of his life. Both Burrows and Champlin had enlisted in the First Rhode Island within a month of the law's passage in 1778 granting freedom to slaves who enlisted during the war.[29]

Most black Revolutionary War veterans were poor and illiterate. They did not have the background needed to organize substantial numbers of people or to take on local authorities, let alone state legislatures. Although a few extraordinary participants in the war, like James Forten and Prince Hall, became formidable characters in the movement to better black people's lives, most veterans of color made their contributions back in their communities, telling their stories, inspiring the young men, and providing evidence of black men's endurance and sacrifice for a growing abolition movement. The one place that these obscure men could rise to the level of written notice and challenge the federal government was in the Revolutionary War pension process. Despite the many avenues closing down to them in early-nineteenth-century American life, black men staked a claim like any other veteran and insisted that they were owed, that they were worthy.

The 1818 Pension Act

On May 18, 1821, John Harris stood in the Petersburg, Virginia, superior court to make a claim on the U.S. government. Whether his palms were moist or his heart beat faster, Harris was there to apply for a pension for his services during the Revolutionary War, some forty years before. The sight of court clerks, witness box, and judge might have inspired little confidence in Harris, an African American man seeking justice in a southern court. Courthouses everywhere, but especially in the South at this time, were hardly associated with blind justice and fair outcomes for black men. Although Harris stood in the Petersburg courthouse thanks to federal legislation that rewarded veterans of the Revolution, he and thousands of other black men were accustomed to laws and promises that by dint of their race did not apply to them. One had only to hearken back to the founding documents of the land for proof of this. And more recently, states in the new republic were redefining words like "inhabitants," "freemen," and "citizens" to deprive black men of basic political rights. So John Harris confronted an unpredictable situation as he waited for the proceedings to begin.[30]

Despite intimidating circumstances, this sixty-nine-year-old "free man of color" dutifully recited what the federal government wanted to know. He had joined the military struggle in 1778 and had immediately been marched to Valley Forge, Pennsylvania, some 250 miles away. After surviving the rigors of that encampment, he went with Washington's army into New Jersey on a grueling march through stifling heat to cut off the British army retreat from Philadelphia to New York. At some part in this march, he was pulled out of the ranks and made to serve a young Virginia major by the name of James Monroe. Together the two soldiers survived heat exhaustion and the British army at the Battle of Monmouth. If Harris provided details of the battle or further adventures of his service, the court clerk did not record them. Harris's narrative closes with his activities in 1780 when he was building barracks at Chesterfield Courthouse back in Virginia. Once Harris finished his story, Judge Richard Parker pronounced himself satisfied as to Harris's veracity and his financial need for a pension. This was enough for the soldier-turned-barrel-maker to collect eight dollars a month, the sum mandated by law for all privates in the continental line during the Revolution.

The federal government, during the presidency of John Harris's commanding officer, Monroe, passed Revolutionary War pension legislation in 1818 that gave support to veterans of the continental line who had served at least nine consecutive months and could prove financial distress. The idea of expanding the pension program from "invalids" and officers to the rank-and-file soldier had been advocated by Monroe himself. Among the issues debated in Congress was the cost of such a program. How many "war-worn relics" could there be? Members of Congress assumed very few. One senator who still had reservations about the cost suggested that the pension system be limited to Continental Army soldiers only. Of that cohort he estimated that only two thousand individuals were still alive, making the program's price tag affordable. As the news of the pension hit the nation's press in early April 1818, the very few veterans of the Revolution thought to remain turned out to be twenty thousand more than that, men who had defied the war's toll and general life expectancy and would climb their county courthouse steps and tell their stories.[31]

In the tiny town of Exeter, New Hampshire, four black veterans from the Second New Hampshire led the way: London Dailey, age seventy; John Cook, age fifty-six; Jude Hall, age sixty-three, and Tobias Cutler, of indeterminate age. These men had all started life as slaves, but three of them later became leaders in Exeter's black community. The year before the pension act, Dailey had placed an ad in the local newspaper, addressing it to "the people of colour throughout the state." All were welcome to convene at Dailey's home for the purpose of forming what sounds like a mutual aid society. Jude Hall, known as "Old Rock," was "remarkable for his powerful physique," claimed an early historian of Exeter. Another local resident said that Jude could lift a barrel of cider and drink from the bunghole. So extraordinary was Hall's strength that another townsman related that around Exeter "it was said that parts of his ribs that [were] usually cartilaginous were of bone." Tobias Cutler's claim to fame in town history was his leadership of fellow blacks at military turnouts honoring abolition in the northern states. What is interesting about this group is that their race appears nowhere in their pension applications. Many black veterans appear in their depositions or in their supporters' testimony with the phrase "man of color" appended to their last names. Whether a strategy of the Exeter court to mask skin color or the result of a scribe who did not think to put it down, the original Exeter pensioners went through the system as any other applicants. Only London Dailey's name might have tipped off the government bureaucrats as to his race. A week after the initial group deposed in court, Prince Light, also of the Second New Hampshire and also a former slave, entered the courtroom. He was described in an early history of Exeter as being "a favorite leader" in the African American community.[32]

With the town's leaders showing the way, other African American veterans from Rockingham County, New Hampshire, faced the imposing courthouse façade and made their entry to proclaim themselves as men of parts, honorable, worthy men. In the pension process, these poor, illiterate men moved from being names on a list to being individuals with stories. And in the telling, these men on society's lowest rung claimed their status as citizens who were owed the rights for which they had fought. They claimed a founding role in the country's birth through their military service. The leaders of the Exeter group were all "during-the-war men," working longer than the average white recruit in the Second New Hampshire. The pension applicants also proclaimed themselves family men in owning last names and describing their families. Although the veterans' stories were mediated by white court clerks, were shaped by what the government wanted to know, and were distant recollections, the pension applications give voice to black veterans like no other source and reveal what happened to them when their soldier days were done. Their experiences with the pension office are part of this picture for in daring to claim their due, these old veterans dealt with problems that were specifically theirs as black men. The soldiers of '76 once again assessed the terrain, utilized allies, and realized what they were up against in the process of moving their claims forward.

At the end of the Revolutionary War, most African American veterans could probably say that, to use Tom Paine's words, they "deserved the love and thanks of man and woman." Certainly, every black man who served in the Revolution had a reasonable expectation that his life would be better after the war. The pension records show, however, that the Revolution's black veterans did not enjoy the same fruits of victory as did whites. These differences reflect not only the lower status held by most blacks at the time of the Revolution but also the effects of increased racism following the war, especially in the nineteenth century, when opportunities for black veterans dramatically dwindled.[33]

Measures of opportunity such as literacy, mobility, and property all indicate that white veterans had a distinct advantage over their African American counterparts. Only 16 percent of the black veterans of this study could sign their name, and those signatures reveal a shaky, tentative hand. New England produced most of the literate veterans. Twenty-one percent of black Yankees could sign their names, compared to only 11 percent each for the southern and Mid-Atlantic states. The pension files indicate that illiterate African Americans were prey to tireless conmen who took advantage of these vulnerable people in making off with their discharge certificates and even pension benefits.[34]

The difference between the geographic mobility of black veterans and that of white veterans is striking. Three-quarters of the black men in this study remained in the state where they enlisted, compared to approximately half of whites. If they did move out of state, it was usually to other seaboard states. Only twenty-three of the pensioners in this study moved to a frontier area such as Ohio, Indiana, Kentucky, or Tennessee. Although the Northwest Ordinance of 1781 declared that all territory north of the Ohio River would be free of slavery, states in that area concocted laws to keep African Americans away from their borders. In addition to concern over racial hostility toward them as strangers, African Americans may also have preferred to stay where they could find other people of color in familiar neighborhoods. Only eight of the five hundred pensioners ended up in a major city. Even in New England, the most liberal area of the country for blacks, poor African Americans recently emancipated would often be warned out of towns they moved to, in fear that they would eventually live at public expense. As a result, most African American Revolutionary War veterans stayed in familiar surroundings.[35]

Another reason for the lack of African American mobility was poverty. John Harris, who served James Monroe during the war, lived on the outskirts of Dinwiddie, Virginia, with two small broken pots, one old basket, one old table, two old chests, and some coopering tools as possessions. Of the black veterans whose property was valuated in their applications, Harris was one of the poorest, with goods totaling $3.62. The inventories of the majority of African American pensioners whose property merited a figure (many had nothing) were valued at less than fifty dollars. Only a handful of pensioners in this study owned a house, most of whom were in New England, and they were described as "shabby . . . old . . . small . . . one story." White veterans, on the other hand, averaged property holdings of $129 and showed more debt than African Americans, an indication that they could get credit more readily. Blacks had knives and forks but no spoons; they had buckets but no washtubs. Whites had more of everything—more animals, more tools, more furniture. The 1818 pension law required that all recipients be "in reduced circumstances," but even in indigence, men of color were poorer than their white counterparts.[36]

The poverty of African American veterans is highlighted in a December 1818 letter written by David Howell, a district judge in Rhode Island. In the wake of the 1818 pension law, there were many abuses of the system, particularly with respect to applicants hiding their property to qualify. In response, the federal government in 1820 stipulated that local courts would have to verify a list of property to be submitted to the pension office. All past cases had to be revisited. Judge Howell was irritated. It was through his court that the veterans of Rhode Island's Black Regiment were processed. Howell had already stated that these veterans were sufficiently poor and for this reason saw no need to call on these men to prove what was already apparent. "It had been a very unpleasant circumstance to me," complained Howell, "that I have been called on for proof of the poverty of so many Negroes whose almost universal poverty is notorious among us here." Identifying them as a group apart, Howell still exhibited sympathy for these veterans, who, according to his lights, deserved to be left in peace. So even among Revolutionary War veterans, the most cherished characters in the nation's memory, skin color denoted the poorest of the poor.[37]

Experiences with the Pension Office

In proving their service, black and white veterans shared some common problems. At forty or fifty years' remove from the events in their declarations, the old men could not, at times, recall dates or could only remember a happening in relation to some other event—for example, "It was the spring after the taking of Burgoyne," or "We arrived there when they were gathering oats." A number of veterans estimated their enlistment on or around what they called the "Dark Day." At mid-morning on May 19, 1780, the sky over New England became dark and this continued to varying degrees throughout the day. People had to light candles. The probable cause was smoke from forest fires coupled with heavy fog, but many citizens figured that the apocalypse was imminent, and perhaps some of those people decided that God had called on them to enlist. Elsewhere, veterans jumbled the order of events and sometimes had to receive help from their fellow comrades in summoning up memories. They lost discharge papers, had difficulty finding witnesses, and received the dispiriting news that certain work performed during the war was not deemed sufficiently military in nature to merit a pension.[38]

In applying for a pension, many African Americans had to cope with complications concerning the basic signifier of identity—their name. Once set free from enslavement, these soldiers often shed as much of their old status as possible, including their master's names. Consequently, the name found on the muster rolls was not necessarily the current identity of the veteran. Some men adopted the names of their fathers at the end of the war. Cuff Cousins enlisted under the name of his master, but once "freed by the laws of the state" of Massachusetts he recovered his father's surname and became Cuff Tindy.[39] Other African American men were encouraged by their officers to change their names. When Ben Roberts applied for a pension in 1818, he had to explain that he enlisted as Benjamin Black, "a name by which he was then called." His captain, Elijah Humphrey, had suggested that he change his name, and so he had dropped "Black" in favor of "Simmons." After the war, Ben learned that his father's name was "Roberts," a name the veteran owned for the rest of his life.[40]

Joseph Johnson's identity issues were even more labyrinthine. While never identifying himself as a slave, Johnson had lived since childhood in Henry Rosekrans's household. Although his father's name was Thomas Peters, Joseph was called only by his first name. Rosekrans's son had asked Joseph to enlist in his company as a substitute for one Thomas Johnson. "I recollect that an officer took hold of my hand," said Joseph in his pension application, "and made me write my name that I would serve during the war and that I would be true to my country." Despite the fact that he was "made" to write down his name, he was known in the company as Joseph Johnson "on account (as I suppose) of my having taken Johnson's place." After the war, Joseph moved around and eventually encountered "a man from Litchfield" who took to calling him Tom. When word got out that "Tom" had served with Major James Rosekrans during the war, Joseph Johnson became "Thomas Rosekrans," and at the end his life he had both his master's and his father's names.[41]

In adopting surnames, the African American community claimed their right to identify themselves, thereby chipping away at the obstacles to full civic participation in their communities. And whether taking a father's name or an officer's name, these veterans, along with newly freed African Americans in general, did more than reject slavery or claim civic rights. They proclaimed that they were members of a family, that they belonged to one another and not to some outsider, and that it was a moral violation to split up parents and children.

Although black veterans chose their own surnames to identify themselves, local courts often fixed them with another identifier when they came to claim a pension—their race. This worked in only one direction, as whites were never labeled as such, their names sufficing to designate them. When "John Harris, a free man of color," entered the Prince George County Courthouse in Virginia, it is highly unlikely that he himself stated the obvious about his appearance. The court clerk, however, found it necessary to label him as such. The African American pension applicants could not but have realized that race was always pertinent to their condition, and so when they cast about to find fellow veterans to testify on their behalf, they overwhelmingly chose white men. At times these white supporters demonstrated ingrained racism when talking about their black neighbors. One of the white men who supported Caesar Shelton's pension application characterized this veteran as "an industrious and good Citizen for a Black Man." A white supporter of Isaac Perkins, a North Carolina veteran, claimed that Perkins would never have falsified his financial situation for "though a man of *Colour*, we do believe him to be too honest in principal to practice anything like a fraud." A prominent pension agent in Rhode Island, Benjamin Cowell, claimed that Reuben Roberts was "more honest and industrious than the blacks in general." These white supporters were all the more notable because they had to skirt their unapologetically racist views to identify black veterans as members of the community who deserved respect and a pension. The camaraderie of the war prevailed over the entrenched views of black men's inferiority and untrustworthiness.[42]

More representative of the support depositions, however, were white veterans who praised their old comrades with no racist qualifiers. The black men were "industrious . . . good soldiers . . . faithful." One neighbor gushed that "no man, no, not James K. Polk himself is of better moral character" than the pension applicant. Aside from complimentary qualities, white veterans could enhance a black comrade's deposition. Pomp Magus, an African American veteran from Massachusetts, recited the bare bones of his three-year stint in the Revolutionary War. Perhaps his eleven-month ordeal as a prisoner of war in British-occupied New York City was too painful or too shameful to resurrect, because he makes no mention of it in his first deposition. It is his white comrade, Asa Hart, who not only tells of their joint confinement but also relates how Magus afforded him "much assistance" while imprisoned. Another New Englander, Jamaica James, started his pension narrative with his enlistment in the Continental Army. One of his former buddies told the pension office that James had forgotten to relate that he was wounded at Bunker Hill. Yet another New Englander, Prince Crosley, had a Revolutionary War captain intercede for him when he wanted to move to a new location. James Cooper, a Virginia veteran of over four years, could move around in a different way thanks to his military past. He included in his pension application a pass that he received in 1787. This allowed him to travel to the Carolinas and Georgia and remain "unmolested so long as he behaves himself well" because he was "an old soldier."

Cooper had lost his discharge certificate when washing clothes, but he treasured this pass that testified to his service.[43]

Black veterans not only secured the support of white veterans, but on occasion they elicited depositions from very prominent white men. Generals, colonels, and captains supported these African Americans. So also did members of Congress, governors, judges, sheriffs, postmasters, and ministers. Future president John Tyler wrote letters in support of two black men in his Charles City County, Virginia, neighborhood. For a local veteran who could not prove the length of his enlistment, Tyler (then a member of the House of Representatives) procured two certificates, one from an orderly sergeant and one from a respectable gentleman, testifying that the veteran had served twelve months. On another occasion, one of Tyler's "near neighbors," Isaac Brown, had applied for a pension and was rejected. Tyler, now a U.S. senator, submitted an amended declaration "with all the deficiencies . . . corrected." To indicate to the Pension Office that his interest in Brown was not of fleeting nature, Senator Tyler had Brown's pension certificate sent straight to him.[44]

When a fellow veteran could not be found to validate a pension applicant's story, the people he had been living next to for decades intervened. Individuals as well as groups testified on behalf of a man who had been regaling them with stories for years. Said one supporter of Israel Pearce of the North Carolina line, "His head and face and body bear the marks of service." Ten of Jehu Grant's neighbors signed their shaky signatures, along with the number of years they had known the veteran, in support of his application. James Wormsley's neighbors, eighty-three of them, signed in support of this upstanding man.[45]

With declarations of their service duly notarized by a local court and depositions from neighbors, local notables, and old veterans, the African American applicants waited for word from Washington. Despite the fact that race directly followed an African American's name in most court documents and racism was rife in the land, a man's race seemed to have had little effect on the administrators of the 1818 act. The rejection rate for white veterans was higher than that of African Americans (8 percent versus 3 percent). This surprising finding could be due to cases of fraud resulting from the 1818 act. It was a national scandal that so many veterans lied about their wealth. Black men did not have to lie about their poverty. They also might have been less likely to hoodwink the system because the consequences of such action would be doubly hard for a black man. In a society riddled with racial prejudice and double standards, this seemingly fair treatment stands as a beacon. How can one account for this? At least during the first general pension legislation in 1818, there were still many veterans in society and government officials who had seen firsthand the significant contributions of black soldiers. Just as the Revolutionary War captain defended

Private Crosley's right to live where he wanted, thousands more veterans could remind their intransigent neighbors of the undeniable service they and other veterans had contributed during the war. While a good number of veterans still lived, the general culture might have been more tolerant with respect to these old, black men whose age made them less threatening to the white community.

A less sanguine explanation of the rejection rates in the 1818 cohort is found in the legislation itself. The pension act required a veteran to tell his story to a local court, "and on its appearing to the satisfaction of the said judge that the applicant served in the Revolutionary War, he [the judge] shall certify and transmit the testimony in the case to the Secretary of the Department of War." The process then, included a threshing operation at the local level that may well have turned away more blacks than whites. We do not know how many black and white men were told to go home. The only evidence we have is from a few African American veterans who explained how it happened to them. James Weeks had served more than three years in New York units during the war. When he approached his local county court years alter, the judge told him he could not assist the veteran, having no copy of the legislation on his person. The judge palmed off the sixty-six-year-old veteran to another judge, who declined to assist him because Weeks did not have the money for the processing of his application. Beyond that technicality, the judge discouraged him from making any further application. Five years later, Weeks tried again, and this time his paperwork reached "the seat of government," which deemed him worthy to join the pension roll.[46]

However discouraging the local climate, once an application reached Washington, D.C., the pension clerks under the 1818 act behaved like true bureaucrats, authorizing pensions according to the evidence presented. Presence on a muster roll or the possession of a discharge from the war period were both considered golden evidence. If such "direct proof" were not available, "two disinterested witnesses" were needed to testify to the veteran's service. There was, then, some room for a judgment call on the part of the Pension Office bureaucrats. It appears that these government clerks exercised this flexibility with astounding color-blind impartiality, at least for the 1818 cohort. By 1832, however, the world had changed such that African American veterans had to clear new obstacles to obtain a pension.[47]

CHAPTER 6

ANOTHER ASSAULT

A FROWNING WORLD AND THE SECOND PENSION ACT

In 1818, the same year that the government passed its first general pension legislation, the Missouri Territory applied to join the Union as a slave state. Up to that time, territories joined the Union in twos—one slave and one free. The balance of power between slave and free states was thus maintained, but Missouri threatened to give slaveholders the upper hand. The furor over Missouri engendered the first national debate on the institution of slavery. Contemplating Missouri, Thomas Jefferson wrote that "this momentous question like a firebell in the night, awakened and filled me with terror . . . I consider it the knell of the Union." It is at this time that Jefferson moved from a "necessary evil" argument with respect to slavery to a precursor of slavery as a positive good. He favored the spread of slavery to the West because the peculiar institution would be diffused over the vast reaches of the continent, making slavery a national problem, not a narrowly sectional one. Slaves would be happier out west, claimed Jefferson. If no solution were in the offing, Jefferson proposed a moral solution—become a humane slaveholder. In response to a fellow Virginian who contemplated emancipating his slaves, Jefferson advised him to keep his slaves and exercise Christian trusteeship because to free slaves not prepared to be free would be evil.[1]

Jefferson's response to developments at the end of his life was more measured than the views of many slaveholders, whose verbiage took on a much uglier tone. Slaveholders everywhere could reinforce their racist notions with then cutting-edge science that maintained that the human species contained varieties within it of varying attributes. Skin color encompassed inherent differences that could never be bridged. Europeans were at the top of the tree of creation, Africans on the bottom. Scientists studied skulls and heads. They measured facial angles to get at human intelligence. They studied bumps on the head. Charts and graphs lent credibility to this pseudoscience. Jefferson was a man ahead of his time in this area as well. In 1783 he held forth on racial differences, preferring the whites' "superior beauty . . . and more elegant symmetry of form" over the blacks' deficiency in forethought, disagreeable odor, emotionless sexual drive, inferior intelligence, and dull imagination. He did admit, however, that more observation would be needed to ascertain whether these differences were environmental or immutable. By the 1820s and 1830s, scientists had come down on the side of fixed traits.[2]

So now when whites wanted separate neighborhoods, and even separate pews in church, they had scientific backing. Inferior blacks could work for next to nothing, edging out whites in unskilled, low-paying jobs That is, until thousands of Irish immigrants arrived in the nineteenth century. They competed with blacks for the marginal jobs in American cities. Such competition fostered ill will between the two groups. Perhaps this is why a French visitor to this country in 1831, Alexis de Tocqueville, wrote that racial prejudice "appears to be stronger in the states that have abolished slavery than in those where it still exists."[3]

Government was not keeping up with the sentiments of the people, reasoned some whites, and so they took matters into their own hands. Tensions exploded in some of the country's major cities. Philadelphia's first major race riot occurred in November 1829 following a noisy black church service. In that same year, Cincinnati mobs convinced more than half the black population to leave the city. The early riots were just the beginning of an increasingly devastating series of race riots in the 1830s and 1840s. And as usual, just the threat of violence kept many of the oppressed in their place. Again, Tocqueville, a prescient observer of American culture and democracy, provided an example of extralegal policing. A Philadelphian had told him that black voters risked maltreatment if they came to the polls. "What becomes of the Reign of law in this case?" asked the Frenchman. "The law with us is nothing," replied the American, "if it is not supported by public opinion.[4]

As African Americans moved through the pension process, conditions in their everyday lives worsened, and not just in the streets where they lived. Major states joined the likes of Connecticut and New Jersey to take back the vote from their citizens of color. More blacks lived in New York than in any other northern state. They tended to vote for Federalists as that party formed the aristocratic class that freed individual slaves and then dominated the state government when gradual emancipation passed in 1799. Federalists also dominated state abolition societies. Black voters rewarded them at the polls, drawing the attention of the rising Democratic-Republican Party. In New York City, African Americans comprised almost 10 percent of the total population. In 1809, Democratic-Republican poll inspectors presumed all black men to be slaves and sent them home. In the closely contested election of 1813, New York's people of color formed a substantial block and put Federalists over the top. In the following year, Democratic-Republicans prevailed and immediately began to throw roadblocks in the way of African American voters. Blacks were obliged to go through an elaborate registration process and then bring full copies of these forms to the officers of election. Later, at the Constitutional Convention of 1821, the committee charged to write the suffrage section recommended the exclusion of blacks altogether from the vote. One of its members opined that blacks were "a peculiar people, incapable in my Judgment, of exercising that privilege with any sort of discretion, prudence or independence." The right to vote had become a privilege, and a decision to vote for the other party had become a lack of independence.[5]

The Federalists, in response, pointed out that blacks had not done anything to merit exclusion in the forty years they had been voting. Peter Augustus Jay, son of Founder John Jay, wondered how his opponents could extend the vote to some while denying it to others who already possessed it. Another Federalist pointed out that black soldiers who had distinguished themselves in the War of 1812 surely ought to vote as well as all white men over twenty-one. After much debate, another suffrage committee relented and ordered a property requirement of $250 for blacks only (the previous property requirement was only $40). Having perhaps learned from previous states' experience, they also stipulated that nonvoters would not be taxed. Meanwhile in Westchester County, New York, John Patterson, a black veteran of Saratoga, Monmouth, and Newtown learned that his assembly had declared him unfit to vote. At least he could find some comfort in his recently acquired federal pension and the plaudits of a federal government that had declared him to be one of the "founders of American independence."[6]

The Quaker State Strikes

One of the last public acts of Benjamin Franklin's life was to affix his signature to a 1789 address that called for "the exercise and enjoyment of civil liberty" to newly freed slaves. In the following year, the Pennsylvania Constitution guaranteed the right to vote to all freemen. But by the time that the Quaker state assembly went to write a new state constitution in 1837–38, most states had abandoned the notion of equality for all, equating white skin with citizenship.[7]

Pennsylvania did not blindly follow the others. In the constitutional convention's first session, the third article concerning voting rights went back to committee after each debate and came back to the floor eleven times with no racial qualifiers. This despite impassioned speeches by those who wanted to deprive all blacks of the vote. Benjamin Martin of Philadelphia was foremost among them. His first foray into debate cast himself as the protector of the black community. From what?—from unrealistic expectations that blacks would ever be equal to whites. Today the vote, he said, tomorrow black legislators in this august body. He chided the "gentle men" on the other side of the issue of talking about equality when not one of them would sit next to a black legislator. "Public sentiment" had thus far prohibited blacks from voting, said Martin, so why endanger the black population by giving them a right of which the general community disapproved?[8]

While most of the debate on suffrage focused on property and residence requirements, the forces of racial exclusion threw up argument after argument. Some legislators wanted some very restrictive qualifiers on black voting. "A free Negro is the freest man on earth," claimed Representative McDowell, "his is freedom unrestrained and irresponsible—unmixed with rational interventions." The current amendment with no racial exclusions whatsoever "would turn loose among us . . . the worthy and the worthless" who would "rush to the polls in senseless and untriumph [sic]."[9]

For all this Armageddon talk, the convention voted down the inclusion of the word "white" in its voting requirements. The indefatigable racists launched additional arguments: Pennsylvania fronted three slave states whose blacks would stream into the Commonwealth; voting would lead to intermarriage; equality would mean that some day the country would suffer from black generals; compare Europe and Africa on the scale of civilization; the vote is not a natural right but rather a matter of regulation; the Bible sanctioned slavery; no amount of education could bring people of color to the requisite level of intelligence. On this last point, Representative Martin pointed out that schools had made it possible for men of color to beg for whiskey from door to door . . . in Hebrew, Greek or Latin. The racists wanted to insert "white" in the constitution and let the people of the state decide.[10]

In the last days of the spring-summer session, the convention received a petition from African Americans in Pittsburgh who had heard about the debates and strenuously protested the loss of the vote. Their strong language offended some legislators. The petition was moot, however, because in mid-July, the convention still stood firm in allowing all freemen to vote. Then came a Pennsylvania Supreme Court decision that changed everything. In *Hobbs et al. v. Fogg*, a black man from Luzerne County said he had been turned away at the polls despite his having fulfilled all the state voting requirements. The election officials did not dispute his story. The court's decision declared that men of color did not have the right to vote. The presiding judge in this case resorted to a 1795 trial whose paperwork could not be found. He had heard about it from another gentleman. He had to reach back to old colonial laws to support his decision as well as provide a convoluted paragraph on what the 1790 Pennsylvania Constitutional Convention meant by "freeman." However flawed the arguments, the Supreme Court had spoken. In the Constitutional Convention's fall-winter session, even more heated debate rocked the legislative chamber, with more speeches from those who did not want to change the constitution. Even so, in late January, the legislators finally voted to insert the word "white" in the voting requirements. It was now up to the people of Pennsylvania to vote on the new constitution. The African American community had nine months to convince the states' voters to reject the new document.[11]

The most famous response came from Philadelphia's black community, which rallied in churches and produced the "Appeal of 40,000 Citizens threatened with Disenfranchisement to the People of Pennsylvania." They led off on page one with a history lesson. "Our fathers bled" on the questions of taxation and representation, they said. Both the Confederation Congress and the 1780 Pennsylvania Constitutional Convention considered the question of black voters and freemen, concluding that "freemen" included people of color. The appeal continued with a scathing assessment of the judge's decision in the *Hobbs v. Fogg* case. Still, the appeal's writers did not advocate universal black suffrage. Realizing that whites had to be won over, they claimed the vote only for "the industrious, peaceable, and useful" part of the colored people." That said, they wanted the same qualifications to apply to whites.[12]

The most impassioned argument came in the appeal's middle section. For over two pages of the eighteen-page pamphlet, the writers reminded Pennsylvanians about black men's military service during the revolution. Not having too many African American veterans from the Quaker State, they concentrated on the First Rhode Island Regiment. One congressman claimed that "no braver men met the enemy in battle." A New York congressman related that he "saw a battalion of them [black soldiers] as fine martial looking men as I ever saw." Yet another congressman reminded the New York Constitutional Convention that "in the war of the Revolution, these people helped to fight your battles by land and by sea." The appeal's writers also reminded its readers that in 1779 the Continental Congress had recommended that Georgia and South Carolina field black units that would be "formidable to the enemy." Black soldiers "hazarded their lives." Black soldiers "shed their blood on the snows of New Jersey." They had "faced British bayonets in the most desperate hour of the revolution." Did they endure the famine at Valley Forge and the horrors of British prison ships so that their children "might be disenfranchised and loaded with insult?" They ended the history lesson with the observation that there were still-living black veterans who would see their civil liberty wrenched from their grasp. In October 1838, the people of Pennsylvania approved the new constitution by thirty-six hundred votes. The elimination of property requirements for whites far outweighed any concern for black voters.[13]

African American Community's Response

The denial of suffrage was not the only contributor to the downward spiral experienced by the black community in the first half of the nineteenth century. Alcoholism, lack of educational opportunities, colonization schemes, and increasingly violent invective also played a role. African American churches again led the way in guiding their communities through the darkening days of the 1820s and 1830s. One of the churches' leading ministers, Jehiel Beman, started as a shoemaker and itinerant preacher in Colchester, Connecticut. He later headed the Cross Street Church in Middletown. Called to lead Zion's Church in Boston, he became a major figure in New England's African American community. Liberation was in his blood. Beman's father, Caesar, had been a slave and a Revolutionary War veteran. Caesar had likely served in his master's stead, joining the Fifth Connecticut Regiment and serving for over two years. When choosing a surname to answer to the roll, he opted not to use his master's name but rather fashioned a new one that spoke to his aspirations. Family lore relates that Caesar wanted to "be a man" and so he became Caesar Beaman (be-a-man), sometimes shortened to Beman.[14]

When the Revolutionary War veteran's son traveled south of the Mason-Dixon line as an adult, he saw slave society in action for the first time, leading him to reflect, "To think that my father faced the cannon's mouth for this country's liberty, and I and my brother [are] still bound." Although a free man, Jehiel was still bound by society's depiction of black people as inherently inferior. That notion covered a multitude of deficiencies that denied people of color equality of opportunity. Reverend Beman not only spoke out about the pressing need for education in his community, he also tried to start a college for blacks in New Haven. He moved his family to Colchester, Connecticut, possibly because there was a good "colored school" there. His children, including a son who would continue in his father's footsteps, benefited from a particularly gifted teacher, Prince Saunders, whose father was also a Revolutionary War veteran. Although uplift of the community centered around education, Jehiel Beman also fought against the drinking problem plaguing all Americans at this time. He founded the Connecticut State Temperance Society for Coloured People. In addition to individual improvement, Beman worked to break down the roadblocks to full citizenship imposed by government. He mustered the community to work on voting rights for blacks, denied by his home state after the War of 1812. He also actively labored in abolition work, once being roughed up by a mob as he exited an antislavery society meeting. As a son of a Fifth Connecticut veteran, Jehiel Beman faced the onslaught of lies, specious arguments, and raw racial hatred fostered by a society dedicated in one way or another to keeping people of color "still bound." He passed on the fight to his son Amos, another tireless minister in the business of liberation, and to a grandson who would fight in the Civil War.[15]

Jehiel Beman was not alone in exhorting equality for all. Other ministers led their congregations in contesting any steps backward, even those under the guise of reform. The idea of the repatriation of blacks to Africa had been circulating since the 1780s. In 1816, a collection of reformers and southern slaveholders founded the American Colonization Society. They argued that whites would never allow African Americans to climb out of their degraded condition, and so a return to Africa or other places outside the United States was the best course. Prominent blacks like Paul Cuffee and James Forten initially supported the idea, but the African American community as a whole rejected the scheme. Later in the 1830s, when a more radical abolition movement stoked strong responses from the anti-abolitionists, William Lloyd Garrison published a book titled *Thoughts on African Colonization*, in which he reproduced responses to the black emigration idea from African American organizations and churches throughout the North. They all referenced revolutionary rhetoric and their grandfathers' participation in the Revolutionary War. New Yorkers highlighted hypocrisy when they said, "The time must come when the Declaration of Independence will be felt in the heart as well as uttered from the mouth." Voices from Nantucket and Pittsburgh borrowed Jefferson's words "we hold these truths to be self evident" as a preface for their anti-emigration argument. Voices from Manhattan, Brooklyn, and New Haven emphasized the blood spilled by the revolutionary generation. "Shall we forsake the tombs and flee to an unknown land? No!" exclaimed Brooklyn activists. A voice from Pennsylvania added that no "conspiring world [would] be able to drive us hence."[16]

While ministerial regiments roused their congregations to action, other activists proved the lie that African Americans could not "rise above the level of narration" by publishing a newspaper owned and edited by black men. Peter Williams Jr., son of a Revolutionary War veteran and himself a minister, was a key supporter of *Freedom's Journal* in 1827, edited by two African Americans, Samuel E. Cornish and John B. Russwurm. Operating out of New York City for two years, the writers made clear that "we wish to plead our own cause." In the first issue of the paper, the editors declared themselves "dedicated exclusively to their [black people's] improvement." So articles about educational issues and temperance filled the paper as well as information about the wider black world. The Republic of Haiti, founded by a revolution of the enslaved, appeared in the first issue, and the paper's editors promised that "everything that relates to Africa shall find a ready admission in our columns," in the hopes that solid information would break down the negative stereotypes about the place. To counter oversimplified prejudices about black people, the paper ran the biography of Paul Cuffee over the first few issues. Cuffee was a black man who had been an illiterate youth but ended up a prosperous ship owner and pillar of the community. Phillis Wheatley, the poet, was later featured for the same reason. And lastly, the editors often used the language of the American Revolution throughout its pages. It began on page one of the first issue with the leadoff article. Citing the Declaration of Independence, they charged American society with the "neglect of self evident truths." Financial and editorial issues closed *Freedom's Journal* at the end of two years of publication. It was followed by another African American–run paper whose publishing life was even shorter. But the idea that black voices had to be heard registered loud and clear, as twenty-four pre–Civil War black newspapers carried on the mission of education and advocacy.[17]

One of the subscription agents for *Freedom's Journal* in Boston was a transplanted North Carolina freeman named David Walker. In his thirties Walker had made his way north to eventually work as a secondhand clothier in Boston. In 1829 he published a pamphlet called *Appeal to the Colored Citizens of the World but in Particular and Very Expressly to Those of the United States of America*. In the same way that Tom Paine used blunt language to convey radical ideas in his pamphlet *Common Sense*, so also did David Walker in his *Appeal*. He threatened the demise of the country if slavery were not abolished—and not only because God would strike but so also would the enslaved rise up and overthrow the evil order of things. The man who would not fight, claimed Walker, ought to be kept in chains. Men who submit rather than fight deserve all the demeaning descriptions propagated by slaveholders, those "pretenders to Christianity . . . avaricious usurpers . . . enemies to God." To insure maximum efficacy, Walker preached planning and readiness when the righteous rose up. "If you commence, make sure [of the] work," advised Walker. "Do not trifle, for they will not trifle with you. They want us for their slaves and think nothing of murdering us . . . therefore—if there is an *attempt* made by us, kill or be killed."[18]

Before the day came when slaveholders would curse their birth, said Walker, every effort had to be made to destroy the poison poured into African Americans' heads about their inferiority and slavery's beneficence. To the argument that slavery existed in the Bible as well as in the great classical civilizations,

Walker pointed out that the slavery that existed in history was not nearly the vicious brand practiced in his country. Joseph, the Israelite slave, rose to prominence just below the Pharaoh. Romans allowed slaves to buy their freedom and move to the "greatest eminence." None of these societies denied the humanity of their slaves. They never considered them "talking apes." Slaves in antiquity could own property, in marked contrast to Walker's contemporaries, who no sooner might buy a patch of land than whites would try to get it, even if it were in a mud hole, he claimed.

Walker reserved special attention to "the very learned and penetrating Mr. Jefferson," whose *Notes on Virginia* should, claimed Walker, be given to every young, black male. The response had to come from the black community, "for you will either have to contradict or confirm him [Jefferson] by your own actions," argued Walker, "and not by what our friends have said or done for us." Walker's voice led the way, countering the Sage of Monticello's contention that blacks were probably inherently inferior. That's like confining one deer to a cage for his lifetime, said Walker, while letting another go free, and then calling the caged animal inferior. How dare this great philosopher pass judgment on men in chains, Walker wrote.

Christian ministers also poisoned the minds of America's blacks by preaching obedience to the master. Walker, himself a devout Christian, called this brand of Christianity the gospel of blood and whips. Slaveholders, while "murdering their slaves by inches" denied the enslaved an education as well as access to the true gospel. Rather than turn to these false men of God, Walker counseled recourse to the English people as "the best friends the coloured people have upon the earth." Even while practicing a horrendous brand of slavery in the West Indies, Walker maintained, they still had done "one hundred times more for the melioration of our condition than all the other nations of the earth put together." Walker did not give specifics, but he could have referred to the *Somerset* decision, the English policy toward the enslaved during the Revolution, and the powerful abolition movement in Britain at that time.[19]

Walker's language is as vibrant and accessible as Tom Paine's. "The Americans have got fat on our blood and groans," he wrote. He characterized slavery as taking another's life "by inches." He knew of thousands of whites in the slave-holding states "as ignorant . . . as horses, the most they know is to beat the coloured people." He distilled the Africa colonization movement into the phrase "the colonizing trick." And he beseeched black men to look higher than "wielding a razor and cleaning boots and shoes." While writing engaging prose himself, Walker admired the inspirational language of another wordsmith, Thomas Jefferson, who, although a slaveholder, could write powerful prose. Walker quoted a large piece of the Declaration of Independence in his *Appeal*, after which he exclaimed, "See your Declaration[,] Americans!!! Do you understand your own language?" Here again is another black man making use of the powerful language of the Revolution and turning it back on the community keeping people of color "under their feet."

Copies of Walker's *Appeal* traveled on ships that made their way to southern ports. Walker the clothier would sew copies into sailors' duds and allegedly had a network of distributors in his native state of North Carolina. Enough copies made their way south to elicit a roar from that region. The mayor of Savannah appealed to the mayor of Boston, Harrison Otis, to arrest Walker. North Carolina levied harsh penalties on circulating seditious publications as well as teaching slaves to read and write. Horrified slaveholders offered three thousand dollars for Walker's head and ten thousand dollars if brought back to the South alive. Walker died a few months after the publication of his pamphlet's third edition. Although the cause of his death remains a mystery, some suspected that he was poisoned, while others believed he died of tuberculosis, as had his daughter. Walker's only son, Edwin Garrison Walker, born after his father's death in 1830, would become the third African American admitted to the legal profession in Massachusetts and the first black man elected to the Massachusetts state legislature.[20]

Southerners were not the only critics of Walker's brand of radicalism. In the second issue of William Lloyd Garrison's *Liberator*, Garrison asserted "that a good end does not justify wicked means." He called for peaceful tactics but acknowledged that Walker was only paying slaveholders back "in their own coin." Indeed, "if any people were ever justified in throwing off the yoke of their tyrants, claimed Garrison, the slaves are that people." As if on cue, a slave in Virginia, Nat Turner, led a revolt in August 1831 that resulted in the death of fifty-five white people before it was quashed. Close to three hundred black people, many of whom knew nothing of the plan, were either executed by the state or strung up by mobs in Virginia and North Carolina.[21]

America had become the land of extremes: far-fetched science, pantomime justice, disenfranchisement, race riots up north, insurrections down south. The vibrations of all these excessive developments reached Washington, D.C., and influenced the implementation of America's second Revolutionary War pension act. In 1832, black veterans, now older and feebler, had to tap deep reserves of determination to confront a bureaucracy that like so much else in American life had hardened toward people of their color.

The 1832 Pensioners

The new 1832 pension legislation broadened the field of potential applicants by admitting those who had served in the militia and state lines, provided they had served a total of at least six months during eight years of war. The poverty requirement was dropped. (The 1818 law limited a pension to Continental Army veterans who had served at least nine consecutive months and could prove indigence). The amount of the pension varied according to rank and length of service. A veteran who had served two years or more received full pay for life according to his rank. All who had served between six months and two years received their annuities in proportion to their length of service.[22]

Under the new legislation, African American former militiamen could apply for a benefit, as could the small number of economically solid black men who had been excluded from pension consideration by the 1818 poverty requirement. While Congress widened the field, the Pension Office created regulations that made it more difficult for African American veterans to actually receive a pension. The 1818 and 1832 regulations stipulated that those who worked for the army through any kind of civil contract were ineligible. For instance, an independent operator who had sold his teamster services to the army was under "a civil contract" and so not eligible for a pension, while the man who belonged to the army and was assigned teamster duties did qualify. The law provided other examples of carefully scrutinized work: "clerks to commissaries and to shopkeepers etc., teamsters, boatmen etc." The rule affected black veterans more than it did whites because black men were far more likely to be ordered into support jobs like commissary duty or service to officers. If muster lists could not be found—a more likely occurrence in 1832 because militia lists were generally not preserved—the assumption was that the applicant fell under the "civil contract" stipulation and so was ineligible, no matter how many support depositions he had that said otherwise.[23]

Whereas the "civil contract" stipulation was printed in the act's official regulations, other practices of the pension office were not. Absent in the 1832 act was the new unwritten rule affecting men who had been servants during their military service. These men did not fall under the civil contract. The 1818 bureaucrats had rejected both white and black men who had worked as servants to officers, usually on the basis of age. An eleven-year-old, argued the office, would never be mustered into a unit. But once these boys attained manhood, the practice in the army had varied according to one's skin color. White boys of military age usually became regular soldiers, but black men of comparable years often remained as servants or served some part of their enlistment as servants. What did the pension office do with such applicants? In 1818 it gave these black men pensions.

The office did not penalize adult males who had enlisted in the services and then were ordered into servant duty. In 1832, with militia muster records largely non-existent, the office rejected veterans with such a record. All those black veterans who were rejected because of servant status fell under the 1832 legislation. As in the case of civil contracts, the system did not set out to purposely discriminate against African Americans, but the result was a higher hurdle for black veterans.

While the servant issue could work against white veterans as well, the last of the new Pension Office policies addressed only black men. In 1832 the office refused pensions to any black man who had enlisted while still enslaved. This proviso appears nowhere in the 1832 act or in the act's regulations. In 1818 veterans who had enlisted while enslaved received pensions. In 1832 enslaved status served as grounds to disqualify black men.

Perhaps these stipulations help explain why the rejection rate for African American applicants is significantly higher than that of white men in 1832. That the rate went up is no surprise. A half-century after the war, memory further failed, the pool of veterans who could support an application dwindled, and militia rolls were harder to obtain than the Continental Army records. In 1818 whites experienced more rejection, but in 1832 the rejection rate for African American applicants was more than double that of white applicants (31 percent versus 13 percent).[24]

After 1832 the Pension Office used both slave status and job type to reject black men. Peter Nash suffered just such a double stroke against his pension. Nash had joined his master in 1778 to guard the Connecticut coast. He had initially served as a waiter but was so well respected that he also acted as a private, manning the field piece on the boat whenever the need arose. The Pension Office rejected Nash's application at first because he "was a slave at the time the duty was performed." The office turned a blind eye to a Connecticut law that exempted any two men who could provide a substitute of any color. Elsewhere, in a letter from the Pension Office, Nash's service was disqualified because the office found one of the support depositions to have claimed that Nash had been a waiter. As the letter stated, that "description of service was not contemplated in any act." Nash's advocate fired back that the Pension Office's version was a "mistake." He reminded the office that there was more than one support affidavit and that one of the veterans pointed out that Nash was "usually attached to the field piece," putting him in the center of the action during any military engagement. Such clarification was in vain. Peter Nash, an active participant in the defense of his state, was denied a pension. As officials saw it, they had adhered to the law's procedures.[25]

Although there are other cases of this sort in the pension records, one case in particular highlights a clear chronology in the shifting reasons for denying a black man a pension. In the case of Primus Hall, however, J. L. Edwards, the commissioner of pensions, met formidable opponents in the persons of Hall and his attorney, Reuben Baldwin. The story begins with Hall's deposition in 1835. He had enlisted in 1776 in the Fifth Massachusetts under Thomas Nixon and fought in the battles for New York City as well as at Trenton and Princeton. Having fulfilled his service requirement after Trenton, he stayed on for six more weeks at the "earnest request" of General Washington. Honorably discharged in early 1777, he enlisted later in that year on a three-month tour of duty that saw him at "the surrender of Burgoyne." At that battle he caught his captain, Samuel Flint, when the officer was shot, and "set him down against a tree" when it was obvious that the wound was mortal. Another three-month hitch took Hall to Rhode Island, where, "with another coloured man," he was detached to a French corps of sappers and miners. Finally, in 1781 and 1782, he served as a steward to Colonel Timothy Pickering, the quartermaster general, and assisted him in accounting for the contents of Cornwallis's war chest after the Battle of Yorktown. While in Virginia, his pocketbook containing his freedom papers and his earlier discharges had been stolen. Like most veterans, he had lost his final discharge. The local court in Massachusetts expressed its belief that Hall was indeed a veteran. He signed his deposition and waited for the bureaucratic process to take its course.[26]

Instead of a pension certificate, Hall received a letter from Edwards, who rejected his application on three counts. First, Edwards required supporting affidavits from fellow veterans or, as Edwards put it, "from the numerous survivors of the revolution still residing in Massachusetts." Second, Hall's service as a steward to the quartermaster in 1781–82 was "not embraced in the provisions" of the pension act. A suspicious Edwards also wondered why Hall had taken so long to apply.

Baldwin, Hall's attorney, wrote back that Hall had thought to apply for the first pension act but had too much property to make an application. Hall had learned of the 1832 act only when informed of such by another pensioner in the fall of 1835. In addition to the two already submitted, Baldwin enclosed more affidavits from fellow veterans who were eyewitnesses of Hall's service. Within a week Edwards replied, but this time he departed from the points he had before made. Edwards's new complaint was that Hall did "not disclose whether he was free-born or emancipated, and if the latter, at what time?" The gatekeeper at the Pension Office demanded another deposition.

Baldwin showed Edwards's correspondence to his client, who "expressed much disappointment . . . particularly of that clause requiring 'evidence whether he was free born or emancipate[d].'" Hall also mentioned his father's name, Prince Hall, which may have raised a flag at the Pension Office as a man with that name had been a prominent abolitionist in Boston. Primus Hall was not brought up by his father, but rather by Ezra Trask, a white man who never treated Primus Hall as a slave. To protect Hall from future challenges, Trask had signed a paper that proclaimed Hall free at age twenty-one. But Hall's attorney did not see how any of this was pertinent. He was "at a loss to conceive how that question can have any influence or bearing on the case under consideration." Baldwin knew of "many coloured persons" who were slaves at enlistment and received pensions. And so Hall and Baldwin appealed.

In a week's time, Edwards fired back that he needed paperwork pertaining to Hall's emancipation. Baldwin responded that it would be "impracticable" to produce evidence from sixty years before. Still, the attorney related that in Dumfries, Virginia, in 1782, Hall had found himself in a crowded tavern, lying on animal skins with many other men. Someone had stolen his pocketbook that night with its freedom papers and discharges therein. In addition to Baldwin's letter explaining the lack of paperwork, Hall once again deposed in court, adding more details about his life.[27]

The new packet of evidence and argument was still not satisfactory. It would have been "more satisfactory," claimed Edwards, if Hall had provided the "instrument which he avers he received from his former master." Edwards further stated that, while he had no doubt that Hall "was with the army," he wondered if Hall had been no more than a waiter in his first three tours of service. Edwards's groundless speculation—Hall had three support affidavits that said otherwise—must have struck Hall as racist rationalization. Just as his lawyer knew of enslaved men at enlistment who had received pensions, Primus Hall personally knew at least one black veteran who served with him in Pickering's quartermaster department and qualified for a pension back in 1818. Hall had testified at that time in support of Asabel Wood's successful application. By 1835, times had changed and called for more energetic measures to successfully secure a pension.[28]

In extreme exasperation, Hall and Baldwin decided to cease their appeals because it seemed the Pension Office was determined to believe that Hall had been a waiter, despite three affidavits that said otherwise (two from veterans and one from the son of Captain Flint, the officer who had died in Hall's arms). Furthermore, Baldwin explained that his client was "not well pleased at the reiterated and often repeated inquiries as to the manner, how, and in what manner he became free since he has been so over 64 years." Before ending his correspondence with Edwards, the attorney felt compelled to point out that when Ezra Trask became too old and poor to support himself, Hall had rented a farm for the white man who raised him. Hall and Baldwin would circumvent the Pension Office to appeal to the "national Legislature," where they hoped for justice "without distinction of colour."

On January 4, 1838, a congressional oversight committee on Revolutionary War pensions found in favor of Hall. The committee noted that the commissioner of pensions had refused "from time to time to allow a pension to this free coloured man on different grounds." While perhaps merited at the time, the committee, said, the objections were "obviated" by the testimony produced. The committee's findings, passed by congressional act in June 1838, would seem the end of the story, but it was not. On August 6, 1838, Baldwin objected to new requirements demanded by the Pension Office. Edwards wanted another formal declaration by Hall that included proof that Hall was who he said he was! Baldwin had had enough. He was not going to submit a fifth declaration that would be *"line by line, word for word, comma for comma"* the same as the first four depositions. He informed Edwards that Congressman Richard Fletcher would "be able to substantiate" Hall's identity. In September 1838, Hall's new advocate sent a copy of the congressional act to Edwards, instructing the Pension Office to forward Hall's certificate to the congressman.

The Hall case highlights both promising and discouraging developments in early-nineteenth-century America. By 1832, African American veterans confronted a much more daunting process in their pursuit of a pension. Hall, as a man who had fought the British Empire and examined the British army's coffer after the decisive Battle of Yorktown, was not about to acquiesce to government bureaucrats. Despite the repeated blockages of 1832, he persisted and won. In this case, military service and a man's determination could trump even the rising racist tendencies in American life.

The sense of confidence imparted by service in the nation's founding military struggle is highlighted in the cases of four veterans for whom more copious documentation exists. Samuel Sutphin, Mark Murry, Hamet Achmet, and Jeffrey Brace fought battles before, during, and after the revolution. Slaves at enlistment, Sutphin, Achmet, and Brace gambled on the probability that fighting for the cause would lead to freedom. Murry, a freeman at enlistment, gambled that risking his life for the American cause would lead to a better day. All encountered sobering experiences after the war that did not prevent them from applying for Revolutionary War pensions. In the process of claiming their right to the nation's gratitude, they encountered setbacks, enlisted the help of white veterans, and in three out of four cases, eventually succeeded in securing official recognition either from a state or the federal government for their sacrifice in the war.[29]

Samuel Sutphin of New Jersey

Samuel Sutphin was born enslaved on January 1, 1747, in Hunterdon County, New Jersey, as noted in his master's Bible. Sometime in 1775 he was sold to a neighbor, Casper Berger, who told Sutphin that if he substituted for Berger in the militia service throughout the war, he could be freed. "I believed the white man's word," Sutphin later recalled. Between 1776 and 1778, the aspiring freeman signed up on eight separate occasions and participated in some of the most significant military actions of the early war. Two hours after his unit arrived on Long Island in 1776, the British and Hessians poured off their ships to start the battle for New York City. Sutphin reported that he fought for six hours as the American army retreated and then enlisted the aid of another black man to ferry Sutphin and some of his comrades to the New Jersey shore. Sutphin was also present at the Battle of Princeton, where he related that a group of British soldiers, cornered in Nassau Hall, were flushed out by American cannon fire. On his fourth tour of duty, Sutphin captured a soldier and received a gun from "General Dickinson" as acknowledgment for his services. Telling of his service in General John Sullivan's campaign, Sutphin remembered the names of the two Indian scouts, Shawnee John and Indian Ben, who helped them defeat the Iroquois warriors who had attacked Cherry Valley, a white settlement on the frontier. On returning from that action, Sutphin related, he had killed a Hessian, whom he "watched fall." Shortly thereafter, in late 1778, he was wounded in the leg, which sidelined him for a few months.

Because his last tour was deemed to be so considerable, Sutphin's master was never called up again, and so ended Sutphin's military career. The master, however, reneged on his promise to free him and instead made more profit on the veteran by selling him. Three masters later, Samuel Sutphin purchased his freedom from Peter Sutphin's widow by selling rabbit, raccoon, and muskrat skins.[30]

In June 1832, at the age of eighty-five, Samuel Sutphin applied for a pension from the federal government. In this first attempt, he mentioned neither his race nor his enslavement, limiting his statement to the information relevant to the pension. He had substituted for a man named Casper Berger, he said, and he listed seven short militia stints and one nine-month tour of service, replete with officers' names in every case. He did not, however, provide any support depositions from fellow veterans. Perhaps it is for this reason that in August 1832 Sutphin was back in court to flesh out the details of his service. Here a racial signifier was placed by his name and the substitution deal with his master was explained. The court made an extraordinary addendum to this deposition, in which the judge explained that Sutphin was a respected church member in his community and no longer lived in the county in which he enlisted, thus making it difficult to obtain support from other veterans. Sutphin's "arduous duties in the revolution ably and nobly performed," claimed the court, made him "highly meritorious of a pension." In accordance with the pension act, which stipulated that if no support depositions could be had, two "respectable persons" (a clergyman was preferable) should testify, the Reverend John C. Van Dermont swore to his belief that Sutphin was indeed a veteran.

Lacking muster rolls for the New Jersey militia and an eyewitness account of Sutphin's service, the Pension Office wanted more details and further evidence. In 1833 Sutphin made two court appearances, the first of which was to explain that extreme age and bodily infirmity made it difficult to recall dates with any precision. Indeed, Sutphin often dated events along the agricultural cycle—at "hay and harvest season" or "about the season of early corn planting." In his second court appearance, Sutphin answered a set of questions required by the government. Here Sutphin mentioned that a former governor of New Jersey, a justice of the peace, and a postmaster could attest to his character. His frustration with the process was evident as the word "again" was underlined when he swore to particulars.[31]

The Pension Office remained unmoved, claiming that "being a slave originally, Sutphin was not bound to serve in the militia and the circumstances of each tour of actual service not having been stated as was required, the claim is rejected." In May 1834, Sutphin was once again in the courthouse to explain himself. Concerning the first argument, Sutphin reiterated the deal with his master. He had not been drafted, he had been a substitute. He admitted that his memory of his commanding officers was often limited to men of Dutch descent as he "could talk but little English" at the time of the war. He was more specific about his wounds. A musket ball had hit him at the bottom of one of his gaiters, lodging button and ball into his flesh. He cited many veterans' names in the Long Island and Sullivan campaigns. After dealing with the particulars of his military service, Sutphin turned his attention to the flawed process at his county courthouse. He fingered the court clerk or, as he put it, "the writer of my story," who was "much hurried" in the first depositions and so provided a sketchy outline of his service. He reminded the Pension Office that he had served in the militia "fighting for the white man's freedom." And at the bottom of the fifth page of miniscule writing, Sutphin closed his deposition by saying that he had told the same story in all his depositions, but he doubted whether court clerks "were willing to hear it" as "they omitted all the particulars, asked me but few questions and hurried over it as soon as possible."

When this latest deposition was sent to Washington, D.C., it was accompanied by the testimony of a doctor (who happened to be a former member of

Congress), validating Sutphin's war injuries. A local justice of the peace attested to Sutphin's scars and the gun Sutphin had been awarded and still treasured from the war. And, finally, a veteran pensioner swore to Sutphin's presence "under arms" at Princeton and around Monmouth. Sutphin had done his best to date his stints by the year and season of their occurrence, specify officers' names for each of his enlistments, obtain testimony of an eyewitness to his service, and obtain support of two character witnesses, one of whom was a clergyman as preferred by the pension legislation.

The office in Washington found the new testimony unpersuasive, but not for the reasons previously stated. Pension officials shifted their objections from the issue of slaves and the draft to a problem with discrepancies in Sutphin's declarations (without specifying what they were), and they expressed skepticism about Sutphin's hitch under Sullivan. A nine-month militia stint, claimed the pension office, was "an improbable length."

Nine months later, Lewis Condict, a former member of Congress, requested a final appeal, highlighting an issue that should have been addressed at the beginning—Sutphin's name. The reason it could not be found on the muster rolls was that, as a slave, "his second name always changed as he changed masters." Sutphin's advocate advised the pension officials to look for "Sam Berger or Bergher" or "Sam, a coloured Man" on the rolls. In a last emotional appeal, the writer pleaded that the government keep its promise to this "sober, industrious, meek, humble, and devout" man. Perhaps this list of adjectives was another strategy meant to appeal to white elites in Washington, who wished that all poor people could behave accordingly. It might have struck a chord with J. L. Edwards, the commissioner of pensions, who was himself a southerner, had black servants in his home according to the census, and whose office denied black men who had been slaves at enlistment, a policy with no authorization from the pension act. Finally Sutphin's advocate noted what was perhaps the real problem at the Pension Office. "Without your aid," he wrote, "his unfortunate color will stand between him and his country's justice."

The Pension Office stood its ground, resuscitating one of its previous objections for the final response. Sutphin was a slave "and was not, of course, bound to serve in the militia." The black man's repeated declarations that he had not been drafted but substituted for another man were in vain. Such an acknowledgment would land the Pension Office squarely against the existence of the May 1777 New Jersey law that rewarded masters economically when they enlisted servants—no race disqualified. The government also claimed that without proof of Sutphin's participation in Sullivan's campaign, he would not meet the six-month requirement under the law. The pension officials did not believe the lengthy militia hitch, part of which had taken place during

General Sullivan's campaign against the Indians. Finally, Edwards's office wanted more officers' names. The names that Sutphin had supplied were not adequate.[32]

Three years and many depositions later, Sutphin gave up, at least at the level of the federal government. In 1835, his supporters asked the return of his papers from the Pension Office so they could prepare a case for the New Jersey legislature. On March 10, 1836, Samuel Sutphin, at age eighty-nine, finally received his due.

Many a man in his eighties would have given up on the first rejection letter, but there is a sense in these sources that Samuel Sutphin would not be denied his right to a pension and the official acknowledgment that accompanied it. On this point, he was adamant—and not, I believe, because of the money. He was, after all, nearly ninety years old when the State of New Jersey approved his pension. Rather, he had children, grandchildren, and neighbors whom he had been regaling with war stories for decades. Nobody was going to tell this wounded veteran that he had not served in the Revolution. Despite a duplicitous master, indifferent court clerks, and from his perspective, an intransigent Pension Office, Samuel Sutphin persevered, buoyed by a fellow veteran, a clergyman, neighbors, a postmaster, judges, and even a member of Congress. Samuel the Meek was also Samuel the Persistent.

Mark Murry from North Carolina

Mark Murry was an extraordinary character in colonial North Carolina. Born in the 1750s, this mulatto man was free, but, unlike most other free mulattoes, no master had released him from slavery. His parents had been free. His grandparents had been free. One has to reach back into the seventeenth century to find the reason for this uncommon line of freemen. Mark's great grandmother, Nancy Murry, left Ireland for the promise of America but did not have the money for her journey. Once landed, she was sold to a Colonel Walk and was bound to work for him for a number of years. She likely shared many a workday with people of color on her master's plantation. Perhaps this contact led to her choice of partner once she had completed her obligation to the colonel. She had children with an African American man. With respect to her offspring, North Carolina law trumped skin color. Her children were born free because slave status descended in the female line. The condition of the mother determined the status of her children. So Nancy's descendants would never have to suffer Nancy's fate—to work for a master who owned her body.[33]

Mark Murry's mother was remarkable as well. She was a midwife, renowned in Halifax County, North Carolina, for her skills, so much so that "respectable" ladies sought her services. Mark worked with his father on a farm, but one day in 1780 the old man interrupted Mark's work splitting rails and conveyed the news that Charles Town, South Carolina, had toppled to the British. Father told son that as a free man Mark had to fight for his country. The older man wanted to see an honorable discharge at the end of his son's service. Off to the militia went Murry to fulfill his father's expectations and perhaps to experience the rush of high adventure and the satisfaction of contributing to the war effort.

After the war, "a great many speculators" invaded Halifax County and told veterans that they would never receive any payment for the IOUs that they held from their military service. As Murry put it, they said, "Boys, I am sorry for you. You will never get nothing" from the government. So the veteran gambled and sold the IOUs from two of his tours for $1. Another speculator paid Murry's taxes for one or two years in exchange for the IOU from another tour of service. Murry explained that he earned his living from hard labor. Although he "could read his bible but could not write," he still had no financial basis to make a go of it in his native state. This might have sparked his move to Tennessee, perhaps as part of a group of veterans who moved west.

Murry's stories appear in his Revolutionary War pension application. In the 1840s he struggled to fulfill the requirements of the federal pension act of 1832 that required at least six months of service as well as proof of service in the form of a written discharge or two witnesses who served with the applicant during the war. As a man in his nineties in Wilson County, Tennessee, Murry claimed that he could not find companions in arms nor did he have any discharge certificate from his multiple three-month militia stints. But he rallied his memory to relate stories that addressed his problems with the pension system.[34]

Regarding the lack of a discharge certificate, Mark was far from alone among Revolutionary War veterans. In his case, his discharges disappeared in his father's possession. When the old man died shortly after the war, Mark could not find them. But he told the Pension Office how he had struggled to procure his first discharge back in 1780. One of his officers, an "overbearing man" named James Cooper, had gone after Murry because the mulatto man would not act as the officer's servant. Murry complained to a higher-up, who asked if Cooper were a rich man in civilian life. When told no, the officer deemed Cooper not worthy of a servant and so told Murry to ignore Cooper. At that moment, Murry had made an enemy. The rebuffed Cooper struck back by denying Murry a discharge. The mulatto man and three of his messmates, all white men, complained to "General Butler," who ordered an honorable discharge for Murry. The militia private had no hesitation in going up the chain of command to obtain a redress of his grievances. Perhaps he needed the support of three white men to trouble a general, but he nonetheless took the risk and succeeded in claiming his due.

A second problem with the Pension Office concerned his name. Few militia muster rolls survived the war years but North Carolina comptroller records that kept track of money paid or owed to veterans did exist in the state capital. Like many men of color, Murry's name on documents did not exactly jibe with his then current name. Murry related that on two tours he had served with a man named Coban, who had created nicknames for the mulatto private, probably, mused Murry, because of his "mixed blood." Coban's creativity did not stretch far, as he called Murry "Meril," "Merrell," and "Marry." Murry did not explain how these names related to his mixed-race self, but he did address the comptroller's records that showed payments made to an M. Marry. Even if the Pension Office admitted that spelling was a free-form exercise, its officials noted that the sheriff of Northampton County distributed the money—not the sheriff of Murry's adjoining county.

Murry's quest for a pension continued from 1845 to 1854. In the end, the Pension Office admitted that he probably had served his country but maintained that he could not prove the length of time he served. This sparked another reminiscence from Murry's trove of war stories. A man in his nineties might not remember exact dates, but like many others he recalled notable events. His father had summoned him to service right after the fall of Charles Town in May 1780. While on the march to South Carolina, his unit spent a crucial day performing a mock battle for the entertainment of some North Carolina grandees and so missed the Battle of Camden (see chapter 2). The fall of Charles Town occurred on May 12, 1780. The defeat at the Battle of Camden, which many soldiers called "Gates's Defeat," took place on August 16, 1780. Murry's unit continued to operate, in retreat mode, for an indeterminate amount of time after the battle. He had established the first three months of the six-month requirement for a pension. Unfortunately he could not bracket future stints in the militia with recognizable events. He claimed to have served in various hitches until after "Cornwallis was taken," for a total of twelve months.[35]

After the government rejected his application a second time, he enlisted the support of people who knew him. Elizabeth Pope, the widow of a white pensioner named Philip Pope, said she lived three miles away from the Murry farm in North Carolina and that Mark had served. "They were respectable," she opined, "for coloured people." Another member of the Pope family declared "to have such confidence in the man that I would believe anything he would state upon any subject." But the supporter went on, as so many whites did, to qualify his full endorsement of the "light mulatto." He labeled Murry a man of first-rate character but could not stop there, adding, "although a mixed coloured man."[36]

A third supporter, Jesse Grimes, made no such limiting racial statements. He was also a North Carolina transplant in Tennessee and had known Murry since Grimes's boyhood, when the veteran, then around fifty years of age, was to Grimes already an old man. Grimes had imbibed the stories that Murry and Murry's mother and sister had told him. But his favorite opportunity to hear war stories occurred when a group of veterans got together to reminisce. Particularly at community events like logrollings and house raisings, young Jesse had hung on to every word these old men, all of whom were white slaveholders with the exception of Murry, let drop about "campaign exploits." Despite indubitable social distinctions, these events in the setting of war memories made these men "companions in arms," Grimes claimed, since they had shared the adventures of their lives in the same company. These stories "made a deep impression upon my mind," recalled Grimes.[37]

He shared one of their jokes with the Pension Office. Henry Kent, a member of this group, was a man of small stature and said that if ever in another battle, he would get behind Mark Murry for protection. Murry would have none of it. Although "a man of uncommon physical power in his more youthful days," according to Grimes, Murry had declared that he would be breastworks for no man—breastworks being temporary fortifications familiar to all soldiers at that time. Murry's joke brought on a burst of laughter from veterans and appreciative neighbors alike. Having heard over the years many of Murry's stories, Grimes offered to provide more of these if the Pension Office deemed it necessary. Unfortunately for future researchers, the bureaucrats in Washington had to ascertain that applicants conformed to the requirements of the law, and no amount of colorful or riveting stories constituted proof of the length of a veteran's service. So although two of Murry's sons had been inspired by their father's stories and went on to serve with Andrew Jackson at New Orleans, and although the Pension Office admitted that Murry probably had served, its officials rejected his pension application for lack of proof that he had soldiered the requisite six months.

The seventy-five pages of Mark Murry's pension application testify to a proud man whose confidence survived the societies in which he lived. As a free man of color, he had to negotiate his way through a slave society that had just deprived African Americans of the vote. In his soldier days he twice went over the head of an officer who wanted Murry as his servant and then tried to deny him a written discharge. After the war, Murry made a high-risk decision in leaving all that was familiar in North Carolina to settle on the Tennessee frontier. From the number of near neighbors back in Carolina who lived in his part of Tennessee, it is likely that a group of veterans moved together. Most black veterans did not go far from their place of enlistment after the war. When Murry first heard of the pension act, he assumed like many others did that he would not qualify, because of his color. But once apprised of his admissibility, Murry faced down the federal government three times to get his due. Ultimately he believed that his color resulted in the Pension Office's decision to reject him. Perhaps he could have gone a fourth time if death had not intervened. He died on the eve of the Civil War but left a large family in Tennessee and a wealth of historical evidence to testify to his determination to be free and equal.

Hamet Achmet—Africa and Connecticut

Like many of the African American veterans, Hamet Achmet's early life is a blur to us. His name might well indicate Muslim origin. The estimate of his age in an 1820 document puts his birth in the 1750s. His very thick accent, even in old age, stymied a court clerk who explained that the veteran was a native of Africa. When exactly Achmet was snatched from his homeland is unknowable. He appears in the Connecticut line as a drummer around 1777. He reckoned that it was a few years before Yorktown, or as he put it, "the capture of Cornwallis." He was described at his enlistment as "young" and small of stature. He listed his participation only at the Battle of Yorktown in his first pension application. Discharged in the state of Delaware, Achmet walked home, presumably to Connecticut.[38]

By 1811 he resided in Bridgeport, where seven years later, he applied for a government pension as a former revolutionary soldier. The fact that he still had his drum and leather cap from the army days did not constitute proof of service to government officials. He exhibited a proactive disposition by procuring his own support depositions, requiring him to find witnesses to his service in different towns. Samuel Fayerweather from Weston, Connecticut, deposed that as a private and NCO during the war he had known Achmet, who spoke English "indifferently" and was quite a character among the men. Fayerweather related a story that still amused him forty years later, although the court clerk was sketchy on the details. It had to do with Fayerweather teasing Achmet on the banks of the Schuylkill River about saving "his allowance of spirits and self respect." The episode ended with Achmet's canteen gone missing, "to the no small amusement of the soldiers" witnessing the event. To "retaliate," Achmet entered Fayerweather's tent that night to head-butt his comrade, only to receive "several strokes of the deponent's heel." These momentary adversaries parted company at the close of the war, only to be reunited in 1814 on the streets of Bridgeport where the white man "instantly" recognized Achmet. Fayerweather lent his newfound status as a captain to support the drummer's pension application in 1818.

Self-portrait of Hamet Achmet, ink on paper. This veteran of the Connecticut line, renowned in Middletown, Connecticut, for his small stature and long hair, drew his own picture, relaxing in old age with his pipe and crowning glory. Courtesy of the Middlesex County Historical Society, Middletown, Connecticut.

Achmet walked from Bridgeport to adjacent Fairfield next to secure Dan Raymond's testimony. Raymond deposed that the "man now present before me" was the same "little black drummer" he had seen at the Battle of Stony Point, adding this engagement to Achmet's list of battles. With two witnesses and his own testimony, Achmet's paperwork moved on to Washington, D.C.

The Pension Office initially rejected the application, saying that the officer cited in Achmet's deposition did not match the right state line. It happened that the court clerk made the error and admitted that this native of Africa was very difficult to understand. In his initial court appearance, Achmet had chattily let drop many officers' names from New England and the middle states and "related many things" concerning his army service. It was too much for the court clerk, who did the best he could. After the Pension Office rejection, the two men (Achmet and the court clerk) met again to get the story right. Still straining to make himself understood, Achmet had to point in the direction where his colonel (Return J. Meigs) lived, in order for the clerk to understand. Once that ordeal was over, Achmet procured another support deposition by walking to Milford, about ten miles from Bridgeport, where Jeffery James testified that Achmet was in the room and "by his particular request, this affidavit is made." When Achmet later had to submit proof of his indigence in 1820, he added another battle to his list, Germantown, where, he reported, he had been wounded and afterward had convalesced at the unenviable encampment of Valley Forge. His wound did not prevent him from serving six more years although in 1820 he claimed it had later oozed blood, preventing him from working as a day laborer. The list of his possessions at that time was valued at $11.71. Half the value of all that he owned consisted of his drum from the war, assessed at $6. About the drum, a court official said that it had "the distinctive markings of the United States painted on it." Achmet's second attempt at a government pension, shortly after the first, was successful. Till the day of his death, he would receive eight dollars per month, a tidy sum for a man whose total wealth had once totaled $11.71.

By 1820, Hamet, at age sixty-two, had moved from Bridgeport to Middletown. He was a superb hustler in later life, claiming that he had been a slave at Mount Vernon and as a boy had held General Washington's bridle. He regaled his neighbors in Middletown with stories of "the fine dinners and grand company" when he had served at Washington's table. From time to time he exhibited mementoes said to be from the general, most notably a lock of hair that he closely guarded and had buried with him. He never explained how a slave at Mount Vernon managed to become a drummer in the Connecticut line. Nowhere in his pension application did he make this connection with Washington. None of the three veterans who had supported his application mentioned it either. But the enterprising Achmet played up alleged Mount Vernon memories to the hilt in later life. As an old man he made toys to supplement his pension. On his cottage door was a sign that read "Drums large and small, made and sold by General Washington's waiter." He had saved his old drum and cap from the war and appeared at public events with them, wearing a dark blue uniform with red stripes and "gay epaulettes." Otherwise he could be seen on the streets, toy drums at his waist, accosting well-heeled men and telling them that he dreamed that they had given him a shilling. If he encountered a likely boy, the shilling became a penny. "Of course, the dream would be realized," wrote his nineteenth-century biographer. It was on Middletown's streets that he likely approached the carriage carrying the Marquis de Lafayette on that man's 1824–25 tour through America. The French general must have recognized such a distinctive man and probably exchanged a few words. Like any veteran recognized by the great Lafayette on that tour, Hamet's personal stock must have soared. In

1827 a number of members of the American Literary, Scientific, and Military Academy, then in Middletown, each pledged to give Hamet ten cents.

Achmet's renown reached showman P. T. Barnum, who tried to lure the veteran into his show, claiming he had already employed another servant from Mount Vernon. Achmet turned him down perhaps, fearing he might be unmasked by a real servant from the old days. As it turned out, the other servant was a hoax as well. In 1839 Achmet merited a small article in a Hartford newspaper that described him as small of stature with long, matted hair. The article mentioned another notable peculiarity—he had a white wife. When a townswoman decided to write a pamphlet on Achmet after his death, she explained that since mixed marriages "were not in favor," the young, white woman who wanted to become the second Mrs. Achmet "washed her face and hands in a decoction of mahogany chips" in anticipation of approaching the Methodist parsonage to tie the knot. The groom was described as very black and very short and thickset. His hair was described as "sooty wool which long manipulation had converted into pipe-stem curls which waved about his face in the most comical way imaginable." One of his wives, after a quarrel, decided to cut off her husband's ringlets as he lay asleep. Which one did the deed? At one juncture during his first marriage, to Jane, a black woman, he took out an advertisement in the local paper advising publicly that he would not pay any more of her debts. Jane died in 1827 to be closely followed by Marian, the second wife. There too marital trouble plagued the Achmet household, as in the spring of 1828 Marian left his bed and board, thus prompting Hamet to put another ad in the paper. The rocky state of affairs in the Achmet household could have induced either wife to cut off Hamet's crowning glory. Achmet's death in 1842 merited an obituary that labeled him "colored" and "a revolutionary pensioner." It also reported of Achmet that "he said" he was a servant of George Washington's.

For Achmet the war did not result in equality or a fair chance at the pursuit of happiness. Hamet made his own happiness. He became a beloved member of the community. His flamboyant personality and winning ways charmed people who saw him as a harmless figure of fun. Beneath the veneer, however, lived a crafty spinner of stories, undoubtedly taking satisfaction in pulling one over on his neighbors. He found a protector of sorts in a prominent local lawyer with whom he consulted on major issues like the P. T. Barnum offer and through whom he received his pension money. (Hamet's pension originally went through the member of congress representing his district). When the government rejected his original pension application, he appealed. The local court clerk admitted that he had made a mistake by not carefully listening to Hamet's thickly accented speech. By 1839 the veteran bragged that he had received between fourteen hundred and fifteen hundred dollars from the Pension Office to date, duly recorded by his biographer. Like many other veterans, he wed a much younger woman the second time around, but he flaunted conventions by marrying a white woman—another piece of this maverick's story recorded by the newspaper and his biographer.

The white citizens of Middletown could appreciate a funny, eccentric old man who was likely viewed as an exception by many who still held strong prejudices. These same white people might have treated Achmet better when alone with him than in group situations. This group dynamic was certainly in play when the State of Connecticut, in whose continental line he served, turned its back on the real-life continental veteran by limiting his options and taking away his right to vote. He, in turn, decided to milk the Revolution for all it was worth. In a way, this small-town P. T. Barnum encapsulated the change in his society from Republican virtue to a nation of self-serving businessmen in that he had both suffered as a rank-and-file soldier in the war and then later capitalized on it. The promise of the Revolution had failed him, but he managed to make the Revolution work for him.

Jeffrey Brace—Africa and Connecticut

Unlike the long and detailed pension files of Sutphin, Murry, and Achmet, the file of Jeffrey Brace contains just the bare essentials from his court appearance in April 1818. He had enlisted in the Connecticut line and fought at the Battles of White Plains, Stamford, Westchester, and Fort Mifflin, where he was wounded. Brace thought he had signed up for a three-year commitment but found that he was expected to serve for the duration. He "cheerfully served" for five years and nine months and received a discharge and badge of merit, which he had lost. Brace was an exceptional pensioner in that he provided posterity with his memoirs, which flesh out these bare details, turning Brace from an abstraction associated with a few battles to a flesh-and-blood man, who, according to his own narrative, "passed through so many varying scenes of life."[39]

Eight years before Brace applied for a pension, he had related his life story to an abolitionist, who published the result in 1810. Like the pension applications, this narrative was filtered through the mind of a white man. Unlike hurried court clerks who transcribed pension applications, however, B. F. Prentiss was truly interested in the pageant of Jeffrey Brace's life, from which he culled colorful details and moral lessons—and no doubt added a stroke or two of his own to drive home his point. Although Brace's memoir was fashioned to sway minds against slavery, the narrative provides unique glimpses into one veteran's life before the war and his experiences afterward.

Born and raised in Africa, Brace was sixteen years old when kidnapped and forced aboard a slave ship bound for the Caribbean. He sailed with the British fleet during the French and Indian War, earned the name Jeffrey for a reckless courage that reminded his superiors of Sir Jeffrey Amherst, and continued to sail the Atlantic until he was sold to a religiously strict Puritan with sadistic tendencies. Several masters later he ended up with a kindly widow in Woodbury, Connecticut, who taught him to read by studying the Bible with him. When the old woman died, Jeffrey "descended like real estate in fee simple" to her son, Benjamin Stiles.

In 1777, at the advanced age of thirty-seven, he entered the Connecticut line with his master and his master's brother. It is unclear whether he entered the service as a servant to his master or whether he took advantage of a 1777 Connecticut law allowing blacks to be hired as substitutes for white men. The latter possibility seems more likely, because shortly after his enlistment he was drafted into a company of light infantry that wanted men above six feet tall. (Brace was six foot three). Whether his editor's sentiments or his own sense of irony, Jeffrey Stiles (as he was now known) wrote, "Alas! Poor African slave to liberate freemen, my tyrants." In the ensuing years, Stiles marched all over the northern theater of war, participating in major battles like Monmouth and minor skirmishes like the one in Horseneck (Greenwich), Connecticut. Unfortunately he provided no details of the battles, perhaps because he felt (or his editor felt) that history books could do a better job of enlightening his readers. Stiles did, however, relate with great relish some stories that feature his ingenuity and daring.

On one occasion, Stiles served as a lookout for a small band of soldiers in search of stolen cattle. Suddenly a man rode up to him with pistol in hand and ordered Stiles to lay down his arms. Fearing that this might be a prank concocted by fellow soldiers who had pulled this kind of thing before on "the soldiers belonging to our line"—and he was in an all-black company—Stiles questioned the man, ascertaining at some point that he was a British light horseman in disguise. Stiles managed to kill the enemy soldier and tore off down the road on the dead man's horse, pursued by men with swords in hand. As the enemy gained on the spur-less Stiles, he saw his captain and comrades up ahead on the road who whistled at seeing the "long shanked negro soldier with a leather cap, mounted on an elegant gelding light horse." Within twenty or thirty rods (165 yards at most) Stiles heard his captain order the men not to fire as they might hit Jeffrey. But the men fired anyway, killing four British soldiers and striking Stiles's coat and bayonet belt. The British had been only within "two or three jumps of me," he says in his memoirs, but suddenly, "being so handsomely saluted" with gunfire, they turned and made the best retreat possible.[40]

Once back in camp, Stiles realized he was wounded, thus effectively sidelining him for three months from service in Meigs's regiment, famous for its leather caps. Stiles's recuperation gave him plenty of time to reflect on the close shave he'd had with death. Why did his pursuers hold their fire as they thundered down the path and came within "two or three jumps" of him? Stiles surmised that his pursuers thought they could question this sentry about the state of the lines. Or perhaps they saw the opportunity to "enrich their coffers" by selling this black man in British-occupied New York. The only person to enrich himself from Stiles's adventure was, ironically, an American officer who agreed to pay Stiles $250 for the horse, saddle, and bridle, and then "thought proper never to pay the same."

At war's end, the newly freed Jeffrey Stiles changed his name to that of his father—anglicized to "Brace"—and moved to Vermont, a sparsely settled area at that time. He hired himself out and was often cheated out of his pay to the point that he wondered whether there was any difference between slavery and freedom. Yet he managed to buy twenty-five acres of uncleared land, though he still had to work for wages to afford the cost of setting up his own farm and to support his African-born wife, who had two children of her own. These children became a source of great concern to Brace and his wife, for as soon as they were old enough to work, white neighbors made the claim that they were not properly raised and so had to be hired out on a long-term contract. Although Brace said that "the majesty of Guinea rose indignant in my breast," the authorities prevailed and the two children were bound away. As he explained it, "The corruption and superstition, mingled with the old Connecticut bigotry and Puritanism, made certain people think a Negro had no right to raise their own children."[41]

Years later, when Brace's own children came of a likely age to be hired out, a white neighbor who coveted the black man's land tried the same trick. By this time Brace was a viable farmer and landholder in the community and had sufficient pull to resist the attempt. The incessant feuding with his white neighbor induced him to consider a move to Kentucky—a Revolutionary War colonel was leading a group of settlers there—but Brace thought the better of it, opting not to live so close to slavery. "They might haul me in," he said, or prosecute him for sedition if he said something out of line. His children did not understand why he tolerated so much abuse. They wanted to avenge his wrongs, while their father counseled that the best chance for redress was to turn the other cheek. "This to them seemed like false doctrine," he said.

Finally he found a reasonably good situation in 1804 when he moved to Georgia, Vermont, a town on Lake Champlain. It was here in 1818 that Brace called on the government to acknowledge his services during the Revolutionary

War by awarding him a pension. His first attempt failed. Even though Brace was supported by the testimony of another soldier, who maintained that "there was no better soldier in the army," the Pension Office did not believe the truth of Brace's deposition and could not find his name on the muster rolls. Brace's supporters managed to interest a member of Congress, Samuel Crafts, into lodging a protest with J. L. Edwards. The tone of Edwards's reply suggests that Congressman Crafts had applied some pressure. No, said a defensive Edwards, his doubt concerning Brace's service did not imply that the judge handling Brace's case was a fraud. (Fraud cases in Vermont were particularly numerous in 1818). Edwards admitted that none of Brace's deposition clashed with the known facts about the regiment to which he belonged. All that was needed, claimed Edwards, was an explanation of the name change and two veterans who would vouch for him. Jeffrey Brace did better than that. He provided testimonies from three more veterans, one who mentioned that Brace was part of an all-black company and another who complicated matters further by relating that Jeff Brace, alias Jeff Stiles, was also nicknamed Pomp London! But this last glitch did not stop the eventual issuance of a pension certificate in July 1821.

By that time, eighty-one-year-old Jeffrey Brace, in his own words, had "passed through so many varying scenes of life." This old, frail man who stood in the Franklin County courthouse had swum the Niger River, survived the Middle Passage and several sadistic masters, sailed around the Atlantic world, fought in the American Revolution, and published his life story to further the abolition movement. This life is completely outside the popular metaphor that stresses the helplessness and incompetency of people of color. He tried to better his lot by moving to a frontier area and purchasing land. Despite rapacious selectmen and neighbors, he continued to soldier on, picking up stakes for greater opportunity. He was helped along the way by men with military titles. A Colonel Lyon provided the opportunity to move to Kentucky, and "Majors Clark and Sheldon" helped him in northern Vermont. Perhaps they felt moved to aid a fellow veteran. Despite a strict Pension Office, which at that time was doubly vigilant about fraud in Vermont applications, Brace reapplied when rejected, enlisting the help of four white veterans and a member of Congress. Although no fuss was made when this extraordinary man passed away in 1827, his children, who did not accept humiliation and injustice so placidly, undoubtedly passed on his stories to their children, providing a strong historical claim to their quest for liberation.

As Jeffrey Brace's memoir attests, court clerks bled out the personality from veterans' pension narratives. And so when one might expect to find differences, for example, between white and black depositions, there is little to be detected.

The same applies when trying to find regional differences among the applicants. The narratives of freemen of Connecticut are strikingly similar to those of enslaved Virginians. Between the two pension acts of 1818 and 1832, the first national debate on slavery took place around the entry of Missouri into the union. In 1832 slavery was once more an issue, abolitionist voices were stronger, and more numerous black voices in the movement were apparent. Yet there is no discernable change in the tone or content between the 1818 applications and the ones in 1832.

The bureaucracy of the pension system itself no doubt accounts for some of this uniformity. But perhaps the veterans' service in the war that forged the nation left a positive memory that transcended regions, national debates, and mounting racism in American life. With few exceptions, the veterans in their old age looked back to their Revolutionary War service as the adventure of their lives. These young recruits burst forth from the confines of their neighborhoods and masters' oversight to experience new locales. Although ordered about in the army, African Americans were used to taking orders, and they could see that white men were subject to the same officer's bark. These men wore uniforms and were part of an organization that had to be respected. Black men were part of units that requisitioned white farmer's corn and shot at men who in civilian life would have lorded over them. Jeff Stiles and his comrades even got away with personally requisitioning a Tory farmer's pig. On many levels, then, military service proved a liberating time in itself. It also often resulted in individual emancipation and sparked a movement to gradually emancipate all slaves in the North. Military service freed the slave and servant from the narrow optic of everyday survival to a broader vision of active participation in a larger cause. And that cause was not only the white man's freedom but also their own. Such was the pride and emotional connection to the revolutionary days that some veterans put up a fight about handing over their discharges to get their pension. Agrippa Hull's attorney requested the prompt return of the discharge signed by George Washington, because his client "had rather forego the pension than lose the discharge." New Jersey veteran Oliver Cromwell remembered a pension agent taking away his discharge thirty-five years before. "He mourns over it much," claimed his local newspaper, "and always speaks of it being taken away from him with tearful eyes." Among the men who lost their discharges—in fires, in the laundry, when they moved—was an old soldier who had destroyed the precious paper himself. His widow explained that her husband "supposed it would never be of use to him." Whether because Kemar Blackman believed that no tangible benefits would result from the paper or because he was disillusioned with the aftermath of the Revolution, he burned the paper.[42]

Although some black men found it harder under the 1832 legislation to obtain a pension, those who succeeded reaped a reward that made an enormous difference in their lives, particularly for penurious veterans under the 1818 legislation. Caesar Wallace, a veteran of Bunker Hill, Monmouth, and Newtown, had no belongings to speak of when he obtained his eight-dollar monthly pension. Two years later, when the government demanded a list of property for every veteran who had received a pension, Wallace noted the presence of one cow as the sum total of his assets, purchased with some of the pension money he had thus far received. Another veteran in slightly better financial shape, Prince Bailey, obtained a pension in 1818 only to have it taken away in 1820, when he, like many other pensioners, did not pass the government means test. He owned thirty-five acres and a small house. When this bad news had gotten out, Bailey's creditors swooped down upon him, necessitating the sale of his house and land. In 1825, Bailey came back to court to apply for another pension because the actions of the federal government had just made him destitute. He was restored to the rolls.[43]

When Bailey reapplied for his pension, his white creditors and the town selectmen verified the sale of his land and praised Bailey's good morals. Their belief in his upstanding character may also have been aided by the fact that a government pension would put the black veteran in a position to pay his remaining debts or, at the very least, take the burden of his upkeep off the local authorities. African American veterans like Bailey understood the value of a white man's word over that of a black man's, and so they tapped their white acquaintances for support. (There are very few support depositions from African Americans, and what few there were often appear in rejected applications.)

For a man whose total wealth totaled $3.62, an eight-dollar-per-month pension was a significant improvement. Bristol Budd, a veteran of the Connecticut line, was a fifty-seven-year-old blind man who walked four hundred miles from Susquehanna, Pennsylvania, to New Canaan, Connecticut, in order to procure the support depositions for his pension. He was led on a string by his fourteen-year-old son. Another old soldier, Charles Cuffey, a seventy-five-year-old veteran of the Eleventh Virginia, walked close to two hundred miles to obtain his depositions. Up in New England, the colonel of the Third Massachusetts Regiment was amazed when a sixty-six-year-old veteran, William Johnson, appeared on his doorstep. Colonel William Hull, in his support deposition, said that Johnson, now a Vermont resident, "traveled several hundred miles to find me." He remembered that at the West Point encampment Johnson had contracted smallpox, the pockmarks of which still spotted the veteran's face forty years later. Aside from procuring support depositions, former soldiers talked among themselves and in the process had their memories refreshed. Benjamin

Cowell, a popular pension agent in Rhode Island, would sometimes have a dozen veterans in his waiting room. It must have been a wonderful occasion to be able to talk of those times with people who understood what that service was all about.[44]

The pension process instigated many reunions, the most poignant of which concerned an applicant named Thomas Gardner. Both white veterans who testified on his behalf said that he was the best drummer at West Point. Both vets also stated that Gardner was known as "Black Tom" and "Black Drummer" in the army. One of the white men, fourteen years old when he met Gardner on Saint Patrick's Day, 1782, subsequently learned the "art of drumming" from the best, he said. Just a month before Gardner's pension hearing, the two men got together again and "beat the drum" with one another. Much to the surprise of the white veteran, Black Tom remembered all "the regular Continental beats."[45]

Other veterans with no fellow former soldiers in their neighborhood sometimes found a veteran who did not remember the pension applicant from forty to fifty years before. But upon exchanging war stories, the applicant proved to his potential supporter that he really was a soldier. Such was the case for Caesar Clark, whose detailed account of the siege of Fort Mifflin (which veterans often called the Mud Fort because it was on Mud Island) convinced Charles Fanning, a former lieutenant of his Connecticut regiment, that Caesar was indeed a veteran. Fanning did another service for Simeon Simons, a Rhode Island veteran who over a period of six years traded war stories, often about Simons's senior officer, Christopher Greene of the First Rhode Island. Fanning had often been in the same brigade as the First Rhode Island and had known Greene well. The two men frequently talked about Greene's death in May 1781. Fanning ultimately wrote a support deposition for Simons that said that Simons "has so particularly stated the circumstances of that event" that Fanning had no doubt that Simons was really a veteran. Widows whose husbands did not go through the pension system had even more challenging obstacles to overcome. They had to prove their husband's service *and* provide proof of marriage. Sarah Green related that shortly after her wedding, she and her husband went to the army. Her husband died in 1786, and his only proof of service was her own memories, now of sixty-year vintage. So she found a veteran and related stories to him that only a person who was there could relate. With the veteran's help, she secured her pension.[46]

In a way that they could never have imagined before the war, a generation of African Americans who remained in this country could see the great leaders and themselves in the same sentence. They say in their pensions, "I fought at Burgoyne's defeat" or "I manned a redoubt at the fall of Cornwallis." Men who had been classed with boys and old men in the beginning of the war had become members of the elite units of the army. The adjectives change too. They are still "faithful" but they are also "noble" and "worthy." As "noble ruins of that splendid period," their war service sometimes elevated them into heady company. Peter Jennings, a veteran of the First Rhode Island and one of the few black veterans to move to the western frontier, was acknowledged by General Lafayette when the famous general passed through Tennessee during his 1826–27 tour. Up in New England, Nancy Daley, daughter of veteran Cato Fisk, testified twice to help her mother obtain a widow's pension. Nancy was not sure of the exact date of her father's death, but she remembered that he died in the same week as a prominent local general—which would put her father's death in March 1824. She distinctly remembered this connection because the following Sunday "the minister preached a sermon on their deaths and mentioned my father before he mentioned the General, and some people in the Parish were offended at it." The minister, whose own father was a Revolutionary War veteran, had paired Nancy's father with a general, resulting in a miffed congregation. This story represents a mixed legacy, but its hopeful side is surely in evidence. Liberation often begins with small stories. The pension reveals that Nancy could sign her name, indicating a certain degree of literacy that her father did not have. She also screwed up her courage and twice appeared in court to help her mother successfully obtain a widow's pension. Could her veteran-father have envisioned this train of events? We don't know. But his actions and the actions of thousands of other men of color inspired the next generation.[47]

The old, undaunted warriors continued to fight well after the cannons were silenced on the battlefield. Although participants in the making of the country, most black veterans were still far away from the world they had dreamed of for their children. The applicants were still largely limited to jobs that paid a pittance. Jack Gardner, a three-year veteran in the Fourth Massachusetts Regiment, was described in 1818 as "a regular perambulator of our streets with wheel barrow and swill tub in search of daily food for himself and swine." But while poor and limited by skin color in the new republic, he and other veterans became celebrities in their own communities, particularly when they aged. Countless neighbors in supporting affidavits testified that they had been listening to the veterans' stories for decades. The veterans talked to their children too, and they could take satisfaction from the strides made by the next generation. The pension files reveal that more than half of the male children of these veterans could write their names. Jeff Brace's sons exhibited less patience than their father over injustices committed by white neighbors. These children joined others who gathered around the old veterans and took inspiration from their actions. Jeremiah Asher, a grandson of an African-born veteran, wrote his memoirs in 1850 as a way to trumpet the evils of slavery and raise money for his church in Philadelphia. The younger Asher characterized the Revolution as an "eventful period [that] will never be forgotten by us whose fathers fought for liberty, not from the yoke of Britain but from the yoke of American slavery." William Wells Brown, the abolitionist-playwright-novelist, had two grandfathers in the war. W. E. B. Du Bois claimed Mumbet as an ancestor. Isaac Brown's descendants fought in the Civil War through World War II. Each enlistment, like that of their Revolutionary War ancestor, was another claim on the nation's promise of liberty and equality for all.[48]

Conclusion

Claiming Their Due

A frowning world was everywhere for people of color before the American Revolution. Slavery was no sooner questioned than the inferiority of Indians and women. The Revolution rattled the way of this world. First of all, it produced chaos that preoccupied white male rulers and diverted their attention away from the daily full-time control of wives, servants, and slaves. To be sure the Founding Fathers worried about a social revolution from below, but the crisis called for all hands on deck. Poor people had to be armed despite the danger all around that that prospect engendered. People of color, fully one-fifth of the population, could not be ignored. The British certainly did not ignore them. Revolutionaries had to think of black people in a novel way—as participants in creating a new world—and it made the people at the top uncomfortable.

Along with the military emergency and the chaos it entailed, the Revolution spawned a language that ended up with a power all its own. The fight on the American side was said to be about slavery—the chains that the king, that "Royal Brute of Britain," wanted to coil around the colonists' hearts and souls. As real-life slaves listened to the revolutionaries' arguments, they found a language tailor-made to their situation: the evil of slavery, the equality of men, the birthright of liberty. And were the revolutionaries' aspirations any more improbable than theirs? Here was a colonial backwater taking on an empire that had just prevailed in a world war. Their white neighbors challenged the divine right of kings. If "divine right" could be toppled, surely the whites might see their way clear to treating people of color as themselves. After all, monarchy in the colonies was as unquestioned in 1763 as slavery was.

First courted by the British, people of color by the thousands risked the unknown and allied themselves with the redcoats. The lists in the *Royal Gazette* showing 666 men and women in the various departments of the British army in Charles Town alone, are an indication of the support rendered to the side that did more to free black people than the liberty-loving patriots. Indeed, the British had more black refugees streaming into town than jobs to give them.

Fewer men of color actively supported the revolutionaries' military effort. By fits and starts, most state governments begrudgingly opened the way for soldierly participation to all, regardless of race. When that happened, muster lists with names like Cato, Cuff, London, and Scipio testified to black men's contributions to the cause that on average was of longer duration than that of their white compatriots.

When black men entered the army, they encountered a world of possibilities unthinkable in civilian life. The uniform they donned on entering the service was the same uniform that white soldiers wore. As military men, they could requisition white farmers' goods. They were part of an armed company that scattered civilians as the soldiers marched down the road. And the road on which they marched often took them to faraway places. Winsor Fry, as a young teenager, marched to Boston in 1775. After enlisting in the Rhode Island continental line in 1777, he marched to New Jersey, where he fought at the Battle of Red Bank. He then proceeded to Valley Forge, Pennsylvania, where he heard about the prospect of an all-black Rhode Island regiment. He marched back home to become part of that experiment and fought at the Battle of Rhode Island. After taking a few months of unauthorized leave, he was back in service to walk to the major army encampment on the Hudson River, and from there he marched with the French and American armies to Yorktown, Virginia. Returning to the Hudson after the battle, he was discharged at Saratoga and walked home. This kind of mobility probably exceeded most people's experiences, and it certainly outpaced the limits of Winsor's civilian life. Private Fry's travels and adventures must have imparted a confidence to this veteran who encountered all manner of trials and challenges during his service.[1]

In addition to mobility, black soldiers found themselves fighting alongside white soldiers for a cause bigger than themselves. Samuel Bell, a freeman from North Carolina, thought it his duty to fight for American independence. Richard Rhodes, born in Africa, married the larger cause with his own situation when he told the pension office years later that he had "entered the army for the purpose of attaining my freedom." Jehu Grant, another enslaved man, heard the "songs of liberty [that] thrilled through my heart," he said. To encamp with thousands of other men, a novel experience on its own for anyone, white or black, must have given black soldiers hope that future alliances were possible with sympathetic whites. Jehu Grant found one such white man who was instrumental in Grant's eventual freedom.[2]

Military service also provided an outlet for men to be forceful, to take initiative, to engage in aggressive behavior. Their wild, young spirits could act out under the watchful eye of their officers. This must have been particularly liberating for black men who had to daily swallow humiliation back in civilian life, whether free or enslaved. With great exhilaration, a North Carolina veteran related that "we whipped the British and Tories." Although meaning "to defeat," the soldier's choice of verb might have been influenced by the fact that he had seen many black men physically whipped back home. Dick Brattle made it a point to say in his pension application that at the Battle of Rhode Island the first unit onto the terrain that would become the battlefield was the Black Regiment, followed by the Second Rhode Island, a white regiment.[3]

Part of coming into one's manhood in the army was the realization that each soldier was engaged in important work with implications that went beyond his personal life. Black men had few opportunities for such employment as civilians. On a muster list, every private who was "on command" found himself involved in some mission outside of camp. Their officers deemed it essential that these soldiers leave their companies to perform their missions and, in so doing, advance the well-being and safety of their fellow soldiers. Every black soldier, however, even if skeptical that the basic rights touted by leaders pertained to him, must have been aware that he was part of a force that would, if successful, topple the mighty British. These British and Hessian professionals were worthy opponents. No matter what life would deliver after the conflict, black men felt the satisfaction that they had fought and they had won.

While acquiring muscularity all their own in the army, black soldiers also interacted with their white cohort in new ways. An army brings together men from all walks of life to act in teams that advance one side's war goals. The serious business of defeating the enemy while defending one's own life calls for soldiers to put aside their prejudices and dislikes in order to coalesce as a unit. This is the ideal. During the Revolutionary War there was a form of fellowship in Washington's forces. The white man and black man were allies in the ranks—even in the presence of dislike and distrust. Holly Mayer's work on the recruitment of French Canadians and Catholics in the continental line addresses this kind of relationship. "The need for allies and soldiers," Mayer pointed out, "forced governments, societies and individuals to reconcile with persons and creeds they formerly rejected." This accommodation "did not mean full acceptance or integration by the parties involved," continued Mayer, "but it did encourage toleration in the name of union for short-term military aims and long term national objectives." Unit cohesion does not eliminate prejudice but it does force a wide variety of individuals to share their lives in close quarters over an extended period of time. There was no other institution in eighteenth-century life, other than the military, that did this. The white veteran who says that "for a black man" Cato was a good soldier is a man who likely did not relish the thought of serving beside black men, but who nonetheless gave grudging approval to an undeniably good soldier as a result of witnessing the black man's comportment and competency over months or years. Some white veterans went even further and underscored extraordinary action on the part of a black veteran. Whereas Pomp Magus, a soldier in the Massachusetts line, chose to give a sparse recitation of his three-year service to the pension office, his white colleague Asa Hart added in his support deposition that Magus had helped him out considerably when they both were prisoners of war in New York City. William Taburn used to carry a short white soldier across deep streams throughout the war. The range of support depositions went from a simple statement that the black pension applicant had been in a certain unit, to a racist but supportive declaration of a black man's qualities, to a statement featuring some warmth and appreciation. The first of the above is by far the most numerous sort, whether because a white man actually said the bare minimum or because the court clerk elected to record the fewest words.[4]

The army assembles men of disparate backgrounds and ultimately deposits them on a battlefield where every soldier prefers the best men around him, regardless of some attributes that mattered in civilian life. After a battle the men might have eaten at different messes or lodged in different tents, but they had shared an extraordinary life experience that connected them in varying degrees for the rest of their lives. After the war, the revolutionary soldiers returned to a society that had not experienced this attachment. Most of the rank and file were poor men who did not have the influence to immediately change their worlds. Racism in the sense of believing in the inferiority of people of color continued unabated in both the military and wider society. Yet years after the war, two drummers of different races got together to drum the old continental beats. A mulatto freeman and white slaveholders, all veterans, reminisced at house-raisings on the Tennessee frontier. A white officer intervened for a black private whose move to a new neighborhood had evinced a general outcry from whites. None of the above scenes would have happened without military service. The shared experiences began the work of chipping away at the hatred and intolerance that is also racism. The war's alliances among its soldiers, however expedient in the 1770s and 1780s, initiated at least sufferance and at best appreciation in some quarters among some people. Unfortunately, this modest advance in the cause of humanity was overwhelmed by the staggering weight of wealth produced by labor-intensive commodities grown in the South.

Rice and indigo defeated John Laurens's eccentric scheme. Even at the height of crisis, South Carolina decisively turned down the idea of black soldiers. Neither the British advance into their state nor the occupation of their major city could nudge state legislators to make soldiers out of slaves. White revolutionaries saw thousands of bondsmen and bondswomen flee to the British side and focused on getting them back rather than doing all they could to conquer the enemy. John Laurens censured his intransigent neighbors dominated, he said, by a triple-headed monster—prejudice, greed, and timidity. His father, Henry, laid the blame more delicately when he said that South Carolina had missed a chance to employ "those miserable Creatures to whom we owe some gratitude." But as much as the Laurenses wanted to pit their enlightened selves against their crass, grasping neighbors, they could not conquer slavery even in their own lives. In 1776, when his father seemed poised to free his slaves, a concerned John advised his father to back off and consider the long process that manumission should entail. Later on, John felt no compunction at the prospect of breaking up slave families in order to create his regiment. After his death, fellow soldiers remarked on the pitiable condition of his two slaves. To his credit, John pressed on for a black regiment. But his attention seemed riveted on what he could not control rather than personal conditions he could act upon. Henry was no better. He could have broken new ground by not separating families or by ceasing to resort to the workhouse. As each new challenge of the Revolution confronted Henry Laurens, whether that be the Thomas Jeremiah case at the beginning of the conflict or his role in the Paris peace negotiations at the end, the weight of his upbringing prevailed. He sided with his neighbors. Even his advocacy of his son's cause might have been disingenuous, a gesture placating his son, full knowing that the idea would go nowhere among the elite he knew so well. Ultimately, a heartbroken Henry lived out his life on the Mepkin Plantation tended to by 298 slaves according to the 1790 census. The weight of the peculiar institution prevailed. No amount of rattling the cages could weaken slavery's hold on the American South.[5]

With respect to the black community, the American Revolution brought liberty to some and equality to none. Whatever openings were required by the war's exigencies were made with fear and expediency in mind. Once the emergency passed, the whites in power reassessed. A quarter-century of the revolution's rhetoric, combined with economic considerations and religious fervor, gradually freed slaves in the north. But otherwise white society methodically went about closing equal opportunity for people of color. The African American community challenged each move, however. This can be seen in the proliferation of aid societies and subscriptions to the *Liberator*, harboring of runaway slaves, David Walker's appeal to action, the Pittsburghers' petition to retain the vote, and the response of the African Methodist Episcopal Church (founded in 1816) to the idea of emigration and African colonization. The black community seized the revolution and made it a weapon in their fight for basic rights.

One of the tactics they used in this struggle was to point to the sacrifice made by their fathers and grandfathers in the Revolutionary War. Although desperately poor and illiterate, these veterans could still tell a story. Their children listened and so also did their neighbors. In 1813, when Pennsylvania flirted with a bill to prevent the immigration of people of color into the state, James Forten, himself a former prisoner of war, lost no time in replying with his pamphlet titled "A Series of Letters by a Man of Color." If the bill were to pass, a black man who could not produce a certificate that he was registered in Pennsylvania would be put in jail for up to six months, and if no one answered the advertisements and claimed him, he would be sold. Forten reminded his readers, "Many of our fathers, many of ourselves, have fought and bled for the Independence of our country. Do not then expose us to sale. Let not the spirit of the father behold the son robbed of that Liberty which he died to establish." The bill, fortunately never became law.[6]

Thomas Jefferson called slavery a state of war, a metaphor whose organizing principle requires an enemy who must be conquered or destroyed. Warfare is seen as pitting the good against the bad. Jefferson's metaphor made the enslaved an enemy army whose members had to be reduced to harmlessness: to chattel, children, ciphers. Metaphors come with entailments. In this case, the freedom of whites was at stake, and woe betide any unpatriotic citizen who did not support this war. The metaphor suited the slaveholders who soldiered against their enslaved targets.

The Revolution's black continentals did not fit into Jefferson's metaphorical construct. They fought a war on the side of the revolutionaries, expecting better treatment with eventual equality for their service. What, after all, separated a slave-turned-soldier from a virtuous militiaman? By talking to their families and neighbors, black soldiers reorganized the thinking of their descendants. African-born soldiers reconceptualized slavery as theft. The next generation created new metaphors for the economic arrangement in the South: crime, national sin, violation of the Commandments, anti-Republicanism. David Walker likened slavery to a deer in a cage. After the war, when new dangerous metaphors sprang up, black abolitionists would move quickly to counter them. Supporters of sending blacks back to Africa called people of color "strangers within the gates." Members of the black community replied, "We are not strangers . . . we are already American citizens." They pointed out that their fathers had "fought and bled and died" for the country's liberties. "Shall we forsake their tombs, and flee to an unknown land?" they asked. "No!" came their emphatic response. The African American revolutionaries' service, combined with gradual emancipation and growing literacy in their community, created new black regiments that hove into view and rang the fire bell in Thomas Jefferson's dreams.[7]

Absent from the history of the early Republic is this amazing cast of African American characters—the soldiers of the Revolution. During the war, black soldiers could proudly manifest a confident assertion of their manhood right alongside white soldiers. Indeed, they earned badges of merit and distinction that many white soldiers did not attain. After the war they mounted a frontal assault in local courthouses throughout the land by proclaiming themselves worthy in a society that went about systematically demeaning anyone of their skin color. Their challenges to the status quo did not make headline news. They occurred in small towns, noted by sons and daughters and neighbors. The frowning world still existed after the Revolution, but the way that people confronted it was different. Instead of fighting alone, African American communities, particularly in the North, banded together and confronted every one of the outrages visited on them as people of color. The Revolution played an important role in that change. "Standing in their own light" went from being a charge worthy of punishment to a declaration of independence. And the black community has never looked back, no matter what the obstacles. In the veterans' old age, the nation envisioned the Revolution as the epochal event in its past, but the African American veterans were involved in forward momentum. The struggle of '76 was an ongoing one, and they passed it along to the next generation, bequeathing the example of their lives to inspire bolder action in the face of even greater risk.

Notes

Abbreviations

AAS   American Antiquarian Society, Worcester, Massachusetts.

DLAR   David Library of the American Revolution, Washington Crossing, Pennsylvania

HLP   Laurens, Henry. *The Papers of Henry Laurens*. 16 volumes. Columbia: University of South Carolina Press, 1968–2003.

RIHS   Rhode Island Historical Society, Providence.

RWP   U.S. Revolutionary War Pension Records, David Library of the American Revolution, Washington Crossing, Pennsylvania.

    BLW—Bounty land warrant

    R—Rejected pension

    S—Soldier's pension

    W—Widow's pension (if dead husband never applied)

Introduction

1. U.S. Revolutionary War Pension Records, David Library of the American Revolution, Washington Crossing, Pennsylvania [hereafter RWP], Peter Adams, W15512.
2. The classic book on black participation in the American Revolution remains Quarles, *The Negro in the American Revolution*. Recent work on blacks in the revolutionary age include Nash, *Forgotten Fifth*; Egerton, *Death or Liberty*; Countryman, *Enjoy the Same Liberty*; Gilbert, *Black Patriots and Loyalists*. For a beautifully illustrated work, see Kaplan and Kaplan, *The Black Presence in the Era of the American Revolution*. In the realm of fiction, see Lawrence Hill, *Someone Knows My Name* (New York: W. W. Norton, 2007). For young adult readers, see Laurie Halse Anderson, *Chains* (New York: Simon & Schuster Books for Young Readers, 2008) and *Forge* (New York: Atheneum Books for Young Readers, 2010). For a picture book for younger children, see Marion T. Lane, *Patriots of African Descent in the Revolutionary War* (Durham, Conn.: Strategic Book Group, 2011).
3. RWP, Primus Tyng, R10795; RWP, Thomas Lively, S38144; RWP, John Lines, W26775; Robert Laurens in Henry Laurens, *The Papers of Henry Laurens* [hereafter HLP], vol. 9, 316–18, 347.
4. *Niles' Register*, November 27, 1819; Nash, *Forging Freedom*, 233–45.
5. Henry Laurens to James Laurens, December 5, 1771, in HLP, 66–67.
6. U.S. Muster Rolls, 1775–1783, David Library of the American Revolution, Washington Crossing, Pennsylvania; Thornton, "Central African Names and African American Naming Patterns," 727–42; Cody, "There Was No Absalom on the Ball Plantations," 563–96; Charles Joyner, *Down by the Riverside*, 219.

7. Nell, *Service of Colored Americans*, 12; R. Wright, *The Continental Army*, 162. It was not uncommon that an officer was commissioned in a specific regiment and then detached for staff service. As soon as Humphreys joined Washington's "family," his company came under the command of his senior lieutenant. See David Humphreys's papers at the New Haven Historical Society.
8. Johnston, *Record of Connecticut Men*, 205–16; Connecticut Legislature, "Act for Regulating the Militia, December 1776," accessed via HeinOnline; Connecticut Legislature, "Act in Addition to and Alteration of an Act Entitled 'An Act concerning Indian, Molatto, and Negro Servants and Slaves,'" October 1777 session, accessed via HeinOnline.
9. On the question of why the unit was formed, Humphreys's biographer, Frank Landon Humphreys, claimed that the colonel "was one of the first men in the country to recognize the possibilities of the negro as a soldier and by his own influence and that of his faithful body servant, Jethro Martin." Humphreys, Life and Times of David Humphreys, 191–92. William Cooper Nell claimed that officers objected to serving in an all-black company, necessitating a member of Washington's staff to head the unit. Nell, *Colored Patriots of the American Revolution*, 133. Within six months of its formation, the company of black privates was joined in the same brigade with the Rhode Island Regiment, notable for its black soldiers who once formed an all-black regiment. David O. White doubts that white prejudice created the all-black company. White claimed that there were more than forty other blacks in the Connecticut regiments, who could have formed a second all-black unit. I've noted that the noncommissioned officers on the muster roll were promoted to this rank early in 1781 at precisely the time that the company of black privates was formed. At a time when nine regiments were reduced to five, there must have been available NCOs to fill this company's slots. Yet Colonel Zebulon Butler had to promote a group of men to serve here. Of the NCOs in this unit who applied for a pension or bounty land, none of them mention service in this company.
10. RWP, Prince Crosley, W24833. On the subject of obtaining freedom after three years' service, an inquiry was made during Mrs. Crosley's application process to the Comptroller Office in Hartford. The office responded that as far as it knew, no such law was passed, although many veterans had made such a claim. Mrs. Crosley obtained her pension.
11. "Inventory of Soldiers Killed at Fort Mercer, Thomas Arnold's company, October 22, 1777," in Revolutionary War Military Records, Series 1, Subseries A, MSS673-sg2, Rhode Island Historical Society (hereafter RIHS).
12. For Salisbury Freeman, see U.S. Census in 1800 and 1810; MacGunnigle, *Regimental Book*, 18.
13. Tiro, *People of the Standing Stone*; Calloway, *American Revolution in Indian Country*; Glatthaar and Martin, *Forgotten Allies*.
14. Piersen, *Black Yankees*, xi.
15. Thanks to Ruth Whitehead, in whose notes at the South Carolina History Room at the Charleston County Public Library I found a reference to this source (*Royal Gazette*, March 10–14, 1781). Thanks also to Carol Jones at the Charleston Library Society who had to go searching in the vault to find the newspaper (it was not on the microfilm). Moultrie, *Memoirs of the American Revolution*, 141–71. Moultrie claimed after the war that all his slaves returned to the plantation. Those in

Charlestown were "carried" there, claimed Moultrie. See Frey, *Water from the Rock*, 114–15.
16. The numbers of blacks joining the British is a contentious issue among historians. The best treatment of the issue is Pybus, "Jefferson's Faulty Math," 261. For "tidal flood," see Frey, *Water from the Rock*, 119.
17. Hodges, *Black Loyalist Directory*. In trying to connect the South Carolina list with the New York one, several factors could account for the absence of the South Carolina names in the New York directory. The freed South Carolinians could have changed their names. Disease claimed many lives, including much of the large group of African Americans who engaged in the ill-fated Cornwallis campaign that culminated in Yorktown. Some on the South Carolina list could have represented sequestered slaves who would not have been eligible for the liberty promised by British proclamations. Others may have opted to stay in South Carolina with their families and familiar surroundings. The problems of loyalist slaves coming into the British lines plagued General Clinton beginning in the early days of the British occupation of Charles Town. See Frey, *Water from the Rock*, 119.
18. RWP, William Johnson, S39786; "An Act to Provide for Certain Persons Engaged in the Land and Naval Services of the United States in the Revolutionary War," approved March 18, 1818, Public Acts of Congress, 2518–19; "An Act Supplementary to the Act for the Relief of Certain Surviving Officers and Soldiers of the Revolution," approved June 4, 1832, U.S. Statutes at Large, 22nd Congress, sess.1, chap. 126, iv, 529–30. For history of widows' pensions, see Glasson, *History of Military Pension Legislation*, 48–49.
19. The number of men of color who participated as soldiers and sailors in the American Revolution has been proclaimed to be five thousand. The statistic is so sacrosanct that historians generally do not provide the source or the methodology used to arrive at the number. It is simply a "fact." As far as I can tell, the number makes its first appearance in 1890 in J. Wilson, *Black Phalanx*, 22. The number is reprised in a short work by Herbert Aptheker in 1940: "One may say in full confidence that the number of Negroes who served as regular soldiers in the American forces during the revolutionary War, at a conservative estimate, was 5000." Herbert Aptheker, *The Negro in the American Revolution* (New York, 1940), 41. The latest Daughters of the American Revolution (DAR) survey—Grundset, *Forgotten Patriots*—notes the presence of 6,611 men of color, including Indians. Approximately 1,100 of this number are only "possible" men of color, because there is no racial descriptor attached to their names. (Assumption was made based on "name, occupation, rank.") Subtracting Indians from this total leaves us with 4,463 African Americans for which there is good evidence. The DAR list is based on many sources, most notably pensions, bounty land warrants, muster lists, and memoirs. We do not have a complete set of muster lists, so the 4,463 number is conservative. The DAR list is by far the best source that we have for numbers and ultimately reinforces the popular estimate of around 5,000. Loyalist pensions are also great sources for blacks on the British side, but there are few of them.
20. The closest occupation in the eighteenth century to a soldier, in terms of range of action, would be a sailor in the merchant marine. See Bolster, *Black Jacks*.
21. RWP, John Ellis, S32233; RWP, Mark Murry, R7523.
22. RWP, Hamet Achmet, S38107; RWP, William Taburn, W18115; RWP, Solomon Bibbie, S6644.

23. RWP, James Dinah or Diner, S38791.
24. RWP, Prince Vaughan, S42603.
25. R. Wright, *Continental Army*, 147–54.

Chapter 1

1. Jefferson, *Thomas Jefferson's Notes on the State of Virginia*, 38; Onuf, *The Mind of Thomas Jefferson*, 205–12.
2. "Presentment of the Grand Jury, March 1733/34," *South Carolina Historical and Genealogical Magazine* 25, no. 4 (October 1924), 193–95; "An Act for Appropriating the Present Workhouse for a Place of Correction," 1768, in McCord, *Statutes at Large of South Carolina*, vol. 7, 90–92; "An Act for Settling a Watch," October 8, 1698, in McCord, *Statutes at Large of South Carolina*, vol. 7, 8; Henry Laurens Account Book, June 30, 1769, College of Charleston, Special Collections; Angelina Grimke Weld, "Testimony," in Weld, *American Slavery as It Is*, 55.
3. Angelina Grimke Weld, "Testimony" in Weld, *American Slavery as It Is*, 55. One should read with care the abolitionist literature of the nineteenth century. These are rhetorical tracts making an argument.
4. RWP, Morgan Griffin, S18844; Gideon Griffin, W8877; Allan Jeffers, S1770 ; Berry Jeffers, W10145.
5. RWP, Isham Carter, S39293.
6. Between the pursuit and subsequent executions, forty blacks paid with their lives for Stono. See Mark M. Smith, introduction to *Stono*, xiv. Some parts of the act were repetitions of previous acts. "An Act for the Better Ordering and Governing Negroes and other Slaves in this Province," May 10, 1740, in McCord, *Statutes at Large of South Carolina*, vol. 7, 397–417.
7. "An Act for the Better Ordering and Governing Negroes and other Slaves in this Province," May 10, 1740, in McCord, *Statutes at Large of South Carolina*, vol. 7, 412. On number of hours worked and Sunday work, see ibid., 404, 413.
8. Ibid., 399.
9. Ibid., 411. For purchase price of slave, see Edgar, *South Carolina: A History*, 80. This part of the code, allowing for punishment of slave owners, was more of a threat than serious legislation meant to be enforced.
10. McCord, *Statutes at Large of South Carolina*, vol. 7, 399, 402, 416.
11. Ibid., 398, 399, 410, 413, 414.
12. Ibid., 407–13; "Account of the Negroe Insurrection in South Carolina, 1739," in M. Smith, *Stono*, 14; Higginbotham, *In the Matter of Color*, 198. In the colony's early years, blacks were allowed to defend white society in wars against the Indians. See Peter Wood, *Black Majority*, 124–30.
13. "An Act for the Better Security of This Province against the Insurrections and Other Wicked Attempts of Negroes and Other Slaves, May 1743," in McCord, *Statutes at Large of South Carolina*, vol. 7, 417. This statute was not a new idea. The assembly had passed a similar law just before the Stono Rebellion. The degree to which this law was enforced is open to interpretation. Even earlier, in the 1720s, the state fretted about vulnerability on a Sunday and passed a similar law but found later on that it was not very effective. Major slave codes pulled together previous laws and added new ones to the mix. South Carolina's first slave laws drew inspiration from the codes of Barbados.

14. "An Additional and Explanatory Act to an Act of the General Assembly of This Province, Entitled 'An Act for the Better Ordering and Governing Negroes and Other Slaves in this Province,' May 17, 1751," in McCord, *Statutes at Large*, vol. 7, 420-25.
15. Ibid., 415; Pinckney, *Letterbook of Eliza Lucas Pinckney*, 57.
16. Peter H. Wood, "Anatomy of a Revolt," in Smith, *Stono*, 69; Edward A. Pearson, "Rebelling as Men," in Smith, *Stono*, 87; "Acts Relating to Slaves," in McCord, *Statutes at Large*, vol. 7, 415, 421.
17. "Diary of Timothy Ford," *South Carolina Historical and Genealogical Magazine* 13 (October 1912): 189-90. Ford later moved to South Carolina in 1785.
18. Pearson, "Rebelling as Men," in Smith, *Stono*, 95; Berlin, "Time, Space, and the Evolution of Afro-American Society on the British Mainland North America," 66; "An Act for Better Ordering and Governing Negroes," in McCord, *Statutes at Large*, vol. 7, 97-417. Berlin's groundbreaking article noted that slavery developed differently in the North, the Chesapeake, and the Deep South, resulting in distinct black cultures.
19. Berlin, "Time, Space, and the Evolution of Afro-American Society," 66; Muller quoted in Littlefield, *Rice and Slaves*, 156; Wood, *Stono*, 69. For black agitation in Charles Town in the decade before the outbreak of war, see P. Wood, "Liberty Is Sweet," 149-84.
20. RWP, Tim Jones, S18063.
21. A. Leon Higginbotham, *In the Matter of Color*, 19; P. Wood, "The Changing Population of the Colonial South, 38.
22. Weld, *American Slavery as It Is*, 26.
23. Hurmence, *Before Freedom*, 7. Since there are very few prerevolutionary sources from slaves, I've used Hurmence's Federal Writers' Project narratives, in the belief that enormities of this order occurred in the eighteenth century as well.
24. Jefferson, *Thomas Jefferson's Notes on the State of Virginia*; Weld *American Slavery as It Is*, 54, 55, 98; Hurmence, *Before Freedom*, 24; J. Smith, *Autobiography of James L. Smith*, 151. There are certainly drawbacks in using nineteenth-century evidence in order to give an idea of eighteenth-century slavery. The abolitionists rarely relate conversations they had with black victims, so one is left in the dark about how the enslaved responded to oppression. But again, it is nineteenth-century sources, this time slave narratives, that speak of work slowdowns, destruction of equipment, petty thievery, tricking the master, et cetera. The abolitionists also tell of the worst they had seen. These were not necessarily everyday occurrences but they could happen on any day of the week.
25. Weld, *American Slavery as It Is*, 22, 54, 55, 98; Hurmence, *Before Freedom* 24; Grimes, *Life of William Grimes*, 65-66.
26. Hurmence, *Before Freedom*, 43, 121; Douglass, *Narrative of Frederick Douglass*, chap. 7; Weld, *American Slavery as It Is*, 172.
27. A. Leon Higginbotham, *In the Matter of Color*, 203; Evans, "A Question of Complexion," 411-15. Ira Berlin points out that Virginia and South Carolina were the only colonies to whip blacks who raised a hand against whites. So also were they (along with North Carolina) the only colonies to ban free blacks from the polls. North Carolina later lifted its ban. See Ira Berlin, *Slaves without Masters*, 8-9.
28. Pinckney, *Letterbook of Eliza Lucas Pinckney*, 12, 34.

29. Isaac, *Landon Carter's Uneasy Kingdom*, 187–97. For more on Jack and black society in the Chesapeake, see Kulikoff, *Tobacco and Slaves*, 317–435.
30. Equiano, *Interesting Narrative of the Life of Olaudah Equiano*, 98, 136, 140. Milton Marshall interview in Hurmence, *Before Freedom*, 41–43.
31. Breen and Innes, *"Myne Owne Ground"*; Berlin, "Time, Space, and the Evolution of Afro-American Society," 69–77.
32. E. Greene and Harrington, *American Population before the Federal Census of 1790*, 102; Burrows and Wallace, *Gotham*, 159–66; Berlin, *Many Thousands Gone*.
33. Burrows and Wallace, *Gotham*, 31–33. In half freedom, children remained enslaved. See A. Leon Higginbotham, *In the Matter of Color*, 114–21.
34. Burrows and Wallace, *Gotham*, 148; Lepore, *New York Burning*, 58.
35. A. Leon Higginbotham, *In the Matter of Color*, 129.
36. Zabin, *Dangerous Economies*, 136–58; Lepore, *New York Burning*; Rediker, *The Many-Headed Hydra*, 174–210. Historians disagree on the question of whether the 1741 rebellion was a conspiracy or not. See Burrows and Wallace, *Gotham*, 198–99. There is not much newspaper coverage of the Golden Hill Riot of January 1770.
37. Fox, *Journal of George Fox*, 277; Dunn and Dunn, "The Founding," 31, 45; William Penn, "To James Harrison, 25 October 1685," in *Papers of William Penn*, vol. 3, 66.
38. Dunn and Dunn, "The Founding," 31; Slaughter, *Beautiful Soul of John Woolman*, 200.
39. A. Leon Higginbotham, *In the Matter of Color*, 281–82; "An Act for the Trial of Negroes (1705)," in Pennyslvania Statutes at Large, vol. 2, 233–36; "Act for the Better Regulation of Negros in the Province (1725–26)," in Pennsylvania Statutes at Large, vol. 4, 59–64.
40. A. Leon Higginbotham, *In the Matter of Color*, 289.
41. "Act for the Better Regulation of Negros in the Province (1725–26)," Pennsylvania Statutes at Large, vol. 4, 61–62; A. Leon Higginbotham, *In the Matter of Color*, 282–84.
42. Nash, *Forging Freedom*, 19–42; Slaughter, *Beautiful Soul of John Woolman*, 132, 149, 172, 395; Jackson, *Let This Voice Be Heard*, 120, 121, 135; Woolman, *Journal of John Woolman*, 190–212; Boudreau, *Independence*, 159.
43. A. Leon Higginbotham, *In the Matter of Color*, 75; "Act for the Better Preventing of a Spurious and Mixt Issue, December 5, 1705," in Massachusetts Acts and Resolves; "Act Relating to Molato and Negro Slaves, July 28, 1703," in ibid.
44. "Act to Prevent Disorders in the Night, 1703," in Massachusetts Acts and Resolves, chap. 11, 5353; ibid., 1752–53 acts, 646; ibid., 1756–57, 991, 997; ibid., February 2, 1744, 219.
45. A. Leon Higginbotham, *In the Matter of Color*, 74, 79.
46. Ibid., 83, 85.
47. Davis, *Problem of Slavery in the Age of Revolution*, 496–501. For coverage in Boston, see *Boston Post-Boy*, July 27, 1772, August 31, 1772, and September 7, 1772; *Connecticut Courant*, July 30, 1772. In the *Connecticut Journal* and *New Haven Post-Boy*, July 31, 1772, and the *Providence Gazette*, July 25, 1772, there is an addendum to the London article, challenging anybody's right to own another human being. See also *Providence Gazette*, September 5, 1772, September 14, 1772; *Newport Mercury*, August 3, 1772.
48. "Felix's Petition." For a more assertive 1773 petition, see P. Wood, *Strange New Land*, figure 8, plate following page 80. Here the writers gently ask the legislature to

remember that all people have natural rights. But since God has permitted slavery, they will disclaim all previous wages and act in a peaceable way to gain their freedom, they say, after which they will voluntarily remove to Africa.
49. A. Leon Higginbotham, *In the Matter of Color*, 86–88; "Petition 1/13/1777."
50. For more on the Atlantic World revolts of the time, see Morgan and O'Shaughnessey, "Arming Slaves in the American Revolution," 180–208.
51. Berlin, *Many Thousands Gone*; Bolster, *Black Jacks*.
52. Lemisch, "Jack Tar in the Streets," 371–407; Carp, *Rebels Rising*, 27–61.
53. Trial transcript, in Adams, *Legal Papers of John Adams*, vol. 3, 268. Newspaper accounts in the week after the massacre related that British soldiers had been out on the streets with swords in hand, bullying boys, before the events reached a crescendo on King Street. See *Boston Gazette*, March 12, 1770; *Boston Newsletter*, March 8, 1770.
54. Trial transcript, in Adams, *Legal Papers of John Adams*, vol. 3, 115, 120, 192, 204.
55. Ibid., 268–69.
56. *Boston Newsletter*, March 8, 1770, supplement; *Boston Chronicle*, March 18, 1770; *Boston Gazette*, March 12, 1770; *Boston Evening Post*, March 12, 1770; *Boston Post-Boy*, March 12, 1770; Pariseau, "Searching for a Martyr," 16–19.
57. *Boston Gazette*, October 2, 1750.
58. Pariseau, "Searching for a Martyr," 18.
59. *Boston Gazette*, March 4, 1771, March 11, 1771, March 9, 1772; *Boston Evening Post*, March 11, 1771, March 9, 1772, March 8, 1773, March 14, 1774.
60. Wheatly, *Collected Works of Phillis Wheatley*, 229, 233, 234, 338.
61. In the Townsend Revenue Act's preamble, the phrase "raise a revenue" was used—a phrase synonymous with "tax." See Tuchman, *March of Folly*, 172; *Boston Weekly Newsletter*, December 23, 1773; *Boston Gazette*, March 4, 1771, December 20, 1773.
62. "An Act for Further Preventing All Riotous, Tumultuous, and Disorderly Assemblies or Companies of Persons, and for Preventing Bonfires in Any of the Streets or Lanes within Any of the Towns of This Province," January 1753, Massachusetts Acts and Resolves, vol. 3, 647–48; DeLoria, *Playing Indian*, 1–9.
63. *Boston Weekly Newsletter*, December 23, 1773.
64. Raphael, *Founding Myths*, 70–72; Ferling, *A Leap in the Dark*, 107; Burrows and Wallace, *Gotham*, 215; Breen, *American Insurgents*, 76–98.
65. Oliver, *Peter Oliver's Origin and Progress of the American Rebellion*, 65, 89, 102; Irvin, *Clothed in Robes of Sovereignty*, 66.
66. "Address to the People of Great Britain," in *Journals of the Continental Congress*, vol. 1, 82–90; "Memorial to the Inhabitants of the Colonies," ibid., 101.
67. "Memorial to the Inhabitants of the Colonies," ibid., 101; Moore, *Notes on the History of Slavery in Massachusetts*, 244.
68. Fischer, *Paul Revere's Ride*, 189–260.
69. RWP, Silas Burdoo, S21099; RWP, Prince Johonnot, S18057; RWP, Archelaus White, S43299; RWP, Sampson Moore, S13961; RWP, Caesar Glover, S32738.
70. "Massachusetts Committee of Safety, May 20, 1775," in Force, *American Archives*, vol. 2, 762; Raphael, *People's History of the American Revolution*, 76.
71. Lockhart, *Whites of Their Eyes*, 54, 170, 194–314.
72. RWP, Prince Johonnot, S18057. Not all the Americans were on top of the hill. See Quintal, *Patriots of Color*, 17.

73. The Board of War was created by the Second Continental Congress. Washington, *Writings of George Washington*, vol. 2, 125, 269, 354, 620, 623; Washington, *Writings of George Washington*, vol. 3, 350.
74. "Proclamation of Earl of Dunmore, 1775"; Frey, *Water from the Rock*, 63–64. The British had been considering the arming of blacks, as evidenced in pamphlets, parliamentary proceedings, and newspapers before Dunmore's Proclamation. See Morgan and O'Shaughnessy, "Arming Slaves in the American Revolution," 187–89.
75. Woody Holton, *Forced Founders*, 145.
76. Dunmore's Proclamation is dated November 7, but it was published on November 14 when Dunmore declared martial law. See Pybus, *Epic Journeys of Freedom*, 9; *Pennsylvania Evening Post*, Norfolk byline, January 13, 1776; Selby, *Revolution in Virginia*, 64. Claims have been made that Dunmore's force consisted mainly of former slaves. I can find no source from the period that backs this contention. British army troop strength (detachment of Fourteenth Regiment), supported by December 1, 1775, muster roll, Norfolk, showed 174 effectives. See Papers of the Continental Congress, roll 65, DLAR; Neal Jamieson to Gordon Glasiford, November 17, 1775, in Papers of the Continental Congress, roll 65, 393, DLAR; Diary of Robert Honyman, p. 4 in Peter Force Collection, 8D1#73, Manuscript Division, Library of Congress.
77. *Pennsylvania Evening Post*, December 12, 19, 26, 1775; ibid., December 14, 1775, for Philadelphia story.
78. *Pennsylvania Evening Post*, December 5, 1775.
79. "George Washington to Col. Joseph Reed, December 12, 1775," in Washington, *Papers of George Washington*, vol. 4, 553; "Lund Washington to George Washington, December 3, 1775," in *Papers of George Washington*, vol. 2, 479–80; McDonnell, *Politics of War*, 145; Pybus, *Epic Journeys of Freedom*, 12.
80. "General Orders, February 21, 1776," in Washington, *Writings of George Washington*, vol. 3, 350; Pybus, *Epic Journeys of Freedom*, 20; Foner, *Give Me Liberty!*, 2–3. While chastising George III for weakening slavery, Jefferson also inserted a clause condemning the king for prohibiting the colonies from ending the slave trade. The Deep South saved Jefferson from this apparent contradiction by having the slave trade clause removed.
81. Pybus, *Epic Journeys of Freedom*, xiii, 19, 150, 218.
82. *North Carolina Watchman* (Salisbury, N.C.), November 11, 1852. The 1850 slave schedule lists a slave of ninety-four, along with female slaves ages forty-five, forty-three, thirty-nine, and thirty, and two males, ages thirty-eight and fifteen. The *Watchman* obituary may have exaggerated Billy's age. In Sarah Ingram's probate inventory, there is no mention of Billy. The sixteen-year-old male in the 1850 slave schedule, named Robert, was sold to pay the debts of the estate. Mrs. Ingram's sister, who had lived with her, died shortly after Mrs. Ingram. She rejected the slaves bequeathed to her "as they were old and far from being profitable." Whatever these slaves meant to her at the end of her life, they were characterized as a "lost or dead expense to her." Note concerning Mrs. Eliazbeth Martin in Sale Accounts of Sarah Ingraram's estate, recorded November 15, 1783, in Norfolk City Circuit Court Record of Reports no. 1, reel 57, pp. 10–12, Library of Virginia. Billy certainly knew these discarded people well—perhaps they were relatives—but he likely remained powerless to help them.

83. Quarles, *The Negro in the American Revolution*, vii; Pybus, *Epic Journeys of Freedom*, xiii–xvi.
84. A. Leon Higginbotham, *In the Matter of Color*, 83.

Chapter 2

1. RWP, Mark Murry, R7523.
2. "An Act to Regulate and Establish a Militia in This State," in Walter Clark, *State Records of North Carolina*, 190–98.
3. RWP, Samuel Bell, S6598. Nat Turner's Rebellion in 1831 was a slave revolt in southern Virginia that resulted in the death of around sixty whites. Amis, *City of Raleigh*, 27, 57. Many thanks to Earl Ijames at the North Carolina Historical Society who explained to me the terrain of the Samuel Bell's Robeson County. Baptist, *The Half Has Never Been Told*.
4. P. Wood, "The Changing Population of the Colonial South, 39; Wells, *Population of the British Colonies in American before 1776*, 71; Sutherland, *Population Distribution in Colonial America*, 211; RWP, Sampson Moore, S13961.
5. RWP, John Foy, S29802; Wells, *Population of the British Colonies in America before 1776*, 265; "An Act for Forming and Regulating the Militia within the Colony of Massachusetts Bay in New England and for Repealing All the Laws Heretofore Made for That Purpose," January 22, 1776, in Massachusetts Acts and Resolves, chap. 10, 445–54; "An Act for Providing a Reinforcement to the American Army," November 14, 1776, in Massachusetts Acts and Resolves, chap. 21, 595–600; "An Act in Addition to an Act Entitled 'An Act for Forming and Regulating the Militia within the Colony of the Massachusetts Bay in New England and for Repealing All the Laws Heretofore Made for That Purpose,'" March 13, 1778, chap. 24, 778–80, in Massachusetts Acts and Resolves. Prior to the revolution, the Massachusetts legislature exempted Indians and blacks in the 1693 militia law. During Queen Anne's War, free blacks were required to report to the local military company "in case of alarm." See "An Act for Regulating of the Militia," November 22, 1693, in Massachusetts Acts and Resolves; "An Act for the Regulating of Free Negroes etc.," June 12, 1707, in Massachusetts Acts and Resolves. The acts and resolves of the Massachusetts legislation during the French and Indian War did not highlight race. With the exception of donors (who lent the province one thousand pounds sterling) and the Quakers, the legislature did not specifically exempt any other group. Perhaps the 1693 militia law was in full force. See "An Act in Addition to an Act intitled 'An Act for the Regulation of the Militia,'" in Massachusetts Acts and Resolves, April 1756, vol. 3, 924–25; "An Act for the Speedy Levying of Soldiers for an Intended Expedition Against Canada," in Massachusetts Acts and Resolve, March 28, 1759, vol. 4, 191–95. On the ground there is evidence that blacks served. See "Order Allowing Eight Pounds Sterling to Jacob Bigelow," in Massachusetts Acts and Resolves, February 16, 1762, vol. 17, 144; Shy, *People Numerous and Armed*, 39; Steele, *Betrayals*, 140.
6. RWP, Elisha Parker, S11211; RWP, Jacob Francis, W459; RWP, Joseph Brown, W1543; RWP, Amos Read, R8628.
7. Virginia Ordinances of Convention, July 1775, in Hening, *Hening's Statutes at Large*, vol. 9, 27–28; "An Act for Regulating and Disciplining the Militia," in Hening, *Hening's Statutes at Large*, May 5, 1777, vol. 9, 268, 273, 275.

8. McDonnell, "Class, Race, and Recruitment in Revolutionary Virginia"; "Act for Speedily Recruiting Virginia Regiments on the Continental Establishment and for Raising Additional Troops of Volunteers," in Hening, *Hening's Statutes at Large*, October 20, 1777, vol. 9, 337; "Act for Raising Volunteers to Join the Grand Army," in ibid., May 4, 1778, vol. 9, 445, "Act for Recruiting for the Continental Army," in ibid., 454; "Act for Speedily Recruiting Virginia Regiments on Continental Establishment," in ibid., October 1778, 588.
9. McDonnell, "Class, Race, and Recruitment in Revolutionary Virginia," 125; "An Act for Recruiting This State's Quota of Troops to Servine in the Continental Army," in Hening, *Hening's Statutes at Large*, October 16, 1778, vol. 10, 326–31.
10. Quarles, *The Negro in the American Revolution*, 56; "An Act to Procure Recruits," Laws of Maryland, chap. 43, October 1780 session, accessed via HeinOnline.
11. "An Act to Regulate the Militia," in Pennsylvania Statutes at Large, March 17, 1777, vol. 9, chap. 750; "An Act Obliging the Male White Inhabitants of This State to Give Assurances of Allegiance to the Same and for Other Purposes Therein Mentioned," in Pennsylvania Statutes at Large, June 13, 1777, vol. 9, chap. 756; "A Further Supplement to the Act Entitled 'An Act to Regulate the Militia of the Commonwealth of Pennsylvania," in Pennsylvania Statutes at Large, December 30, 1777, vol. 9, chap. 781; "An Act for the Regulation of the Militia of the Commonwealth of Pennsylvania," in Pennsylvania Statutes at Large, March 20, 1780, chap. 902; "An Act for the Greater Ease of the Militia and the More Speedy and Effectual Defence of This State," in Pennsylvania Statutes at Large, May 26, 1780, vol. 10, chap. 908; "An Act to Complete the Quota of the Federal Army Assigned to This State," in Pennsylvania Statutes at Large, December 23, 1780, vol. 10, chap. 926; Alexander Scammel, "Return of the Negroes in the Army," August 4, 1778, Series 4, General Correspondence, George Washington Papers, Library of Congress, http://memory.loc.gov/.
12. Quarles, *The Negro in the American Revolution*, 56; Calloway, *The American Revolution in Indian Country*, 51–53; "An Act to Raise Troops for the Defense of the Frontier," in *Laws of the State of New York*, March 11, 1780, chap. 53; "An Act for Raising Two Regiments for the Defense of the State on Bounties of Unappropriated Land," in ibid., March 20, 1781, chap. 32; "Act for Completing the Four Battalions of this State for Continental Service," in *Acts of the General Assembly of the State of New Jersey*, May 28, 1777, chap. 29, accessed via HeinOnline. For New Jersey law, see also *Pennsylvania Packet*, June 3, 1777.
13. Neimeyer, *America Goes to War*, 21–26; RWP, London Atis, W23468; RWP, Richard Leet, S38908; RWP, Pomp Sherbourne, W17297; RWP, Jeremiah Virginia, S19141.
14. RWP, Prime Coffin, S44499; RWP, Prince Light, S44511; Bell, *History of the Town of Exeter*, 253; RWP, Abednego Jackson, S10909; RWP, Samuel Dunbar, S15106. For the Mashpee men, see James Keeter, S92942, John Francis, S34887; Isaac Wickham, S34534, Simon Perpeaney, BLW 1941; Joel Taburn, S42037; William Taburn, W18115; Burwello Tabourn, S7694; Lycus Simms, R9584 (although designated R, he got a pension; later relatives got rejected).
15. RWP, John Lines, W26775. Judith also had a letter from her first husband. She claimed that John Lines's letter was written in his own hand. Mayer, *Belonging to the Army*, 68, 103, 125, 126, 129.
16. RWP, Prince Hull, S36596; Aaron Brister, W17341; Richard Fortune, S37933; Joseph Johnson, R5636.

17. Van Buskirk, "Claiming Their Due," in Resch and Sargent, eds., *War and Society in the American Revolution*, 136.
18. Quarles, *The Negro in the American Revolution*, 54; RWP, Cicero Sweat, S43189; RWP, Edward Sands, S W16148; RWP, Nicholas Hawwawas, S17997; RWP, Caesar Shelton, S19764; RWP, Peter Jennings, S4436; RWP, James Kersey, S8788. Jennings's memory might have failed him when he mentioned the "Fifth Regiment of Artillery." In 1776, the army's corps of artillery numbered no more than four regiments. Perhaps he was in a continental regiment with an all-black company. Another possible all-black company hailed from Boston and is known as "the Bucks of Massachusetts." There is no evidence that they existed during the Revolutionary War, however. The first sign we have of them is in the 1780s when they received a flag from John Hancock's son. This information is provided by nineteenth-century historian William Cooper Nell, who also tells us that a nineteenth-century abolitionist, Lydia Maria Child, lived across the street from the black man who led the unit. She called him "Colonel." Unfortunately Nell provides no date for Child's testimony. The Bucks were most certainly not in the Continental Army. They could have been a militia unit. It is also possible that they formed after the war at a time when Bostonians were launching private militia companies. A prominent African American in town, Prince Hall, called on black men to join the effort to suppress Shays' Rebellion. The unit could have reflected African Americans' bid to become full citizens in the wake of the war. Thanks to J. L. Bell, a consultant for the National Park Service and writer on Massachusetts in the revolution, for the postwar thesis.
19. Graydon, *Alexander Graydon's Memoirs of His Own Time*; Frazer, "Extracts from Papers of General Persifor Frazer," 134.
20. "Alexander Hamilton to John Jay, March 14, 1779," in Hamilton, *Papers of Alexander Hamilton*, vol. 2, 17–19; Thomas Wentworth Higginson, who commanded a black regiment in the Civil War, took exception to the notion, still current in his time, that slavery provided good recruits because the enslaved were used to obeying a master. Obedience, he said, was very important, but self-respect was essential, and that latter attribute had to be instilled in slave recruits. "The more strongly we marked the difference between the slave and the soldier, the better for the regiment," Higginson claimed. See Higginson, *Army Life in a Black Regiment*, 244.
21. Quarles, *The Negro in the American Revolution*, 58; "James Madison to Joseph Jones, November 28, 1780," in Madison, *Papers of James Madison*, vol. 1, 209–10; "Joseph Jones to James Madison, December 8, 1780," in ibid., 232–33.
22. RWP, Jacob Francis, W459.
23. RWP, Benjamin Lattimore, S13683.
24. For Saratoga statistics: "History and Culture," Saratoga National Historical Park, nps.gov/sara/historyculture; for Yorktown statistics, thanks to Karen Rehm, chief historian, Yorktown Colonial National Historical Park; for Gettysburg, "Experience Gettysburg National Military Park: Facts at a Glance," Gettysburg National Military Park, www.nps.gov/gett/planyourvisit/upload/Gettysburg-NMP-Facts-at-a-Glance-Sheet-4-12.pdf. The number 165,000 represents only the effectives.
25. Middlekauf, *Glorious Cause*, 323; Headrick, *Tools of Empire*, 85; Neumann, *History of Weapons of the American Revolution*, 14–15.

26. Webster, *American Socket Bayonets*, 7; Neumann, *History of Weapons of the American Revolution*, 48–51; RWP, Jacob Francis, W459; Jerome Waldron's and John Manners's depositions in RWP, Jacob Francis, W459.
27. Johnston, *Storming of Stony Point on the Hudson*; George Washington to John Sullivan, August 1, 1779, in Washington, *Writings of George Washington*, vol. 16, 31.
28. RWP, John Roe, S39045; RWP, Primus Tyng, R10795.
29. On September 16, 1776, the Continental Congress authorized the creation of eighty-eight infantry regiments or battalions to serve for three years or the duration. On May 27, 1778, the Congress reduced the number of infantry regiments in the continental line to eighty, but it decreed that each one of these units form a light infantry company (giving each regiment a complement of nine companies containing a total of 585 officers and men at full strength). Continental light infantry became the elite of the army, its troops training for skirmishing in open order (like British light infantry) and storming fortified positions (like British grenadiers). Following the British practice, General Washington detached the light companies from his various regiments to serve together in a separate corps of light infantry. General Wayne led four provisional regiments composed of these companies against Stony Pont. In the following year, the light companies were formed into six battalions to operate under the Marquis de Lafayette. The fact that black men served in the elite companies of the Continental Army says something about that force's integrated nature. Thanks to historian Greg Urwin for this information. The Stony Point site today is quite forested. The site's historian, Ray Russell, tells me that at the time of the battle it would not have been. The British would have want to see what was coming.
30. Order of Battle, July 15, 1779, in Johnston, *Storming of Stony Point*, 401; Johnston, *Storming of Stony Point*, 176, 178, 192; Anthony Wayne to George Washington, July 16, 1779, in Stillé, *Major-General Anthony Wayne*, 96. Controversy would ensue about who did what (and when) in the great victory of Stony Point. One officer maintained that he had been in the British works a full ten minutes before the arrival of the officer who garnered a special medal after the battle. Others thought that General Wayne, a Pennsylvanian, unjustly lauded the men from his state. A Virginia colonel mentioned the overwhelming number of Virginians in the vanguard who were overlooked. A Connecticut colonel dared to correct Wayne's version by urging Wayne to recognize two or three others who entered the British works "at the same instant" as Fleury. A flurry of claims and counterclaims flew from field officers. "Our feelings in these matters are exquisite," explained a miffed colonel. The officers neglected the critical role of the rank-and-file soldiers, however, until one of their number, Tyng, spoke up in his pension application forty years later.
31. 1790 Federal Census, Andover, Vermont, David Drury. For the controversy, see Col. Febiger to Thomas Jefferson, July 21, 1779; Col. Febiger to Col. Heth, September 13, 1779; Lt. John Gibbon to [Capt.] Allen McLane, November 27, 1821; Col. Meigs to General Wayne, August 22, 1779, all in Johnston, *Storming of Stony Point*, 188, 189, 197, 407.
32. RWP, Pompey Woodward W4867; Ketchum, *Saratoga*, 292–93, 326; "John Stark to New Hampshire Council, April 18, 1777," in Gabriel and Resch, *Battle of Bennington*, 34–36; "Benjamin Lincoln to Philip Schuyler, August 18, 1777," in *Collections of the Massachusetts Historical Society*, 120–21; Horatio Gates to John Hancock, August

20, 1777, Papers of the Continental Congress, DLAR, vol. 174, 232. Gates, who had been a British soldier during the French and Indian War, was an American army commander at the battles of the Saratoga campaign.
33. RWP, James Depuy, R2894; Tiedemann, *The Other New York*.
34. Knouff, *Soldier's Revolution*, 247.
35. RWP, Morgan Griffin, S18844; RWP, Caesar Godfrey, S32739; RWP, Elisha Hunt, S13486; RWP, Tim Jones S18063; RWP, Caesar Shelton, S19764; RWP, Thomas Lively, S38144.
36. Morris, *New Jersey Medicine in the Revolutionary Era*, 7; Cowan, *Medicine in Revolutionary New Jersey*, 22–32, Washington quote from p. 32; *Medicine and Surgery during the American Revolution* (Morristown, N.J., 1977), pamphlet 385 at DLAR; Blanco, *Physician of the American Revolution*, 150; Purvis, *Almanacs of American Life*, 195. The life expectancy of fifty-five began at the age of eleven, not at birth.
37. RWP, Morgan Griffin, S18844; Blanco, *Physician of the American Revolution*, 150.
38. Cowan, *Medicine and Surgery during the American Revolution*, 26, 33; Gould, *Times of Brother Jonathan*, 208, 209.
39. RWP, Allan Jeffers, S1770; RWP, Peter Jennings, S4436; RWP, Andrew Pebbles, S38297; Edward Sorrell, W26493.
40. RWP, William Taburn, W18115.
41. Van Buskirk, *Generous Enemies*, 73–105; RWP, Prince Light, S44511; RWP, Cuff Ashport, W27332; RWP, Oxford Tash, W16155; RWP, John Foy, S29802; RWP, Primus Coburn, S34703; Martin, *Private Yankee Doodle*.
42. RWP, Jeffrey Brace, S41461; Brinch, *Blind African Slave*.
43. RWP, Jacob Francis, W459, Pomp McCuff, S36084.
44. Whitehead, "The Autobiography of Peter Stephen Du Ponceau," 221–23. For more on honorific names, see Irvin, *Clothed in Robes of Sovereignty*, 184–90.
45. RWP, Mark Murry, R7523.
46. Egleston, *Life of John Paterson*, 142–44.
47. RWP, William Taburn, W18115.
48. RWP, Pomp Sherbourne, W17297; RWP, Cuff Wells, W18103; RWP, Mingo Pollock, W17469.
49. RWP, Aaron Carter, W22726.
50. RWP, Caesar Bassett, W16827; RWP, Mingo Pollock, W17469; RWP, Aaron Brister, W20772.
51. RWP, Aaron Carter, W22726; RWP, Joseph Green, W27415.
52. RWP, Prince Bailey, W17230; RWP, Peter Maguira, R6830; RWP, Hamet Achmet, S38107. Charles Neimeyer presented findings from various surveys and came up with the following on percentage of foreign-born members of Washington's forces: Massachusetts: 9 percent, based on analysis of 396 soldiers; Pennsylvania: 67 percent, based on analysis of 582 soldiers who listed their places of birth; Maryland: 40 percent, based on Smallwood's recruits; South Carolina: 40 percent based on First Regiment of Provincials; Virginia: from 1 percent, based on 419 Virginia pension records, to 39 percent, for Morgan's riflemen. Neimeyer, *America Goes to War*, 16–51.
53. RWP, Caesar Shelton, S19764; RWP, Thomas Gardner, W7500.
54. RWP, Plato Turner, S33832; RWP, Isham Scott, S42004; RWP, Agrippa Hull, W760; RWP, John Harris, S37997; RWP, William Walton, S22035; RWP, Pomp Magus,

S33059; RWP, James Hawkins, S37991; RWP, Joel Taburn, S42037; RWP, Reuben Bird, S37776.
55. RWP, James Harris, S38006; RWP, Nicholas Hawwawas, S17197. Both 1778 muster rolls for Captains Payne and Mennis (officers cited in Harris's pension) label Harris a private. U.S. Muster Rolls, DLAR.
56. RWP, Drury Walden, R11014; RWP, George Buley, W27576; RWP, Silas Burdoo, S21099; RWP, John Pinn, R8264; RWP, Andrew Pebbles, S38297; RWP, Moses Knight, W10182; RWP, Samuel Dunbar, S15106; RWP.
57. RWP, Daniel Williams, R11569; RWP, Amos Robinson, S36265; "General Instructions for the Colonels, December 1777," in Washington, *Writings of George Washington*, vol. 10, 240–41.
58. RWP, Primus Slocum, S39844; Neagles, *Summer Soldiers*, 35–36; RWP, Caesar Babcock, R339; "General Orders, October 27, 1776," in Washington, *Papers of George Washington*, vol. 6; "General Orders, August 8, 1782," in Washington, *Papers of George Washington*, vol. 24, 489; RWP, Jim Capers R1669 (he got a pension); RWP, Thomas Gardner W7500; Cuff Wells, W18103; RWP, Sampson Cuff, S34616.
59. RWP, Record Prime, R8486; RWP, Oliver Cromwell, S34613; George Sambo on First Rhode Island muster list in Thomas Cole's company, October, November, and December 1778 and August 1779, U.S. Muster Rolls, DLAR.
60. "George Washington to the President of Congress, December 24, 1779," in Washington, *Writings of George Washington*, vol. 17, 312; "George Washington to the President of Congress, January 5, 1780," in Washington, *Writings of George Washington*, vol. 17, 357–58; "literally starved": Martin, *Ordinary Courage*, 104; RWP, Cato Boose, S15342; RWP, Edward Harman, S36000.
61. For postwar Virginia, see Alan Taylor, *Internal Enemy*.

Chapter 3

1. Samuel Tenny to Elihu Greene, January 16, 1778, and April 8, 1778, Nathanael Greene Papers, American Antiquarian Society (hereafter AAS).
2. Nathanael Greene to unknown recipient, January 5, 1778, Nathanael Greene Papers, AAS.
3. "George Washington to Nicholas Cooke, January 2, 1778," in Washington, *Writings of George Washington*, vol. 10, 257.
4. Samuel Tenny to Elihu Greene, January 16, 1778; Greene to unknown recipient, January 5, 1778, Nathanael Greene Papers, AAS.
5. Rappleye, *Sons of Providence*; Santmier, *Little History of Smithfield Monthly Meeting of Friends*.
6. RWP, Andrew Frank, S21207. The black pensioners who served before 1778 are Peter Jennings (1776), Richard Potter (1776), Esek Roberts (June 1777), Philip Rodman (Oct. 1776), Pero Mowry (1777), Winsor Fry (1775), Robert Green (1777), London Hazard (1777), Henry Tabor (1777), James Profit (1776), William Wanton (1777), Andrew Frank (1775), Caesar Babcock (1775), Edward Hopps (1775), Prosper Gorton (1777), Doming Earl (1776), Peleg Runnels (1777), and Thomas Ray (1777). Five other pensioners had conflicting dates of service, one date before February 1778 and one after. They could have come from militia units or a state line. There were more men in muster lists before the spring of 1778 who did not live long enough to claim a pension.

7. RWP, Philip Rodman, S39835; Fischer, *Washington's Crossing*, 141 (Paine quote), 271–73. General Mifflin also assembled soldiers and asked them to stay. At Princeton in early December, a soldier estimated Washington's forces at twenty-five hundred, as men whose enlistments had expired peeled off by the hundreds. See Fischer, *Washington's Crossing*, 131.
8. RWP, Peter Jennings, S4436; Fischer, *Washington's Crossing*, 215, 317, 332, 334. The Hessian colonel was Johann Rall. The American captain was William Washington.
9. RWP, Peter Jennings, S4436; *Providence Gazette*, November 15, 1777.
10. RWP, Peter Jennings, S4436; Edward Colimore, "The Nightmare Lingers: 67 Years Later, the Carnage of Iwo Jima Remains Fresh for New Jersey Marine," *Philadelphia Inquirer*, February 19, 2012; Seymour I. Toll, "Human Cost of WWII Still Sears 68 Years Later," *Philadelphia Inquirer*, December 16, 2012; Edward Colimore, "Survivor of a Dark Day: Center City Man Saw Nazi Massacre," December 22, 2012, *Philadelphia Inquirer*; Fischer, *Washington's Crossing*, 213.
11. RWP, Richard Potter, R838 (rejected because he deserted); Fremont-Barnes and Ryerson, eds., *Encyclopedia of the American Revolutionary War*, vol. 2, 427–28; Londahl Smidt, "German and British Accounts on the Assault on Fort Mercer," 9, 13.
12. Selesky *Encyclopedia of the American Revolution*, vol. 1, 373–74; Samuel Ward to George Washington, October 23, 1777, in Papers of the Continental Congress, roll 168, 153, DLAR; Walter H. Covell, "Colonel Christopher Greene," Roger Williams Family Association, www.rogerwilliams.org (thanks to Peter Flagg Maxson for this source).
13. RWP, Esek Roberts, W2351; Selesky, *Encyclopedia of the American Revolution*, vol. 2, 1099.
14. Louis Wilson, "The First Rhode Island Regiment, 1777 to 1783: The Formation of the Black Regiment," typescript in author's possession.
15. "Bill Permitting Slaves to Enlist into the Continental Battalions, Acts and Resolves of the Rhode Island Assembly," accessed via HeinOnline.
16. Ibid. Lorenzo Greene contends that prospective recruits had to get the master's permission but provides no source for this. See Greene, "Some Observations on the Black Regiment of Rhode Island," 156.
17. Acts and Resolves, Rhode Island Assembly, February 1778, 14–18, Rhode Island Historical Society.
18. *Providence Gazette and Country Journal*, February 7, 1778 through March 14, 1778; *Newport Gazette*, February 5, 1778. The Tory newspaper *Newport Gazette* had excellent sources within the Rhode Island legislature to be able to report so early on this story. The article did not explain its mention of "dishonorable terms." No further stories on this subject appeared in the *Gazette* through the end of February.
19. The June/July muster lists of Dexter's, Lewis's, Flagg's, and Coles's units total 123 privates and 6 musicians of color. (Thomas Arnold's company numbered fifty-three privates, all veterans.) U.S. Muster Rolls, DLAR. The General Treasurers' List complied by Ken Carlsen of the Rhode Island State Archives shows seventy-three slaves whose masters were reimbursed. An undated scrap from the Second Company of Foot in the Rhode Island Historical Society shows twenty-nine soldiers who had enlisted as slaves, fourteen of whom enlisted from February to June 1778 and are not on the treasurer's list. So at least 87 of the 129 new men in the First Rhode Island were slaves who responded to the February 1778 act. Given that fourteen men from

only one company are not on the treasurer's list, it is likely that other slaves-turned-soldiers are also not on that list.

20. Bartlett, *Census of the Inhabitants of Rhode Island and Providence Plantations*. For black Babcocks in the regiment, see Primus Babcock in Captain Lewis's company, July 1778, and William Babcock in Captain Dexter's company, July 1778, in U.S. Muster Rolls, DLAR, "Rhode Island Slaves Enlisted into Continental Battalions, 1778," compiled by Kenneth S. Carlson and drawn from the General Treasurer's Accounts, Rhode Island State Archives.
21. William Greene to Nathanael Greene, March 6, 1778, in Nathanael Greene Papers, AAS.
22. Elijah Lewis to the Speaker of the Assembly, March 13, 1778, in Letters to the Governor, vol. 12, letter 39, in Rhode Island State Archives.
23. There is a Thomas Hazard in the 1777 Rhode Island Military Census. Of the five who signed up in South Kingston, four were slaves. Other men from South Kingston did sign up later. The regiment was not at this time commonly known as the Black Regiment. Most Revolutionary War sources labeled it the First Rhode Island, Colonel Greene's Regiment, or the Rhode Island Regiment. The nineteenth century saw "the Black Regiment" come into vogue. Newport Champlain made it to the end of the war: Captain John Dexter muster list, August 1778, Revolutionary War Military Records, B6, F22, RIHS. Later calculations based on the Rhode Island Regimental Book of 1781 corroborates the average age of twenty-five for enlistees. MacGunnigle, *Regimental Book*, 132.
24. Rhode Island Acts and Resolves, February, 1778, March, 1778, and May 1778 sessions.
25. Scrap dated March 27 or 17, 1778, Beriah Brown Papers, RIHS; RWP, Scipio Brown, S38584.
26. Rhode Island Acts and Resolves, October 1778 session, 23. For Frank's service before the establishment of the Black Regiment, see Captain William Tew's muster list, February 1778, U.S. Muster Rolls, DLAR. Noted Rhode Island historian Sidney S. Rider found that Eyres was reimbursed.
27. Chamberlain, *Rhode Island Military Census*, 97–105. Some of the men mentioned in the census (Cesar Rose, Tony Rose, Ned Rose, Dick Champlin, July Champlin, Jack Champlin, Tom Reynolds, Mingo Reynolds, and Samson Reynolds) appear on muster lists.
28. Rhode Island Acts and Resolves, May 1778 session; muster list, John S. Dexter, July 1778, U.S. Muster Rolls, DLAR. For substitution laws with no racial qualifier, see Rhode Island Acts and Resolves, August 1777, 18.
29. Covell, "Colonel Christopher Greene"; Rappleye, *Sons of Providence*, 195; U.S. Muster Rolls, DLAR, record group 93, film #4, roll 136, "Prisoners Taken at Quebec." Greene was taken prisoner along with other Rhode Island men, including Jeremiah Greenman, who was later taken prisoner by the British at Pines Bridge, where Greene died.
30. Wells, *Population in the British Colonies*, 265.
31. Captain Flagg's muster list, July 1778, U.S. Muster Rolls, DLAR; MacGunnigle, *Regimental Book*, xviii; Greenman, *Diary of a Common Soldier*, 102. There is one muster list noting Prince Ingraham enlisting on February 2, which was before the act was passed.

32. Flagg's muster list, June 1778, U.S. Muster Rolls, DLAR.
33. Angell, *Diary of Colonel Israel Angell*, xii.
34. RWP, Winsor Fry, S38709; Flagg's muster list, April 1778, U.S. Muster Rolls, DLAR.
35. Flagg's muster list, July 6, 1778, U.S. Muster Rolls, DLAR; Thomas Arnold's muster list, May 1778, U.S. Muster Rolls, DLAR.
36. William Humphrey's muster list, May 1778, U.S. Muster Rolls, DLAR; Arnold's muster list, May 1778, U.S. Muster Rolls, DLAR; Thanks to Greg Urwin for the insight on model companies.
37. For example of blank space under "corporal," see Elijah Lewis muster, July 6, 1778, U.S. Muster Rolls, DLAR; "Order, East Greenwich, June 9, 1779," in Revolutionary War Military Records, Box 2, RIHS. Confusion exists with respect to rank when white and black men have the same name. Ebenezer Slocum, for example, has sometimes been identified as a noncom officer. There were two men of that name in the Rhode Island line, one a private who died on December 29, 1781, the other a corporal in John Holden's May 1779 company. The 1790 federal census for Rhode Island lists an Ebenezer Slocum who is white, likely the noncom officer. Similarly, Benoni Bates has been tagged as a black noncom, but here too there were two men with the same name—a white corporal (RWP, S39961) and a black private (RWP, S38515). The inspector general's report was contradicted by musters that have no corporals listed through 1779 and into 1780. In Captain Lewis's company, three appear in January 1780: one deserted, one on command, one reduced (something deemed impossible by the inspector general because of race). David Potter, the corporal relegated to private status, was a private (if the same man) on the April 1779 list. Could he have been African American? For inspector general's report, see U.S. Muster Rolls, record group 93, film 4, roll 136, frame 192, DLAR—"Return of the Brigade of Foot commanded by Brigadier General Stark as reviewed by the Inspector General, Sept. 6, 1779."
38. "Mrs. Mary Almy's Narrative," typescript, in Ellery Papers, box 1, folder 11, Newport Historical Society. Although Mrs. Almy was married to an officer in the revolutionary forces, her sympathies lay definitely with the British. While her husband was off soldiering, she stayed behind in Newport with six children, her mother, and a younger sister.
39. Whittemore, *General of the Revolution*, 5; RWP, Dick Brattle, R1167.
40. "John Sullivan's Report to Congress, August 31, 1778," in Amory, *Military Services and Public Life of Major-General John Sullivan*, 84–89; RWP, Boomer Jencks, S15902; Whittemore, *General of the Revolution*, 3, 105–8; Dearden, *Rhode Island Campaign of 1778*, 124; Benjamin Cowell Papers, RIHS. Accounts of the Battle at Newport include Deardon, *Rhode Island Campaign of 1778*; Blanco and Sanborn, *American Revolution*, vol. 2, 1386–96; Cowell, *Spirit of '76 in Rhode Island*, 167; quote from "narrative" of Battle of Rhode Island, Benjamin Cowell Papers, RIHS.
41. Blanco and Sanborn, eds. *American Revolution*, vol. 2, 1392; Amory, *Military Services and Public Life of Major-General John Sullivan*, 88, 93, 280; John Sullivan to George Washington, August 29 & 31 1778, Papers of the Continental Congress, DLAR; undated chart titled "A Return of the Killed, Wounded & missing of the Army . . . in the Action of 29 August 1778," Papers of the Continental Congress, DLAR. In his August 31 letter, Sullivan enclosed a casualty report to the Congress.

The First Rhode Island killed in action comes from the unit's muster lists. To most accurately assess the First Rhode Island's casualties in the context of Sullivan's entire army, it is necessary to know when on the August 31 Sullivan's casualty report was generated, but that is impossible.

42. After Orders, RIHS, B1, F22, S1,' SSA, 1778, John Holden Orderly Book, June 1–September 24, 1778, RIHS.

43. "Return of Purchases," Military Returns—Revolutionary War, no. 2, 107, Rhode Island State Archives; John Holden Orderly Book, June 1, 1778 to September 24, 1778, RIHS; Risch, *Supplying Washington's Army*, 189–201. Shortly after a mutiny in 1779, the men of the Second Rhode Island were given a weekly allowance of three days' fresh meat, three days' salt meat, and one day's salt until further notice. If the mutiny had something to do with provisions, Colonel Angell might have been trying to approximate the official army ration. "August 3, 1779," Second Rhode Island Orderly Book of Colonel Israel Angell, B1, F114, S1, SSB, July 1779–February 1780, RIHS; Preserved Pearce Ledger, box 2, F4, RIHS; John Holden Orderly Book, September 3, 1778, September 6, 1778, RIHS.

44. Account of Clothing, 1780, made out by John S. Dexter in Revolutionary War, no. 5, second section, p. 1, Rhode Island State Archives; "Order from William Pecke, June 9, 1779," Revolutionary War Military Records, RIHS; Rhode Island Acts and Resolves, March 1780 to September 1780; Jeremiah Olney to Coggeshall Olney, January 1, 1782, Jeremiah Olney Papers, RIHS; Stephen Olney to Mr. Hazzard, February 17, 1780, Revolutionary War Military Records, B2, F4, RIHS.

45. March 2, 1780, Second Rhode Island muster lists, DLAR; John Holden Orderly Book, August 10, 117, RIHS; Jabez Bowen to J. Olney, July 16, 1781, Jeremiah Olney Papers, RIHS; "Return of the Sick," September 17, 1778, and February 18, 1779, Revolutionary War Military Records, box 4, folder 7, RIHS.

46. Thomas Cole's muster list, October 1778, May 1779, April 1779, June 1779, August 1779, September 1779, October 1779, U.S. Muster Rolls, DLAR; Orders, Colonel Christopher Greene, October 30, 1779, DLAR; Orderly Book, Israel Angell, September 17, 1779, Revolutionary War Military Records, RIHS; John Holden Orderly Book, September 8, 1778, September 22, 1778, September 9 and 11, 1778, Revolutionary War Military Records, RIHS. During the Civil War, Thomas Wentworth Higginson, the commander of the first all-black regiment (the First South Carolina Volunteers) said that his men had a limited command of proper names and places, so confusion would ensue. One night, the countersign was "Fredericksburg" which had no meaning for the rank and file, so the sergeant of the watch substituted "Crockery-ware," a familiar word. "Carthage" would be familiarized to "Cartridge" and "Concord" became "Corncob." Perhaps the First Rhode Island experienced the same problem and supplemented their stock of proper names and places with phrases in everyday use.

47. Noah Robinson Diary, October 3 and 27, 1777; March 3, 1778, RIHS; Greenman, *Diary of a Common Soldier*, 139.

48. "Rules and Regulations," *Journals of the Continental Congress*, vol. 2, 111. In the Book of Deuteromy no more than forty lashes are imposed. Later on in the Continental Army, one thousand stripes was the standard punishment for desertion, while theft could go up to fifteen hundred lashes. See Anderson, *People's Army*, 122–40; "George Washington to William Heath, September, 1776," Washington, *Papers of*

George Washington, vol. 6, 398–99; "Articles of War," September 20, 1776, *Journals of the Continental Congress*, vol. 5, 788.
49. Neagles, *Summer Soldiers*, 77, 187, 221, 254; Angell, *Diary of Colonel Israel Angell*, 66–73; scrap, July 31, 1779, Revolutionary War Military Records, vol. 2, 143, RIHS; Greenman, *Diary of a Common Soldier*, 138–39.
50. Court Martial, September 5, 1779, and July 6, 1779, Revolutionary War Military Collection, RIHS; Court Martial, May 1779, in Orderly Book, Colonel Christopher Greene Papers, DLAR; court-martial proceedings, September 4, 1781, Revolutionary War Military Records, box 1, folder 91, RIHS; Orderly Book, Colonel Christopher Greene Papers, July 14, 1779, June 15, 1779, June 21, 1779, DLAR.
51. Court Martial, July 6, 1779, Revolutionary War Military Records, RIHS; Court Martial, June 15, 1779, Orderly Book, Colonel Christopher Greene Papers, DLAR.
52. The Fry story comes from many sources whose dates do not always jibe. See Elijah Lewis muster lists, February–July 1780 and August 1780–January 1781, U.S. Muster Rolls, DLAR; George Washington to Christopher Greene, April 12, 1780, May 31, 1780, October 21, 1780, George Washington Papers, Library of Congress, http://memory.loc.gov/; Christopher Greene to George Washington, October 14, 1780, Revolutionary War Military Records, box 1, folder 69, RIHS; "Return of Casualties since 24 December 1779," Colonel Christopher Greene Papers, DLAR; MacGunnigle, *Regimental Book*, 111, The difference between June and October 1780 is likely due to General Heath's arrival in June, which caused an upheaval in the regiment, calling for them to be relocated with the main army in the state of New York. A flurry of desertions occured through July.
53. Orderly Book, Israel Angell, September 17, 1779, September 13, 1779, Revolutionary War Military Records, RIHS; Angell, *Diary of Colonel Israel Angell*, 27. It should be noted that there are fewer numbers of orderly book pages for the First Rhode Island than for the Second so any generalizations are made with caution. Olney letter, August 4, 1782, Papers of the Continental Congress, #149, I, folder 563, DLAR. See also "George Washington to Secretary of War, August 5, 1782," in Washington, *Papers of George Washington*, vol. 24, 467; 1790 and 1800 federal censuses.
54. Court Martial, undated (but scrap indicates that it occurred between June 1779 and February 1780), Revolutionary War Military Records, B1, F53, S1, SSA, RIHS.
55. Ibid.
56. Ibid.
57. Angell, *Diary of Colonel Israel Angell*, 47, 66; Orderly Book, Israel Angell, September 12, 1779, Revolutionary War Military Records, RIHS.
58. Orderly Book, Israel Angell, January 5, 1779, September 23, 1779, September 16, 1779; December 1, 1779, Revolutionary War Military Records, RIHS; Angell, *Diary of Colonel Israel Angell*, 37.
59. Court Martial, September 5, 1779, Revolutionary War Military Records, RIHS.
60. "Regimental Orders, July 15, 1779," in Orderly Book, Colonel Christopher Greene Papers, DLAR.
61. "Court Martial, June 5, 1782," in Washington, *Writings of George Washington*, vol. 24, 311; Court Martial, October 14, 1782, Washington, *Writings of George Washington*, vol. 25, 259–60.

62. Angell, *Diary of Colonel Israel Angell*, 79–85; Court Martial, June 5, 1782, in Washington, *Writings of George Washington*, vol. 24, 311; Court Martial, October 14, 1782, Washington, *Writings of George Washington*, vol. 25, 259–60.
63. Angell, *Diary of Colonel Israel Angell*, 88; "George Washington to Horatio Gates, November 13, 1779," in Washington, *Writings of George Washington*, vol. 18, 894.
64. *Providence Gazette*, June 16, 1780.
65. Heath to George Washington, June 20, 1780, William Heath Papers, reel 16, DLAR; George Washington to Christopher Greene, May 15, 1780, George Washington Papers, Library of Congress, http://memory.loc.gov/.
66. *Providence Gazette*, June 16, 1789; William Heath to George Washington, June 20, 1780, William Heath Papers, DLAR (originals at the Massachusetts Historical Society); George Washington to Colonel Greene, May 15, 1780, George Washington Papers, Library of Congress, http://memory.loc.gov/; "Act for Raising and Sending into the Field 600 Men to Recruit the Continental Battalions Raised by this State under the Command of Colonel Christopher Greene and Col. Israel Angell," General Assembly, State of Rhode Island and Providence Plantations, June session, 1780; William Heath to George Washington, June 21, 1780, William Heath Papers, DLAR; William Heath to George Washington, June 23, 1780, William Heath Papers, DLAR; William Mumford to William Heath, June 25, 1780, William Heath Papers, DLAR.
67. William Heath to George Washington, June 25, 1780, William Heath Papers, DLAR; George Washington to Captain Holden, June 26, 1780, William Heath Papers, DLAR; William Heath to Major Flagg, June 27, 1780, William Heath Papers, DLAR; William Heath to Col. Greene, June 27, 1780, William Heath Papers, DLAR; Heath to Flagg, July 1, 1780, William Heath Papers, DLAR.
68. "George Washington to William Heath, June 29, 1780," in Washington, *Writings of George Washington*, vol. 19, 92; "George Washington to Governor William Greene, June 29, 1780," in Washington, *Writings of George Washington*, vol. 19, 96–97; William Heath to Flagg, July 7, 1780, Heath Papers; Rider, *Historical Inquiry*, 28. In 1782 Colonel Olney issued a call for recruits in which he spurned any potential recruits of color. "It has been found from long and fatal experience that Indians, Negroes and Mulattoes do not (and from a total want of Perseverance and Fortitude to bear the various fatigues Incident to any Army) and cannot answer the public service; they will not therefore on any account be received." *Providence Gazette and Country Journal*, March 9, 1782. This might have been issued because of white men's refusal to fight with blacks.
69. Muster list, John Dexter, February–July 1780 (this unit combined Dexter's and Flagg's men), U.S. Muster Rolls, DLAR; muster list, Elijah Lewis, February–July 1780 (this unit combined men from Lewis's, Cole's, and Slocum's companies), U.S. Muster Rolls, DLAR.
70. Muster list, Elijah Lewis, February–July 1780, U.S. Muster Rolls, DLAR.
71. William Heath to George Washington, July 12, 1780, Heath Papers; "George Washington to William Heath, July 27, 1780," in Washington, *Writings of George Washington*, vol. 19, 269. See also *Newport Mercury*, July 15, 1780. George Washington issued a similar pardon to the Massachusetts line at about the same time.
72. *Newport Mercury*, July 15, 1780; *American Journal and General Advertiser*, July 12, July 19, 1780, August 30, 1780; Heath, *Memoirs of Major-General Heath*, 232; Heath

to ?, July 10, 1780, William Heath Papers, DLAR; Heath to George Washington, July 12, 1780, William Heath Papers, DLAR; Heath's Proclamation, July 13, 1780, William Heath Papers, DLAR; muster list, John Dexter, February–July 1780, U.S. Muster Rolls, DLAR; muster list, Elijah Lewis, February–July 1780, U.S. Muster Rolls, DLAR; Forbes and Cadman, *France and New England*, 108.

73. "George Washington to Heath, June 2, 1780," in Heath, *Memoirs of Major-General Heath*, 218; George Washington to Heath, July 5, 1780, July 15, 1780, August 3, 1780, August 17, 1780, August 28, 1780, in Washington, *Writings of George Washington*, vol. 19, 122, 176, 307, 390, 460; "October 1, 1780," Heath, *Memoirs of Major-General Heath*, 233; George Washington to Christopher Greene, November 27, 1780 and George Washington to the Comte de Rochambeau, November 27, 1780, in Washington, *Writings of George Washington*, vol. 20, 410, 414.

74. "Christopher Greene to George Washington, October 14, 1780," George Washington Papers, Library of Congress, http://memory.loc.gov/.

75. "Resolutions," October 3, 1780, *Journals of the Continental Congress*, vol. 18, 894; George Washington to Christopher Greene, November 27, 1780, George Washington Papers, Library of Congress, http://memory.loc.gov/; muster list, Captain Zephaniah Brown, January 1, 1782, U.S. Muster Rolls, DLAR; muster list, Captain Dulee Jerauld, February 1782, U.S. Muster Rolls, DLAR. There were a couple of men of color in Olney's light infantry. See muster list, Captain Stephen Olney, January 1782, U.S. Muster Rolls, DLAR.

76. For skirmishing between De Lancey's men and the Continental army, see Heath, *Memoirs of Major-General Heath*, 247–80; Kim, "The Limits of Politicization," 868–89. For a good map of the area and the location of both armies' lines and the no-man's-land in between, see Swanson, *Between the Lines*, 1.

77. Greenman, *Diary of a Common Soldier*, 200; Van Buskirk, *Generous Enemies*, 44–72; Heath, *Memoirs of Major-General Heath*, 247.

78. Greenman, *Diary of a Common Soldier*, 208–9. For more recent but brief accounts of this action, see Anthony Walker, *So Few the Brave*, 78–79; Hufeland, *Westchester County during the American Revolution*, 378.

79. Christopher Greene to Sam Ward, April 16, 1781, Papers of Christopher Greene, DLAR.

80. Christopher Greene to William Heath, May 8, 1781, William Heath Papers, DLAR; "George Washington to Heath, May 8, 1781," in Washington, *Writings of George Washington*, vol. 22, 58; William Heath to Christopher Greene, May 10, 1781, William Heath Papers, DLAR.

81. Heath, *Memoirs of Major-General Heath*, 267; Greenman, *Diary of a Common Soldier*, 208. Estimates of casualties vary. Historian Harold Peckham recorded fourteen killed and thirty captured, with an estimate of ten wounded. Peckham, *Toll of Independence*, 86. James Thacher, a Continental Army doctor at the main camp said that thirty-one were killed and twenty-two taken prisoner. See Thacher, *Military Journal of the American Revolution*, 262. *New-York Gazette and Weekly Mercury*, May 21, 1781, reported twenty-two killed, two wounded, and thirty-six prisoners. *American Journal and General Advertiser* (patriot newspaper based in Providence), July 4, 1781, reported ten dead, two wounded, and twenty-four prisoners. De Lancey's pension contains a list of those captured at the Croton River: thirty-six from Rhode Island, three from New Hampshire, five from the New York Militia.

82. Lippett, *Reminiscences of Francis J. Lippett*, 28 (thanks to Peter Flagg Maxson for this source); MacGunnigle, *Regimental Book*, 58, 62; Arnold Muster List, December 1777, U.S. Muster Rolls, DLAR, for Childs's enlistment.
83. RWP, William Wilkinson, W3748. Dexter was promoted to a major as a result of the fatalities of May 14.
84. Flagg, *Founding of New England*, 101; "Captain Stephen Olney's Account of That Part of the Revolutionary War in Which He Took Part from the Battle of Bunker Hill in 1775 to the Capture of Yorktown in 1781," copied by Sandford B. Smith, RIHS.
85. RWP, Prince Robinson, R8894 (widow rejected, not soldier); MacGunnigle, *Regimental Book*, 58.
86. Van Buskirk, *Generous Enemies*, 73–105; Greenman, *Diary of a Common Soldier*, 209–18.
87. Henry Collins Flagg's narrative in Flagg, *Founding of New England*, 101; *Providence Gazette*, May 26, 1781; *American Journal and General Advertiser*, July 4, 1781, reproduced in MacGunnigle *Regimental Book*, 58.
88. *New-York Gazette and Weekly Mercury*, May 21, 1781.
89. Ibid.
90. Heath, *Memoirs of Major-General Heath*, 247–67; Col. James De Lancey's pension application, Public Records Office, A013, vol. 113, part 1, folio 271–90 on microfilm, DLAR. On De Lancey's not leading most of his unit's raids, see Hufeland, *Westchester County during the American Revolution*, 382.
91. Greenman, *Diary of a Common Soldier*, 200. The three deserters were Privates Francis Williams (April 19, 1781), Elijah Woggs (March 18, 1781, William James (March 18, 1781), and Sergeant William Kipp (March 15, 1781). One of De Lancey's officers, a Captain Kipp, led the detachment to Widow Griffin's house. He was not the same individual who deserted Greene's unit, and there is no indication that the Kipps were related.
92. RWP, Benjamin Lattimore, S13683; RWP, Jack Rowland, S17018; Peckham, *Toll of Independence*, 61. For coverage of the monument's installation, see Nancy Gerbino, "Black Sons of the Revolution Remembered," *North Country News* (Yorktown, N.Y.), May 19–25, 1982.
93. Closen, *Revolutionary Journal of Baron Ludwig von Closen*, 92. Closen noted in his journal that three-quarters of the Rhode Island line were "Negroes." Perhaps the men he saw that day were primarily African Americans, but the musters reveal that 80 percent were white.

Chapter 4

1. "George Washington to Nicholas Cooke, February 2, 1778," in Washington, *Writings of George Washington*, vol. 10, 257. For more on the Laurenses, see Wallace, *Life of Henry Laurens*; Hargrove, "Portrait of a Southern Patriot"; Massey, *John Laurens and the American Revolution*; Kelly, "Henry Laurens," 82–123.
2. Bridenbaugh, "Charlestonians at Newport, 1767–1775," 43. For a sample of Carolina arrivals, see *Newport Mercury*, June 1, 1767; June 13, 1768; June 26, 1769; May 28, June 4, and June 11, 1770; June 17, 1771; May 18, 1772. For Henry Laurens and Brown University, see Rawley, "Henry Laurens and the Atlantic Slave Trade," 82–97. Population stats for Charles Town in Fraser, *Patriots, Pistols and Petticoats*, 2. The

population in revolutionary South Carolina was 60 percent white and 40 percent black. Edgar, *South Carolina*, 78. For Newport, see Crane, *A Dependent People*, 76. New York City had close to the same percentage of blacks as Newport.
3. "James Laurens to Henry Laurens, December 22, 1773," in Laurens, *The Papers of Henry Laurens* [hereafter HLP], vol. 9, 204; "John Laurens to Henry Laurens, October 26, 1776," in HLP, vol. 11, 275–77; "John Laurens to Henry Laurens," January 14, 1778, in HLP, vol. 12, 305; Edgar, *South Carolina*, 78. For distinction between a slave society and a society with slaves, see Berlin, *Many Thousands Gone*, 8.
4. "Henry Laurens to William Brisbane, August 14, 1776," in HLP, vol. 11, 225; "Appendix to the Extract, July 20, 1769," HLP, vol. 7, 99–100. This admission of Laurens occurred in a heated public exchange with a fellow South Carolinian. Laurens's opponent had sarcastically pointed to Laurens's goodness of heart as he claimed that Laurens saw the trade as an "unlawful Traffic" and got out of it as a salve to his conscience.
5. B. Wood, *Origins of American Slavery*, 40–93. On the labor process necessary for these two crops, see P. Wood, *Black Majority*, 61, 75.
6. P. Wood, *Taking Care of Business in Revolutionary South Carolina*, 289; Smith *Stono*, xiii–xv.
7. Wood, *Black Majority*, 134–42; Rogers, *Charlestown in the Age of the Pinckneys*, 56.
8. "Henry Laurens to Peter Nephew, December 20, 1771," in HLP, vol. 8, 111; "James Laurens to Henry Laurens, September 18, 1773," in HLP, vol. 9, 112; "Henry Laurens to James Baillie, September 23," 1774 in HLP, vol. 9, 576; "James Laurens to John Laurens, December 5, 1771," in HLP, vol. 8, 84; "Henry Laurens to Lachlan McIntosh, August 20, 1772," in HLP, vol. 8, 431.
9. "James Laurens to Henry Laurens, May 29, 1772," in HLP, vol. 8, 355. For wages received for hiring out of Scaramouche, see Henry Laurens Account Book, February and March, 1772, 461–70, College of Charleston, Special Collections, MS 0027. For confinement in workhouse, see Henry Laurens Account Book, June 1772 Account Book, 48, College of Charleston, Special Collections; "Henry Laurens to James Laurens, December 5, 1771," in HLP, vol. 8, 66–67. On Mary, see "Henry Laurens to William Brisbane, October 17, 1777," in HLP, vol. 11, 561–64; "Henry Laurens to Alexander Hamilton, April 19, 1785," in HLP, vol. 16, 553–56; "Henry Laurens to John Loveday, June 21, 1777," in HLP, vol. 11, 181.
10. "J. L. Gervais to Henry Laurens, July 26, 1777," in HLP, vol. 11, 407–8.
11. "Henry Laurens to William Brisbane, October 17, 1777," in HLP, vol. 11, 562; "J. L. Gervais to Henry Laurens, July 2, 1778," in HLP, vol. 13, 540; "J. L. Gervais to Henry Laurens, August 17, 1778," in HLP, vol. 14, 181.
12. "Henry Laurens to Lachlan McIntosh, February 10, 1770," in HLP, vol. 7, 228; "Henry Laurens to George Appleby, February 28, 1774," in HLP, vol. 9, 317; "Henry Laurens to William Cowles, May 2, 1772," in HLP, vol. 8, 286; "Henry Laurens to George Appleby, February 28, 1774," in HLP, vol. 9, 317; "Henry Laurens to James Laurens, October 10, 1771," in HLP, vol. 8, 4; "Henry Laurens to William Cowles, May 2, 1772," in HLP, vol. 8, 286; "Henry Laurens to Henry Carver, May 28, 1772," in HLP, vol. 8, 343; "Henry Laurens to J. L. Gervais, May 29, 1772," in HLP, vol. 8, 353. Inoculation: "Henry Laurens to William Cowles, October 31, 1771," in HLP, vol. 8, 26–27. Henry Laurens's surprisingly accommodating behavior could be explained by the possibility that Scipio (Robert) was his son. However, Laurens says later that he had bought Scipio.

13. "Henry Laurens to William Cowles, October 31, 1771," in HLP, vol. 8, 26–27; "Henry Laurens to James Laurens, November 19, 1771," in HLP, vol. 8, 47; "Henry Laurens to George Appleby, May 28, 1772," in HLP, vol. 8, 342.
14. "Henry Laurens to Robert Deans, December 28, 1772," in HLP, vol. 8, 515; "Henry Laurens to George Austin, Sr., April 19, 1773," in HLP, vol. 8, 696–97; "Henry Laurens to William Howell, April 19, 1773," in HLP, vol. 8, 697.
15. "Henry Laurens to J. L. Gervais, May 29, 1772," in HLP, vol. 8, 353.
16. "Henry Laurens to Alexander Garden, August 20, 1772," in HLP, vol. 8 435–36; "Henry Laurens to Peter Nephew, March 15, 1773," in HLP, vol. 8, 620; "Henry Laurens to James Laurens, March 22, 1773," in HLP, vol. 8, 635; "Henry Laurens to William Gambell, March 15, 1773," in HLP, vol. 8, 621.
17. "Henry Laurens to George Appleby, February 28, 1774," in HLP, vol. 9, 316–18; "Henry Laurens to George Appleby, March 10, 1774," in HLP, 347; Massey, *John Laurens and the American Revolution*, 30–95; Gilbert, *Black Patriots and Loyalists*, 73–81.
18. "Henry Laurens to James Laurens, December 5, 1771," in HLP, vol. 8, 66–67; "Henry Laurens to J. L. Gervais, March 22 to April 7, 1773," in HLP, vol. 8, 635; "Henry Laurens to Peter Nephew, March 15, 1773," in HLP, vol. 8, 620; "Henry Laurens to William Gambell, March 15, 1773," in HLP, vol. 8, 621.
19. "Henry Laurens to Paul Preston, November 22, 1771," in HLP, vol. 8, 48; "Henry Laurens to Felix Warley, February 3, 1772," in HLP, vol. 8, 169; "Henry Laurens to Samuel Brailsford, February 25, 1772," in HLP, vol. 8, 188–89; "Henry Laurens to J. L. Gervais, February 28, 1772," in HLP, vol. 8, 197; "Henry Laurens to Ross and Mill, May 20, 1772," in HLP, vol. 8, 358; "Henry Laurens to Henry Bright & Co., October 31, 1769," in HLP, vol. 7, 192.
20. "Henry Laurens to James Laurens, December 5, 1771," in HLP, vol. 8, 67; "Henry Laurens to John Laurens," February 21, 1774," in HLP, vol. 9, 304; "Henry Laurens to J. L. Gervais, November 7, 1771," in HLP, vol. 8, 37.
21. "Henry Laurens to John Laurens, June 18, 1775," HLP, vol. 10, 184–85; "Henry Laurens to John Laurens, June 23, 1775," HLP, vol. 10, 191–92. For more on this case, see Ryan, *World of Thomas Jeremiah*; Harris, *Hanging of Thomas Jeremiah*. For more on rumors of slave revolt in South Carolina, see Piecuch, *Three Peoples, One King*, 76–83.
22. "Thomas Hutchinson to the Council of Safety, July 5, 1775," in HLP, vol. 10, 206–8.
23. "Council of Safety to St. Bartholomew Committee, July 18, 1775," in HLP, vol. 10, 231–32.
24. "Henry Laurens to James Laurens, July 19, 1775," in HLP, vol. 10, 234–35.
25. "Henry Laurens to James Laurens, August 20, 1775," in HLP, vol. 10, 321–32.
26. "Henry Laurens to Alex Innes, August 20, 1775," in HLP, vol. 10, 331; *Public Advertiser*, December 16, 1775; "John Laurens to Henry Laurens, October 4, 1775," in HLP, vol. 10, 450.
27. "Henry Laurens to Col. Stephen Bull, March 16, 1776," *South Carolina Historical and Genealogical Magazine* 11 (1910), 171–73, 204–5.
28. "Henry Laurens to John Laurens, August 14, 1776," in HLP, vol. 11, 224–25.
29. Ibid.
30. "John Laurens to Henry Laurens, October 26, 1777," in HLP, vol. 11, 275–77.
31. "John Laurens to Henry Laurens, January 14, 1778," in HLP, vol. 12, 305; "Henry Laurens to John Laurens, January 22, 1778," in HLP, vol. 12, 328; "Henry Laurens to John Laurens, January 28, 1778," in HLP, vol. 12, 367–68.

32. "John Laurens to Henry Laurens, February 2, 1778," in HLP, vol. 12, 390–92; "John Laurens to Henry Laurens, February 9, 1778," in HLP, vol. 12, 430.
33. "Henry Laurens to John Laurens, February 6, 1778," in HLP, vol. 12, 412–13.
34. "John Laurens to Henry Laurens, February 15, 1778," in HLP, vol. 12, 446–47; "Henry Laurens to John Laurens, March 1, 1778," in HLP, vol. 12, 494–95.
35. "John Laurens to Henry Laurens, February 15, 1778," in HLP, vol. 12, 446–47; "John Laurens to Henry Laurens, March 10, 1779," in HLP, vol. 15, 64–65.
36. "George Washington to Henry Laurens, March 20, 1779," in Washington, *Writings of George Washington*, vol. 14, 370–31; "An Act to Prevent Sedition and Punish Insurgents and Disturbers of the Public Peace," April 11, 1776, in McCord, *Statutes at Large of South Carolina*, vol. 7, 345.
37. "Committee Report, March 25, 1779," in HLP, vol. 15, 72; *Journals of the Continental Congress*, vol. 13, 385–87; "Henry Laurens to John Laurens, April 3, 1779," in HLP, vol. 15, 76–77; "J. L. Gervais to Henry Laurens, March 16, 1778," in HLP, vol. 13, 5.
38. "Christopher Gadsden to Samuel Adams, July 6, 1779," in Gadsden, *Writings of Christopher Gadsden*, 165–66; "Henry Laurens to John Laurens, September 21, 1779," in HLP, vol.15, 172; Mattern, *Benjamin Lincoln and the American Revolution*, 60–61, 71, 79, 81; Russell, *American Revolution in the Southern Colonies*, 117–23; RWP, Allan Jeffers, S1770.
39. "An Ordinance to Direct the Manner of Procuring Negroes to be Employed in the Public Service, #1025, October 9, 1776," in McCord, *Statutes at Large of South Carolina*, vol. 7, 428–29; "An Ordinance to Carry into Effect the Above-cited Ordinance, #1053, February 14, 1777," in McCord, *Statutes at Large of South Carolina*, vol. 7, 394; *Gazette of the State of South Carolina*, December, 30, 1778; January 20, 1779; February 3, 1779; "An Act for the Alteration and Amendment of an Act Entitled 'An Act for the Regulation of the Militia . . . ,'" #1116, February 13, 1779," in McCord, *Statutes at Large of South Carolina*, vol. 4, 465; *Gazette of the State of South Carolina*, March 3, 1779.
40. "An Act for Completing the Quota of Troops to be Raised by this State for the Continental Service and for Other Purposes Herein Mentioned, March 28, 1778," #1075, in McCord, *Statutes at Large of South Carolina*, vol. 4, 410; "An Ordinance for Completing Six Continental Regiments Raised in this State," January 29, 1779, #1112in McCord, *Statutes at Large of South Carolina*, vol. 4, 186; *Gazette of the State of South Carolina*, March 24, 1779; August 25, 1779; September 29, 1779; "An Ordinance for Authorizing the Governor or Commander in Chief for the Time Being to Embody Foreigners, Resident in This State, and to Form the Same into Separate Independent Companies or a Battalion, for the Public Service, February 17, 1779," #1118, in McCord, *Statutes at Large of South Carolina*, vol. 7, 469.
41. *South-Carolina and American General Gazette*, October 29; *Gazette of the State of South Carolina*, February 17, 1779; March 24, 1779.
42. "Henry Laurens to James Laurens, January 6, 1776," in HLP, vol. 11, 4–5; "Henry Laurens to Lachlan McIntosh, August 27, 1776," in HLP, vol. 11, 262; "J. Custer to Henry Laurens," March 4, 1780, HLP, vol. 15, 238–39.
43. "J. L. Gervais to James Laurens, January 6, 1776," in HLP, vol. 11, 414–15; *Gazette of the State of South Carolina*, October 16, 1777; April 19, 1778; "J. L. Gervais to Henry Laurens, July 2, 1778," in HLP, vol. 13, 540.

44. "J. L. Gervais to Henry Laurens, June 26, 1778," in HLP, vol. 13, 518–21; "Henry Laurens to James Laurens, June 7, 1777," in HLP, vol. 11, 345; "Samuel Massey to Henry Laurens, June 12, 1780," in HLP, vol. 15, 304–5; Piecuch, *Three Peoples, One King*, 161–62. When Laurens describes pursuit of another planter's runaway slaves, he uses the active voice.
45. *Gazette of the State of South Carolina*, December 28, 1778; March 31, 1779; August 25, 1779; *South-Carolina and American General Gazette*, December 10, 1779; *South Carolina Gazette*, November 7, 1775.
46. Samuel Elliot, March 16, 1777, Record of Wills, Charlestown County, vol. 17, 622, Charleston County Public Library; William Raven will, October 14, 1765, Record of Wills, Charlestown County, vol. 10, 728.
47. *South Carolina Gazette*, February 3, 1779, February 10, 1779, November 3, 1779; *South-Carolina and American General Gazette*, October 29, 1779, December 17, 1779, January 19, 1780; *Gazette of the State of South Carolina*, January 20, 1779, August 25, 1779.
48. "Henry Laurens to William Manning, February 27, 1776," in HLP, vol. 11, 123; Van Buskirk, *Generous Enemies*, 136; Braisted, "The Black Pioneers and Others"; "J. L. Gervais, to Henry Laurens, April 28, 1780," in HLP, vol. 15, 282–89.
49. "John Laurens to Henry Laurens, January 27, 1780," in HLP, vol. 15, 232; Haw, *John and Edward Rutledge of South Carolina*, 132; Mattern, *Benjamin Lincoln and the American Revolution*, 90–92; footnote to "John Laurens to Henry Laurens, January 27, 1780," in HLP, vol. 15, 233n11.
50. "John Laurens to Henry Laurens, March 26, 1780," in HLP, vol. 15, 261–62; Braisted, "The Black Pioneers and Others," 22; Mattern, *Benjamin Lincoln and the American Revolution*, 91–109. For prominent Whigs who congratulated Clinton on the restoration of royal control, see Frey, *Water from the Rock*, 111.
51. RWP, Charles Hood, S41659; RWP, James Kersey, S878; RWP, William Clark, W6687; RWP, John Womble, S42083; RWP, Ambrose Lewis, S36041; RWP, Elisha Hunt, S13486; RWP, Thomas Lively, S38144; RWP, Drury Scott, S35644; RWP, Ephraim Hearn, S38020; RWP, Morgan Griffin, S18844; RWP, Gideon Griffin, W8877; RWP, Allan Jeffers, S1770; RWP, Berry Jeffers, W10145.
52. "Henry Laurens to South Carolina Delegates in Congress, May 14, 1780," in HLP, vol. 15, 295–96.
53. *Royal Gazette*, March 10–14, 1781, July 14, 1781. Moultrie claimed that all his slaves carried down to the British lines subsequently returned to him. See Frey, *Water from the Rock*, 114–15. Larger estimates of African Americans working in the British departments appear in British sources. See Frey, *Water from the Rock*, 121–22; Piecuch, *Three Peoples, One King*, 221.
54. RWP, George Russel, S39059; RWP, Mark Murry, R7523; Pancake, *This Destructive War*, 106; Russell, *American Revolution in the Southern Colonies*, 173.
55. Golway, *Washington's General*, 209; Richard Hargrove, "Portrait of a Southern Patriot," 199.
56. RWP, Peter Jennings, S4436; Ketchum, *Victory at Yorktown*, 251.
57. Closen, *Revolutionary Journal of Baron Von Closen*, 89, 92; muster rolls of the Rhode Island Regiment, record group 93, U.S. Muster Rolls, DLAR. Lieutenant Jean Francois de Lesquevin, Comte de Clermont Crevecoeur, quoted in Selig, *March to Victory*, 18. For the proximity of the Fourth Connecticut and the Rhode

Island Regiments, see Lesser, *Sinews of Independence*, 204–6. The two regiments were also listed side by side in the July 1781 "Order of Battle." See Johnston, *Record of Connecticut Men*, 304.

58. On Olney's participation in the battle, see Cowell, *Spirit of '76 in Rhode Island*, 236–37; J. Greene, *Guns of Independence*, 240–45; "George Washington to the President of Congress, October 16, 1781," in Washington, Writings of George Washington, vol. 23, 228. For Olney's company, see "Roll and Muster of the Light Infantry Company in the Rhode Island Regiment of Foot for the month of January 1782," U.S. Muster Rolls, DLAR. There is the possibility that two more names on the light infantry list could represent men of color. Many historians assume that the Rhode Island Regiment of 1781 is the old First Rhode Island, a unit of African American privates. They consequently give undue credit to black men in the assault of Redoubt 10. The Rhode Island Regiment including two companies of African Americans were at Yorktown, but they played no starring role in the taking of Redoubt 10.
59. Ewald, *Diary of the American War*, 335–36; Martin, *Private Yankee Doodle*, 241; Riley, "St. George Tucker's Journal," 387. Another veteran in the American army, Josiah Adkins, attributed the number of African American bodies to "Cornwellsian cruelty." He maintained that Cornwallis had about five hundred blacks inoculated for smallpox and released them to the countryside just as they were growing sick, in order to spread the contagion among the Americans. See Atkins, *Diary of Josiah Atkins*, 32–33.
60. RWP, Abraham Ailstock, S6475.
61. Addington, *Patterns of War*; Neumann, *History of Weapons of the American Revolution*, 22; Alexander, "The Forgotten French," 13; Hure, "The French Artillery at the Battle of Yorktown," 34–37.
62. *Royal Gazette*, March 2, 1782; "Nathanael Greene to George Washington, March 9, 1782," in Greene, *Papers of General Nathanael Greene*, vol. 10, 471.
63. "Nathanael Greene to John Rutledge, December 9, 1781," in Greene, *Papers of General Nathanael Greene*, vol. 10, 202–23.
64. "An Act to Procure Recruits and Prevent Desertions, February 26, 1782," #1151, in McCord, *Statutes at Large of South Carolina*, 513–14; "Nathanael Greene to John Martin, February 2, 1782 in Greene, *Papers of General Nathanael Greene*, vol. 10, 304.
65. John Laurens to George Washington, May 19, 1782, and George Washington to John Laurens, July 10, 1782, in George Washington Papers, Library of Congress, http://memory.loc.gov/. Laurens wrote a near identical letter to his friend Alexander Hamilton.
66. Massey, *John Laurens and the American Revolution*, 207–9; John Laurens to George Washington, May 19, 1782, Founders Online, National Archives, http://founders.archives.gov/; George Washington to John Laurens, July 10, 1782, Founders Online, National Archives, http://founders.archives.gov/.
67. John Laurens to George Washington, June 11, 1782, Founders Online, National Archives, http://founders.archives.gov/.
68. "Thaddeus Kosciuszko to Nathanael Greene, September 2, 1782," in Kosciuszko, *Autograph Letters of Thaddeus Kosciuszko*, 77. The "naked" condition of Laurens's two slaves was not out of the ordinary for slaves on southern plantations.
69. RWP, Andrew Pebbles, S38297. On Pebbles's recollection, Lee had left the army shortly after Yorktown because of issues having to do with honor. He did

subsequently marry in April 1782. Perhaps this was part of the reason for his departure given to soldiers, as Pebbles remembers it this way. John Laurens inherited command of Lee's accomplished light infantry legion. See Massey, *John Laurens and the American Revolution*, 226–28; Boyd, *Light Horse Henry Lee*. There are divergent opinions as to whether Laurens disobeyed orders at Chehaw Neck. Gregory Massey, John Laurens's biographer, says Laurens's departure from his camp was a "dereliction of duty." Richard Hargrove in his essay on Laurens says he was "in disregard of his orders" when he marched out to intercept the British. Jim Piecuch, on the other hand, claims that Laurens was obeying General Green's order to "do everything possible to thwart the British expeditions." See Massey, *John Laurens and the American Revolution*, 225; Hargrove, "Portrait of a Southern Patriot," 200; Piecuch, *Three Peoples, One King*, 323.

Chapter 5

1. Caesar Tarrant will, September 1797, in Deeds and Wills (Virginia), v. 34, reel 7, Library of Virginia, Richmond.
2. Arthur Zilversmit, "Quock Walker," 614–24.
3. "Constitution of Massachusetts, 1780"; Blanck, "Seventeen Eighty-Three," 24–51; Zilversmit, "Quock Walker," 614–24.
4. Blanck, "Seventeen Eighty-Three," 28–38.
5. C. Sedgwick, "Mumbett." Sheffield was one of one hundred Massachusetts towns that responded to the Boston Committee of Correspondence invitation to weigh in on what they perceived to be their rights and current violations of them.
6. Ibid., 64. Mumbet loved her master, John Ashley, and referred to him as "Master" until she died. Her mistress, on the other hand, was imperious and cruel. Once when Mumbet's sister was about to be chastised by Mrs. Ashley, who threatened with a hot iron, Mumbet put herself between sister and mistress, receiving the blow on her arm. Mumbet said she never covered the awful wound and that when visitors came to the house they would ask what happened. Mumbet said she replied, "Ask Missus." See C. Sedgwick, "Mumbett," 7; T. Sedgwick, "The Practicability of the Abolition of Slavery." Another source of inspiration could have come from a fellow slave of Ashley. Zach Mullen took Ashley to court under circumstances similar to Quock Walker. See Zilversmit, "Quock Walker," 618. On Brom's identity, see court records in Rosenthal, "Free Soil in Berkshire County, 1781," 781–85. See also Zilversmit, "Quock Walker," 619.
7. Zilversmit, "Quock Walker," 622–24.
8. A. Leon Higginbotham, *In the Matter of Color*, 82–88; Blanck, "Seventeen Eighty-Three," 27; RWP, Humphrey Hubbard, W25539; James Storm, in *Massachusetts Soldiers and Sailors in the Revolutionary War (Images Online)*, www.ancestry.com. Neither the *Boston Gazette* nor the *Worcester Spy* carried any story about the Mumbet decision in August and September 1781. Similarly, the final Walker case in the spring of 1783 did not rise to the level of public notice. On African American networks, John Adams learned from a Georgia congressional delegate that "Negroes have a wonderful art of communicating intelligence among themselves: it will run several hundreds of miles in a week or a fortnight." See Moore, *Historical Notes on the Employment of Negroes*, 14.

9. "An Act for the Gradual Abolition of Slavery, 1780," in Ronald Garet, University of South California Law School, http://weblaw.usc.edu/users/rgaret/documents/AnActfortheGradualAbolitionofSlavery.pdf; Fogleman, "From Slaves, Convicts, and Servants to Free Passengers," 43–76; Herndon and Murray, *Children Bound to Labor*, 17.
10. "An Act to Authorize the Manumission of Slaves," in Hening, *Hening's Statutes at Large*, May 1782, vol. 11, 39; "Act Directing the Emancipation of Certain Slaves Who Have Served as Soldiers in This State and for the Emancipation of the Slave Aberdeen," in Hening, *Hening's Statutes at Large*, vol. 11, 308. A phrase similar to Patrick Henry's "Give me liberty, or give me death!" appears in a popular play of the time, *Cato, A Tragedy*, by Joseph Addison ("It is not now time to talk of aught / But chains or conquest, liberty or death"). The same play likely inspired Nathan Hale's last words, "I regret that I have but one life to lose for my country." Quoted in Taylor, *Internal Enemy*, 36.
11. RWP, Oliver Cromwell, S34613. Thanks to Glenn Williams for his description of Badges of Merit versus Badges of Distinction. For Badges of Distinction, see "General Orders, August 7, 1782," in Washington, *Writings of Washington*, vol. 24, 487; for badges of merit, see "General Orders, June 8, 1783," in Washington, *Writings of Washington*, vol. 26, 481.
12. RWP, Humphrey Hubbard, W25539; RWP, Isaac Wickhams, S34534; RWP, James Keeter, S32942; RWP, John Francis, S34887; RWP, Agrippa Hull, W760. Robert Gould Shaw, colonel of the Massachusetts Fifty-Fourth Regiment in the Civil War, reported home that when black recruits donned their uniforms for the first time, they felt "as big as all creation." See Shaw, *Blue-Eyed Child of Fortune*, 297.
13. Taylor, *The Internal Enemy*, 1–54; Wolf, *Race and Liberty in the New Nation*, 5, 111–21.
14. Wesley, "Negro Suffrage in the Period of Constitution Making," 143–68; Fox, "The Negro Vote," 32; Horton, *Connecticut Constitution*, 9–11; *Laws of Connecticut*, May session, 1814, 162, accessed via HeinOnline; "Constitution of Delaware, 1776"; Berlin, *Slaves without Masters*, 90–91, 190–91.
15. Wright, "Negro Suffrage in New Jersey," 172–76; RWP, Jacob Francis, W459.
16. "Constitution of Maryland, 1776," articles 5 and 23; Wesley, "Negro Suffrage in the Period of Constitution Making," 154; Maryland Session Laws, 1783, chap. 23, accessed via HeinOnline; "Maryland Constitution, 1792."
17. "An Act to Alter Such Parts of the Constitution and Form of Government as Relate to Voters and Qualifications of Voters," chap. 90, passed December 31, 1801, and ratified in 1802, Session Laws Library Maryland, accessed via HeinOnline; "An Act to Alter Such Parts of the Constitution and Form of Government as Relate to Voters and Qualifications of Voters," chap. 83, passed and ratified in 1810, Session Laws Library Maryland, accessed via HeinOnline.
18. RWP, Thomas Carney, S35203; Nash, "Thomas Peters."
19. "An Act in Further Addition to the Act Entitled an 'Act for Regulating the Election of the Governor, Lt. Governor, and Assistants,'" Connecticut Session Laws, May 1814, chap. 15, accessed via HeinOnline. The people of Connecticut had their chance to strike out the word "white" in 1847 and 1865. Both times the voters declined to do so. Not until the federal government forced its citizens to acknowledge an African

American's right to vote with the Fifteenth Amendment did Connecticut and other northern states acquiesce. *Connecticut Courant*, September 22, 1818; *American Mercury*, June 9, 1818; "The Constitution of Connecticut, 1818," article 5, sections 1 and 2; *Connecticut Courant*, October 13, 1818; Horton, *Connecticut Constitution*, 10–11.

20. RWP, Robin Starr, S36810; Ann J. Arcari, "Freeman in Name Only: The African Americans in Colonial Farmington, Connecticut," master's thesis, Trinity College, 1998; General Assembly Papers, RG002, Rejected Bills—African Americans, 1810–1869, folders 3, 10, 12, 13, Connecticut State Library.

21. Gary Nash, *Forging Freedom*, 63–64; *Freeman's Journal*, September 21, 1781. It is unlikely that the Cato piece was written by a black man named Cato. It may well be the work of French-born American abolitionist Anthony Benezet, who lived until mid-1784.

22. A. Leon Higginbotham, *In the Matter of Color*, 89–90.

23. Egerton, *Gabriel's Rebellion*.

24. "Act to Emancipate James, a Negro Slave, the Property of William Armistead, Gentleman, 1786," in Hening, *Hening's Statutes at Large*, vol. 12, 380.

25. "An Act for the Manumission of a Negro Named Saul," November 13, 1792, in, Hening, *Hening's Statutes at Large*, vol. 13, 619; "An Act for the Purchase and Manumitting Negro Caesar, November 14, 1789, in Hening, *Hening's Statutes at Large*, vol. 13, chap. 84, 102.

26. Nash, *Forging Freedom*, 186, 187.

27. "An Act in Further Addition to an Act Entitled an 'Act for Regulating the Election of the Governors, Lt. Governor, Assistants,'" Connecticut Session Laws, May 1814, chap. 15, accessed via HeinOnline; Bias Stanley and William Lanson, "Petition Against a Legislative Act, October 1815," in Public Records of the State of Connecticut (1814), Connecticut State Library. Thanks to Debra Pond of Law and Legislative Reference Services, Connecticut State Library, for this source.

28. General Assembly Papers, RG002, African Americans, box 1, folders 16 and 23, Connecticut State Library; General Assembly Papers, RG002, Rejected Bills, box 2, folders 2, 3, 7, 10–13, 15–17, Connecticut State Library.

29. Nash, *Forging Freedom*, 43; Col. Jeremiah Olney to the Abolition Society, May 20, 1791, in Abolition Society Minutes, 1789–1827, Rhode Island Historical Society. Jack Burrows was captured at Crompond and taken to New York City as a prisoner. He is listed in the regimental book as having deserted a month later. It is unclear whether he was still a prisoner in June 1781, whether he took off for a limited time, or whether he indeed did desert. It did not seem to matter to his commanding officer in 1791. William H. Robinson, *Proceedings of the Free Africa Union Society and the African Benevolent Society: Newport, Rhode Island, 1780–1824*, ix (accessed at the Newport Historical Society).

30. RWP, John Harris, S37997. Sections on the 1818 and 1832 pension material originally published in Van Buskirk, "Claiming Their Due," in Resch and Sargent, *War and Society in the American Revolution*, used here with permission of Northern Illinois University Press.

31. Resch, *Suffering Soldiers*, 113–14.

32. RWP, London Dailey, W5260; RWP, Tobias Cutler, S45710; RWP, John Cook, S45694; RWP, Jude Hall, W23238; *Exeter Watchman*, July 22, 1817; Perry, *Exeter in*

1830, 1–25; Sawyer, *History of Kensington*; Bell, *History of the Town of Exeter*; RWP, Prince Light, S44511.
33. Paine, "The American Crisis," 69; Resch, *Suffering Soldiers*, 178; Judith Van Buskirk, "Claiming Their Due," 132–62.
34. The white literacy rate has been calculated at 91 percent in 1840. See Cremin, *American Education*, 491. For examples of veterans who were duped, see RWP, Job Primus, W10256; RWP, Scipio Watson, W18240.
35. Litwack, *North of Slavery*, 70–71; Crackel, "Revolutionary War Pension Records," 155. See also Resch, *Suffering Soldiers*, 218.
36. Resch, *Suffering Soldiers*, 179. Resch's estimate includes white veterans with no dollar value. My estimates for blacks do not include this cohort.
37. RWP, Levi Caesar, S39269.
38. RWP, David Howland, W22298; RWP, Jacob Francis, W459; RWP, James Jones, S41701; Strauss, "Ten Notable Apocalypses."
39. RWP, Cuff Tindy, S33804.
40. RWP Ben Simmons, W24974.
41. RWP, Joseph Johnson, R5636.
42. RWP, John Harris S37997; RWP, Caesar Shelton S19764; RWP, Isaac Perkins, S41953; RWP, Reuben Roberts, S39834.When race is mentioned, the most frequently used terms are "man of color" and "coloured." Two-thirds of my sample are identified as "man of color," one-fourth as "coloured man" (particularly popular in the middle states), 8 percent use the term "black," and 2 percent designate "Negro."
43. RWP, Pomp Magus, S33059; Prince Crosley, W24833; Jamaica James, S44984; James Cooper, S39362.
44. RWP, James Harris, S38006; RWP, Isaac Brown, S39214.
45. RWP, Israel Pearce, S3660; RWP, Jehu Grant, R4197; RWP, James Wormsley, S23498.
46. RWP, James Weeks, S33269.
47. "An Act to Provide for Certain Persons Engaged in the Land and Naval Service of the United States, in the Revolutionary War, March 18, 1818," U.S. Statutes at Large, 15th Cong., Sess. 1, chap. 19, 410–11.

Chapter 6

1. Jefferson quoted in Ellis, *American Sphinx*, 264–65.
2. Jefferson, *Thomas Jefferson's Notes on the State of Virginia*, 138–41; Wolf, *Race and Liberty in the New Nation*, 174.
3. Litwack, *North of Slavery*, 65, 161.
4. Nash, *Forging Freedom*, 275; Litwack, *North of Slavery*, 84 (Tocqueville quote), 100.
5. R. Fox, "The Negro Vote in Old New York," 255–68 (including "peculiar people"); White, *Somewhat More Independent*, 4, 26.
6. Fox, "The Negro Vote in Old New York," 258–60; RWP, John Patterson, S43783.
7. For recent interpretation of Franklin's motivations concerning abolition, see Waldstreicher, *Runaway America*.
8. E. Guyer, *Daily Chronicle and Convention Journal*, 309.
9. Ibid., 327.
10. Ibid., 331, 353, 454.
11. Ibid., 452; *Hobbs et al. v. Fogg*, 1837, accessed via LexisNexis Academic.
12. Purvis, *Appeal of Forty Thousand Citizens*, 1–14.

13. Ibid., 11–14; *Pennsylvania Freeman*, November 1, 1838.
14. Kathleen Housley, "Yours for the Oppressed," 17–29.
15. Ibid.; RWP, Caesar Beaman, S39130; RWP, Cuff Wells, W18103.
16. Garrison, *Thoughts on African Colonization*, 17–50; Nash, *Forging Freedom*, 233–45; Newman, *Transformation of American Abolitionism*, 96–104.
17. *Freedom's Journal*, March 16, 1827, accessed online via Wisconsin Historical Society, www.wisconsinhistory.org/; Dann, *The Black Press*, 15–46; "Newspapers, Biographies," in *Black Press: Soldiers without Swords*, PBS Online, www.pbs.org/blackpress/news_bios/index.html. The paper's founding editors, Cornish and Russwurm, fell out in the first six months, with Cornish leaving the paper. Russwurm carried on until he decided to join the colonization campaign and moved to Africa.
18. Walker, *Walker's Appeal*.
19. Ibid., 47.
20. "David Walker, 1796–1830." Harrison Gray Otis, mayor of Boston in 1829–31, was the nephew of revolutionaries James Otis and Mercy Otis Warren.
21. *Liberator*, January 8, 1831; "Nat Turner's Rebellion."
22. "An Act Supplementary to the Act for the Relief of Certain Surviving Officers and Soldiers of the Revolution," June 4, 1832, U.S. Statutes at Large, 22nd Congress, sess. 1, chap. 126, 529–30.
23. "Execution of the Act Providing for Persons engaged in the Land and Naval Service of the Revolution, January 4, 1820," in *American State Papers*, vol. 9, *Claims*, 682–84. For 1832 regulations, see "Pension Act of 1832 with the Instructions of the War Department for Carrying It into Effect," June 7, 1832, ProQuest U.S. serial set digital collection, no. 221 H.doc. 298.
24. The rejection rates for African American veterans are based on the men of this study. The white veterans are based on a random sample of six hundred white veterans.
25. RWP, Peter Nash, R7558; Quarles, *The Negro in the American Revolution*, 54.
26. RWP, Primus Hall, S43677. Primus's attorney, Reuben Baldwin, is not to be confused with Roger Sherman Baldwin, who defended the Amistad group.
27. Nash, *Race and Revolution*, 65–67; Nell, *Colored Patriots of the American Revolution*, 29–30.
28. RWP, Asabel Wood, S22947.
29. RWP, Samurel Sutphin, R10321; RWP, Jeffrey Brace, S41461; RWP, Mark Murry, R7523. Murry died and so was unsuccessful in obtaining a pension from the federal or state government.
30. RWP, Samuel Sutphin, R10321; Lender, *New Jersey Soldier*, 10.
31. Resch, *Suffering Soldiers*, 167–68.
32. Quarles, *The Negro in the American Revolution*, 70. By 1777, "New Jersey even gave up asking for freemen in its appeals. Any able-bodied and effective volunteers would do." See Lender, *New Jersey Soldier*, 17.
33. RWP, Mark Murry, R7523. Thanks to Ronald A. Lee of the Tennessee State Library and Archives for help accessing the 1834 state constitution.
34. Murry certainly knew Philip Pope, who was a pensioner and lived in Tennessee. Later, after Pope's death, Murry would get Pope's family members to testify for him.
35. According to other sources, Gates was said to have run the fastest away from Camden. With regard to the start of Murry's first stint, the Pension Office said

that it would have taken two or three weeks for news of Charlestown's fall to reach North Carolina. This was an 1854 letter from the office. Murry might have been exhausted by this point and did not challenge this estimate. Many American soldiers had not quite made it to Charles Town by the time of the city's fall and very likely fled north through Murry's county with the news.
36. RWP, Mark Murry, R7523.
37. Ibid.
38. For this and the following paragraphs: RWP, Hamet Achmet, S38107; Stedman, *Hammet Achmet*. Stedman's sources were the oldest person then living in Middletown and stories from her grandfather, a lawyer who had taken Achmet under his wing. Thanks to Debbie Shapiro from the Middlesex County Historical Society for providing sources connected to Hamet. Thanks to Mary Thompson at the Washington Library at Mount Vernon (officially the Fred W. Smith National Library for the Study of George Washington) who told me that there is no evidence that Hamet was ever at Mount Vernon. Mary has collected names of Washington's slaves not on the plantation censuses of 1783 and 1799. She said that after Washington's death, his will (freeing his slaves), appeared in most newspapers. Following on this news came many elderly African Americans who garnered local celebrity by claiming that they had worked for Washington, sometimes allegedlly having taken Billy Lee's place as Washington's manservant during the war. There is also no evidence that Washington freed slaves during the war so they could join the Continental Army, let alone a regiment from another state. Concerning the lock of Washington's hair, Stedman says it was buried with Hamet, but there are a few strands in a gold frame at the Middlesex County Historical Society that purport to be Washington's. The label reads that these few strands were given to "Mrs. Hart" by Hamet Achmet. See "The Strange Case of Hammet Achmet and Washington's Hair," *Middletown (Conn.) Press*, February 16, 1985; Nell, *Colored Patriots of the American Revolution*, 134–35; *Middlesex Gazette*, July 5, 1821, April 9, 1828; *Boston Courier*, December 5, 1842; *Daily Atlas*, December 5, 1842.
39. RWP, Jeffrey Brace, S41461; Brinch, *Blind African Slave*.
40. Brinch, *Blind African Slave*, 164–65.
41. Ibid.; Nash and Soderlund, *Freedom by Degrees*, 175–86.
42. RWP, Agrippa Hull, W760; RWP, Artillo Freeman, S44853. See also RWP, Oliver Cromwell, S34613; Powell and Persico, *My American Journey*, 114.
43. RWP, Caesar Wallace, S43250; RWP, Prince Bailey, W17230.
44. RWP, Bristol Budd, W25304; RWP, Charles Cuffey, W9402; RWP, William Johnson, S39786; Cowell, *Spirit of '76 in Rhode Island*.
45. RWP, Thomas Gardner, W7500. He remembers St. Patrick's Day because there was an "affray" between the artillery troops and the regular soldiers in the Connecticut line.
46. RWP, Caesar Clark, S37871; RWP, Simeon Simons, R9587; RWP, Joseph Green, W27415.
47. RWP, Peter Jennings, S4436; RWP, Cato Fisk, W14719.
48. RWP, Jack Gardner, W1593; Asher, *Incidents in the Life of Jeremiah Asher*, 18; Nell, *Services of Colored Americans*; Nell, *Colored Patriots of the American Revolution*; Nell, *Property Qualification or No Property Qualification*. Literacy rate for the children of black veterans calculated by examining those children who supported their mother's widow pension application. The women had to prove their marriage, and

often children would depose in court, either signing their names or marking an *X*. Isaac Brown information supplied by his descendant, Marion T. Lane, author of *Patriots of African Descent in the Revolutionary War, Part 1.*

Conclusion

1. RWP, Winsor Fry, S38709.
2. RWP, Samuel Bell, S6598; RWP, Richard Rhodes, W22060; RWP, Jehu Grant, R4197.
3. RWP, Dick Brattle, R1167.
4. Mayer, "Canada, Congress, and the Continental Army," 503-35; RWP, Pomp Magus, S33059; RWP, William Taburn, W18115. Thanks to Holly Mayer and Rick Herrera, former soldiers and current scholars of the American Revolution, for their thoughts on this section.
5. Federal census of 1790 under Henery Laurance (Henry Laurens), St. John's, Charleston, South Carolina. Mepkin is currently in Berkeley County. In 1790 it was part of the Charleston District.
6. Newman, *Transformation of American Abolitionism*, 95; quoted in Nash, *Race and Revolution*, 192; Julie Winch, "The Making and Meaning of James Forten's Letters from a Man of Color, William & Mary Quarterly 64, no. 1 (January 2007): 129-38.
7. "Sentiments of People of Color," in Garrison, *Thoughts on African Colonization*, 27; "Thomas Jefferson to John Holmes," April 22, 1820, Library of Congress, www.loc.gov/exhibits/jefferson/159.html.

Bibliography

Manuscript Collections

American Antiquarian Society, Worcester, Massachusetts
    Nathanael Greene Papers
    South Carolina newspapers
Burlington County Historical Society, Burlington, New Jersey
    New Jersey Abolition Society
Charleston County Public Library, Charleston, South Carolina
    John Lewis Gervais to Henry Laurens folder
    Probate Records
    Record of Wills
    South Carolina newspapers
    Workhouse Folder
College of Charleston, Special Collections, Charleston, South Carolina
    Henry Laurens Account Book
    Henry Laurens Collection
    Drayton Papers
Connecticut State Library, Hartford, Connecticut
    Comptroller's Records
    Connecticut Archives, Revolutionary War
    General Assembly Papers
    Public Records of the State of Connecticut
David Library of the American Revolution (DLAR), Washington Crossing, Pennsylvania
    Christopher Greene Papers
    Early American Orderly Books
    Eighteenth- and nineteenth-century newspapers
    Horatio Gates Papers
    William Heath Papers
    Papers of the Continental Congress
    Records of Revolutionary War Soldiers
    U.S. Muster Rolls
    U.S. Revolutionary War Pension Records (RWP)
    U.S. Service Records
Exeter Historical Society, Exeter, New Hampshire
    Genealogy Collection
    Pauper Records
Library Company, Philadelphia, Pennsylvania
    South Carolina newspapers (Brigham)
    Library of Congress, Washington, D.C.
    George Washington Papers
Library of Virginia, Richmond
    Legislative Petitions

BIBLIOGRAPHY

    Wills and Administration
    Virginia State Pension Records
Massachusetts Historical Society, Boston
    City directories
    Deeds-Suffolk County
    Probate and Family Court
Massachusetts State Archives, Boston
    Massachusetts Probate Records
    Massachusetts Soldiers and Sailors
    Revolutionary War Pensions (state file)
National Archives and Records Administration
New England Historic Genealogical Society, Boston
    Cemetery records
    City directories
New Hampshire Historical Society, Concord
    Congregational Church Records
New Haven Historical Society, New Haven, Connecticut
    City directories
    New Haven Military Collections
Newport City Hall, Newport, Rhode Island
    Probate records
    Proceedings of the Free Africa Union Society and the Africa Benevolent Society
Newport Historical Society, Newport, Rhode Island
    Ellery Family Papers
Providence City Hall, Providence, Rhode Island
    Town Meeting records
Rhode Island Historical Society, Providence
    Abolition Society Minutes
    William Arnold Papers
    Bowen Family Papers
    Beriam Brown Papers
    Moses Brown Papers
    Benjamin Cowell Papers
    Deed Book Collection
    Theodore Foster Papers
    Colonel Christopher Greene Papers
    John Holder Orderly Book
    Esek Hopkins Papers
    David Howell Papers
    Jeremiah Olney Papers
    Preserved Pearce Papers
    Perkins Papers
    Reverend John Pitman Papers
    Providence Town Papers
    Revolutionary War Military Records
    Reynolds Family Papers
    Noah Robinson Diary
    Rhode Island Citizens Historical Society

Rhode Island State Archives, Providence
    Military Returns—Revolutionary War, Books 1, 2, 5
    Regimental Book—First Rhode Island
South Carolina Historical Society, Charleston
    Bowen-Cooke Papers
    DeSaussure Family Papers
    Grimke Family Papers
    Ford-Ravenel Papers
    John Laurens Correspondence
    Miscellaneous manuscripts 1 and 2
    Pinckney Family Papers
    Roger P. Saunders Orderly Book
State Archives of North Carolina, Raleigh
    Probate records
Virginia Historical Society, Richmond
    Preston Family Papers
    Randolph Family Papers
    Virginia Negro Soldiers and Sailors in the Revolutionary War

Primary Sources

Adams, John. *Legal Papers of John Adams*. 3 vols. Edited by L. Kinvin Wroth and Hiller B. Zobel. Adams Papers, series 3. Cambridge, Mass.: Belknap Press of Harvard University Press, 1965.

American State Papers. Library of Congress. http://memory.loc.gov/ammem/amlaw/lwsp.html.

Angell, Israel. *Diary of Colonel Israel Angell*. New York: Arno Press, 1971.

Asher, Jeremiah. *Incidents in the Life of Jeremiah Asher*. London: C. Gilpin, 1850.

Atkins, Josiah. *The Diary of Josiah Atkins*. Edited by Steven E. Kagle. New York: Arno Press, 1975.

Bartlett, John R., ed. *Census of the Inhabitants of Rhode Island and Providence Plantations, 1774*. Baltimore: Genealogical Publishing, 1990.

Brinch, Boyrereau. *The Blind African Slave, or Memoirs of Boyrereau Brinch, Nicknamed Jeffery Brace*. Edited by Benjamin F. Prentiss. Electronic ed. Chapel Hill, N.C.: Documenting the American South, 2004. http://docsouth.unc.edu/neh/brinch/menu.html.

Calhoun, John C. *The Papers of John C. Calhoun*, vol. 5, *1820–1821*. Edited by W. Edwin Hemphill. Columbia: University of South Carolina Press, 1971.

Chamberlain, Mildred M., ed. *The Rhode Island Military Census—South Kingston*. Baltimore: Genealogical Publishing Company, 1985.

Clark, Walter, ed. *The State Records of North Carolina*, vol. 24, *Laws 1777–1788*. Goldsboro, N.C.: Nash Brothers, 1905.

Closen, Ludwig von. *The Revolutionary Journal of Baron Ludwig von Closen, 1780–1783*. Edited by Evelyn M. Acomb. Chapel Hill: University of North Carolina Press, 1958.

Collections of the Massachusetts Historical Society, vol. 2. 7th series. Boston: Massachusetts Historical Society, 1902.

"The Constitution of Connecticut, 1818." Connecticut General Assembly. www.cga.ct.gov/asp/Content/constitutions/1818Constitution.htm.

"Constitution of Delaware, 1776." Yale Law School. Avalon Project. avalon.law.yale.edu/18th_century/de02.asp.

"Constitution of Maryland, 1776." Yale Law School. Avalon Project. http://avalon.law.yale.edu/17th_century/ma02.asp.

"Constitution of Massachusetts, 1780." Center for Constitutional Studies, Source Documents. National Humanities Institute. www.nhinet.org/ccs/docs/ma-1780.htm.

Dann, Martin E., ed. *The Black Press, 1827–1890: The Quest for National Identity.* New York: Putnam, 1971.

Douglass, Frederick. *Narrative of Frederick Douglass, An American Slave, Written by Himself.* Electronic ed. Chapel Hill, N.C.: Documenting the American South, 2004. http://docsouth.unc.edu/neh/douglass/douglass.html. First published 1845.

Emilio, Luis F. *A Brave Black Regiment: The History of the 54th Regiment of Massachusetts Volunteer Infantry, 1863–1865.* New York: Da Capo Press, 1995. Unabridged republication of the second and enlarged edition first published in Boston in 1894.

Equiano, Olaudah. *The Interesting Narrative of the Life of Olaudah Equiano.* Edited by Robert J. Allison. New York: Arno Press, 2007.

Ewald, Johann. *Diary of the American War: A Hessian Journal.* Edited by Joseph P. Tustin. New Haven: Yale University Press, 1979.

Forbes, Allan, and Paul F. Cadman. *France and New England.* Boston: State Street Trust, 1925.

Force, Peter, ed. *American Archives.* Reprint, New York: Johnson, 1972. First published 1837–53.

Ford, Thomas. "The Diary of Timothy Ford." *South Carolina Historical and Genealogical Magazine,* July 1912, 132–47, and October 1912, 181–204.

Fox, George. *The Journal of George Fox.* Edited by Norman Penney. New York: E. P. Dutton, 1948. First published 1924.

Frazer, Persifor. "Extracts from the Papers of Persifor Frazer." *Pennsylvania Magazine of History and Biography* 31 (1907): 129–44.

Gadsden, Christopher. *Writings of Christopher Gadsden.* Edited by Richard Walsh. Columbia: University of South Carolina Press, 1966.

Garrison, William Lloyd. *Thoughts on African Colonization.* New York: Arno Press, 1968. First published 1832.

Gillespie, Joanna Bowen. *The Life and Times of Martha Laurens Ramsay, 1759–1811.* Columbia: South Carolina University Press, 2001.

Gooding, James Henry. *On the Altar of Freedom: A Black Soldier's Civil War Letters from the Front.* Edited by Virginia M. Adams. Amherst: University of Massachusetts Press, 1991.

Graydon, Alexander. *Alexander Graydon's Memoirs of His Own Time.* Edited by John S. Littell. Philadelphia: Lindsay and Blakiston, 1846.

Greene, Nathanael. *The Papers of General Nathanael Greene.* Edited by Dennis Conrad. Chapel Hill: University of North Carolina Press, 1998.

Greenman, Jeremiah. *Diary of a Common Soldier in the American Revolution: An Annotated Edition of the Military Journal of Jeremiah Greenman.* Edited by Robert C. Bray and Paul E. Bushnell. DeKalb: Northern Illinois University Press, 1978.

Grimes, William. *Life of William Grimes, the Runaway Slave.* Edited by William L. Andrews and Regina E. Mason. New York: Oxford University Press, 2008.

Grundman, Claudia B., ed. *Continental Congress Papers*. Richmond: Virginia State Library, 1976. (Viewed on microfilm at DLAR.)

Grundset, Eric G., ed. *Forgotten Patriots: African Americans and the American Indian Patriots in the Revolutionary War*. Washington, D.C.: Daughters of the American Revolution, 2008.

Guyer, E., ed. *The Daily Chronicle and Convention Journal: Containing the Substance and Spirit of the Proceedings of the Convention . . . May 2, 1837 to Alter and Amend the Constitution of the State of Pennsylvania*. Harrisburg, 1837. (Accessed at the Biddle Law Library at the University of Pennsylvania.)

Hamilton, Alexander. *The Papers of Alexander Hamilton*, vol. 2. Edited by Harold C. Syrett. New York: Columbia University Press, 1962.

Heath, William. *Memoirs of Major-General Heath, Containing Anecdotes, Details of Skirmishes, Battles, and other Military Events during the American War*. Boston: I. Thomas and E. T. Andrews, 1798.

Hening, William Walker. *Hening's Statutes at Large*. Transcribed by Freddie L. Spradlin. VAGenWeb, July 19, 2009. http://vagenweb.org/hening/.

Hodges, Graham Russell. *The Black Loyalist Directory: African Americans in Exile after the American Revolution*. New York: Garland, 1996.

Higginson, Thomas Wentworth. *Army Life in a Black Regiment*. New York: W. W. Norton, 1984. First published 1870.

Hurmence, Belinda, ed. *Before Freedom, When I Just Can Remember: Twenty-Seven Oral Histories of Former South Carolina Slaves*. Winston-Salem: John F. Blair, 1989.

Jefferson, Thomas. *Thomas Jefferson's Notes on the State of Virginia*. Edited by William Peden. Chapel Hill: University of North Carolina Press, 1955.

Johnston, Henry P., ed. *Record of Connecticut Men of the Military and Naval Service during the War of the Revolution, 1775–1783*. Baltimore: Clearfield, 1997.

Journals of the Continental Congress. 34 vols. Washington, D.C.: Government Printing Office, 1904–37.

Kalm, Peter. *Peter Kalm's Travels in North America*. Edited by Adolph B. Benson. New York: Dover, 1964.

Kosciuszko, Thaddeus. *Autograph Letters of Thaddeus Kosciuszko in the American Revolution*. Edited by Metchie Budka. Chicago: Polish Museum of America, 1977.

Laurens, Henry. *The Papers of Henry Laurens*. 16 vols. Columbia: University of South Carolina Press, 1968–2003.

Laws of the State of New York Passed at the Sessions of the Legislature Held in the Years 1777–[1801]. Albany: Weed, Parsons, 1886.

Lesser, Charles H., ed. *Sinews of Independence: Monthly Strength Reports of the Continental Army*. Clements Library Bicentennial Studies 2. Chicago: University of Chicago Press, 1976.

Lippett, Francis J. *Reminiscences of Francis J. Lippett*. Providence: Preston and Rounds, 1902.

MacGunnigle, Bruce. *Regimental Book: Rhode Island Regiment for 1781 etc.* East Greenwich, R.I.: Rhode Island Society of the Sons of the American Revolution, 2011.

Madison, James. *The Papers of James Madison*, vol. 1. Edited by William T. Hutchinson and William M. E. Rachal. Chicago: University of Chicago Press, 1962.

Madison, James. *The Writings of James Madison*. 9 vols. Edited by Gaillard Hunt. New York: G. P. Putnam, 1900–1910.

Martin, Joseph Plumb. *Private Yankee Doodle: Being a Narrative of Some of the Adventures, Dangers and Sufferings of a Revolutionary Soldier by Joseph Plumb Martin.* Edited by George F. Scheer. New York: W. R. Scott, 1962.

———. *Ordinary Courage: The Revolutionary War Adventures of Joseph Plumb Martin.* New York: Brandywine Press, 1993.

"Maryland Constitution, 1792." Archives of Maryland Online, Maryland State Archives. http://msa.maryland.gov/megafile/msa/speccol/sc2900/sc2908/000001/000416/html/am416--1.html.

Massachusetts Acts and Resolves. Commonwealth of Massachusetts, Executive Office for Administration and Finanance. www.mass.gov/anf/research-and-tech/over sight-agencies/lib/massachusetts-acts-and-resolves-1692-to-1959.html.

McCord, David, ed. *Statutes at Large of South Carolina*, vol. 7. Columbia: A. S. Johnston, 1840.

Moultrie, William, *Memoirs of the American Revolution.* New York: D. Longsworth, 1968.

Neagles, James C. *Summer Soldiers: A Survey and Index of Revolutionary War Courts-Martial.* Salt Lake City: Ancestry Inc., 1986.

Oliver, Peter. *Peter Oliver's Origin and Progress of the American Rebellion: A Tory View.* Edited by Douglass Adair and John A. Schutz. Stanford: Stanford University Press, 1961.

Paine, Thomas. "The American Crisis, December 23, 1776." In *Common Sense and Other Writings*, 81–96. Edited by Gordon S. Wood. NY: Modern Library, 2003.

Peckham, Howard, ed. *Toll of Independence: Engagements and Battle Casualties of the American Revolution.* Chicago: University of Chicago Press, 1974.

Penn, William. *The Papers of William Penn.* Edited by Richard Dunn and Mary Maples Dunn. Philadelphia: University of Pennsylvania Press, 1986.

Pinckney, Elise, ed. *The Letterbook of Eliza Lucas Pinckney, 1739-1762.* Chapel Hill: University of North Carolina Press, 1972.

Purvis, Thomas, ed. *Almanacs of American Life: Revolutionary America, 1763-1800.* New York: Facts on File, 1995.

———. *Appeal of Forty Thousand Citizens, Threatened with Disenfranchisement, to the People of Pennsylvania.* Philadelphia: Merrihew and Gunn, 1838.

Quintal, George, Jr. *Patriots of Color: "Peculiar Beauty and Merit": African Americans at Battle Road and Bunker Hill.* Boston: Boston National Historical Park, and Washington, D.C.: Government Printing Office, 2004.

Riley, Edward M. "St. George Tucker's Journal of the Siege of Yorktown, 1781." *William and Mary Quarterly* 5, no. 3 (1948): 375–95.

Robinson, William H. *The Proceedings of the Free Africa Union Society and the Africa Benevolent Society: New Port, Rhode Island, 1780-1824.* (Accessed at the Newport Historical Society, Newport, Rhode Island)

Sedgwick, Theodore. *The Practicability of the Abolition of Slavery: A Lecture Delivered at the Lyceum of Sturbridge, Massachusetts, February 1831.* New York, 1831. http://archive.org/details/practicabilityofoosedg.

Shaw, Robert Gould. *Blue-Eyed Child of Fortune: The Civil War Letters of Colonel Robert Gould Shaw.* Edited by Russell Duncan. Athens: University of Georgia Press, 1992.

Smith, James L. *Autobiography of James L. Smith.* Norwich: Press of the Bulletin, 1881.

Smith, Mark M., ed. *Stono: Documenting and Interpreting a Southern Slave Revolt.* Columbia: University of South Carolina Press, 2005.
Smithfield Monthly Meeting. "A Little History of Smithfield Monthly Meeting of Friends." In *213th Anniversary of Smithfield Meeting of Friends.* Woonsocket, R. I.: Smithfield Meeting, 1932. (Unpaginated pamphlet at Friends Historical Library of Swarthmore College, Swarthmore, Pennsylvania.)
Southern, Ed, ed. *Voices of the American Revolution in the Carolinas.* Winston-Salem, N.C.: John P. Blair, 2009.
Sutcliffe, Andrea. *Mighty Rough Times, I Tell You: Personal Accounts of Slavery in Tennessee.* Winston-Salem: John F. Blair, 2000.
Thacher, James. *Military Journal of the American Revolution.* New York: New York Times and Arno Press, 1969. First published 1862.
United States Statutes at Large. Library of Congress. www.loc.gov/law/help/statutes-at-large.
Walker, David. *Walker's Appeal, in Four Articles.* First published 1830. Electronic ed. Chapel Hill, N.C.: Documenting the American South, 2004. http://docsouth.unc.edu/nc/walker/walker.html.
Washington, George. *Papers of George Washington.* 22 vols. Edited by Philander Chase and Dorothy Twohig. Revolutionary War Series. Charlottesville: University Press of Virginia, 1985–2013.
———. *The Writings of George Washington, 1745–1799.* 39 vols. Edited by John C. Fitzpatrick. Washington, D.C.: Government Printing Office, 1931–44.
Watson, Judith Green, compiler. *South Kingston, Rhode Island Tax Lists, 1730–1799.* Rockland, Maine: Picton Press, 2007.
Weld, Theodore Dwight. *American Slavery As It Is.* New York: American Anti-Slavery Society, 1833.
Wheatley, Phillis. *The Collected Works of Phillis Wheatley.* Edited by John C. Shields. New York: Oxford University Press, 1988.
Whitehead, James L. "The Autobiography of Peter Stephen Du Ponceau." *Pennsylvania Magazine of History and Biography* 63, no. 3 (April 1939): 432–61.
Woolman, John. The Journal of John Woolman. Boston: Houghton Mifflin, 1871.

Newspapers

American Journal and General Advertiser (Providence, R.I.)
American *Mercury*
Boston *Chronicle*
Boston *Courier*
Boston *Evening Post*
Boston *Gazette*
Boston *Newsletter*
Boston *Post Boy*
Connecticut Courant
Daily Atlas
Exeter (N.H.) Watchman
Freedom's Journal (New York)
Gazette of the State of South Carolina (Charleston, S.C.)
Liberator (Boston)

New-York Gazette and Weekly Mercury
New Hampshire Gazette
Newport (R.I.) Gazette
Newport (R.I.) *Mercury*
Pennsylvania Evening Post (Philadelphia)
Pennsylvania *Freeman* (Philadelphia)
Public Advertiser (London)
Providence Gazette
Providence Gazette *and Country Journal*
Royal Gazette (Charleston, S.C.)
South-Carolina and American General Gazette (Charleston, S.C.)

Secondary Sources

Addington, Larry H. *The Patterns of War since the Eighteenth Century.* Bloomington: Indiana University Press, 1994.

Alexander, Dennis. "The Forgotten French: As Our First Allies, They Shared the Victory at Yorktown," *American History Illustrated*, October 1981, 10–17.

Amis, Moses. *City of Raleigh: Historical Sketches.* Raleigh, N.C.: Edwards and Broughton, 1887.

Amory, Thomas C. *The Military Services and Public Life of Major-General John Sullivan.* Port Washington, N.Y.: Kennikat Press, 1868.

Anderson, Fred. *A People's Army: Massachusetts Soldiers and Society in the Seven Years' War.* Chapel Hill: University of North Carolina, 1984.

Aptheker, Herbert. *The Negro in the American Revolution.* New York: International Publishers, 1940.

Babits, Lawrence, and Joshua Henry. "Fortitude and Forbearance": The North Carolina Continental Line in the Revolutionary War. Raleigh: North Carolina Department of Cultural Resources, 2004.

Baptist, Edward E. *The Half Has Never Been Told: Slavery and the Making of American Capitalism.* New York: Basic Books, 2014.

Barrett, Frank J., and Theodore R. Sarbin. "Rhetoric of Terror: 'War' As Misplaced Metaphor." Unpublished paper.

Bell, Charles. *History of the Town of Exeter, NH.* Exeter, N.H.: J. E. Farwell, 1888.

Berlin, Ira. *Many Thousands Gone: The First Two Centuries of Slavery in North America.* Cambridge, Mass.: Harvard University Press, 1998.

———. *Masters without Slaves: The Free Negro in the Antebellum South.* New York: Random House, 1975.

———. "Time, Space, and the Evolution of Afro-American Society on the British Mainland North America." *American Historical Review* 85 (February 1980): 44–78.

Berlin, Ira, and Ronald Hoffman. *Slavery and Freedom in the Age of the American Revolution.* Urbana: University of Illinois Press, 1983.

Blanck, Emily. "Seventeen Eighty-Three: The Turning Point in the Law of Slavery and Freedom in Massachusetts." *New England Quarterly* 75, no. 1 (March 2002): 24–51.

Blanco, Richard. *Physician of the American Revolution: Jonathan Potts.* New York: Garland, 1979.

Blanco, Richard, and Paul J. Sanborn. *The American Revolution, 1775–1783.* 2 vols. New York: Garland, 1993.

Bolster, Jeffrey. *Black Jacks: African American Seamen in the Age of Sail.* Cambridge, Mass.: Harvard University Press, 1977.
Boudreau, George W. *Independence: A Guide to Historic Philadelphia.* Yardley, Pa.: Westholme, 2012.
Boyd, Thomas. *Light Horse Henry Lee.* New York: C. Scribner's Sons, 1931.
Braisted, Todd. "The Black Pioneers and Others: The Military Role of Black Loyalists in the American War for Independence." In *Moving On: Black Loyalists in the Afro-Atlantic World*, edited by John W. Pulis, 3–27. New York: Garland, 1999.
Breen, T. H. *American Insurgents, American Patriots.* New York: Hill and Wang, 2011
———, and Stephen Innes. *"Myne Owne Ground": Race and Freedom on Virginia's Eastern Shore, 1640–1676.* New York: Oxford University Press, 1982.
Bridenbaugh, Carl. "Charlestonians at Newport, 1767–1775." *South Carolina Historical Magazine* 41 (April 1940): 43–47.
Brown, Christopher Leslie Brown. "The Problems of Slavery." In *The Oxford Handbook of the American Revolution*, edited by Edward G. Gray and Jane Kamensky, 427–46. New York: Oxford University Press, 2012.
Burrows, Edwin G., and Mike Wallace. *Gotham: A History of New York City, 1898.* New York: Oxford University Press, 1999.
Calloway, Colin. *The American Revolution in Indian Country: Crisis and Diversity in Native American Communities.* New York: Cambridge University Press, 1995.
Carp, Benjamin. *Rebels Rising: Cities and the American Revolution.* New York: Oxford University Press, 2007.
Carp, Wayne. *To Starve the Army at Pleasure: The Continental Army Administration and American Political Culture, 1775–1783.* Chapel Hill: University of North Carolina Press, 1984.
Cody, Cheryll Ann. "There Was No Absalom on the Ball Plantations: Slave Naming Practices in the South Carolina Low Country, 1720–1865." *American Historical Review* 29, no. 3 (June 1987): 563–96.
Countryman, Edward. *Enjoy the Same Liberty: Black Americans and the Revolutionary Era.* Lanham, Md.: Rowman & Littlefield, 2012.
Cowan, David, L. *Medicine in Revolutionary New Jersey.* Trenton: New Jersey Historical Commission, 1975.
Cowell, Benjamin. *Spirit of '76 in Rhode Island.* Baltimore: Genealogical Publishing Company, 1973.
Crackel, Theodore J. "Revolutionary War Pension Records and Patterns of American Mobility, 1780–1830." *Prologue* 16 (Fall 1984): 155–67.
Crane, Elaine Forman. *A Dependent People: Newport, Rhode Island in the Revolutionary Era.* New York: Fordham University Press, 1985.
Cremin, Lawrence A. *American Education: The National Experience, 1783–1876.* New York: Harper and Row, 1980.
Crews, Ed. "Play Ball! Colonial Games and America's National Pastime." *Colonial Williamsburg*, Spring 2008. www.history.org/Foundation/journal/Spring08/ball.cfm.
Crow, Jeffery J. *The Black Experience in Revolutionary North Carolina.* Raleigh: Division of Archives and History, 1977.
"David Walker, 1796–1830." In *Africans in America.* WGBH/PBS. www.pbs.org/wgbh/aia/part4/4p2930.html.

Davis, David B. *The Problem of Slavery in the Age of Revolution, 1770–1823*. Ithaca: Cornell University Press, 1999.
Dearden, Paul F. *The Rhode Island Campaign of 1778: Inauspicious Dawn of Alliance*. Providence: Rhode Island Bicentennial Foundation, 1980.
Deloria, Philip J. *Playing Indian: Otherness and Authenticity in the Assumption of American Indian Identity*. New Haven: Yale University Press, 1999.
Dunn, Mary Maples, and Richard S. Dunn. "The Founding, 1681–1701." In *Philadelphia: A 300 Year History*, edited by Russell F. Weigley, 1–32. New York: W. W. Norton, 1982.
Edgar, Walter. *South Carolina: A History*. Columbia: University of South Carolina, 1998.
Egerton, Douglas R. *Death or Liberty: African Americans and Revolutionary America*. New York: Oxford University Press, 2009.
———. *Gabriel's Rebellion: The Virginia Slave Conspiracies of 1800 and 1802*. Chapel Hill: University of North Carolina Press, 1993.
Egleston, Thomas. *The Life of John Paterson: Major General in the Revolutionary Army*. New York: G. P. Putnam's Sons, 1898.
Ellis, Joseph. *American Sphinx: The Character of Thomas Jefferson*. New York: Alfred A. Knopf, 1997.
Evans, Emory G. "A Question of Complexion: Documents concerning the Negro and the Franchise in Eighteenth-Century Virginia." *Virginia Magazine of History and Biography* 71 (October 1963): 411–15.
Farrow, Anne, Joel Lang, and Jennifer Frank. *Complicity: How the North Promoted, Prolonged, and Profited from Slavery*. New York: Ballantine Books, 2005.
"Felix's Petition." In *Africans in America*, WGBH/PBS. www.pbs.org/wgbh/aia/part2/2h22t.html.
Ferling, John. *A Leap in the Dark: The Struggle to Create the American Republic*. New York: Oxford University Press, 2003.
Fischer, David Hackett. *Paul Revere's Ride*. New York, Oxford University Press, 1994.
———. *Washington's Crossing*. New York: Oxford University Press, 2004.
Flagg, Ernest. *The Founding of New England: My Ancestors' Part in That Undertaking*. Hartford: Genealogical Publishing Company, 1926.
Fogleman, Aaron S. "From Slaves, Convicts, and Servants to Free Passengers: The Transformation of Immigration in the Era of the American Revolution." *Journal of American History* 85 (June 1998): 43–76.
Foner, Eric. *Give Me Liberty! An American History*. New York: W. W. Norton, 2011.
Fox, Ryan Dixon. "The Negro Vote in Old New York." *Political Science Quarterly* 32 (1917): 255–68.
Fraser, Walter J., Jr. *Patriots, Pistols and Petticoats: "Poor Sinful Charles Town" during the American Revolution*. 2nd ed. Columbia: University of South Carolina Press, 1993.
Fremont-Barnes, Gregory, and Richard Alan Ryerson, eds. *Encyclopedia of the American Revolutionary War: A Political, Social and Military History*. 5 vols. Santa Barbara: ABC-CLIO, 2006.
Frey, Sylvia R. *Water from the Rock: Black Resistance in a Revolutionary Age*. Princeton: Princeton University Press, 1991.
Gabriel, Michael P., and Tyler Resch. *The Battle of Bennington: Soldiers and Civilians*. Charleston, S.C.: History Press, 2012.

Gerbino, Nancy. "Black Sons of the Revolution Remembered." *North Country News*, May 19–25, 1982.
Gilbert, Alan. *Black Patriots and Loyalists: Fighting for Emancipation in the War for Independence*. Chicago: University of Chicago Press, 2012.
Glasson, William Henry. *History of Military Pension Legislation in the United States*. New York: Columbia University Press, 1900.
Glatthaar, Joseph T., and James Kirby Martin. *Forgotten Allies: The Oneida Indians and the American Revolution*. New York: Hill and Wang, 2007.
Golway, Terry. *Washington's General: Nathanael Greene and the Triumph of the American Revolution*. New York: H. Holt, 2005.
Gould, Dudley C. *Times of Brother Jonathan: What He Ate, Drank, Wore, Believed in and Used for Medicine during the War for Independence*. Middletown, Conn.: Southfarm Press, 2001.
Greene, Evarts B., and Virginia Harrington. *American Population before the Federal Census of 1790*. Baltimore: Genealogical Publishing Company, 1977.
Greene, Jerome A. *The Guns of Independence: The Siege of Yorktown, 1781*. New York: Savas Beatie, 2005.
Greene, Lorenzo. "Some Observations on the Black Regiment of Rhode Island in the American Revolution." *Journal of Negro History* 37, no. 2 (April 1952): 142–72.
Hall, John. "An Irregular Reconsideration of George Washington and the American Military Tradition." *Journal of Military History* 78 (July 2014): 961–93.
Hargrove, Richard. "Portrait of a Southern Patriot: The Life and Death of John Laurens." In *The Revolutionary War in the South: Power, Conflict, and Leadership*, edited by W. Robert Higgins, 182–202. Durham: Duke University Press, 1979.
Harris, J. William. *The Hanging of Thomas Jeremiah: A Free Black Man's Encounter with Liberty*. New Haven: Yale University Press, 2011.
Haw, James. *John and Edward Rutledge of South Carolina*. Athens: University of Georgia Press, 1997.
Headrick, Daniel R. *The Tools of Empire: Technology and European Imperialism in the 19th Century*. New York: Oxford University Press, 1981.
Herndon, Ruth Wallis, and John E. Murray. *Children Bound for Labor: The Pauper Apprentice System in Early America*. Ithaca: Cornell University Press, 2009.
Herrera, Ricardo A. *For Liberty and the Republic: The American Citizen as Soldier, 1775–1861*. New York: New York University Press, 2015.
Higginbotham, A. Leon, Jr. *In the Matter of Color: Race and The American Legal Process: The Colonial Period*. New York: Oxford University Press, 1978.
Higginbotham, Don. *War and Society in Revolutionary America: The Wider Dimensions of Conflict*. Columbia: University of South Carolina Press, 1988.
Hodges, Graham Russell. *Root and Branch: African Americans in New York and East Jersey, 1613–1863*. Chapel Hill: University of North Carolina Press, 1999.
Holton, Woody. *Forced Founders: Indians, Debtors, Slaves, and the Making of the American Revolution in Virginia*. Chapel Hill: University of North Carolina Press, 1999.
Horton, Wesley W. *The Connecticut Constitution: A Reference Guide*. Westport, Conn.: Greenwood, 1993.
Housely, Kathleen. "'Yours for the Oppressed': The Life of Jehiel Beman." *Journal of Negro History* 77, no. 1 (Winter 1992): 17–29.

Hufeland, Otto. *Westchester County during the American Revolution.* White Plains, N.Y.: Westchester County Historical Society, 1926.

Humphreys, Frank London. *Life and Times of David Humphreys, Soldier-Statesman-Poet, "Belov'd of Washington."* New York: G. P. Putnam's Sons, 1917.

Hurd, D. Hamilton. *History of New London County, Connecticut.* Philadelphia: Lippincott, 1882.

Hure, Henri. "The French Artillery at the Battle of Yorktown." *Field Artillery Journal* (September/October 1986): 34–37.

Irvin, Benjamin H. *Clothed in Robes of Sovereignty: The Continental Congress and the People Out of Doors.* New York: Oxford University Press, 2011.

Isaac, Rhys. *Landon Carter's Uneasy Kingdom: Revolution and Rebellion on a Virginia Plantation.* New York: Oxford University Press, 2004.

Jackson, Maurice. *Let This Voice Be Heard: Anthony Benezet, Father of Atlantic Abolitionism.* Philadelphia: University of Pennsylvania Press, 2009.

Johnston, Henry P. *The Storming of Stony Point on the Hudson.* New York: J. T. White, 1900.

Jones, George Fenwick. "The Black Hessians: Negroes Recruited by the Hessians in South Carolina and Other Colonies." *South Carolina Historical Magazine* 83 (October 1982): 287–302.

Joyner, Charles. *Down by the Riverside: A South Carolina Slave Community.* Urbana: University of Illinois Press, 1985.

Kaplan, Sidney, and Emma N. Kaplan. *The Black Presence in the Era of the American Revolution.* Greenwich: New York Graphic Society, 1973.

Kelly, Joseph P. "Henry Laurens: The Southern Man of Conscience." *South Carolina Historical Magazine* 107 (April 2006): 82–103.

Ketchum, Richard. *Saratoga: Turning Point of America's Revolutionary War.* New York: Holt, 1999.

———. *Victory at Yorktown: The Campaign That Won the Revolution.* New York: Henry Holt, 2004.

Kim, Sung Bok. "The Limits of Politicization in the American Revolution: The Experience of Westchester County, New York." *Journal of American History* 80 (December 1993): 868–89.

Knoblock, Glenn A. *"Strong and Brave Fellows": New Hampshire's Black Soldiers and Sailors of the American Revolution, 1775–1784.* Jefferson, N.C.: McFarland, 2003.

Knouff, Gregory T. *The Soldier's Revolution: Pennsylvanians in Arms and the Forging of Early American Identity.* University Park: Penn State University Press, 2004.

Kulikoff, Allan. *Tobacco and Slaves: The Development of Southern Cultures in the Chesapeake, 1680–1800.* Chapel Hill: University of North Carolina Press, 1986.

Kwasny, Mark. *Washington's Partisan War, 1775–1783.* Kent, Ohio: Kent State University Press. 1996.

Lemisch, Jesse. "Jack Tar in the Streets: Merchant Seamen in the Politics of Revolutionary America." *William and Mary Quarterly* 25, no. 3 (July 1968): 371–407.

Lender, Mark W. *The New Jersey Soldier.* Trenton: New Jersey Historical Commission, 1975.

Lepore, Jill. *New York Burning: Liberty, Slavery, and Conspiracy in 18th Century Manhattan.* New York: Alfred A. Knopf, 2005.

Littlefield, Daniel C. *Rice and Slaves: Ethnicity and the Slave Trade in Colonial South Carolina*. Urbana: University of Illinois Press, 1981.
Litwack, Leon F. *North of Slavery: The Negro in the Free States, 1790–1860*. Chicago: University of Chicago Press, 1961.
Lockhart, Paul D. *The Whites of Their Eyes: Bunker Hill, the First American Army, and the Emergence of George Washington*. New York: Harper, 2011.
Londahl-Smidt, Donald M. "German and British Accounts on the Assault on Fort Mercer at Redbank, New Jersey, in October 1777." *Hessians: Journal of the Johannes Schwalm Historical Association* 16 (2013): 1–31.
MacGunnigle, Bruce. *Regimental Book: Rhode Island Regiment for 1781 etc.* East Greenwich: Rhode Island Society of the Sons of the American Revolution, 2011.
Malcolm, Joyce Lee. *Peter's War: A New England Slave Boy and the American Revolution*. New Haven: Yale University Press, 2009.
Mason, Matthew. *Slavery and Politics in the Early Republic*. Chapel Hill: University of North Carolina Press, 2006.
Massey, Gregory D. *John Laurens and the American Revolution*. Columbia: University of South Carolina Press, 2000.
Mattern, David B. *Benjamin Lincoln and the American Revolution*. Columbia: University of South Carolina Press, 1995.
Mayer, Holly. *Belonging to the Army: Camp Followers and Community during the American Revolution*. Columbia: University of South Carolina Press, 1996.
———. "Canada, Congress, and the Continental Army: Strategic Accommodations, 1774–1776." *Journal of Military History* 78 (April 2014): 503–35.
McDonnell, Michael A. "Class, Race, and Recruitment in Revolutionary Virginia." In Resch and Sargent, *War and Society in the American Revolution*, 103–26.
———. *The Politics of War: Race, Class, and Conflict in Revolutionary Virginia*. Chapel Hill: University of North Carolina Press, 2007.
McInnis, Maurie D. *The Politics of Taste in Antebellum Charleston*. Chapel Hill: University of North Carolina Press, 2005.
Melish, Joanne Pope. *Disowning Slavery: Gradual Emancipation and "Race" in New England, 1780–1860*. Ithaca: Cornell University Press, 1998.
Middlekauf, Robert. *The Glorious Cause*. New York: Oxford University Press, 2007.
Moore, George Henry. *Historical Notes on the Employment of Negroes*. New York: C. T. Evans, 1862.
———. *Notes on the History of Slavery in Massachusetts*. New York: Negro Universities Press, 1968. First published 1866.
Morgan, Philip D., and Andrew Jackson O'Shaughnessy. "Arming Slaves in the American Revolution." In *Arming Slaves: From Classical Times to the Modern Age*, edited by Christopher Leslie Brown and Philip D. Morgan, 180–208. New Haven: Yale University Press, 2006.
Morris, Robert Charles. *New Jersey Medicine in the Revolutionary Era, 1763–1787: An Exhibition*. Newark: New Jersey Historical Society, 1976.
Nash, Gary B. *Forging Freedom: The Formation of Philadelphia's Black Community, 1720–1840*. Cambridge, Mass.: Harvard University Press, 1988.
———. *The Forgotten Fifth: African Americans in the Age of Revolution*. Cambridge, Mass.: Harvard University Press, 2006.
———. *Race and Revolution*. Madison, Wisc.: Madison House, 1990.

———. "Thomas Peters: Millwright and Deliverer." In *Struggle and Survival in Colonial America*, edited by David G. Sweet and Gary B. Nash, 69–85. Berkeley: University of California Press, 1981.

Nash, Gary B., and Graham Russell Gao Hodges. *Friends of Liberty: Thomas Jefferson, Tadeusz Kosciuszko, and Agrippa Hull: A Tale of Three Patriots, Two Revolutions, and a Tragic Betrayal of Freedom in the New Nation*. New York: Basic Books, 2008.

Nash, Gary B., and Jean R. Soderlund. *Freedom by Degrees: Emancipation in Pennsylvania and Its Aftermath*. New York: Oxford University Press, 1991.

"Nat Turner's Rebellion." In *Africans in America*, WGBH/PBS. www.pbs.org/wgbh/aia/part3/3p1518.html.

Neimeyer, Charles Patrick. *America Goes to War: A Social History of the Continental Army*. New York: New York University Press, 1996.

Nell, William Cooper. *Colored Patriots of the American Revolution*. New York: Arno Press, 1968.

———. *Property Qualification or No Property Qualification: A Few Facts from the Record of Patriotic Services of the Colored Men of New York, during the Wars of 1776 and 1812*. New York: T. Hamilton and W. H. Leonard, 1860.

———. *Services of Colored Americans in the Wars on 1776 and 1812*. New York: AMS Press, 1976. First published 1851.

Neumann, George C. *The History of Weapons of the American Revolution*. New York: Harper and Row, 1967.

Newman, Richard S. *The Transformation of American Abolitionism: Fighting Slavery in the Early Republic*. Chapel Hill: University of North Carolina Press, 2002.

Onuf, Peter. *The Mind of Thomas Jefferson*. Charlottesville: University of Virginia Press, 2007.

Pancake, John S. *This Destructive War: The British Campaign in the Carolinas, 1780–1782*. Montgomery: University of Alabama Press, 1985.

Pariseau, Justin. "Searching for a Martyr: Crispus Attucks and Historical Memory of the Boston Massacre." *Historic Nantucket* 62 (Winter 2012): 16–19.

Perry, Willam Gilman. *Exeter in 1830*. Hampton, N.H.: P. E. Randall, 1972.

"Petition 1/13/1777." In *Africans in America*, WGBH/PBS. www.pbs.org/wgbh/aia/part2/2h32t.html.

Piecuch, Jim. *Three Peoples, One King: Loyalists, Indians, and Slaves in the Revolutionary South, 1775–1782*. Columbia: University of South Carolina Press, 2008.

Pierson, William Dillon. *Black Yankees: The Development of an Afro-American Subculture in 18th Century New England*. Amherst: University of Massachusetts Press, 1988.

Powell, Colin, and Joseph Persico. *My American Journey*. New York: Ballantine Books, 2003.

"Proclamation of Earl of Dunmore, 1775." In *Africans in America*. WGBH/PBS. www.pbs.org/wgbh/aia/part2/2h42.html.

Pybus, Cassandra. *Epic Journeys of Freedom: Runaway Slaves of the American Revolution and Their Global Quest for Liberty*. Beacon Press: Boston, 2006.

———. "Jefferson's Faulty Math: The Question of Slave Defections in the American Revolution." *William and Mary Quarterly* 62, no. 2 (April 2005): 243–64.

Quarles, Benjamin. *The Negro in the American Revolution*. New York: W. W. & Norton, 1961.

Rael, Patrick. *Black Identity and Black Protest in the Antebellum North.* Chapel Hill: University of North Carolina Press, 2002.
Raphael, Ray. *Founding Myths: Stories That Hide Our Patriotic Past.* New York: New Press, 2004.
———. *A People's History of the American Revolution: How Common People Shaped the Fight for Independence.* New York: HarperCollins, 2001.
Rappleye, Charles. *Sons of Providence: The Brown Brothers, the Slave Trade, and the American Revolution.* New York: Simon and Schuster, 2006.
Rawley, James A. "Henry Laurens and the Atlantic Slave Trade." In *London, Metropolis of the Slave Trade*, edited by James A. Rawley. Columbia: University of Missouri Press, 2003.
Rediker, Marcus. *The Many-Headed Hydra: Sailors, Slaves, and Commoners and the Hidden History of the Revolutionary Atlantic.* Boston: Beacon Press, 2000.
Resch, John. *Suffering Soldiers: Revolutionary War Veterans, Moral Sentiment, and Political Culture in the Early Republic.* Amherst: University of Massachusetts Press, 2000.
Resch, John, and Walter Sargent, eds. *War and Society in the American Revolution.* DeKalb: Northern Illinois University Press, 2007.
Rider, Stanley S. *An Historical Inquiry Concerning the Attempt to Raise a Regiment of Slaves in Rhode Island.* Providence: S. S. Rider, 1880.
Risch, Erna. *Supplying Washington's Army.* Washington, D.C.: Center of Military History, United States Army, 1981.
Rogers, George C. *Charlestown in the Age of the Pinckneys.* Columbia: University of South Carolina Press, 1980.
Rosenthal, James M. "Free Soil in Berkshire County, 1781." *New England Quarterly* 10 (December 1937): 781–85.
Ruddimann, John A. *Becoming Men of Some Consequence: Youth and Military Service in the Revolutionary War.* Richmond: University of Virginia Press, 2014.
Russell, David Lee. *The American Revolution in the Southern Colonies.* Jefferson, N.C.: McFarland, 2000.
Ryan, William R. *The World of Thomas Jeremiah: Charlestown on the Eve of the American Revolution.* New York: Oxford University Press, 2010.
Saillant, John. *Black Puritan, Black Republican: The Life of and Thought of Lemuel Hayes, 1753–1833.* New York: Oxford University Press, 2003.
Santmier, Arthur. *A Little History of Smithfield Monthly Meeting of Friends.* www.oftedahl.com/SmithfieldFriends/history.htm.
Sawyer, Roland. *History of Kensington, NH.* Farmington, Maine: Knowlton and McLeary Company, 1946.
Schama, Simon. *Rough Crossings: Britain, the Slaves and the American Revolution.* New York: Harper Collins, 2006.
Selby, John E. *Revolution in Virginia.* Charlottesville: Colonial Williamsburg Foundation, 2007.
Selesky, Harold E., ed. *Encyclopedia of the American Revolution.* 2nd ed. 2 vols. Detroit: Charles Scribner's Sons, 2006.
Selig, Robert. *March to Victory: Washington, Rochambeau, and the Yorktown Campaign of 1781.* Center of Military History publication 70-104-1. Washington, D.C.: Government Printing Office, 2005.

Shy, John. *A People Numerous and Armed: Reflections on the Military Struggle for American Independence.* New York: Oxford University Press, 1990.

Slaughter, Thomas P. *The Beautiful Soul of John Woolman, Apostle of Abolition.* New York: Hill and Wang, 2009.

Stedman, Emilie T. *Hammet Achmet: A Servant of George Washington.* Middletown, Conn.: E. T. Stedman, 1900.

Steele, Ian K. *Betrayals: Fort William Henry and the "Massacre."* New York: Oxford University Press, 1990.

Stillé, Charles J. *Major-General Anthony Wayne and the Pennsylvania Line in the Continental Army.* Port Washington, NY: Kennikat Press, 1968.

Strauss, Mark. "Ten Notable Apocalypses That (Obviously) Didn't Happen." *Smithsonian.com*, November 12, 2009, www.smithsonianmag.com/history/ten-notable-apocalypses-that-obviously-didnt-happen-9126331.

Sutherland, Stella H. *Population Distribution in Colonial America.* New York: AMS Press, 1936.

Swanson, Susan Cochran. *Between the Lines: Stories of Westchester County, New York, during the American Revolution.* Pelham, N.Y.: Junior League of Pelham, 1975.

Taylor, Alan. *The Internal Enemy: Slavery and War in Virginia, 1772–1832.* New York: W. W. Norton, 2013.

Thornton, John. "Central African Names and African-American Naming Patterns." *William and Mary Quarterly* 50 (October 1993): 727–42.

Tiedemann, Joseph S., ed. *The Other New York: The American Revolution beyond New York City, 1763–1787.* Albany: State University of New York Press, 2006.

Tiro, Karim. *The People of the Standing Stone: The Oneida Nation from the Revolution through the Era of Removal.* Amherst: University of Massachusetts Press, 2011.

Tuchman, Barbara. *The March of Folly: From Troy to Vietnam.* New York: Ballantine Books, 1985.

Urwin, Gregory. "When Freedom Wore a Redcoat." *Army History* (Summer 2008): 6–23.

Van Buskirk, Judith L. "Claiming Their Due: African Americans in the Revolutionary War and Its Aftermath." In Resch and Sargent, *War and Society in the American Revolution*, 133–60.

———. *Generous Enemies: Patriots and Loyalists in Revolutionary New York.* Philadelphia: University of Pennsylvania Press, 2002.

Waldstreicher, David W. *Runaway America: Benjamin Franklin, Slavery, and the American Revolution.* New York: Hill and Wang, 2004.

Walker, Anthony. *So Few the Brave: Rhode Island Continentals, 1775–1783.* Newport: Seafield Press, 1981.

Wallace, David Duncan. *The Life of Henry Laurens, with a Sketch of the Life of Lt. Col. John Laurens.* New York: Russell and Russell, 1915.

Waselkov, Gregory A., ed. *Powhatan's Mantle: Indians in the Colonial Southeast.* Lincoln: University of Nebraska Press, 1989.

Webster, Donald B., Jr. *American Socket Bayonets, 1717–1873.* Alexandria Bay, N.Y.: Museum Restoration Service, 1986.

Weigley, Russell F. *Philadelphia: A 300-Year History.* New York: W. W. Norton, 1982.

Wells, Robert V. *The Population of the British Colonies in America before 1776.* Princeton, N.J.: Princeton Univbersity Press, 1975.

Wesley, Charles H. "Negro Suffrage in the Period of Constitution Making, 1787–1861." *Journal of Negro History* 31, no. 2 (April 1947): 143–68.
White, David O. *Connecticut's Black Soldiers, 1775–1783*. Chester, Conn.: Pequot Press, 1973.
White, Shane. *Somewhat More Independent: The End of Slavery in New York City*. Athens: University of Georgia Press, 1991.
Whittemore, Charles P. *A General of the Revolution: John Sullivan of New Hampshire*. New York: Columbia University Press, 1961.
Wilson, Ellen Gibson. *The Loyal Blacks*. New York: G. P. Putnam, 1976.
Wilson, Joseph. *Black Phalanx*. New York: Arno Press, 1968. Reprint of the 1890 edition.
Winch, Julie. *A Gentleman of Color: The Life of James Forten*. New York: Oxford University Press, 2002.
———. "The Making and Meaning of James Forten's Letters from a Man of Color." *William & Mary Quarterly* 64, no. 1 (January 2007): 129–38.
Wolf, Eva Sheppard. *Race and Liberty in the New Nation*. Baton Rouge: Louisiana State University Press, 2006.
Wood, Betty. *The Origins of American Slavery: Freedom and Bondage in the English Colonies*. New York: Hill and Wang, 1997.
Wood, Peter H. *Black Majority: Negroes in Colonial South Carolina from 1670 through the Stono Rebellion*. New York: W. W. Norton, 1975.
———. "The Changing Population of the Colonial South: An Overview by Race and Region, 1685–1790." In *Powhatan's Mantle: Indians in the Colonial Southeast*, edited by Gregory A. Waselkov, 57–132. Lincoln: University of Nebraska Press, 2006.
———. "'Liberty Is Sweet': African American Freedom Struggles in the Years before White Independence." In *Beyond the American Revolution: Explorations in the History of American Radicalism*, edited by Alfred F. Young, 149–84. DeKalb: Northern Illinois University Press, 1993.
———. *Strange New Land: Africans in Colonial America*. New York: Oxford University Press, 2003.
———. "Taking Care of Business in Revolutionary South Carolina: Republicanism and the Slave Society." In *The Southern Experience in the American Revolution*, edited by Jeffrey J. Crow and Larry E. Tise, 268–93. Chapel Hill: University of North Carolina Press, 1978.
Wright, Marion T. "Negro Suffrage in New Jersey, 1776–1878." *Journal of Negro History* 33, no. 2 (April 1948): 172–76.
Wright, Robert K., Jr. *The Continental Army*. Washington, D.C.: Center of Military History, United States Army, 1983.
Young, Alfred F., ed. *Beyond the American Revolution: Explorations in the History of American Radicalism*. DeKalb: Northern Illinois University Press, 1993.
———. *The Shoemaker and the Tea Party: Memory and the American Revolution*. Boston: Beacon Press, 1999.
Zabin, Serena. *Dangerous Economies: Status and Commerce in Imperial New York*. Philadelphia: University of Pennsylvania Press, 2009.
Zilversmit, Arthur. "Quock Walker, Mumbet, and the Abolition of Slavery in Massachusetts." *William and Mary Quarterly* 25 (October 1968): 614–24.

Index

Achmet, Hamet, 20, 88, 94, 220–24
Adams, John, 46–50
Adams, Rachel, 3, 16
African Americans: battle experiences, 79; differences and similarities with white soldiers, 78, 79, 83, 88, 119, 211; motivation for enlistment, 60–69, 213, 217; postrevolution activism, 158, 188, 190, 201–4, 206, 207, 237; relationship with officers, 17–18, 67, 68, 81–85, 210; relationship with rank and file, 94, 111, 235, 236; as servants, 18, 90; soldier vs. civilian life, 92, 93; supporters of the British, 13–15, 19, 53–58, 68, 100, 161, 163–65, 168, 233, 236; wounded, 79–81
Ailstock, Absolom, 120–21
Allen, Richard, 16
Andre, John, 82
Angell, Israel, 120–21
Armistead, James, 187
Arnold, Benedict, 107, 129
Arnold, Thomas, 11, 110, 111
Ashley, John, 176
Ashport, Cuff, 83
Attis, London, 66
Attucks, Crispus, 45–48, 188

Babcock, Caesar, 92
Babcock, Primus, 104
Bacon's Rebellion, 36
badges of merit, 21, 179, 224
Bailey, Prince, 88, 229
battles: Bennington, 76; Brandywine, 99; Bunker Hill, 52, 53, 97, 125; Camden, 32, 79, 84, 93, 94, 166; Canadian campaign, 107; Charles Town, 13, 26, 164–65; Freeman's Farm, 72; Germantown, 99; Guilford Courthouse, 92; Kemp's Landing, 54; Lexington and Concord, 51, 107; Monmouth, 71, 190; Princeton, 93, 213; Red Bank, 11, 96, 100–101, 108, 111, 234; Rhode Island, 113–116; Saratoga, 78, 82, 113; Savannah, 26, 156, 158, 163; Stony Point, 73–76, 159, 221, 224; Trenton, 67, 92, 98, 99; White Plains, 72, 97; Yorktown, 32, 57, 61, 72, 78, 141, 166, 212, 220
bayonets, 73–75, 136, 168
Bell, Samuel, 61
Beman, Jehiel, 203–4
Berlin, Ira, 32, 37
Bibbie, Solomon, 20
Billy (slave, d. 1852), 56
Bird, Reuben, 90
Blackman, Kemar, 228
Boose, Cato, 93
Boston Massacre, 45–48
Boston Tea Party, 48–50
bounties, 22, 64, 66, 158–59, 170
Brace, Jeffrey, 83, 224–29
Brandt, Joseph, 77
Brister, Aaron, 67
Brown, Joseph, 63
Brown, Scipio, 106
Bucklin, Prince, 120
Buley, George, 90
Burdoo, Silas, 51, 90
Burke, Africa, 110
Burnet, John, 151, 152

Capers, Jim, 92
Carney, Thomas, 184
Carter, Aaron, 87
Carter, Isham, 24, 26
Carter, Landon, 35
Champlain, July, 120
Champlin, Newport, 105, 120
Charles Town, S.C., 13, 25–26, 30, 143, 145, 158–160, 163, 164
Chehaw Neck, S.C., 171, 268

293

294 INDEX

Chastellux, Francois-Jean de, 139, 140
Clark, William, 164
Childs, Prince, 133
Clinton, Sir Henry, proclamation of 1779, 163
Coburn, Primus, 83
Coddington, Jack, 110
Coffin, Primus, 66
Cole, Thomas, 112, 130
colonization, 204, 206
Connecticut: 4th Connecticut Regiment, 6–11; enlistment laws, 9, 10
Continental Congress, 50, 157, 162–64
Cook, Louis, 84
Cowell, Benjamin, 195
Cornish, Samuel, 204
"Crompond." *See* Pines Bridge, N.Y.
Cromwell, Oliver, 92
Crosley, Prince, 10, 195, 197
Cuff, Sampson, 92
Cuffee, Paul, 186, 188, 204, 205
Cushing, William, 175

Davidson, William Lee, 82
De Lancey, James, 130, 132, 134, 136
Democratic Party,182, 183, 199, 200
Depuy, James, 77, 94
D'Estaing, Comte, 114
Dexter, John S., 107, 133
Dimond, Ezekiel, 122
Dinah, James, 20
discharges, military, 179, 196, 210, 217, 224, 228
Douglass, Frederick, 34
Drury, David, 74, 75
Dunbar, Samuel, 66, 90
Dunmore, Lord, 53, 153

Edwards, J. L. , 210–12, 215, 227
Eldridge, Caesar, 115
Ellis, John, 19
enlistment. *See* laws, enlistment
Ewald, Johann, 168
Exeter, N.H., veteran's group, 190–91

Federalist Party, 183, 100
Fisk, Cato, 231

Flagg, Ebenezer, 110, 111, 124, 126, 127, 131, 133, 135, 136
Fleury, Francois, 75
Ford, Timothy, 30
Forton, James, 187, 189, 238
Fortune, Richard, 67
Foy, John, 62, 83
France, and French support, 128–29, 163, 166
Francis, Jacob, 63, 71, 72, 83, 168, 183
Frank, Andrew, 97
Frazer, Persifor, 70
Freedom, Cato, 19
Freedom's Journal, 204–5
Freeman, Elizabeth (Mumbet), 176–77
Freeman, Peter, 185
Fry, Windsor, 110, 111, 121, 234
furloughs, 85–88

Gadsden, Christopher, 158, 170
Gardner, Prince, 120
Gardner, Sharper, 121
Gardner, Thomas, 89, 92, 230
Gates, Horatio, 84, 166
George, Sampson, 118
Gervais, John L., 150, 157, 160
Glover, Caesar, 51
Gould, Frank, 106, 122
Graydon, Alexander, 70
Greene, Cato W., 108, 110, 111, 129
Greene, Christopher, 96, 166; background, 107–8; Battle of Rhode Island, 113–14; discipline, 116–17, 121; First Rhode Island, 102, 104; Pines Bridge, N.Y., 130–38, 188, 230; Red Bank, N.J., 100–101; relationship with Gates, 125–26, 129
Greene, Nathanael, 105, 171; on the army, 95, 102; background, 107, 166; Battle of Rhode Island, 113; on black soldiers, 96,169, 187; southern campaign, 166
Greenman, Jeremiah, 132, 134, 137
Griffin, Anthony, 120
Griffin, Morgan, 26, 79, 80, 165
Grimes, William, 34
Grimke, Angelina, 25
Griswold, Matthew, 10

Hall, London, 107
Hall, Primus, 210–12
Hall, Prince, 189, 210
Hamilton, Alexander, 70
Harman, Edward, 93–94
Harris, James, 90
Harris, John, 89, 189
Hawkins, James, 89
Hawwawas, Nicholas, 68, 90
Hazard, Peter, 105, 122
Hazard, Pharaoh, 105
Hearn, Ephraim, 165
Heath, William, 119, 125–29, 131, 132
Holden, John, 126
Hood, Charles, 164
Howell, David, 193
Hubbard, Humphrey, 177, 180
Hull, Agrippa, 79, 164
Hull, Prince, 67
Hull, William, 17
Humphreys, David, 6–10
Hunt, Elisha, 79, 164

Jackson, Abednego, 66
James, Jamaica, 195
Jeffers, Allan, 26, 81, 158, 165
Jeffers, Berry, 165
Jeffers, Osborne, 26, 165
Jefferson, Thomas: Democratic Republican Party, 184; Missouri Compromise, 198; *Notes on the State of Virginia*, 206; on slavery, 4, 24, 25, 26, 33, 37, 59, 238
Jennings, Peter, 69, 81, 98, 166, 168, 237
Jeremiah, Thomas, 151–52
Johnson, Joseph, 67, 194
Johnson, Violet, 18
Johnson, William, 16, 229
Johonnot, Prince, 51–53
Jones, Tim 24, 32
Jordan, Thomas, 20

Kersey, James, 69, 164
Kirk, William, 11
Knight, Moses, 90
Kosciuszko, Thaddeus, 85, 171–72

Lafayette, Marquis de: at Battle of Rhode Island, 113–14; and black veterans, 187, 231; at Brandywine, Pa., 81, 99; Pines Bridge, N.Y., recollections, 132; Yorktown, Va., 166, 168
Lanson, William, 181
Lattimore, Benjamin, 72, 137
Laurens, Henry: on black soldiers, 142, 154–56, 158, 163–165; as president of Continental Congress, 143; on Thomas Jeremiah, 151–52; and Robert Scipio, 148–149; on slavery, 6, 35, 144, 150, 151, 153, 160, 162; Somerset case, 149; Tybee Island, Ga., 152–53
Laurens, James, 149, 160
Laurens, John: Battle of Rhode Island, 114; on black soldiers, 142, 154–57, 163, 164, 169, 170, 171, 236, 237; death of, 81, 171–72; in Europe, 149, 151, 152; on slavery, 143–44, 154; at Yorktown, 171, 172
Laurens, Robert (Scipio), 4, 142, 147–49, 154
laws, enlistment, 53, 55, 61–66
Lay, Asa, 11
Lee, Henry, 172
Leet, Richard, 66
Lewis, Ambrose, 164
Lewis, Elijah, 105
Lexington and Concord, Mass., 51
Light, Prince, 66, 83
Lincoln, Benjamin, 158, 163–64
Lines, John, 67
Lines, Judith 4, 67
Lively, Thomas, 4, 79, 164
Lomack, William, 165

Madison, James, 70
Maguira, Peter, 88
Magus, Pomp, 90, 195
March (Henry Laurens's slave), 146, 147, 160
Martin, John, 170
Mashpee Indians, 66, 180
Mathews, Saul, 187
Mary (Henry Laurens's slave), 142, 146
McCuff, Pomp, 84

Mepkin Plantation, 145, 147, 160, 237
Missouri debate, 198
Mirchell, Nahum, 184
Moody, Pero, 185, 188
Moore, Sampson, 51, 61
Moultrie, William, 14
Murry, Mark, 19, 60, 84, 216–20
musicians, 91–92, 126

Nash, Peter, 209
Newport, R.I., 102, 108, 118, 124, 127, 128, 143
New York, 37–38

Oliver, Peter, 50
Olney, Jeremiah, 122, 127, 141, 188
Olney, Steven, 117, 134, 141
Oneida (Native American tribe), 129

Paine, Thomas, 98, 135, 174, 191, 205, 206
Parker, Elisha, 63
Patterson, John, 200
Pebbles, Andrew, 81, 90, 172
Pennsylvania: Act for the Gradual Abolition of Slavery, 177–78; Quakers, 40, 41; slavery, 39–41
pensions, 18, 21, 78, 228; 1818 Pension Act, 16, 20, 189–93; 1832 Pension Act, 18, 20, 208–12, 213; challenges in 1818 cohort, 194–97, 209, 221–22; challenges in 1832 cohort, 208–212, 214–16, 217–20; widows, 16, 86–88, 228, 231
Perkins, Isaac, 105
Pierce, Titus, 110
Pinckney, Eliza, 35
Pines Bridge, N.Y., 131–39
Pinn, John, 90
Pollock, Mingo, 87
Pomp, John, 120
Potter, Richard, 100
Prime, Record, 92
Prosser, Gabriel, 186
Providence, R.I., 125, 127, 129
Pulaski, Casimir, 158

Quakers (Society of Friends), 39–41, 96–97

racism: inherent inferiority, 35, 103, 201, 203, 236; limited occupations, 21, 90, 91; postwar treatment of African Americans, 181, 192–95, 197, 204, 207; race, 53, 78, 136, 215; reneging on suffrage, 182–85, 199–203; treatment in army, 89, 116, 122, 127, 140
Raymond, Daniel, 20, 94
Read, Amos, 63
Rhode Island: Act to Enlist Slaves, 102, 103; courts martial, 119–24; Battle of Rhode Island, 113–15; First Rhode Island Regiment, 11, 12, 96, 97, 101–141, 157, 202; noncommissioned officers, 112, 113; Rhode Island Regiment, 130; Second Rhode Island Regiment, 111, 112, 118, 120–23, 126
Roberts, Esek, 101
Robinson, Amos, 91
Robinson, Prince, 134, 136
Rochambeau, Comte de, 129–30, 139, 168, 169
Rodman, Mingo, 105
Rodman, Philip, 98
Roe, John, 73–74
Rose, Francis, 15
Rose, Ned, 122
Rosswurm, John B., 204
Rowland, Jack, 137
runaways, 47, 106, 161–62, 176
Rush, Benjamin, 41, 81
Rutledge, John, 157, 160, 163, 169, 170

Sam (Henry Laurens's slave), 6, 142, 146
Sampsom, George, 93, 110, 118
Sands, Edward, 68
Santo Domingo, Haiti, 186, 187
Saunders, Prince, 203
Scaramouche (Henry Laurens's slave, later freeman), 142, 146
Scott, Drury, 165
Sedgwick, Theodore, 176–77
Sharper, William 11–13
Shelton, Caesar, 68, 80, 89, 195
Sherbourne, Pomp, 66, 86
Shrewsberry (Henry Laurens's slave), 171
Simon, Lycus, 67

slavery, 24–26, 31–32, 86–87, 142–143, 160; South Carolina, 26–30, 58, 170; Virginia, 32–37, 173, 181, 198, 238; Middle Colonies, 37–41; Massachusetts, 41–44, 174–79, 206
Slocum, Primus, 91
Somerset decision, 43, 148, 149
Sorrell, Edward, 81
South Carolina, 143–44, 153, 157–59, 164, 170
Stanley, Tobias, 188
Starr, Robin, 185
Stoddard, Fortune, 122
Steuben, Friedrich von, 84, 112, 187
Stono Rebellion, 27–30, 144–45
Sullivan, John, 65, 78, 113–15, 213
Sutphen, Samuel, 213–16
Sweatt, Cicero, 68

Taburn, Joel, 89
Taburn, William, 20, 82, 85
Taggert, Flora, 86
Tarrant, Caesar, 173, 187
Tash, Oxford, 83
task system, 31, 32
Tenny, Samuel, 95–97
Thompson, London, 121
Tocqueville, Alexis de, 199
Turner, Nat, 207
Turner, Plato, 89
Tybee Island, Ga., 152, 153
Tyler, John, 196
Tyng, Primus, 4, 74, 75

uniforms, significance of, 179–81
Updike, Caesar, 123

Valley Forge, Pa., 95, 96, 101, 107–8, 111, 189
Varnum, James, 96, 102, 108
Vaughan, Prince, 21
Virginia, Jeremiah, 66

Walker, David, 205–207
Walden, Drury, 90
Walker, Quock, 174–77
Walton, William, 89
Ward, Samuel, 114, 115, 131
Washington, George: on African American soldiers, 53, 67, 102; and Hamet Achmet, 222–23; British use of black soldiers, 55, 156–57; discharge certificates, 21, 179; First Rhode Island, 96, 115, 121, 122, 125–30, 142; proposed South Carolina regiment, 155–57, 170–71; and Gabriel Prosser, 187; revolutionary war, 79, 80, 81, 91, 98, 99, 113, 119, 132, 210; Sullivan's Campaign, 78
Washington, Harry, 56
Wayne, Anthony, 74, 80
Wells, Cuff, 87, 92
Wheatley, Phillis, 16, 48, 205
White, Archelaus, 51
Williams, Daniel, 91
Womble, John, 164
Wood, Peter, 32
Woodward, Pompey, 76
workhouse, Charles Town, S.C., 146, 151, 160

www.ingramcontent.com/pod-product-compliance
Lightning Source LLC
Chambersburg PA
CBHW031429160426
43195CB00010BB/668